The Tyranny of Human Rights:
From Jacobinism to the United Nations

THE TYRANNY OF HUMAN RIGHTS

From Jacobinism to the United Nations

BY

KERRY R. BOLTON

With Forewords by

Dr. Tomislav Sunić & Prof. Edward Dutton

ANTELOPE HILL PUBLISHING

Copyright © 2022 Kerry R. Bolton

All rights reserved. Second printing 2025.

Cover art by Swifty.
Edited by Sam and Margaret Bauer
Formatted by Margaret Bauer.

Antelope Hill Publishing
www.antelopehillpublishing.com

Paperback ISBN-13: 978-1-956887-05-1
EPUB ISBN-13: 978-1-956887-06-8

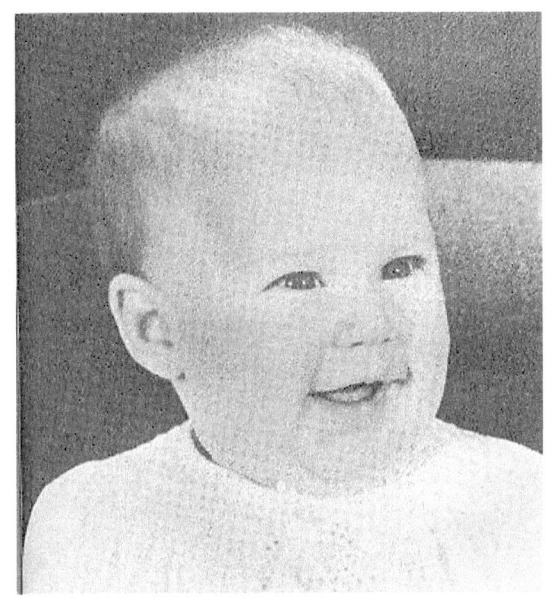

In Memory of

NATASHA GLENNY

Sacrificed on the Altar of "Human Rights"
Rhodesia, 1977

Contents

Foreword by Dr. Tomislav Sunić ix
Foreword: Envy Wears the Mask of Love by Dr. Edward Dutton xiii

Introduction 1
Liberty, Equality, Fraternity…Death 7
English Antecedents: John Locke 15
Rousseau's Social Contract 29
Neo-Jacobinism: From the USSR to the UN 47
"Legacy of Enlightenment" 67
In the Shadow of the Nuremberg Gallows: Raphael Lemkin and the
    Meaning of "Genocide" 73
"Human Rights" as a Social Control Mechanism 99
The Role of the Oligarchs: The Rockefeller Foundation and
    Black Riots 119
The Place of BLM: Funds from the Oligarchs 133
Martin King and Nelson Rockefeller 143
Prelude to the Fall of Africa: Haiti and America 153
The Curtain Falls on White Africa 163
South Africa's Road to Hell 177
Mandela: Another False God 191
Multiculturalism and Social Trust: The Social Consequences of
    Ethnic Diversity 199
The Sociology of Snowflake Liberalism 209

Pied Pipers 219

UNICEF "Playbook": Manual for Globalizing Children 247

Globalization of Labor: Origins and Aims of the United Nations
    Global Migration Compact 271

Kalergi's Plan? Europe and Antieurope 289

Antipodean Social Laboratory: A Case Study of Official Europhobia
    and Slow-Motion Anglocide 301

Humpty Dumpty Laws 309

Behind the Global Witch-Hunt 323

Multiculturalism in Practice: First Annual Europhobic Hatefest
    Turns on Itself 339

Hate Speech and Human Rights: Imposing the Europhobic State 349

Heresy 365

Denigration of Western Science 383

Erasure of Memory: Delenda est Europaeus 399

"Taking the Knee": Reintegrative Shaming 411

Conclusion 417

Bibliography 421

Foreword

By Dr. Tomislav Sunić

Kerry Bolton's book might just as well carry the title *The Decline of the West, Part 2,* or short of that, it can be catalogued as a sequel to Oswald Spengler's work. By using a descriptive and theoretical approach in his heavily footnoted prose, the author describes the endtimes of what was once known as Western civilization. The only problem is that each passage of this book could easily evolve into a separate volume. Each page of the book is replete with dozens of proper names and names of a variety of political organizations to the point that the reader must take a break and read each passage twice. Moreover, given Bolton's usual custom of providing a massive amount of bibliographic references, the following pages aren't designed for an ad hoc perusal or some passing right-wing coffee shop entertainment. This is a very serious piece of scholarly work which requires from a reader of the following pages at least some background in different fields of social science. For those lacking time or patience, or those who might find the book too heavy-handed, it may serve as a good reference for studying the rise and fall of the West.

Bolton is at his best when providing the causal nexus leading up to the catastrophe unfolding now in the West. The Sovietization of the Western politics, the resurgence of primal mannerism among masses of Westerners, the primitivization of conduct in citizens' mutual relationship, the brutalization of the English langue—all these new social pathologies did not drop from the moon. Neither are these signs of the ongoing decay a product of a single special interest group. The chapters of the book trace the historical origins of this chaos. The merit of the author is his willingness to demolish the myth of the much-lauded social contract theorists, the founding fathers of the modern replacement mystique: Jean Jacque Rousseau, John Locke, and their future liberal-leftist fellow travelers. Their daydreams of an expendable man, man as a blank slate, man as a tabula rasa creature, waiting to be perpetually reborn in an imaginary Lalaland, was bound to give birth to what came to be known first as the Lysenkoist-Bolshevik experiment and which we know today under the name of multicultural SJW, BLM, Antifa, LGTB, including hundreds of other outlets of "world-improvers" in the West. In fact, the communist Soviet Union collapsed in the early 1990s because its own egalitarian multiracial aspirations had been better achieved in practice in the Western liberal global village.

The chapters dealing with the distortion of language are particularly important, all the more as language generates political concepts and the way how we communicate with each other. The much used abstract expressions, such as "human rights" or "humanity," having originated during the American and French revolutions, are critically analyzed by the author. Similar upsurge in lexical imprecisions, such as the expressions "ethnic sensitivity training," or "affirmative action," being now part of the US legalese, are directly borrowed from the now defunct Sovietspeak. A separate book could be devoted by Bolton to his brief passage on Alice behind the Looking Glass and her encounters with the polysemic Humpty Dumpty. The Orwellian double-talk used by Humpty Dumpty had its natural outcome somewhat later in the Soviet Union—albeit not as a nursery rhyme but as a deadly legal procedure against wrong-thinkers.

Other than providing a theoretical framework for his analyses Bolton prods into chapters of daily politics and illustrates his prose with the description of current Western movers and shakers. Chapters that follow read often as detailed police reports on the moral corruption, coupled with self-denial of the political class in the West. New Zealand, a country of the author's actual residence, is also briefly discussed as a small tip of the melting iceberg. The old Rousseauistic imagery of the "noble savage" transpires now in the general self-abnegation process by New Zealand Whites toward the Māori people. The "noble savage" in the Pacific Rim must be treated now as a new superego of Whites; he must be hailed as a new deity guiding the sinful White into the glorious future—regardless whether his or her name is Nelson Mandela or George Floyd or Nanaia Mahuta. In fact, even the so-called great replacement in the West, that is, storms of Afro-Asian migrants on their way to Europe, is a logical process that perfectly ties in with the doctrine of liberalism and its twin brother communism.

In hindsight one may wonder whether the political heavyweights mentioned in the book and their disciples sitting now in DC, London, and Brussels are engaged in a deliberate process of lying, or whether they are just unwilling subjects of their own self-delusion. Whichever way they have chosen, the whole course of Western civilization appears nevertheless to have been, over the last two hundred years, a patent exercise in Western self-destruction.

Dr. Tomislav Sunić

Tomislav Sunić, Ph.D. (Political Science) taught at California State University; University of California; Juniata College, Pennsylvania, and the Anglo-American College, Prague. He has served in diplomatic positions for Croatia in Zagreb, London, Copenhagen, and Brussels. Books include: *Homo Americanus*; *Postmortem Report: Cultural Examinations from Postmodernity*; *Titans are in Town*; *Against Democracy and Equality*. (http://www.tomsunic.com/).

Foreword:
Envy Wears the Mask of Love

By Prof. Edward Dutton

The Wisdom of Tennyson

One of the essays in Dr. Kerry Bolton's stimulating collection *The Tyranny of Human Rights: From Jacobinism to the United Nations* begins with a quote from Alfred, Lord Tennyson, a quote that crisply encapsulates most of the movements which the collection explores: "Envy wears the mask of Love and, laughing, sober facts to scorn." Taken from Tennyson's poem "Locksley Hall, Sixty Years Later," there could hardly exist a better summary of the kind of psychology examples of which Dr. Bolton tackles in such gripping detail.

Whether it is Cromwellian Puritans, French Libertines and Jacobins, Marxists, or the multiculturalists, the psychology of the left—and especially of the virtue-signaler—is the same across history, across the interrelated history of political thought through which Dr. Bolton so skilfully guides us. Being liberal correlates with being low in altruism, low in impulse control, and high in neuroticism; that is mental instability: feeling negative feelings strongly.[1] These negative feelings include anger and jealousy, and it is also to be found that the main motivation for wanting to bring about greater "equality" is "malicious envy."[2]

---

[1] Verhulst, "Corrigendum to 'The nature.'" and Kirkegaard, "Mental Illness and the Left."
[2] Lin, "Each is to count for one."

Power Hunger Disguised as Virtue

Related to this, being on the far left is associated with Machiavellianism and narcissism, that is, with desiring power and with believing that you deserve power and praise.[3] Virtue-signaling and victimhood-signaling are also associated with the same "Dark Triad" traits.[4] Liberals are concerned with individualizing moral foundations—which ultimately promote the benefit of the individual over the group—such as "equality" and "harm avoidance," but care little for group-oriented foundations, such as obedience to authority, in-group loyalty and sanctity (v disgust). Conservatives care about all of these foundations.[5] Indeed, despite what they may signal about kindness, leftists—though there may be exceptions; people who are so altruistic that they are drawn towards leftist causes—are not only low-altruism individualists, but when they feel hard done by they will turn on their in-group, possibly even collaborating with an out-group to do so, whereas conservatives will turn on an out-group in the same circumstances.[6]

These disparate relationships all make a great deal of sense. The liberal is, to a great extent, adapted to an unpredictable world, a world in which you "live fast, die young," a so-called "fast life history strategy."[7] In such a world, kindness may never be repaid, because the other person could be wiped out at any minute. So, those who survive in such an ecology will be selected to be selfish and impulsive and to see the world as a dangerous place. In such a perilous environment, they need to get to the top, as only those at the top survive. So they must be Machiavellian. You're more likely to be power-hungry if you're angry, envious, paranoid of others (such that you feel a strong need to control them with an eternal revolution) and unhappy with the state of the world, depressed and anxious, providing you with an incentive to attain power in order to make yourself feel better.

---

[3] Moss, "The Dark Triad traits."
[4] Ok, "Signaling Virtuous Victimhood as Indicators."
[5] Graham, "Liberals and Conservatives Rely."
[6] Waytz, "Ideological differences in the expanse."
[7] See: Rushton, *Race, Evolution, and Behavior*.

Why Do They Virtue-Signal?

But, paranoid and even low in self-esteem as you are, you fear directly playing for status. So you do so covertly. Rather than overtly assert power, you signal your concern with "harm" and "equality."[8] In doing so, as Tennyson noted, you dress up your essential enviousness—as well as low altruism, mental instability, Dark Triad traits and individualism—as "Love": as a desire to make the world better for the "marginalized," with whom you may also identify. Conservatives will cede ground to you, because they are also concerned with individualizing foundations. They, however, are more balanced. As pack animals, who must also ascend the hierarchy to attain resources and so, in prehistory, pass on our genes, we must be concerned with both sets of foundations. It has been shown that pack-orientation becomes more salient the harsher and more stable are the conditions, as this leads to group-selection and the group which is more positively than negatively ethnocentric will tend to dominate.[9] In such predictable circumstances, reciprocity will be repaid, altruism will build up alliances, and individuals will be better able to survive as part of groups, groups that can better solve the problems of the harsh yet predictable environment. Leftists are simply adapted to a more primitive situation in which you need be less concerned about the group.

Accordingly, the thinkers who developed the ideas explored by Dr. Bolton—in essence, equalitarian dogmas—may appear contradictory, as may their less risk-taking followers. It may seem contradictory to propose "freedom" and also propose that they define what "freedom" is and that those who disagree with their desired freedom, or even disagree that they should be in charge of the new free world, should be compelled to be "free" or simply executed. But "logic" has little to do with these movements. They are simply attempts, via covert means, to attain power. Power is far more important to these people than logic.

In pursuit of it, high status Finns will criticize the kind of Romantic peasant nationalism, in some respects inspired by Rousseau, of Finland every day of the year, except on Finnish Independence Day. On this day, they will be proud to be Finns and clearly signal this. This is because they have aspects of Dark Triad traits, meaning logic does not matter. However, they also have low self-esteem, in certain respects, meaning that they are cowardly, and they will tend towards covert plays for status.

---

[8] Benenson, "The development of human."
[9] Dutton, *Making Sense of Race*.; Hammond, "The evolution of ethnocentric behaviour."

Lynn and I

Dr. Bolton looks, in this regard, at what happened to Richard Lynn in the wake of Britain's minor moral panic of 2018 when it came to light that the "London Conference on Intelligence" had been openly taking place at University College London, under the very noses of its leftist administrators, for three years, and had been discussing such forbidden issues as race differences in intelligence. In impotent rage, the leftist mob had this man, at that time nearly ninety years old, stripped of his Emeritus Professorship at the University of Ulster. Lynn had helped organize the conference and had widely published on the "crime think" areas. His defenestration had to occur because all that matters is power and, for leftists, you listen to a person purely because of their credentials; these are means via which society delegates power. Leftists, though low in the moral foundation of disgust, are high in "moral disgust."[10] If one is low in generalized disgust, one will have no problem attacking the "sacred" areas that uphold the system that you do not dominate. However, if one is morally self-righteous, one is more likely to virtue-signal, covertly attack opponents by whom one is disgusted due to their relative lack of individualistic moral foundations, and thus attain power. Lynn had to be publically shamed because his presence besmirched the moral sanctity of (leftist) academia.

Interestingly, something similar had occurred in 2016, as explored in my book *The Silent Rape Epidemic: How the Finns Were Groomed to Love Their Abusers*.

In 2013, Lynn and I had produced a paper in the journal *Intelligence* in 2013 showing that IQ in Finland was declining.[11] Thus it showed that the Lynn-Flynn Effect, co-discovered by Richard Lynn[12] and referring to a rise in IQ, had gone into reverse in Finland. It had drawn upon a table in a Finnish master's thesis, forwarded to us by the Finnish army. We understood this table to simply be reporting the army's data, conveniently forwarded to us by an army representative. I felt it best to cite the thesis anyway, even though we understood it to merely be quoting the army, but Lynn, a very elderly man with some of the issues expected in that regard, disagreed, so the citation was removed, he being the more senior of us. The thesis was, however, cited for other information that could be clearly

---

[10] Graham, "Liberals and Conservatives Rely."
[11] Dutton, "A Negative Flynn Effect."
[12] Kanazawa, *The Intelligence Paradox*.

understood though in Finnish, and cited in my own book[13] as the source for the negative Flynn Effect data via the army.

The result was that in 2016 there was a minor panic in Finland. The largest newspaper, *Helsingin Sanomat*, reported that two academics, who researched intelligence differences and other highly controversial issues, may have been leaked military data. The military concluded that this was not so and there was then a plagiarism investigation by Oulu University in northern Finland, to whom I was affiliated as a "docent," a kind of "Adjunct Senior Lecturer," a qualification in Nordic countries above doctorate and below full professor which renders you affiliated to the university that bestows it. I was granted this, by the Department of Cultural Anthropology, two years prior to becoming seriously interested in intelligence research.

Lynn publicly took full responsibility for the mistake. I pleaded with the committee: Which is more likely, that there had been some kind of genuine confusion or that the co-discoverer of the Flynn Effect, and his colleague, had deliberately plagiarized an obscure master's thesis on this subject and, concomitantly, drawn attention to the fact that they knew of the existence of the master's thesis, as if desiring to be caught? Apparently, it was the latter. The university, toothless to do much, simply requested that I issue a correction, send out a press release, and also send their findings to the University of Ulster. It seemed obvious to me why such an extraordinary conclusion had been reached by an academia that we know is now dominated by leftists, as society has reached a tipping point of leftism, tipped leftist, and has now adopted runaway leftism, with intelligent people competing to signal how leftist they are. This is because intelligence predicts understanding the nature of the dominant worldview, understanding the benefits of adopting it, and having the effortful control to force oneself to adopt it.[14]

My honorary affiliation with Oulu University came under attack again in 2019. My book *The Silent Rape Epidemic: How the Finns Were Groomed to Love Their Abusers* was published on March 7th, 2019. The book explored the epidemic of rapes committed against Finnish girls by Muslim refugees and drew upon evolutionary psychology to make sense of this and of why Finland had flipped from Romantic nationalism to multiculturalism so rapidly. As I wrote in the epilogue to the Finnish translation of *The Silent Rape Epidemic*:

---

[13] Dutton, *Religion and Intelligence*.
[14] See: Dutton, *The Past is a Future Country*.

> *By the end of March 2019, a Tajik man Museo Aseov (b. 1975) had been found guilty of sexually abusing a 10-year-old girl in Oulu's mosque between July and October 2018. He received 3 years and 8 months in prison and had to pay the victim 10,500 euros. The mosque's imam, Abdul Mannan (whom we met earlier), claimed to have been oblivious to what was taking place (Kaleva, 20th March 2019). Around the same time, Abdullhadi Barhum received 2 years and 6 months in prison, and had to pay a 3600 euro fine, for raping a 14-year-old girl. He also forced her to fellate him (Ranta, 26th March 2019). The public fury surrounding this indirectly led to the fall of the government and resurgence for the anti-immigrant True Finns party, who nearly came first in the subsequent election.*

In September 2019, the English-language version of *The Silent Rape Epidemic* was reviewed in True Finns' online newspaper *Suomen Uutiset*. Possibly partly due to the Finns being so fascinated by what foreigners think of them, it spread like wildfire on Finnish-speaking Twitter. It caused a predictable uproar among the Finns who had helped to bring about the silent rape epidemic that it described. A website called *AntroBlogi* vociferously condemned it, with a piece entitled "Pseudo-scientific notions of national nature" on September 24th, 2019. They explained that:

> *Perceptions of Finnishness have political consequences, but Finnishness is also an ideological fiction.... The role of anthropologists, according to the scientific consensus, is not to take prevalent stereotypes seriously or to reinforce them, but to critically examine these perceptions and their connections to power structures. The reasoning represented by Dutton is not based on current anthropological research, and presenting it as such is frustrating not only the entire discipline but also perceptions of humanity. Talking about multiculturalism as a threat demonizes some people. It is a means of reproduction that normalizes racist and discriminatory structures and is based on historical hierarchies of power.*

They then got in touch with Oulu University on Twitter. Oulu University was left with no choice on September 24th but to admit their own impotence: "Edward Dutton does not work at Oulu University. Under current legislation it is not possible to cancel a docentship." I had last done paid teaching for them in early 2016.

Indeed, in June 2019, they had tweeted the same, only in English, in response to leftist criticism of a video I had made critiquing a leftist book on "race" in which I was mentioned. This book was *Superior: The Return of Race Science* by British ethnically Indian journalist Angela Saini.[15] In other words, there was nothing the poor woke dears could do. So, in January 2020, they, rather childishly and without contacting me, removed my name from the list of Docents on the website of Oulu University's Cultural Anthropology Department. This is utterly misleading, of course, because there is no question about the title having been withdrawn, as they have publically admitted.[16] This was a covert act, done secretly, to avoid overt conflict: a covert "cancelation," even.

Locksley Hall

Dr. Bolton's book is an excellent guided tour through the minds of people who think in this way, and what their thinking has accomplished. In Tennyson's early poem, "Locksley Hall," the eye of the poem has his heart broken by a girl. As a result, in a stream of consciousness, he rejects European civilization, embraces Rousseau's Romantic ideas about primitive peoples, and, in effect, virtue-signals about primitive peoples and becomes despairing and self-centered: "Mated with a squalid savage— what to me were sun or clime? I the heir of all the ages, in the foremost files of time." Only the call of war from his comrades—to defend a civilized homeland about to be destroyed—shakes him out of this leftist stupor and makes him realize anew the importance of self-discipline for the good of the group.[17] He realizes that his leftism is an expression of selfishness, envy, and melancholy. "Not in vain the distance beacons. Forward, forward let us range,/ Let the great world spin for ever down the ringing grooves of change./ Thro' the shadow of the globe we sweep into the younger day;/ Better fifty years of Europe than a cycle of Cathay."

Dr. Bolton's book is a timely reminder of just how crucial it is, for those of us who value understanding the true nature of the world, to never stop fighting the intellectual descendants of Rousseau, be they Black Lives Matter thugs, or those who espouse "human rights" without truly

---

[15] Saini, *Superior*.
[16] See: Dutton, *Suomen vaiennettu raiskausepidemia, Jälkikirjoitus*.
[17] Adams, *Dandies and Desert Saints*, 117.

exploring, as Dr. Bolton does, what these truly mean, and the many sinister dimensions to the ideology behind them.

Prof. Edward Dutton
Asbiro University, Poland

Edward Dutton has served as guest researcher in the Psychology Department, Umeå University, Sweden; academic consultant, Psychology Department, King Saud University, Riyadh; Visiting Lecturer in the Anthropology of Religion, Riga Stradins University, Latvia; *docent at* Oulu University, Finland; and editor of the scholarly journal, *Mankind Quarterly*. In 2020 he was appointed Professor of Evolutionary Psychology, Asbiro University, Łódź, Poland. As of 2021, Dutton has authored sixteen books on anthropology, religion, psychology, etc., and numerous papers.

Introduction

"The concept of humanity is an especially useful ideological instrument of imperialist expansion, and in its ethical-humanitarian form it is a specific vehicle of economic imperialism. Here one is reminded of a somewhat modified expression of Proudhon's: 'whoever invokes humanity wants to cheat.' To confiscate the word humanity, to invoke and monopolize such a term, probably has certain incalculable effects, such as denying the enemy the quality of being human and declaring him to be an outlaw of humanity; and a war can thereby be driven to the most extreme inhumanity."

Carl Schmitt (1932)[18]

There is seldom more perfect a justification for propaganda against a state, or a people, as suggested by Schmitt, than the claim that it is mistreating migrants or ethnic minorities. NATO bombed Serbia into submission on the pretext that they were helping the Kosovar Muslims, whom, it was claimed, were being "ethnically cleansed." The war demands of NATO happened to feature the privatization and globalization of the mineral resources of Kosovo, with the Trepca Mine being a special prize, using the demand for the self-governance of the Kosovar Albanians as a pretext for war. The principles that were demanded were drawn from the UN Charter. Economic subjugation by international capitalism proceeded behind the bloodied flag of "human rights":

> *The Parties to the present Agreement:*
> *Reaffirming their commitment to the Purposes and Principles of the United Nations, as well as to OSCE principles, including the Helsinki Final Act and the Charter of Paris for a new Europe...*

---

[18] Schmitt, *The Concept of the Political*, 54.

Recognizing the need for democratic self-government in Kosovo, including full participation of the members of all national communities in political decision-making...

Desiring to ensure the protection of the human rights of all persons in Kosovo, as well as the rights of the members of all national communities...

Have agreed as follows:

Framework

Article I: Principles

1. *All citizens in Kosovo shall enjoy, without discrimination, the equal rights and freedoms set forth in this Agreement.*
2. *National communities and their members shall have additional rights specified in Chapter 1. Kosovo, Federal, and Republic authorities shall not interfere with the exercise of these additional rights. The national communities shall be legally equal as specified herein, and shall not use their additional rights to endanger the rights of other national communities or the rights of citizens, the sovereignty and territorial integrity of the Federal Republic of Yugoslavia, or the functioning of representative democratic government in Kosovo.*
3. *All authorities in Kosovo shall fully respect human rights, democracy, and the equality of citizens and national communities.*
4. *Citizens in Kosovo shall have the right to democratic self-government through legislative, executive, judicial, and other institutions established in accordance with this Agreement. They shall have the opportunity to be represented in all institutions in Kosovo. The right to democratic self-government shall include the right to participate in free and fair elections.*
5. *Every person in Kosovo may have access to international institutions for the protection of their rights in accordance with the procedures of such institutions.*[19]

---

[19] *Interim Agreement for Peace and Self-Government in Kosovo*, 3-4

After much posturing about the welfare of "humanity" the actual aims were pronounced under "economic issues." It took a great deal of rhetoric to serve as a preamble to obscure the starkness of the aim: globalist predation via the dismembering and fracturing of the Yugoslav state.

Article I:

1. *The economy of Kosovo shall function in accordance with free market principles.*
6. *Federal and other authorities shall within their respective powers and responsibilities ensure the free movement of persons, goods, services, and capital to Kosovo, including from international sources. They shall in particular allow access to Kosovo without discrimination for persons delivering such goods and services.*[20]

US foreign policy, including the "color revolutions" and "regime change" it instigates, is conducted under the guise of "human rights," like the Jacobins had their "revolutionary wars" in Europe in the name of "liberty, equality, fraternity," and the Bolsheviks had their abortive war pushing West in the name of "liberation." Woodrow Wilson took the USA into war in Europe stating before Congress: "The world must be made safe for democracy. Its peace must be planted upon the tested foundations of political liberty."[21]

Wilson's Fourteen Points insisted on a post-war world in which the economy was based on free trade and the scuttling of the European imperial blocs as a hindrance to international capital:

> III. *The removal, so far as possible, of all economic barriers and the establishment of an equality of trade conditions among all the nations consenting to the peace and associating themselves for its maintenance.*
> V. *A free, open-minded, and absolutely impartial adjustment of all colonial claims, based upon a strict observance of the principle that in determining all such questions of sovereignty the interests of the populations concerned must have equal weight with the equitable claims of the government whose title is to be determined.*[22]

---

[20] Ibid., 46
[21] Wilson, *War Message to US Congress.*
[22] Wilson, *Fourteen Points.*

The final point urged the establishment of the League of Nations, as a world government, the predecessor to the United Nations:

> *XIV. A general association of nations must be formed under specific covenants for the purpose of affording mutual guarantees of political independence and territorial integrity to great and small states alike.*[23]

Here we begin to see the actual reasons for wars and revolutions behind the rhetoric about "human rights" and "making the world safe for democracy." We see it repeated in Franklin Roosevelt's Atlantic Charter, again predicated on free trade and the scuttling of the European powers from their empires:

> *Third, they respect the right of all peoples to choose the form of government under which they will live; and they wish to see sovereign rights and self-government restored to those who have been forcibly deprived of them;*
>
> *Fourth, they will endeavor, with due respect for their existing obligations, to further the enjoyment by all States, great or small, victor or vanquished, of access, on equal terms, to the trade and to the raw materials of the world which are needed for their economic prosperity.*[24]

The United Nations Declaration on the Rights of Indigenous Peoples (UNDRIP) enables such intervention in the affairs of states on the pretext of "human rights" for indigenes. Will the signatory states to UNDRIP be subjected to UN embargoes and ultimately UN military intervention on the pretext of defending the rights of indigenes, so long as these are of course "people of color"? Certainly, the indigenous peoples of Europe—let alone the indigenous Afrikaners—will not be granted protection, unless some globalist purpose is served. Likewise, the signatories of the United Nations Global Compact for Migration, and an increasing array of other UN global treaties and declarations are fastening the grip of "international law" in the name of "human rights." Yet the UN Migration Compact serves as a justification for intervening on issues this time not of "indigenous peoples," but of migrant peoples.

---

[23] Ibid.
[24] Roosevelt and Churchill, *Atlantic Charter*, 7

Hence, UNDRIP is supposed to protect indigenous peoples, when they are "people of color," while the UN Compact for Migration is supposed to protect not indigenous peoples—when these are Whites—but migrants, when these are, again, "people of color." There is consistency insofar as the globalist laws are formulated to ostensibly protect migrants when they are "people of color," and on the other hand to protect indigenes only when they are, again, "people of color." Whites, whether as migrants or as indigenes, whether as minorities or majorities, are forever the pariahs, outside of international law, other than when, as with Kosovar Albanians, they might be used against other Whites.

The manner by which the Afrikaner was dispossessed and the South African economy globalized followed such a pattern of demands for "human rights." The original pretext was that of the "human rights" not of Blacks but of "*Uitlanders*," mainly British mine workers backed by wealthy investors in the Transvaal, an independent Afrikaner republic. *Uitlanders* had become if not a majority then at least on par in numbers with the Boers, a lesson in what can happen when economics drives migration. However, occupants of the Transvaal were not entitled to vote until a naturalization process requiring fourteen years of residence. On the pretext of "Uitlander rights" agitation was initiated, leading to the abortive Jameson Raid of 1895. Four years later the Second Anglo-Boer War erupted in a grab for South Africa's wealth, using the *Uitlander* issue as the pretext.

The Afrikaner could not be left in peace, despite having secured his independence after two bloody conflicts with Britain. Agitation was resumed in the name of "human rights," this time in regard to the myriad of ethnic communities lumped together as "Black." Between decades of terrorism, internal subversion, business and political maneuvering, and high level pressures from UN rostrums, corporate boardrooms, and Western embassies, the Afrikaners relented and South Africa was delivered to international capitalism behind the facade of "majority rule."

When Nelson Mandela returned from a meeting of the World Economic Forum at Davos in January 1992 he did so as a convert to privatization and globalization.[25] South Africa's economy, resources, and state utilities, after years of Afrikaner struggle, persecution, denigration, and martyrdom,[26] were opened up to capitalist predation courtesy of the

---

[25] Ferguson, *The Square & the Tower*, 311-314.
[26] "Women and Children in White Concentration Camps.": "Boer women, children and men unfit for service were herded together in concentration camps by the British forces during the Second Anglo-Boer War (1899–1902). The first two of these camps (refugee camps) were established to house the families of burghers who had surrendered voluntarily, but very soon, with families of combatant burgers driven forcibly into camps established all over the

African National Congress, and with the help of the multitudes of vacuous do-gooders who shouted *"Amandla"* through the streets of Western cities. Harry Oppenheimer got his vast new consumer and labor market once apartheid was dismantled, albeit reduced to a typically African shambles, and the Afrikaner Nationalism which plutocracy had despised and fought[27] since the nineteenth century, was obliterated.

After the long drama of South Africa, the process of European dispossession has recently been accelerated by three events: the inauguration of President Trump in 2017, showing that Populist-Nationalism persists en masse even in the citadel of globalism; the killing of fifty-one Muslims in Christchurch, New Zealand in 2019; the accidental death of Black criminal George Floyd while resisting arrest in 2020.

Each event unleashed forces that had hitherto worked usually through a gradual, subtle process, into a worldwide reaction of fear and rage. The Trump presidency shocked the oligarchy into the realization that there were still millions of Americans who rejected globalist agendas.

The killing and wounding of Muslims at two mosques in far-off New Zealand provided a pretext for repression that was unleashed from the Antipodes to Austria against all things deemed "Right."

The killing of Floyd provided a further means of reinforcing White self-loathing to the point that it remains a common practice for Whites to bend their knees in atonement and repentance at public events, while bringing rampaging mobs onto the streets.

Europhobia has assumed a religious quality, and dissent is heresy.

---

country, the camps ceased to be refugee camps and became concentration camps. The abhorrent conditions in these camps caused the death of 4,177 women, 22,074 children under sixteen and 1,676 men, mainly those too old to be on commando, notwithstanding the efforts of an English lady, Emily Hobhouse, who tried her best to make the British authorities aware of the plight of especially the women and children in the camps."

[27] For a detailed exposition on this by Harry Oppenheimer, at the time South Africa's leading oligarch, see: Oppenheimer, "Portrait of a Millionaire."

Liberty, Equality, Fraternity...Death

"The effect of liberty to individuals is that they may do what they please; we ought to see what it will please them to do, before we risk congratulations which may be soon turned into complaints."

Edmund Burke (1790)[28]

"Human rights" is the harbinger of death. The premise of "equality" is only possible by leveling. One cannot level upwards, but only downwards. One cannot maintain equality without a continual purging of anyone who rises above the lowest denominator. Paradoxically, a dictatorship of bureaucrats, technocrats and managers, overseen by a cabal of unbalanced intelligentsia, must be imposed to assure the process continues in an orderly fashion. Hence, "human rights" and its "equality" predicate cannot be enacted without tyranny. Jacobinism and Bolshevism were the ultimate doctrines of "equality" in the name of "human rights."

George Washington and Alexander Hamilton sought to avoid the tyranny of equality by a constitutional Republic that recognized that "liberty" is not premised on equality. In this they were vigorously opposed by the party of Thomas Jefferson which sought to introduce Jacobinism to the USA and inaugurate a second revolution. Hamilton's biographer, Ron Chernow, writes of this period, during Washington's second term as president (1793) that it:

> *Revolved around inflammatory foreign policy issues. The French Revolution forced Americans to ponder the meaning of their own revolution, and followers of Hamilton and Jefferson drew diametrically opposite conclusions. The continuing turmoil in Paris added to the caution of Hamiltonians, who were trying to*

---

[28] Burke, *Reflections*, 8.

> *tramp down radical fires at home. The same upheavals encouraged Jeffersonians to stoke the fires anew. Americans increasingly defined their domestic politics by either their solidarity with the French Revolution or their aversion to its incendiary methods. The French Revolution thus served to both consolidate the two parties in American politics and deepen the ideological gulf between them.*[29]

American diplomat William Short wrote from The Hague of the situation in France, where he had been stationed, that the Parisian streets "literally are red with blood." Fourteen hundred political prisoners were slaughtered in the "September Massacres," Robespierre stating that "it is the most beautiful revolution that has ever honored humanity." Marat responded, "Let the blood of traitors flow."[30] In America James Madison exclaimed that the Jacobin Revolution was "wonderful in its progress… stupendous in its consequences."[31] In 1793 French Ambassador Genêt landed in Philadelphia and was feted by Democratic Party crowds which passed around "liberty caps" and sung "The Marseillaise" with gusto.[32] It is these matters that prompted Washington to declare in his "Farewell Address to the American People" (which Hamilton had drafted) that America should maintain a neutral foreign policy and not become embroiled with foreign ideologies and states.

While the USA was spared a bloody Jacobin Revolution, the crypto-Jacobins have for the most part had the upper hand since at least the time of Woodrow Wilson, who sought a world revolution led by the USA, and declared his "Fourteen Points" as a global revolutionary doctrine. Whether Republican or Democrat, liberal or conservative, US Administrations have since then regarded the USA as the custodian of a democratic revolution that imposes an American-Jacobin ideology over the world in the name of the motto on the Great Seal of the USA: *Novus ordo seclorum;* or "a new world order," as President George H. W. Bush termed it in his "State of the Union Address" in 1991:

> *What is at stake is more than one small country, it is a big idea, a new world order where diverse nations are drawn together in common cause to achieve the universal aspirations of mankind: peace and security, freedom, and the rule of law. The world can*

---

[29] Chernow, *Alexander Hamilton*, 430.
[30] Ibid., 432.
[31] Ibid., 433.
[32] Ibid., 439.

therefore seize this opportunity to fulfil the long-held promise of a new world order where brutality will go unrewarded, and aggression will meet collective resistance.[33]

Bush reiterated the same year:

We can see a new world coming into view. A new world in which there is the very real prospect of a new world order...a world where the United Nations, freed from Cold War stalemate is poised to fulfil the historic vision of its founders. A world in which freedom and respect for human rights find a home among all nations.[34]

This is the neo-Jacobin doctrine that premises US foreign policy; its use of "human rights" is a moral facade for both invasion and "color revolution," fomenting revolutionary disorder in Jacobin manner, in what foreign policy adviser Ralph Peters lauded as the USA's world mission of "constant conflict."[35]

The premise of these doctrines, including those posing as empirical sciences, is that there is a "natural state" into which the individual is born, that of absolute freedom and equality; that he is corrupted by imposed institutions and that he can return to his pristine nature of absolute happiness when these institutions (or "primary ties" as the critical theorists say) are broken. Indeed, while the Jacobin's slogan was *Liberty, Equality, Fraternity*, the American humanist slogan was and remains: *Life, Liberty and the Pursuit of Happiness*. That elusive utopian happiness is the outcome of the *perfectibility* of Man (with a capital "M"). It is a predicate of the US Declaration of Independence. The doctrine is proto-Jacobin and a product of the British Enlightenment, as shown in the preamble:

When in the Course of human events it becomes necessary for one people to dissolve the political bands which have connected them with another and to assume among the powers of the earth, the separate and equal station to which the Laws of Nature and of Nature's God entitle them, a decent respect to the opinions of mankind requires that they should declare the causes which impel them to the separation.

---

[33] Bush, *State of the Union*.
[34] Bush, *Persian Gulf Conflict*.
[35] Peters, "Constant Conflict."

> *We hold these truths to be self-evident, that all men are created equal, that they are endowed by their Creator with certain unalienable Rights, that among these are Life, Liberty and the pursuit of Happiness—That to secure these rights, Governments are instituted among Men, deriving their just powers from the consent of the governed—That whenever any Form of Government becomes destructive of these ends, it is the Right of the People to alter or to abolish it, and to institute new Government, laying its foundation on such principles and organizing its powers in such form, as to them shall seem most likely to effect their Safety and Happiness.*[36]

The primary author of the Declaration of Independence, Thomas Jefferson, whose "revolutionary heroism" never extended to seeing a British Redcoat for dust, was later to become a zealous advocate of Jacobinism. Jefferson held John Locke, the English Enlightenment philosopher, to be one of the three greatest men—a "trinity," as he called them—in history, the others being Francis Bacon and Newton.[37]

We see in the Declaration of Independence the precursor of the Jacobin Declaration of the Rights of Man, and of the UN Declaration on Human Rights. Given the US and French sources for the UN Declaration this is no coincidence, as will be seen.

In the Declaration of Independence can be seen the deism of Jefferson that was a feature of Jacobinism, and indeed of the Enlightenment, with the appeal being to the "Laws of Nature and of Nature's God." As will be seen, the Jacobins, in the name of "enlightenment" established the "Cult of the Supreme Being." An unquestioned dogma is laid down, that cannot be challenged because it is predicated on the "God and Laws of Nature," that there are "truths" that are "self-evident," and among these are "that all men are created equal," and that all men are given "unalienable Rights," by the "God of Nature," including "Life, Liberty and the pursuit of Happiness." As will be shown, France's Declaration on the Right of Man refers in the first point to "Men" who are "born and remain free" and with "equal rights." These "rights," according to the French model, are enacted "under the auspices of the Supreme Being."

When the USA was threatened with a Jacobin-style revolution at the end of the eighteenth century, it was widely believed that the crypto-Masonic Order of the Illuminati had infiltrated the USA. Whether true or

---

[36] Jefferson, *Declaration of Independence*.
[37] Boyd, *Thomas Jefferson Papers*, 14:561.

not, and it would be naive to dismiss such ridiculed "conspiracy theories," Jefferson and his party were regarded as the harbingers of Illuminati doctrines. With the Federalists accusing Jefferson and his followers of *illuminism*, Jefferson responded in 1800 by calling Adam Weishaupt "an enthusiastic philanthropist," and alluding to his own adherence to *perfectibilism*:

> *He is among those...who believe in the infinite perfectibility of man. He thinks he may in time be rendered so perfect that he will be able to govern himself in every circumstance, so as to injure none, to do all the good he can, to leave no government the occasion to exercise their powers over him, and, of course, to render political government useless.... The means he proposed to effect this improvement of human nature are "to enlighten men, to correct their morals and inspire them with benevolence."*38

Utopia: The Endless Wait

Likewise, and contrary to assumptions about communism, Karl Marx believed that the state, so far from being omniscient, would eventually wither away after going through a dialectical historical process, of which socialism was an intermediate phase. This would require a long transition period during which man would be gradually perfected through the change of his institutions, as Jefferson termed it, to "improve human nature" and "correct man's morals." Robespierre and the Committee of Public Safety tried it, as did Mao Zedong, Pol Pot, and "human rights" icon Jim Jones. Lenin assured us:

> *The expression "the state withers away," is very well chosen, for it indicates both the gradual and the elemental nature of the process.... Only communism renders the State absolutely unnecessary, for there is no one to be suppressed—no one in the sense of a class, in the sense of a systematic struggle with a definite section of the population."*39

This "withering away of the state" can only be achieved with absolute equality, and that can only be achieved by a prolonged period of the

---

38 Porter, *Illuminati*, 105. The Porter book is a rather banal attempt to ridicule conspiracy theories with the usual *reductio ad absurdum*.
39 Lenin, *The State and the Revolution*, 74, 75.

"dictatorship of the proletariat," under which "class enemies" are destroyed. But the latter can only mean also destroying their institutions: religion, property, nationality (for the proletariat has none, according to Marxism), and family; the same institutions that are called enemies of freedom by the critical theorists.[40]

Again, the predicates even of the most vicious forms of tyranny go back to the same foundations as liberalism, the Enlightenment, with its "rights of man," and its present-day emanation, "human rights"; that "Man" is perfectible through a change of institutions, and thereby a change of his character and morals. The Jacobins and communists have sought this through the liquidation of "class enemies," mass imprisonment, forced labor; the destruction of traditional culture and religion; and the elimination of the family, as "bourgeoisie institutions." Where does the liberal, the United Nations "humanitarian," and the facilitator of "human rights" differ in ideology from the bloody-handed Jacobins and Bolsheviks? All seek the reconstruction of humanity through an imposed equality. This shall become more evident as we examine some of the methods used by the democratic enforcers of "human rights." The difference is in the degrees of enforcement, but even that is becoming less so, the ultimate sanction of violence and warfare being within the purview of the UN, NATO, the USA, or a combination thereof, with the additional option of fomenting "color revolutions."

Jacobin fanatics, around 130 years prior to Bolshevism, and around 150 years prior to the founding of the United Nations Organization, were zealously proclaiming in France's National Assembly the advent of a new epoch of the Universal Republic, Jean Baptiste (alias Anacharsis Cloots) declaring in 1793:

> *We are not free as long as there is a single moral obstacle to our physical advance at a single point anywhere in the world. The Rights of Man are extended to the totality of men. A state that calls itself sovereign grievously wounds humanity, it is in full rebellion against commons sense and happiness, it cuts the channels of universal prosperity, its Constitution faulty at its root, is contradictory, uncertain and ready to fall.*
>
> *We will have no other master than the expression of the general will, absolute and supreme. No, if I encounter on this earth a particular will which resists the universal instinct, I am against it; such resistance spells universal war and servitude,*

---

[40] See: Bolton, *The Perversion of Normality*, 153-184.

and mankind, the Supreme Being, will sooner or later treat it as it deserves.[41]

Here we have the primary elements of present-day cosmopolitan humanism on which liberalism and communism are ideologically based, along with their UN, European Union, and US excrescences:

1. The aim of imposing a humanist doctrine—expressed in the Jacobin Declaration of the Rights of Man, the US Declaration of Independence, the UN Declaration on Human Rights, the Charter of the Fundamental Rights of the European Union, and so on—over "the totality of men."
2. The destruction of any state that resists globalist hegemony, which is dehumanized as a "rogue state," and subjected to economic embargoes, and ultimately military action or a "color revolution."
3. The justification for destructive actions in the name of a universal "general will" or "the international community" as it is today called, including war; Cloots predicting "universal war."
4. The homocentric elevation of "Man" as the "supreme being," replacing God.

---

[41] Anacharsis Cloots, cited by Denis de Rougemont, *The Idea of Europe*, 181.

English Antecedents: John Locke

"You ask what I have found and wide I go,
Nothing but Cromwell's house and Cromwell's murderous crew,
The lovers and the dancers are beaten into the clay
And the tall men and the swordsmen and the horsemen, where are they?
And there is an old beggar wandering in his pride
His fathers served their fathers before Christ was crucified
O what of that, O what of that?
What is there left to say?
All neighborly content and easy talk are gone,
But there's no good complaining, for money's rant is on.
He that's mounting up must on his neighbor mount,
And we and all the Muses are things of no account.
They have schooling of their own, but I pass their schooling by,
What can they know that we know that know the time to die?
O what of that, O what of that,
What is there left to say?..."

W. B. Yeats, "The Curse of Cromwell"

While we might assume that the rot of the present epoch has its origins amidst the decadence of the French aristocrats and the rise of the bourgeoisie that preceded the French Revolution, we can look to the origins, even of Jacobinism, in England. We can trace the first great tumult in the process to the English Revolution of Cromwell, starting in 1642, where the remnants of tradition were dealt a death blow, and money assumed authority over politics in the name of Puritanism. Here we see ideological antecedents of the French Revolution, where property relations—or civil society as it is called—replaced the organic social community and, like the Jacobins, a tyranny was erected in the name of "democracy."

Well might we ponder Yeats's words today of what emerged from England in the seventeenth century in the name of parliament and democracy: *"All neighborly content and easy talk are gone, but there's no good complaining, for money's rant is on."* In the name of "human rights," as we now call "money's rant," there is no "easy, neighborly talk," for on pain of imprisonment or financial ruin, and public vilification by the kept media, none dare speak their own mind or heart, and of "progressive education," "what can they know?"

It is with the English Civil War that we can trace the origins, in the Anglophone world, of "left" and "right," of conservative and liberal. The notion that libertarianism, free trade, and Whig-liberalism are somehow "right-wing" and "conservative"—represented for example by British Prime Minister Margaret Thatcher, or US President Ronald Reagan, or economic theorists such as Friedrich Hayek, Milton Friedman, Ludwig von Mises, the "Chicago School," "the Austrian School," and in Marx's day the "Manchester School"—is testament to the muddle that masquerades as academia. The genuine conservative philosopher Anthony Ludovici, explained:

> *...and it is not astonishing therefore that when the time of the Great Rebellion the first great national division occurred, on a great political issue, the Tory-Rural-Agricultural party should have found itself arrayed in the protection and defence of the Crown, against the Whig-Urban-Commercial Trading party. True, Tory and Whig, as the designation of the two leading parties in the state, were not yet known; but in the two sides that fought about the person of the King, the temperament and aims of these parties were already plainly discernible.*
>
> *Charles I...was probably the first Tory, and the greatest Conservative. He believed in securing the personal freedom and happiness of the people. He protected the people not only against the rapacity of their employers in trade and manufacture, but also against oppression of the mighty and the great...*[42]

A point to be noted from the above is that the Tory Party became "Whig," as did similar parties throughout the world, and even certain regimes such as Pinochet's in Chile, under the catastrophic influence of the Friedmanian

---

[42] Ludovici, *Defence of Conservatism*, 80-81.

"Chicago Boys." The "Right," especially in the Anglophone states, was long ago subverted by liberals, espousing free trade.[43]

As for the central premise of liberalism, it is to John Locke (1632–1704) that the Western culture primarily owes its notion of the individual as a "blank slate" (*tabula rasa*). Locke lived his youth under the Cromwell regime. His mentor was Anthony Ashley Cooper, later the Earl of Shaftesbury, leader of the Whig Party, the predecessor of the Liberals. In dispute over the restoration of a Catholic to the Throne, Cooper and Locke relocated to Holland. Locke returned to England in 1689, the year after the Glorious Revolution that placed William of Orange on the throne. The intrigues of merchants in Holland in regard to both the support for Cromwell and later for William will not detain us here, other than to say that both were examples of oligarchic intrigue.[44]

Locke's *tabula rasa* is an enduring premise of liberalism, leftism, and their oligarchic patrons. It also continues to premise the social sciences, sociology, and social and cultural anthropology, which dogmatically assert that the individual is born *tabula rasa*, and those blanks are filled in through experience. Hence, we see also the notion that environment molds the individual without any input from the innate intelligence or character.

The once well-known anti-liberal author Dr. Lothrop Stoddard summarized the rise of this intellectual milieu, the Enlightenment, which continues to dominant the modern world:

> *All the great thinkers of the eighteenth century (who still influence our ideas and institutions to a far greater degree than we may imagine*[45]*) were convinced believers in "natural equality." Locke and Hume, for example, taught that at birth "the human mind is a blank sheet, and the brain a structureless mass, lacking inherent organization or tendencies to develop in this way or that; a mere mass of undefined potentialities which, through experience, association, and habit, through education in shirt, could be moulded and developed to an unlimited extent and in any manner or direction."*[46] *The doctrine of natural equality was brilliantly formulated by Rousseau, and was explicitly*

---

[43] When the philosopher Christopher Lasch, disillusioned with the modernist conformity of the left, looked for the "American Right" during the 1970s, he found only the same type of anti-traditional libertarianism. See: Lasch, "What's Wrong with the Right?" Also: Bolton, "Lasch Dissents," in *Perversion of Normality*, 249-263.
[44] Bolton, *Banking Swindle*, 16-26. Ultimately the rise of an oligarchy on the ruins of Tradition in England can be traced to Henry VIII, where another Cromwell, Thomas, was Secretary of State. Ibid., 16).
[45] Immeasurably more so today than when Stoddard was writing in 1922.
[46] Stoddard is quoting from W. McDougall, *Is America Safe for Democracy?*, 21.

stated in the American Declaration of Independence and in the French Declaration of the Rights of Man. The doctrine, in its most uncompromising form, held its ground until well past the middle of the nineteenth century.[47] *At that period so notable a thinker as John Stuart Mill could declare roundly: "Of all vulgar modes of escaping from the consideration of the effect of social and moral influences on the human mind, the most vulgar is that of attributing diversities of conduct and character to inherent mental differences."* [48]

The "progressives" of today still shout back at any dissent with the platitudes of the seventeenth century.

Blank Minded Liberalism

Once born, the mind of the child can be filled with anything required to mold the individual into whatever is desired. That is how the modern world has proceeded. The *perfectibility* of "Man" is the aim of liberal, Masonic, and Marxist doctrines. There is nothing innate to be overcome, but only that which has been instilled and which can be purged through re-education. The younger the person the better, since there is not so much to purge. Whether in a liberal-democratic-parliamentary society or that of Pol Pot, the techniques differ in degree, but the process is one of brainwashing. Liberal democracy relies on indoctrination as much as North Korea or China, and is predicated ultimately on the same doctrine of the nature of the mind.

Locke presented a detailed speculative case for the doctrine of the *tabula rasa* (blank slate) mind in 1689. Until then character and intelligence were regarded as innate. As the subsequent sciences of genetics, ethology, epigenetics, and Jungian psychology now tell us, our forebears—prior to the so called "Enlightenment"—had it right in the first place. However, this has not dissuaded much of the present-day social sciences from maintaining Locke's fiction for the sake of their ideological foundations, rendering as nonsense their facade of "empiricism." Such "empiricism" was nothing other than salon speculation among the debased and self-destructive aristocracy and their intellectual protégés,

---

[47] Stoddard lived to see the doctrine's resumption to dominance with the Franklin D. Roosevelt regime a decade later, which the American anti-liberal thinker Yockey termed the "American revolution of 1933." Yockey, *Imperium*.
[48] Stoddard, *Revolt*, 35-36.

but it remains the basis of our modern laws and education. A blatant example of the latter is New Zealand's "new school histories curriculum," beginning in 2022, and premised on another speculative assumption of liberalism, that of the noble savage. Locke introduces his intention:

> *It is an established opinion amongst some men, that there are in the understanding certain INNATE PRINCIPLES; some primary notions, KOIVAI EVVOIAI, characters, as it were stamped upon the mind of man; which the soul receives in its very first being, and brings into the world with it. It would be sufficient to convince unprejudiced readers of the falseness of this supposition, if I should only show (as I hope I shall in the following parts of this Discourse) how men, barely by the use of their natural faculties may attain to all the knowledge they have, without the help of any innate impressions; and may arrive at certainty, without any such original notions or principles.*[49]

Locke here rejects "natural faculties" or "innate principles" in the shaping humans. Where Locke rejects the idea that the *soul* can be inherited by the embryonic *mind*, the reader might refer to the *unconscious* and the *psyche*. One might also apply genetics and epigenetics to the remark by Locke when he criticizes the then common belief about "the constant impressions which the souls of men receive in their first beings, and which they bring into the world with them, as necessarily and really as they do any of their inherent faculties."[50]

In short, Locke was among those Enlightenment philosophers who formulated the still dominant position of sociology, that intelligence and character traits are not, and cannot be, inherited. Mendelian genetics, behavioral epigenetics, and ethology have not changed that view, because it is a dogma fundamental to liberalism.

Drawing on the example of "children and idiots," whose minds are assumed to be blank at birth, Locke proceeds with a dialectical discussion:

> *For to imprint anything on the mind without the mind's perceiving it, seems to me hardly intelligible. If therefore children and idiots have souls, have minds, with those impressions upon them, THEY must unavoidably perceive them, and necessarily know and assent to these truths; which since they do not, it is*

---

[49] Locke, *Human Understanding*, I: 1.
[50] Ibid., I: 2.

> *evident that there are no such impressions. For if they are not notions naturally imprinted, how can they be innate?*[51]

He arrives at the speculative conclusion that what is known to the "mind" is only to be gained by the perception of outside stimuli. The content of the "mind" only contains what is filled from the outside. What philosophers intuited or observed as innate to the "soul" or "mind," which Locke aimed to repudiate with this essay, was more in line with what we now know through psychology, epigenetics, genetics, and ethology.

What Locke confuses with innate abilities is the reception of *knowledge*. Hence, he states the obvious as some type of revelation in proving his position. He uses the straw man argument, which remains the predominate method of the left before resorting to banal abuse or suppression:

> *A child knows not that three and four are equal to seven, till he comes to be able to count seven, and has got the name and idea of equality; and then, upon explaining those words, he presently assents to, or rather perceives the truth of that proposition.*[52]

The question however is whether this hypothetical child has the innate ability to utilize mathematical formulae when taught; not whether a newborn baby can immediately recite mathematical equations between dribbling and breast-feeding. This is an important question for the present, because it is now framed in terms of learned behavior, including whether gender is a social construct that is independent of innate biological sex, and whether "Whiteness" is nothing more than a recent social construct to justify slavery.[53]

These are the types of questions that are now framed to deconstruct authentic—innate, organic—identities. Entire schools of ideology presented as social science pervade and dominate academia as a protected orthodoxy, against which any questioning is condemned as heresy.[54] Ultimately, much of it can be traced to seventeenth century philosophers such as Locke.

Marx is no better, since his doctrine holds that the blank canvas of the human mind is shaped by the forces of social production. Mendelian

---

[51] Ibid., I: 5.
[52] Ibid., I: 16.
[53] For a litany of straw man arguments on this see: Coates, "Race a Social Context."
Of course, it is only "Whiteness" that requires deconstructing, while every other race-identity is not only acceptable but laudable.
[54] See chapters below: "Heresy," and "Denigration of Western Science."

genetics was for long condemned in the USSR as "reactionary" and "fascist," because it means that certain human characteristics are hardwired and are not readily susceptible to change without the use of the most draconian intrusions, including mass liquidation; which is precisely what occurred.[55] Stalin's suppression of genetics was premised on the same doctrine as liberalism: the repudiation of the "innate" that had been inaugurated by Locke, et al. While heretical scientists do not yet face death in the liberal democracies, they are nonetheless *purged* from academia.

Locke continues with a repudiation on the innate by rejecting the primordial quality of *memory*:

> *To which let me add: if there be any innate ideas, any ideas in the mind which the mind does not actually think on, they must be lodged in the memory; and from thence must be brought into view by remembrance; i.e. must be known, when they are remembered, to have been perceptions in the mind before; unless remembrance can be without remembrance. For, to remember is to perceive anything with memory, or with a consciousness that it was perceived or known before.*[56]

Today we know something of the inherent layers of memory, including the *collective unconscious*, thanks especially to the work of Jungian psychology. Dream analysis in particular has shown that the unconscious is multi-layered, and composed of *archetypes* or symbolic images that are common to all of humanity at the most primordial level, but differentiating into later ethnic and racial diversifications. What we are, is the accumulation of what we have inherited from our ancestors, and this is reflected in our memories, and the symbols that reside in our unconscious. To Locke, *archetypes* were understood as only "fantastical" and "chimerical," with "no foundation in nature, nor [with] any conformity with that reality of being to which they are tacitly referred, as to their archetypes."[57]

The mechanism by which memories and archetypes, including the collective or what might be called "racial," are passed through generations can be seen in the science of epigenetics. Often mistakenly regarded as a

---

[55] Witkowski, "Stalin's War."
[56] Locke, *Human Understanding*, III: 21.
[57] Ibid., XXX: 1.

repudiation of genetics,[58] *behavioral epigenetics* explains how the experiences of a generation can be inherited without a change to DNA.[59]

Friedrich Nietzsche presaged behavioral epigenetics, and repudiated Enlightenment assumptions when writing: "That which his ancestors most liked [60] to do and most constantly did cannot be erased from a man's soul… This constitutes the problem of race."[61] Dr. Rupert Sheldrake's *Morphic Field Theory* adds a fascinating dimension to the question of the innate, Sheldrake stating that "through morphic resonance, each member of a species draws upon, and in turn contributes to, a pooled or collective memory…"[62] Hence experiences do not have to be continually relearned by each new generation.

While the drawing-room philosophers and their wealthy patrons of the eighteenth and nineteenth centuries might be forgiven for their ignorance, what is outright malevolent is the present-day fanatical maintaining of these same doctrines by the brutal suppression for heresy of any dissidents in the name of "human rights," "equality," and "democracy."

Lockean Sociology

Of what Locke regarded as the "natural state of man" he wrote:

> *To understand political power right, and derive it from its original, we must consider, what state all men are naturally in, and that is, a state of perfect freedom to order their actions, and dispose of their possessions and persons, as they think fit, within the bounds of the law of nature, without asking leave, or depending upon the will of any other man.*
>
> *A state also of equality, wherein all the power and jurisdiction is reciprocal, no one having more than another; there being nothing more evident, than that creatures of the same species and rank, promiscuously born to all the same advantages of nature, and the use of the same faculties, should also be equal one amongst another without subordination or subjection, unless the lord and master of them all should, by any manifest*

---

[58] The word was coined by the geneticist C. H. Waddington in 1942.
[59] For discussion on behavioral epigenetics see: Bolton, *The Decline and Fall of Civilisations*, 135-150.
[60] Conversely, catastrophes and traumas also play their role in epigenetically shaping character.
[61] Nietzsche, *Good and Evil*, 184.
[62] Sheldrake, "Formative Causation."

declaration of his will, set one above another, and confer on him, by an evident and clear appointment, an undoubted right to dominion and sovereignty.[63]

Here we have the doctrine of "perfect freedom and equality" as decreed by "nature," men "without rank," without innate attributes, until someone illicitly sets himself up as master to reorganize this state of nature. But such authority is a usurpation of nature, as Locke had shown that "*Adam had not, either by natural right of fatherhood, or by positive donation from God, any such authority over his children, or dominion over the world, as is pretended.*"[64]

As in seemingly all doctrines professing liberty and equality, there is a *BUT*: such a utopia cannot be maintained unless somebody has the ability to punish transgressors. Anyone who would undermine the regime of liberty and equality must be liable to punishment, including the death penalty. Locke explains:

And that all men may be restrained from invading others rights, and from doing hurt to one another, and the law of nature be observed, which willeth the peace and preservation of all mankind, the execution of the law of nature is, in that state, put into every man's hands, whereby every one has a right to punish the transgressors of that law to such a degree, as may hinder its violation: for the law of nature would, as all other laws that concern men in this world be in vain, if there were no body that in the state of nature had a power to execute that law, and thereby preserve the innocent and restrain offenders. And if any one in the state of nature may punish another for any evil he has done, every one may do so: for in that state of perfect equality, where naturally there is no superiority or jurisdiction of one over another, what any may do in prosecution of that law, every one must needs have a right to do.[65]

...the offender declares himself to live by another rule than that of reason and common equity, which is that measure God has set to the actions of men, for their mutual security; and so he becomes dangerous to mankind...[66]

---

[63] Locke, *Second Treatise*, II:4.
[64] Ibid., I: 1.
[65] Ibid., II: 7.
[66] Ibid., II: 8.

Locke's prescription for maintaining the "Common-wealth," or what the Jacobins called the "general will," was reflected in France's Declaration of the Rights of Man:

> *Liberty consists in the freedom to do everything which injures no one else; hence the exercise of the natural rights of each man has no limits except those which assure to the other members of the society the enjoyment of the same rights. These limits can only be determined by law.*[67]

There is invariably an outlaw liable to punishment in the name of "reason and equity"; a "class enemy," "fascist," "racist," "Nazi," "White supremeacist," "abusive parent," "war criminal," "terrorist," or collectively, a "rogue state," for such types have "quit the principles of human nature... to be a noxious creature,"[68] such as the mass of American Trump supporters whom Hilary Clinton called "the deplorables," whom she categorized as "racist, sexist, homophobic, xenophobic, Islamophobic."[69] The opponent is dehumanized and delegitimized, and the way is open for his elimination.

We now have not only NATO, US, and UN bombs and troops, but "race relations," and "human rights" laws, and laws imposing international regulations and punishments for the ostensible rights of children (but not the unborn), women, indigenes, "persons of color" (since "white" is not a color), cripples, little people, homosexuals, migrants, LGBT, and about 120 variations thereof...

Locke established the doctrinal premise for the Committee of Public Safety, Cheka/NKVD/KGB, Nuremberg War Crimes Tribunal, UN War Crimes Tribunal, and the war against "rogue states" in the name of "human rights" by sanctioning the death penalty, since:

> *Every man has a power to punish the crime, to prevent its being committed again, by the right he has of preserving all mankind, and doing all reasonable things he can in order to that end: and thus it is, that every man, in the state of nature, has a power to kill a murderer, both to deter others from doing the like injury, which no reparation can compensate, by the example of the punishment that attends it from every body, and also to secure men from the attempts of a criminal, who having renounced*

---

[67] *Declaration of the Rights of Man*, Point 4.
[68] Locke, *Second Treatise*, II: 10.
[69] Rilley, "Read Hilary Clinton."

> *reason, the common rule and measure God hath given to mankind, hath, by the unjust violence and slaughter he hath committed upon one, declared war against all mankind, and therefore may be destroyed as a lion or a tyger, one of those wild savage beasts, with whom men can have no society nor security: and upon this is grounded that great law of nature, Whoso sheddeth man's blood, by man shall his blood be shed...*[70]

Here we have all the elements for the classification and punishment of those who go against what Jean-Jacques Rousseau was later to call the "general will," which is today expanded in the name of the "international community." Locke refers to what has come to be called "crimes against humanity"—having "declared war against all mankind"—who may be put to death.

Locke's treatise is a convoluted and pretentious justification for the creation of a tyranny in the name of "nature," "liberty and equality," masquerading as "philosophy." Lockean doctrine is a rationalization for the notion that man can be perfected through the elimination of traditional institutions. Emanating from this is a galaxy of doctrines, including:

- *Perfectibilism*: the perfectibility of humanity espoused by the Order of the Illuminati and Freemasonry (capping the pyramid,[71] squaring the *Ashler*[72]) proceeding to...
- *Jacobinism:* with its guillotine and extermination of the Vendee.
- *Positivism*: founded by Auguste Comte, the founding figure of *sociology*, who saw the modern era as uniquely "progressive."
- *Behaviorism*: behavior modification of Pavlovian punishment-and-reward that interested the Bolsheviks.
- *Cultural Anthropology*: rejecting any conception of innateness in shaping human society and the individual, an ideology that predicates United Nations doctrines on race.[73]

---

[70] Locke, *Second Treatise*, II: 11.
[71] The capstone hovering above the body of a pyramid depicted on the Great Seal of the USA represents in Masonic symbolism the mission of the Masons to unite the parts, completing the perfection of society. See: Bolton, *The Occult and Subversive Movements*, 130-131.
[72] In Masonic symbolism an *Ashler* is a roughhewn block that represents the present imperfect state of humanity; the aim of the Masons being to bring humanity to perfection by the chiseling out of imperfections.
[73] See "Statement on the Nature of Race and Race Differences," in UNESCO, *The Race Concept*. Among the ideological conclusions is that "man is born a social being" with an "ethic of universal brotherhood." 103.

- *Critical Theory:* that regards the *primary ties* of family, homeland, religion and ethnos, as repressing the rights of the individual to absolute liberty, as detached, autonomous beings.
- *Social Constructionism:* whereby authentic—organic—identities such as race and gender are reduced to being social constructs based on power relationships and societal expectations, that can be deconstructed at will.

Whiggery and Jacobinism

The support of the London Revolution Society, a group of Whig Members of Parliament, aristocrats, merchants and religious dissenters, and other "Revolutionary societies" of the well-heeled, inspired the formation of the Paris Jacobin Club in 1789, and Radical Republican Abolitionists in the USA; universalism and equality being the common factors. These wealthy Whigs aimed to support the French in their Glorious Revolution. They postured about being "world citizens" and their commitment to the common man, especially the Black man, while the London Revolution Society ensured that membership fees were sufficiently high to keep away the English proletariat. A scholarly study of the relationship between English Whig-liberalism and Jacobinism states:

> *The London Revolution Society's entry into French Revolutionary politics helped inspire the creation of the Jacobin Club network. In the French National Assembly on November 25, 1789, the session's President read a letter from the British club, which "disdaining National partialities," declared its approbation of France's revolution and "the prospect it gives to the two first Kingdoms in the World of a common participation in the blessings of Civil and Religious Liberty." By asserting the "inalienable rights of mankind," revolution could "make the World free and happy." The address produced a "great sensation and loud applause in the Assembly, which wrote back to London declaring it had seen the "aurora of the beautiful day" where the two nations could place aside their differences and "contract an intimate liaison by the similarity of their opinions, and by their common enthusiasm for liberty." Within a week, growing Anglophilia inspired the founding of Paris' own Société de la Révolution, which only in January 1790 adopted the better-*

known Société des amis de la Constitution, retaining the English-style nickname Club des Jacobins.[74]

Referring to the arrival of the French ambassador, Genêt, to the USA, as mentioned previously, Professor Alpaugh states that Jacobinism had a lasting impact on the USA. The Democratic Party was established.

> *The French Revolution set off a second wave of still more radical changes. France's revolutionary Jacobin founders took explicit inspiration from the preceding groups, and the unprecedented power of their nationwide network helped inspire new movements for free blacks' political rights in the French colonies (that soon helped galvanize the Haitian Revolution), radical reform mobilization in Britain, a nonsectarian independence movement by the United Irishmen, and the rise of the Democratic-Republican Societies (and soon political party) in the United States.*[75]

Edmund Burke explained to a young French enthusiast for the Jacobin Revolution the genuinely conservative-right outlook on society, contrasting the fluid character of the "social contract" with the permanence of the "state." Here is the genuinely rightist conception of society explained with cogency and exactitude, applicable to the situation today where *neo-Jacobinism* assumes the course for destruction unleashed in France over 230 years ago:

> *Society is indeed a contract. Subordinate contracts for objects of mere occasional interest may be dissolved at pleasure—but the state ought not to be considered as nothing better than a partnership agreement in a trade of pepper and coffee, calico, or tobacco, or some other such low concern, to be taken up for a little temporary interest, and to be dissolved by the fancy of the parties. It is to be looked on with other reverence, because it is not a partnership in things subservient only to the gross animal existence of a temporary and perishable nature. It is a partnership in all science; a partnership in all art; a partnership in every virtue and in all perfection.*

---

[74] Alpaugh, "Friends of Freedom."
[75] Ibid.

> As the ends of such a partnership cannot be obtained in many generations, it becomes a partnership not only between those who are living, but between those who are living, those who are dead, and those who are to be born. Each contract of each particular state is but a clause in the great primeval contract of eternal society, linking the lower with the higher natures, connecting the visible and invisible world, according to a fixed compact sanctioned by the inviolable oath which holds all physical and all moral natures, each in their appointed place.
>
> This law is not subject to the will of those who by an obligation above them, and infinitely superior, are bound to submit their will to that law. The municipal corporations of that universal kingdom are not morally at liberty at their pleasure, and on their speculations of a contingent improvement, wholly to separate and tear asunder the bands of their subordinate community and to dissolve it into an unsocial, uncivil, unconnected chaos of elementary principles....[76]

Under neo-Jacobinism—or whatever it is called today—all is fluid and nothing is permanent; identities are constructed, reconstructed, and shelved. Those that are authentic and organic are supplanted by the artificial and the fleeting. This is called "human rights" and "progress." It is the "progress" of a pathogen eating at the organs of the social body; "to dissolve it into an unsocial, uncivil, unconnected chaos of elementary principles," to quote Burke.

What irony that many of those who embrace this fluidity as "liberty" are now called "conservatives" and "right-wingers" when they are as much part of the legacy of Jacobinism as their left-wing counterparts, causing Charles Lasch, as mentioned above, to wonder whether the "Right" still existed. Now Hayek and Ayn Rand are quoted, and the conception of society by the pseudo-right is of "a partnership agreement in a trade of pepper and coffee, calico, or tobacco, or some other such low concern," as Burke stated. Actual conservative-right thinkers such as Edmund Burke, Thomas Carlyle, and Joseph de Maistre are forgotten.

---

[76] Burke, *Reflections*, 80-81.

Rousseau's Social Contract

"There is nothing so absurd but some philosopher has said it."

Cicero, De Divinatione[77]

"Thomas Carlyle, the eminent Scottish essayist and sometime philosopher, was once scolded at a dinner party for endlessly chattering about books: 'Ideas, Mr. Carlyle, nothing but ideas!' To which he replied, 'There once was a man called Rousseau who wrote a book containing nothing but ideas. The second edition was bound in the skin of those who laughed at the first.'"

Benjamin Wiker (2008)[78]

While the Swiss-born Jean-Jacques Rousseau is given a prime place in the philosophical fermentation that resulted in the French Revolution, what he wrote was foreshadowed by Locke and other British Enlightenment philosophers. Rousseau, as with Locke, premised his doctrine on what was speculated as the "natural state of man." He opens his philosophical treatise, *The Social Contract*, published in 1762, with a familiar Lockean theme:

> *Man is born free; and everywhere he is in chains. One thinks himself the master of others, and still remains a greater slave than they. How did this change come about? I do not know. What can make it legitimate? That question I think I can answer.*[79]

---

[77] Cicero, *Divinatione*, Bk. 2, Ch.58: 119.
[78] Wiker, *10 Books*.
[79] Rousseau, *Social Contract*, I: 1.

From this first premise, to the next, that of family as the first form of social organization,[80] Rousseau comes so close to Locke as to be suggestive of plagiarism. To the question on the origins of authority beyond the primordial authority of parents over children, which even here is conditional—as children "are born men and free; their liberty belongs to them"[81]—Rousseau finds that authority over the free-born is usurped by force: "Since no man has a natural authority over his fellow, and force creates no right, we must conclude that conventions form the basis of all legitimate authority among men."[82] One soon comes to a conclusion that authority is unnatural and is maintained by "conventions," or what one might call morals and religion, and the institutions deriving therefrom. We are on familiar ground, with the "primary ties" condemned by the critical theorists as inhibiting "freedom."[83]

At a time when the Divine Right of Kings was still a vestige of the primordial character of traditional societies, when the King was the nexus between the community and the godhead,[84] Rousseau stated that, "it is an empty and contradictory convention that sets up, on the one side, absolute authority, and, on the other, unlimited obedience." [85] It is only through authority, Rousseau theorizes, that war arises, for none is possible in a state of "nature":

> *But it is clear that this supposed right to kill the conquered is by no means deducible from the state of war. Men, from the mere fact that, while they are living in their primitive independence, they have no mutual relations stable enough to constitute either the state of peace or the state of war, cannot be naturally enemies. War is constituted by a relation between things, and not between persons; and, as the state of war cannot arise out of simple personal relations, but only out of real relations, private war, or war of man with man, can exist neither in the state of nature, where there is no constant property, nor in the social state, where everything is under the authority of the laws.*[86]

---

[80] Ibid., I: 2.
[81] Ibid., I: 4.
[82] Ibid., I: 4.
[83] Erich Fromm, *Escape from Freedom*. On the "Critical Theorists" and their attack on organic social bonds as "repressive" see: Bolton, *The Perversion of Normality*, 153-184.
[84] Evola, *Revolt*, passim.
[85] Rousseau, *Social Contact*, I: 4.
[86] Ibid.

Origins of Society

While the assumptions of the eighteenth century salon would be laughable in normal society, they remain the premises of present day social sciences. It was precisely to "prove" such assumptions that Margaret Mead was sent by Franz Boas, the iconic figure in cultural anthropology, to briefly study Samoan society, and write a book that would show conflict ravaged Western society that Samoans in their pristine state of nature, did indeed live happy, peaceful, and free. While it seems extraordinary that her book, *The Coming of Age in Samoa*, published in 1928, established an enduring reputation, in 1983 her findings were shown to be nonsense by Derek Freeman in his *Margaret Mead and Samoa*. Not only was Freeman an anthropologist but he was an honorary Samoan chief, with an intimate forty years knowledge of Samoan society. Yet Freeman was lambasted. For example, Mead claimed that Samoan society is based on cooperation without social hierarchy, where free love is the norm. Freeman showed that Samoan society is deeply competitive, with high rates of rape and murder, and a strict hierarchy whereby any sleight towards a chief, however unintentional, can cause violence.[87]

For Rousseau, as for Locke, individuals in their state of nature (the noble savage[88]) reach a stage of existence when they must combine to more efficiently share resources for their survival, "and the primitive condition can then exist no longer."[89] Here according to Rousseau and other social contract theorists, we have the beginnings of social organization. The problem becomes one of how individuals can come together in "aggregate" without sacrificing their supposedly inborn "liberty." Rousseau phrases the problem:

> *"The problem is to find a form of association which will defend and protect with the whole common force the person and goods of each associate, and in which each, while uniting himself with all, may still obey himself alone, and remain as free as before."* This is the fundamental problem of which the Social Contract provides the solution.[90]

---

[87] The controversy is discussed in Bolton, *The Perversion of Normality*.
[88] Although Rousseau is often credited with the term, he did not use it, but did refer to the same concept.
[89] Rousseau, *Social Contract*, I:6.
[90] Ibid., I: 6.

Society, nation, and state are matters of property relations among individuals, according to the social contract theory. Here we see the materialistic antecedents of both free trade and socialism. They are problems of commerce and of the merchant. The state-forming, nation-forming and race-forming processes[91] are rendered as matters of contractual agreement as though in a lawyer's office:

> *The clauses of this contract are so determined by the nature of the act that the slightest modification would make them vain and ineffective; so that, although they have perhaps never been formally set forth, they are everywhere the same and everywhere tacitly admitted and recognized, until, on the violation of the social compact, each regains his original rights and resumes his natural liberty, while losing the conventional liberty in favor of which he renounced it.*[92]

Civil Society Replaces Organic Community

What emerges is a conflict between the traditional, "organic community" (*Gemeinschaft*) and "civil society" (*Gesellschaft*). The "civil society" concept of the eighteenth century is presented today as the modern method of government: what George Soros and his teacher Karl Popper call "the open society."[93] A table of comparisons gives clarity of definitions (see below).

The concept was developed by the sociologist Ferdinand Tönnies (1855–1936). What Rousseau and Locke, et al. describe in the formation of society is analogous to the formation of a business corporation, with individuals contracting for the protection of their mutual economic interests. While the organic community arises and maintains the family bond, in a social hierarchy Locke and Rousseau both stated that society develops by superseding this. Marx said much the same.

As Spengler pointed out, Marx formulated his ideas under the impress of the same *zeitgeist* or spiritual epoch as Whig ideologues such as Locke. Hence, Marxism became a mirror image of liberal capitalism and not a transcendence of it. Marx condemned as "reactionists," including other

---

[91] For an examination on such processes as organic see: Bolton, *The Decline and Fall of Civilisations*.
[92] Ibid.
[93] For an example of this theory see: Bolton, *The Perversion of Normality*.

socialists, those who sought a return to the organic community.[94] Such ideological background provides a basis for the nexus that exists between the left and oligarchy. The American Spenglerian philosopher, Yockey, explained:

> ...Capitalistically, all is economics. Self-interest means: economics. Marx differed on this plane in no way from the non-class war theoreticians of capitalism—Mill, Ricardo, Paley, Spencer, Smith. To them all, Life was economics, not Culture.... All believe in Free Trade and want no "State interference" in economic matters. None of them regard society or State as an organism. Capitalistic thinkers found no ethical fault with destruction of groups and individuals by other groups and individuals, so long as the criminal law was not infringed. This was looked upon as, in a higher way, serving the good of all. Marxism is also capitalistic in this.[95]

Comparison of Gemeinschaft and Gesellschaft[96]

Gemeinschaft Relationships	Gesellschaft Relationships
Personal	Impersonal
Informal	Formal and contractual
Intimate and familiar	Task-specific
Traditional	Utilitarian
Sentimental	Realistic
Emphasis on ascribed statuses	Emphasis on achieved statuses
Less tolerance to deviance	Greater tolerance to deviance
Holistic relationships	Segmental (partial) relationship
Long duration	Transient and fragmented
Relatively limited social change	Very evident social change
Predominance of informal social control	Greater formal social control
We-feeling	They-feeling
Typifies rural life	Typifies urban life

---

[94] Marx, *Communist Manifesto*, 57.
[95] Yockey, *Imperium*, 114-115.
[96] Tönnies, *Gemeinschaft und Gesellschaft*.

Social Contract

As noted in the table above in the contrast between organic communities and civil societies, the former is based on "informal social control," that is to say what we can call "customs" and "traditions," sustained by a community's religion, and the nexus between God, throne, and people. Civil societies on the other hand, despite their foundation in the theoretical contract between individuals combining to protect their safety, rights of property and commerce, are held together by "greater formal social control." That is because once it is decided on what basis individuals will be contracted together into a society (called the "general will"), as in commercial contracts, there are laws that are upheld by punishments for those who breach them. Rousseau explained that these clauses of the "social contract":

> ...properly understood, may be reduced to one—the total alienation of each associate, together with all his rights, to the whole community; for, in the first place, as each gives himself absolutely, the conditions are the same for all; and, this being so, no one has any interest in making them burdensome to others.[97]

In theory, since individuals give themselves "freely" in joining the "social compact," as it is also called, they subsume their "rights" to the greater good. When a revolt by a cabal such as the Jacobins or the Bolsheviks assumes power, whether the Vendee peasants or the *Kulaks* have ever given themselves freely to the "general will" is questionable. Theoretically, there can be no injustice or coercion because everyone is equal:

> Finally, each man, in giving himself to all, gives himself to nobody; and as there is no associate over whom he does not acquire the same right as he yields others over himself, he gains an equivalent for everything he loses, and an increase of force for the preservation of what he has.[98]

In practice, equality can only be achieved by eliminating any part that rises above the level established by the social contract as the "general will." The individual *personality* expressed in the organic community, especially

---

[97] Rousseau, *Social Contract*, I: 6.
[98] Ibid.

during the Western Medieval epoch, through the guilds, and the autonomy of townships, is liquidated to establish this republic of equals.

General Will

Of the "general will" Rousseau asserts: "Each of us puts his person and all his power in common under the supreme direction of the general will, and, in our corporate capacity, we receive each member as an indivisible part of the whole."[99] "Liberty, Equality, Fraternity" are proclaimed under the "supreme direction of the general will," under which there is "supreme direction," which was later called the "dictatorship of the proletariat," and is today called the "international community." This "supreme direction" in the interests of the "general will" is maintained by ultimate sanction to violence, whether under the direction of the Committee of Public Safety, Cheka, United Nations, NATO, or US armed forces, the latter three acting under euphemistically termed "policing actions." The character of the "general will" is set out by the Declaration of the Rights of Man, the Soviet Constitution, the UN Declaration on Human Rights, and its multiple emanations.

While Rousseau alludes to each individual being an "indivisible part of the whole," this seemingly organic concept is precisely what is abolished by the doctrine, as the imposition of "equality" eliminates the differentiation that is a necessary basis of authentic "corporate" (organic: *corpus*) community. When the French Republic prohibited the guilds what they eliminated was the final vestige of the traditional organic community that allowed each member to be "an indivisible part of the whole." The French Assembly abolished the guilds in 1791.[100] Any form of association among the trades, arts, or professions, was seen as an obstacle to free trade, and was declared to be "unconstitutional, prejudicial to liberty and the Declaration of the Rights of Man."[101]

> *In place of guilds, the National Assembly, in the name of liberty and as a fiscal measure, enacted an occupational license (patente) that allowed its holder to practice whatever trade he wished. Problems quickly developed—so much so that the abolition of guilds and the inauguration of the occupational license became indelibly associated in the public's mind with a*

---

[99] Ibid., I: 6.
[100] "Chapelier Law."
[101] Ibid., Article 4.

> *sharp decline of standards in both production and commerce. Disaffection with the unregulated market and workplace took hold, prompting a favorable recollection of the era of guilds. Indeed, the fact that the commission appointed by the National Convention in 1795 to draft a new constitution believed it necessary to include an article maintaining the proscription of guilds indicates that the sentiment to return to a system of guilds was more than idle longing. Despite some opposition, the Convention approved it, and it became article 355 of the Constitution of the Year III, which established the Directory.*
>
> *...The extraordinarily difficult winter of 1795–1796 only encouraged favorable memories of guilds; amid hardship and dearth, the public associated the era of corporations with a time of adequate supply, market stability, and good quality.*[102]

Despite prolonged debate on the reestablishment of the guilds under Napoleon, this was not undertaken. It was left to the Catholic Church to reformulate a traditional social doctrine contra what was seen as a double-headed hydra of materialism: free trade and socialism. Of the process Leo XIII wrote in 1891:

> *[F]or the ancient workingmen's guilds were abolished in the last century, and no other protective organization took their place. Public institutions and the laws set aside the ancient religion. Hence, by degrees it has come to pass that working men have been surrendered, isolated and helpless, to the hardheartedness of employers and the greed of unchecked competition.*[103]

Double-Speak

Rousseau dialectically justified repression in the name of liberty by arguing that once the "general will" is contracted into, any deviance therefrom legitimizes repression:

> *In order then that the social compact may not be an empty formula, it tacitly includes the undertaking, which alone can give force to the rest, that whoever refuses to obey the general will*

---

[102] Fitzsimmons, "Debate on Guilds."
[103] Leo XIII, *Rerum Novarum*.

> *shall be compelled to do so by the whole body. This means nothing less than that he will be forced to be free; for this is the condition which, by giving each citizen to his country, secures him against all personal dependence. In this lies the key to the working of the political machine; this alone legitimizes civil undertakings, which, without it, would be absurd, tyrannical, and liable to the most frightful abuses.*[104]

Society is reduced to being a legalistic state, the citizen subject to punishment for breach of contract. He will be "forced to be free," according to the definition of "freedom" decreed by the "general will," framed by lawyers (e.g. Robespierre, Danton) and other bourgeoisie. The regime is enacted by detachment from tradition. The allusion to the citizen being "forced to be free" pre-empts the doctrine of the critical theorists when they wrote of cutting "primary ties" to be "free."

Where problems might arise is when the "general will" is deemed to be in error. "Our will is always for our own good, but we do not always see what that is; the people is never corrupted, but it is often deceived, and on such occasions only does it seem to will what is bad." Rousseau differentiates between the "will of all" and the "general will." The term "general will," posturing as liberty, becomes, like the "dictatorship of the proletariat," a facade for tyranny, because someone must determine what the true "general will" actually is.[105]

Fracture of the General Will

Societies might fracture into "associations" in conflict, and one faction might become dominant, which is precisely what occurred in France, which fractured into bloody conflict until order was established by Napoleon.

Rousseau's answer is that to prevent factions, each citizen should think only "his own thoughts." Conversely, if this is not possible, the other option is to actually increase the factional associations, so that no faction becomes dominant.

This artificially-contrived social fracturing is not merely the left's strategy of "intersectionality" and what is referred to as "identity politics," but it is vigorously promoted by Soros, Rockefeller, Ford, and other

---

[104] Rousseau, *Social Contract*, I:7.
[105] Ibid., II: 3.

oligarchic money, in the name of "human rights," "democracy," "equality," "social justice," and of course an "inclusive economy," summed up with the term "open society."

In Rousseau's republic the social body-corporate becomes analogous to an organism whose cells and organs are being eaten away by disease. Having destroyed the organic social community in the name of freedom, those two options when the "general will" threatens anarchy, are Rousseau's solution: "These precautions are the only ones that can guarantee that the general will shall be always enlightened, and that the people shall in no way deceive itself." [106]

Ultimately order must be restored by a Napoleon, Stalin, or Mussolini, to avoid total fracture into chaos, and whatever blood is shed by these is minor compared to the hell on earth that would be enacted under the continuation of Jacobinism or the Bolshevism of Trotsky, Mao Zedong, and Pol Pot.

Rousseau also states that the death penalty is sanctioned for those who break the social contract. In so doing they are being suicidal, since it is in every individual's interests to abide by the contract. Rousseau is for a change clear:

> *Again, every malefactor, by attacking social rights, becomes on forfeit a rebel and a traitor to his country; by violating its laws be ceases to be a member of it; he even makes war upon it. In such a case, the preservation of the State is inconsistent with his own, and one or the other must perish; in putting the guilty to death, we slay not so much the citizen as an enemy.*[107]

Here is the ideological justification for the guillotine, the Cheka firing squad and, since we now have a "world community" signed to global social contracts (the myriad UN covenants, treaties, and declarations), NATO/US bombs, and UN occupation forces. Rousseau established the premise for this, stating that *"doubtless there is a universal justice emanating from reason alone."* [108] In order for these laws to be effective, *"Conventions and laws are therefore needed to join rights to duties and refer justice to its object."*[109]

---

[106] Ibid., II: 3.
[107] Ibid., II: 5.
[108] Ibid., II: 8.
[109] Ibid.

People Might Get It Wrong

Rousseau sees the problem arising from being able to maintain what is the "enlightened" "general will," since the populace might get it wrong. Therefore, the public, in order to recognize the true "general will" needs, for its own good, the "guidance" of politicians. However, there is also a need for indoctrination, or what is in the liberal democracies such as New Zealand simply called "education" and subsidized "public interest journalism." The public must be "compelled," and "must be shown the good road" (sic). What Rousseau gives us is a totalitarian state in the name of "freedom," ruled over by a cabal that has the power to "change" (sic) the character of every citizen:

> He who dares to undertake the making of a people's institutions ought to feel himself capable, so to speak, of changing human nature, of transforming each individual, who is by himself a complete and solitary whole, into part of a greater whole from which he in a manner receives his life and being; of altering man's constitution for the purpose of strengthening it; and of substituting a partial and moral existence for the physical and independent existence nature has conferred on us all. He must, in a word, take away from man his own resources and give him instead new ones alien to him, and incapable of being made use of without the help of other men.[110]
>
> The general will is always in the right, but the judgment which guides it is not always enlightened. It must be got to see objects as they are, and sometimes as they ought to appear to it; it must be shown the good road it is in search of, secured from the seductive influences of individual wills, taught to see times and spaces as a series, and made to weigh the attractions of present and sensible advantages against the danger of distant and hidden evils. The individuals see the good they reject; the public wills the good it does not see. All stand equally in need of guidance. The former must be compelled to bring their wills into conformity with their reason; the latter must be taught to know what it wills. If that is done, public enlightenment leads to the union of understanding and will in the social body: the parts are

---

[110] Ibid., II: 7.

made to work exactly together, and the whole is raised to its highest power. This makes a legislator necessary.[111]

Oligarchy

These new legislators would be an "elective aristocracy" that would replace "hereditary aristocracy," which is regarded as the worst form of government.[112] What Rousseau is advocating is an *oligarchy* (government by the few). Its totalitarian authority is sanctified by the "general will" and popular franchise. A monarchy however is inherently "wicked" (sic).[113]

Of "democracy," that can never really exist, and the fewer the hands in government the better, as efficiency will be expedited. *"Were there a people of gods, their government would be democratic. So perfect a government is not for men."*[114]

> If we take the term in the strict sense, there never has been a real democracy, and there never will be. It is against the natural order for the many to govern and the few to be governed. It is unimaginable that the people should remain continually assembled to devote their time to public affairs, and it is clear that they cannot set up commissions for that purpose without the form of administration being changed. In fact, I can confidently lay down as a principle that, when the functions of government are shared by several tribunals, the less numerous sooner or later acquire the greatest authority, if only because they are in a position to expedite affairs, and power thus naturally comes into their hands.[115]

The five-member *Directoire* (1795–99) of the French Republic was established as a dictatorship, to suppress the intrinsic anarchy of Jacobinism. Prior to that, Cromwell had dispensed with Parliament and established himself as "Lord Protector" (1653–58) with an appointed assembly. "All power to the Soviets" was replaced by the Central Committee of the Bolshevik Party.

---

[111] Ibid., II: 6.
[112] Ibid., III: 5.
[113] Ibid., III: 6.
[114] Ibid., III: 4.
[115] Ibid.

Rousseau states that when the regime has assured that no citizen can survive without conforming, *"legislation is at the highest possible point of perfection."*[116] In a communist state life itself can be liquidated for the sake of the "general will"; in liberal democracies a dissident can be denied his livelihood, boycotted, dismissed, smeared, and become a pariah.

One might wonder how Rousseau would have fared in the present. Of Peter the Great, he said, like Spengler, that this Czar's "first wish was to make Germans or Englishmen, when he ought to have been making Russians; and he prevented his subjects from ever becoming what they might have been by persuading them that they were what they are not."[117] Further, "Liberty, not being a fruit of all climates, is not within the reach of all peoples."[118] According to Rousseau, differences between races were caused by climate. Therefore, literally some races were not climatically adapted to liberty: "We find then, in every climate, natural causes according to which the form of government which it requires can be assigned, and we can even say what sort of inhabitants it should have."[119] Barren lands should remain populated only by "savage people." Lands that only render subsistent living for one's labors should be populated by "barbarians," lands which provide a "middling surplus" over labor are fit for "free peoples," and those that render great surpluses are suitable for monarchies, enabling princes [rulers] to live on excess wealth without the destitution of the people. "In point of climate, despotism is suitable to hot countries, barbarism to cold countries, and good polity to temperate regions."[120]

Civil Religion

There seems to be the antecedents of fascism[121] in Rousseau's social contract, while liberals assert that fascism and the right are synonymous. Right traditionalists such as Julius Evola critiqued the liberal elements in fascism,[122] and the Catholic Church's social doctrine conflicted with what

---

[116] Ibid., III: 4.
[117] Ibid., II: 8.
[118] Ibid., III: 8.
[119] Ibid.
[120] Ibid.
[121] As a cogent ideology; not a term of abuse.
[122] For example, when Evola was tried by the Italian state for being an influence on youth in the "revival of Fascism," (for which he was found not guilty) Evola stated to the court: *"I am opposed to totalitarianism, counterposing to it the ideals of an organic, differentiated State, and considering 'fascist hierarchism' as a deviation."* Evola's Self-Defence Statement, in Evola, *Men Among Ruins*, 295.

it saw as the fascist idolization of the state. Under liberalism, the state is idolized literally, since Rousseau advocates a "civil religion" (sic), which:

> ...unites the divine cult with love of the laws, and, making country the object of the citizens' adoration, teaches them that service done to the State is service done to its tutelary god. It is a form of theocracy, in which there can be no pontiff save the prince, and no priests save the magistrates. To die for one's country then becomes martyrdom; violation of its laws, impiety; and to subject one who is guilty to public execration is to condemn him to the anger of the gods: Sacer estod.[123]

This was the inspiration for the rival cults of Nature and of the Supreme Being in Jacobin France, erected on the ruins of the Church and the killing of priests. Marxism assumed cultic forms in the communist states; in liberal democracies equality and "human rights" have assumed the role of a "civil religion" that is dogmatically imposed with "public execration" for those who dissent.

Like leftist prelates of the present, Rousseau spoke of "true Christianity," but also stated that there can be no "Christian republic" since:

> Christianity preaches only servitude and dependence. Its spirit is so favourable to tyranny that it always profits by such a régime. True Christians are made to be slaves, and they know it and do not much mind: this short life counts for too little in their eyes.[124]

In this he was a precursor of Marxist atheism, which analyzes Christianity as a means of bourgeoisie social control. Yet Rousseau's "civil religion" is, as the name itself states, for the purpose of maintaining loyalty to the republic. Hence, the Declaration of the Rights of Man was depicted as being inscribed on stone tablets, like the Ten Commandments. This "civil profession of faith," as Rousseau calls it, would have "articles" of "social sentiment" enabling the republic to:

> ...banish from the State whoever does not believe them.... it can banish him, not for impiety, but as an anti-social being,

---

[123] Rousseau, *Social Contract*, IV: 8.
[124] Ibid.

incapable of truly loving the laws and justice, and of sacrificing, at need, his life to his duty. If any one, after publicly recognising these dogmas, behaves as if he does not believe them, let him be punished by death: he has committed the worst of all crimes, that of lying before the law.[125]

Of religion per se, Rousseau had only "one" complaint: *"intolerance, which is a part of the cults we have rejected."*[126] If the results of Rousseau's doctrine were not so soaked in blood, he would be comedic.

Rousseau Honored by UN

Such is Rousseau's continuing influence that Claude Lévi-Strauss, the founder of structuralist anthropology, called him "the father of anthropology" in an essay by that name, published in a commemorative issue of the *UNESCO Courier* devoted to him.[127] Lévi-Strauss lauded Rousseau for predicting that students of mankind would be sponsored to study the various nations, *"of which we know only the names. And we presume to judge mankind!"* Rousseau cited those such as Diderot, saying that such individuals would be sponsored by the wealthy to travel the world and study remote areas. As detailed in *The Perversion of Normality*, the wealthy do indeed lavish funds on anthropologists to study mankind to compile data for planning methods of political and economic control. The UN features prominently in such plans. Rousseau's acknowledgement that the realities of faraway lands were not known to himself and the other *philosophes* of liberalism did not dissuade them from formulating dogmas based on unfounded speculations, that continue to be *imposed* by the UN, NATO, USA, EU and others.

Lévi-Strauss explained that Rousseau was the father of anthropology for two reasons:

> *But Rousseau did not just foresee anthropology, he actually founded it. Firstly, he did so in practice by writing the Discourse on the Origin and Foundations of Inequality Among Men which posed the question of the relationship between nature and culture, and is perhaps the first treatise produced on general anthropology. Secondly, he founded the science in theory by*

---

[125] Ibid.
[126] Ibid.
[127] Lévi-Strauss, "Rousseau."

setting down with remarkable clarity and precision the aims of the anthropologist as **distinguished from those of the moralist** and the historian: "When one wishes to study men, one must look close at hand; but to study man, one must learn to look into the distance; one must first observe the differences in order to discern the properties." (Essay on the Origin of Languages, Chapter VIII.)[128]

It takes a remarkable degree of self-delusion for Lévi-Strauss not to see—or should that be, pretending not to see?—that Rousseau, Diderot, et al. were nothing if not "moralists." What one gets from this inspiration is pseudo-science of the Margaret Mead type, whose purpose was to provide a moral comparison between Samoa and Western civilization. Yet Lévi-Strauss presents Rousseau as modern man's moral judge, writing:

> It is today, I repeat, because he put civilization on trial, pointing a finger at its iniquities and abuses and denied that these could possibly lead to the exercise of virtue in man, that Rousseau can help us to shatter an illusion the deadly effects of which we are now able alas to observe in ourselves and on ourselves.[129]

The Jacobins spoke much of civic virtue, and here we have their herald, Rousseau, who attained sainthood within the civic religion of the French Republic, which established the Committee of Public Safety to maintain that "virtue."

Lévi-Strauss betrayed his own moral posturing when lauding Rousseau for providing the present day social scientist with self-insight for his role as the "involuntary agents of the profound transformation he has wrought within them and which all mankind has come to find in the person of Jean-Jacques Rousseau." Thus, Rousseau as Messiah, not only for anthropologists, by for "all mankind," for through him comes self-realization. Like Buddha, Rousseau had attained self-realization, as Lévi-Strauss explained:

> But if Rousseau's experience helps us to see that of anthropology in a clearer light, it is because Rousseau's temperament, his personal history and circumstances spontaneously placed him in a situation which is precisely that of the anthropologist. And like

---

[128] Ibid., 11. Emphasis added.
[129] Ibid., 14.

the anthropologist, Rousseau did not fail to note at once the consequences that this situation had on him personally...[130]

Lévi-Strauss was writing a hagiography. The real Rousseau had a narcissistic personality disorder, was passive-aggressive, paranoid, and bipolar.[131]

In 2012 he was honored by the UN High Commission on Refugees, on the 300th anniversary of his birth. Writing for the UNHCR Rachel Humphris[132] stated that "Rousseau made many key contributions to the theory and practice of modern politics. One question occupied his thoughts more than any other: How can humans live freely within society?"[133]

Humphris commented: "Inequalities, he argued, were the artificial creations of social systems based on private property and organized labour—systems that allowed the domination and exploitation of some people by others."[134]

On the influence of Rousseau's doctrine on the UN, Humphris stated that "Rousseau's life and work remain highly relevant to the work of UNHCR and the many other humanitarian organizations that are based in the city where he was born [Geneva]." He had "made many key contributions to the theory and practice of modern politics." Rousseau, states Humphris, through his doctrine on the "freedom" of humanity in its "natural state," "contributed to the modern notion that people have inalienable rights, regardless of their place in society. This notion is clearly reflected in 20th century documents such as the United Nations Charter and the Universal Declaration of Human Rights."[135]

So, apparently, according to Dr. Humphris, an eminent ethnographer, present day anthropologists and ethnographers have not learned anything on the actual character of societies and races since the seventeenth and eighteenth century salon speculations about the noble savage. If that is the case, it is little wonder that the "eminent scientists" who wrote the UN Statement on Race made such an absurd job of it, having recourse to Enlightenment banalities.

---

[130] Ibid., 11.
[131] Bolton, *The Psychotic Left*, 49-63.
[132] Humphris is a sociologist and ethnographer of note, specializing in migration issues. She has been "a consultant for numerous UN and international agencies including UNHCR, International Organisation on Migration, World Health Organisation and the OECD. She was the UK Coordinator for the European Website on Integration 2016–2019."
[133] Humphris, "Relevance of Rousseau."
[134] Ibid.
[135] Ibid.

Neo-Jacobinism: From the USSR to the UN

"The French Revolution took place in the name of an intrinsically contradictory and impractical slogan: liberty, equality, fraternity. But in social life, freedom and equality tend to be mutually exclusive, and are antagonistic to each other! Freedom destroys social equality—this is even one of the roles of freedom—while equality restricts freedom, otherwise it cannot be achieved. As for the fraternity, it is not part of their family. This is just an adventurous addition to the slogan and it is not social arrangements that can make true brotherhood. It is spiritual."

Alexander Solzhenitsyn
News of Christendom, (1993)

Alexander Solzhenitsyn pointed out the Jacobin lineage of Bolshevism in an address in 1993 at the opening of a memorial in honor of the Vendée revolt. The peasantry of that region rose to fight the Jacobin tyranny, and the Jacobin state, in the name of *Liberty, Equality, Fraternity*, sought the total elimination of the population, for having breached the "social contract" and fractured the "general will." Solzhenitsyn saw the doctrine of equality as premising these twin tyrannies, Jacobinism and Bolshevism, that sprang from the seventeenth and eighteenth century notion that man can become equal if sufficient force is applied.

The Jacobin Declaration of the Rights of Man reflects the same doctrine as the American Declaration of Independence, Roosevelt's Atlantic Charter, Wilson's Fourteen Points, the Soviet Constitution, the UN Charter, the EU Charter, and so on. The Jacobin declaration states:

The representatives of the French people, organized as a National Assembly, believing that the ignorance, neglect, or contempt of the rights of man are the sole cause of public calamities and of the corruption of governments, have determined to set forth in a solemn declaration the natural, unalienable, and sacred rights of man, in order that this declaration, being constantly before all the members of the Social body, shall remind them continually of their rights and duties; in order that the acts of the legislative power, as well as those of the executive power, may be compared at any moment with the objects and purposes of all political institutions and may thus be more respected, and, lastly, in order that the grievances of the citizens, based hereafter upon simple and incontestable principles, shall tend to the maintenance of the constitution and redound to the happiness of all. Therefore the National Assembly recognizes and proclaims, in the presence and under the auspices of the Supreme Being,[136] the following rights of man and of the citizen:

1. *Men are born and remain free and equal in rights. Social distinctions may be founded only upon the general good.*
2. *The aim of all political association is the preservation of the natural and imprescriptible rights of man. These rights are liberty, property, security, and resistance to oppression.*
3. *The principle of all sovereignty resides essentially in the nation. No body nor individual may exercise any authority which does not proceed directly from the nation.*
4. *Liberty consists in the freedom to do everything which injures no one else; hence the exercise of the natural rights of each man has no limits except those which assure to the other members of the society the enjoyment of the same rights. These limits can only be determined by law.*
5. *Law can only prohibit such actions as are hurtful to society. Nothing may be prevented which is not forbidden by law, and no one may be forced to do anything not provided for by law.*
6. *Law is the expression of the general will. Every citizen has a right to participate personally, or through his representative, in its foundation. It must be the same for all, whether it protects or punishes. All citizens, being equal in the eyes of the law, are equally eligible to all dignities and to*

---

[136] The Supreme Being was a Deist conception that repudiated the Christian conception of God, and manifested as a religious cult in Jacobin France. See: Bolton, *The Occult and Subversive Movements*, 181-183.

all public positions and occupations, according to their abilities, and without distinction except that of their virtues and talents.
7. No person shall be accused, arrested, or imprisoned except in the cases and according to the forms prescribed by law. Any one soliciting, transmitting, executing, or causing to be executed, any arbitrary order, shall be punished. But any citizen summoned or arrested in virtue of the law shall submit without delay, as resistance constitutes an offense.
8. The law shall provide for such punishments only as are strictly and obviously necessary, and no one shall suffer punishment except it be legally inflicted in virtue of a law passed and promulgated before the commission of the offense.
9. As all persons are held innocent until they shall have been declared guilty, if arrest shall be deemed indispensable, all harshness not essential to the securing of the prisoner's person shall be severely repressed by law.
10. No one shall be disquieted on account of his opinions, including his religious views, provided their manifestation does not disturb the public order established by law.
11. The free communication of ideas and opinions is one of the most precious of the rights of man. Every citizen may, accordingly, speak, write, and print with freedom, but shall be responsible for such abuses of this freedom as shall be defined by law.
12. The security of the rights of man and of the citizen requires public military forces. These forces are, therefore, established for the good of all and not for the personal advantage of those to whom they shall be intrusted.
13. A common contribution is essential for the maintenance of the public forces and for the cost of administration. This should be equitably distributed among all the citizens in proportion to their means.
14. All the citizens have a right to decide, either personally or by their representatives, as to the necessity of the public contribution; to grant this freely; to know to what uses it is put; and to fix the proportion, the mode of assessment and of collection and the duration of the taxes.
15. Society has the right to require of every public agent an account of his administration.

16. A society in which the observance of the law is not assured, nor the separation of powers defined, has no constitution at all.
17. Since property is an inviolable and sacred right, no one shall be deprived thereof except where public necessity, legally determined, shall clearly demand it, and then only on condition that the owner shall have been previously and equitably indemnified.[137]

The USSR assured the same type of "rights" and with the same recourse to mass murder, and suppression of religion, as the Jacobins. The Constitution of the USSR (1936) stated:

In conformity with the interests of the working people, and in order to strengthen the socialist system, the citizens of the USSR are guaranteed by law:
(a) Freedom of speech;
(b) Freedom of press;
(c) Freedom of assembly, including the holding of mass meetings;
(d) Freedom of street processions and demonstrations.[138]

The preamble of the UN Universal Declaration of Human Rights (1948) reflects the same doctrine as the Jacobin Declaration of the Rights of Man:

Whereas recognition of the inherent dignity and of the equal and inalienable rights of all members of the human family is the foundation of freedom, justice and peace in the world,

Whereas disregard and contempt for human rights have resulted in barbarous acts which have outraged the conscience of mankind, and the advent of a world in which human beings shall enjoy freedom of speech and belief and freedom from fear and want has been proclaimed as the highest aspiration of the common people,

Whereas it is essential, if man is not to be compelled to have recourse, as a last resort, to rebellion against tyranny and oppression, that human rights should be protected by the rule of law,

---

[137] *Declaration of the Rights of Man.*
[138] Stalin, *Constitution*, Article 15.

> *Whereas it is essential to promote the development of friendly relations between nations,*
>
> *Whereas the peoples of the United Nations have in the Charter reaffirmed their faith in fundamental human rights, in the dignity and worth of the human person and in the equal rights of men and women and have determined to promote social progress and better standards of life in larger freedom,*
>
> *Whereas Member States have pledged themselves to achieve, in co-operation with the United Nations, the promotion of universal respect for and observance of human rights and fundamental freedoms,*
>
> *Whereas a common understanding of these rights and freedoms is of the greatest importance for the full realization of this pledge,*
>
> *Now, therefore,*
>
> *The General Assembly,*
>
> *Proclaims this Universal Declaration of Human Rights as a common standard of achievement for all peoples and all nations, to the end that every individual and every organ of society, keeping this Declaration constantly in mind, shall strive by teaching and education to promote respect for these rights and freedoms and by progressive measures, national and international, to secure their universal and effective recognition and observance, both among the peoples of Member States themselves and among the peoples of territories under their jurisdiction.*[139]

Like the Jacobin declaration, the UN manifesto is a "universal declaration." It establishes a universal law for the entirety of humanity; "a common standard of achievement for all peoples and all nations." Like Jacobinism it is predicated on a moral dogma, asserting that "disregard and contempt for human rights have resulted in barbarous acts which have outraged the conscience of mankind," yet it is precisely this imposition of "universal" ideas that are supposed to be applicable to "all peoples and all nations" that has resulted in the bloodiest of regimes: that of Jacobinism, and that of Bolshevism, and in our own epoch there have been continual wars and revolutions fought in the name of "democracy" and "human rights." As in 1789 France copious amounts of blood are spilled, and

---

[139] *Declaration of Human Rights,* Preamble.

justified by high sounding rhetoric delivered from rostrums, editorial offices, and parliamentary assemblies.

The parallels between the Jacobin Declaration of the Rights of Man, imposed on France by mass murder 230 years ago, the Constitution of the USSR, and the Declaration of Human Rights and other UN documents, are striking. In each case the purpose is to erect a tyranny behind the facade of "liberty," and the worst of all is the UN, whose doctrine is imposed on a global scale. In each case, the state giveth and the state taketh away. The same process is codified in the Race Relations and Human Rights laws of present-day Western states.

The Jacobin declaration assures its "citizens":

10. No one shall be disquieted on account of his opinions, including his religious views, **provided their manifestation does not disturb the public order established by law**.
11. The free communication of ideas and opinions is one of the most precious of the rights of man. Every citizen may, accordingly, speak, write, and print with freedom, **but shall be responsible for such abuses of this freedom as shall be defined by law**.[140]

Point 10 of the Jacobin declaration is most illustrative. "No one shall be disquieted on account of his opinions, including his religious views." This is the regime that while instituting state cults based on "Reason" and "Nature," publicly defrocked the bishop of Paris, placed an actress, dubbed "Liberty, Goddess of Nature," on the High Altar of Notre Dame Cathedral, deconsecrated Notre Dame, rededicated it to the Goddess of Reason, and smashed the glass chalice containing holy oil that had been used to consecrate the monarchs of France since 496 AD. When the Vendée region rose in revolt in 1793 a long campaign of extermination was undertaken by the Jacobin regime.[141] When searching for the origins of the West's current exaltation of "human rights" as a secular religion, the specter of Jacobinism becomes manifest.

The Jacobin declaration, Article 1 states that, "All human beings are born free and equal in dignity and rights. They are endowed with reason and conscience and should act towards one another in a spirit of

---

[140] *Declaration of the Rights of Man.*
[141] Bolton, *The Occult*, 179-185.

brotherhood." It is the imposition of universal equality, which results in the equality of tyranny.

Article 3 states, "Everyone has the right to life, liberty and security of person." Article 127 of the 1936 Soviet Constitution guaranteed "inviolability of the person." So did point 9 of the Jacobin declaration.

Article 17 of the UN declaration states that, (1) "Everyone has the right to own property alone as well as in association with others." (2)"No one shall be arbitrarily deprived of his property." So does the same point 17 of the Jacobin declaration.

Article 18 of the UN declaration states: "Everyone has the right to freedom of thought, conscience and religion; this right includes freedom to change his religion or belief, and freedom, either alone or in community with others and in public or private, to manifest his religion or belief in teaching, practice, worship and observance." Point 10 of the Jacobin declaration gives the same guarantees. So did article 124 of the Soviet Constitution in guaranteeing the right to both belief and non-belief.

Article 19 of the UN declaration assures us that; "Everyone has the right to freedom of opinion and expression; this right includes freedom to hold opinions without interference and to seek, receive and impart information and ideas through any media and regardless of frontier." Article 11 of the Jacobin declaration is precisely the same: "The free communication of ideas and opinions is one of the most precious of the rights of man. Every citizen may, accordingly, speak, write, and print with freedom, but shall be responsible for such abuses of this freedom as shall be defined by law." The Soviet Constitution guaranteed the same rights under Article 15, cited above. Article 29 (2) of the UN declaration states:

> *In the exercise of his rights and freedoms, everyone shall be subject only to such limitations as are determined by law solely for the purpose of securing due recognition and respect for the rights and freedoms of others and of meeting the just requirements of morality, public order and the general welfare in a democratic society.*

The Jacobin declaration states: "5. Law can only prohibit such actions as are hurtful to society." What is "hurtful" to society is determined by having established the "general will." The United Nations establishes a universal "general will" under which in the same clause 29 (3) it is stated: "These rights and freedoms may in no case be exercised contrary to the purposes and principles of the United Nations." Here, the UN establishes itself as a global government with ultimate sanction to punish those states that do not confirm to the global "general will," just as the Jacobin guillotines ran bloody red, and the Bolsheviks assured as many "rights" also, so long as none were "exercised contrary to the purposes and principles" of Bolshevism. The final point of the UN declaration establishes the authority of the UN affirming that:

> *Nothing in this Declaration may be interpreted as implying for any State, group or person any right to engage in any activity or to perform any act aimed at the destruction of any of the rights and freedoms set forth herein.*[142]

While petty tyrants postured at the rostrums of the UN, South Africa was declared a pariah, having been deemed to have contravened the sacrosanct principle of the UN Declaration, Article 16, that:

> *Men and women of full age, without any limitation due to race, nationality or religion, have the right to marry and to found a family. They are entitled to equal rights as to marriage, during marriage and at its dissolution.*[143]

It is notable how the seventeen articles of "human rights" proclaimed by the Jacobins as the "universal rights of man," could so readily be contorted as a moralistic sanction for tyranny. Each of the "articles" of the United Nations Declaration of Human Rights, so obviously inspired by the Jacobin declaration, has added "declarations," "treaties," and "covenants," until a mountainous corpus of "international law" has accumulated, each with its own UN bureaucracy, monitoring agency, and blueprints for laws that are expected to be enacted and enforced by member states. We see this with the human rights, race relations and "hate speech" laws that are becoming increasingly draconian, enacted in nominally White states on the basis of UN declarations on "human rights," "race relations," and immigration; in the laws that destroy the authority of parents, in the name of the "rights of the child," and of "anti-discrimination," and the imposition of ethnic interests against the European, whether as a minority or as a majority, in the name of "eliminating all forms of racial discrimination," or of "the rights of indigenous peoples." So it continues, until the legal edifice of an international tyranny, in the name of "human

---

[142] *Declaration of Human Rights*, Article 30.
[143] Ibid., Article 16 (1).

rights" and under the sanction of "global governance" is imposed over the world.

While indoctrination, intimidation, and increasingly pervasive laws are the preferred method for enforcing compliance by individuals and groups, the ultimate recourse remains violence. The USA, NATO and the UN, alone or in combination, will bomb a state—a "rogue nation"—into submission; use terrorist proxies as in Syria and Libya; a combination of bombs and terrorism as in Serbia; or well-orchestrated "spontaneous" (sic) "color revolutions" as in the former Soviet bloc state and North Africa.

Liberty and Equality in Practice

How the high sounding moral dogmas of the Bolsheviks and Jacobins were implemented in the course of establishing and perpetuating "equality" provided a precedent for the UN, NATO and the USA in seeking to impose the same doctrine.

The French Revolution was a manifestation of the sickness of the West[144] under whose *zeitgeist* both liberalism and Marxism emerged. During this epoch, which we might call the Age of Materialism, under which we remain, the notion arose that man is subjected not to divine laws, but to the laws of nature. These laws are not in themselves, as the Church meant by "natural law," manifestations of the divine. They are autonomous. Added to this is that man is matter. These "laws of nature" were not the result of empirical observation, but of intellectualizing within salons and Masonic lodges.[145]

With this came the equally spurious assumption of the noble savage, a purely speculative being that was said to exist in Africa, Oceania, and the Americas, living in happy freedom, because he was not subjected to the restraints of civilization, such as Church, family, property, hierarchy, marriage, homeland, and Crown. If man could be liberated from civilization, he could return to a natural idyll.

Karl Marx sought to give this fanciful intellectual current a scientific basis, stating that ultimately communism, after the transition through socialism, aimed to eliminate all of those elements of civilization deemed repressive.

---

[144] For the theory that the Western Civilisation has entered a long process of cyclical decay see Bolton, *The Decline and Fall of Civilisations*; Spengler, *The Decline of The West*.
[145] Bolton, *The Occult and Subversive Movements*.

From a Catholic viewpoint Dr. Charles J. McFadden cogently explained the common outlook of liberalism and Marxism, and I can do no better than quote him on this:

> *The general nature of the future Communistic society is readily portrayed in a few lines. It will be a society which will need no organized institution of government. The vast social-minded majority will handle whatever abuses may occasionally take place. It will be a classless society, that is, no distinctions of rank will prevail. Men will work without compulsion, produce according to their capacity, and take from the great abundance of wealth in the common-store-house only in accordance with their needs....*
>
> *The problem which Communism is here endeavouring to solve is, of course, the extremely important problem of the equality of men. The problem is not new, except in the specific form it takes.*
>
> *In the days preceding the French Revolution this same problem of exaggerated inequality was present in France. At the time it was the inequality of privilege which concerned men, that is, inequality before the law, political inequality....*
>
> *Once the inequality of privilege was abolished, a new freedom came into being which developed into an amazing rapidity into liberalism. The solution of the French Revolution eradicated the inequalities of the social past but gave birth to the inequalities of the industrial future.... It paved the way for Liberalism which, when coupled with the Industrial Revolution, created in society greater inequalities of wealth than had ever previously existed.*
>
> *The equality born of the French Revolution was equality in a negative sense. For the most part it meant equal freedom from constraint by the State, Church or Religion in economic affairs.*
>
> *Thus, the attempt of the French Revolution to establish economic equality by destroying political inequalities was a complete failure. Actually, it created a rank Liberalism which made real equality an impossibility.*
>
> *...It reduced the function of the State to that of a policeman whose duty was to protect the freedom of individuals. It forgot that man is a member of society, and thus that he can never act with a freedom which takes only himself into consideration...*

> Today, Communism is very much concerned over the problem of economic inequality...and the solution of this problem, says Communism, lies in the complete destruction of all classes.... Reduce all men to an equal footing, and economic equality will necessarily result....[146]

Communism and liberalism ultimately sought a return to the noble savage; the hypothetical happy individual unencumbered by civilization:

> *I am as free as nature first made man,*
> *Ere the base laws of servitude began,*
> *When wild in woods the noble savage ran.*[147]

Both erected tyrannies.

Amidst the moral decay of France, Edmund Burke commented on the mediocrity of the many lawyers who led the revolutionaries; the intelligentsia who had through some personality quirk found the norms of civilized behavior a burden. There came to prominence the Marquis Donatien Alphonse François de Sade, who epitomizes the *zeitgeist*. It is apt that the individual who embodied the spirit of liberalism should also give his name to sadism.

With the triumph of Jacobinism Donatien de Sade was released from an asylum in 1790. Despite his infamy as a brutalizer of women among the poor, he was elected to the National Assembly where he aligned with the most extreme wing of the revolution, led by Marat. His doctrine of sex and death pre-empted Freud's premise of Eros and Thanatos as the primary motivators of human behavior.

In the *Philosophy in the Bedroom* de Sade condemned in the name of "Nature" "insipid moralists." He called maidenly virtue "absurd" and a product of "dangerous bonds," imposed by "a disgusting religion," and "imbecilic parents." He pre-empted the left in stating that family bonds are "repressive"; what the critical theorists 150 years later called the incubator "fascism"[148]:

> *It is not in this age of preoccupation with the rights of man and general concern for liberties that girls ought to continue to believe themselves their families' slaves, when it is clearly*

---

[146] McFadden, *Philosophy of Communism*, 319-321.
[147] John Dryden, *Conquest of Granada*.
[148] Adorno, *Authoritarian Personality*.

established that these families' power over them is totally illusory.[149]

It seems that de Sade's actual interest was the "liberation" of girls at the earliest possible age from the protection of the family, so that they could be left to the mercies of debased "aristocrats" such as himself. All these elements we can see as integral to today's liberalism, leftism, and feminism. Here we see the irony of feminists espousing the doctrines that were all embodied in the philosophy of de Sade, who purveyed his sociopathy behind the facade of "liberty, equality, fraternity," while writing philosophical rationalizations on the brutalization and humiliation of women. For this liberation he counseled:

[T]o trample upon all the prejudices of her childhood...the most formal disobedience to her family's orders...that among all the bonds to be burst, I ought very surely to recommend that the very first be those of wedlock.[150]

De Sade next establishes himself as the father of "population control," preceding Margaret Sanger by 120 years. Here he supports buggery, for which he had a personal preference, abortion, and contraception, in the name of "liberty":

Madame de Saint-Ange: Do you know, Dolmancé, that by means of this system [mass buggery] you are going to be led to prove that totally to extinguish the human race would be nothing but to render Nature a service?

Dolmancé: Who doubts of it, Madame?[151]

Childbirth and child rearing are to be abhorred as infringing on women's freedom, and abortion and infanticide are "no crimes of Nature."

Madame de Saint-Ange: Propagation is in no wise the objective of Nature; she merely tolerates it; from her viewpoint, the less we propagate, the better; and when we avoid it altogether, that's best of all. Eugénie, be the implacable enemy of this wearisome child-getting, and even in marriage incessantly deflect that

---

[149] de Sade, *Philosophy in the Bedroom*, Dialogue the Third.
[150] Ibid.
[151] Ibid.

perfidious liquor whose vegetation serves only to spoil our figures, which deadens our voluptuous sensations, withers us, ages and makes us fade and disturbs our health; get your husband to accustom himself to these losses; entice him into this or that passage, let him busy himself there and thus keep him from making his offerings at the temple; tell him you detest children, point out the advantages of having none. Keep a close watch over yourself in this article, my dear, for, I declare to you, I hold generation in such horror I should cease to be your friend the instant you were to become pregnant. If, however, the misfortune does occur, without yourself having been at fault, notify me within the first seven or eight weeks, and I'll have it very neatly remedied. Dread not infanticide; the crime is imaginary: we are always mistress of what we carry in our womb...[152]

De Sade invents every cliché and slogan of feminism in his defense of abortion. "We are always mistress of what we carry in our womb," says this liberal champion of "women's health issues." He compares the child to excrement that might be purged with no more meaning than a daily toilet routine. Here we have the life-wary slogan of feminism; that a woman's body is her own regardless of any responsibility one's gender incurs, since genders are but social constructs and fluid according to one's whim.

...as we are of the nails we pare from our fingers, or the excrements we eliminate through our bowels, because the one and the other are our own, and because we are absolute proprietors of what emanates from us.[153]

Here is the liberal creed of freedom laid bare and unequivocal. In the name of "Nature," de Sade wrote, "destruction" was one of her "chief laws," under which "nothing that destroys can be criminal." "Murder" he described as "altering forms." Man was matter, without spirit, and Nature was "conflict."[154] Under the republican utopia of Nature, there would be few actions that are "criminal"[155] when the foundations of society are "liberty and equality." Moreover, there is nothing divine about the child,

---

[152] Ibid.
[153] Ibid.
[154] Ibid.
[155] Ibid.

nothing of the spirit about "it." It is not merely a "thing"; it is literally akin to "shit." Here we see the attitude of the abortionist in theory and practice.

La Droit Humain

The French revolutionists set the course for how human rights would be applied. The implementation of Point 10 of the sacrosanct Declaration of the Rights of Man, "No one shall be disquieted on account of his opinions, including his religious views," was put into effect:

> *All ecclesiastics, not just those in charge of parishes, would now be required to take an oath of allegiance to a regime of "liberty and equality," and any who refused would be immediately deported or—if they were aged or infirm—placed in detention. Most of the remaining church property was put up for sale, and all religious houses were emptied and closed. Even the "constitutional" clergy, those who had taken the oath and supported the Revolution, would be forbidden to wear clerical garb in public and would lose their right to register births, marriages, and deaths—a task henceforth assumed by the municipal administration.[156]*
>
> *...[In 1793] Local militants built a bonfire of sacred books and vestments, and "a philosopher gave a speech announcing that there was no more religion and no more God, and that everything was a question of Nature." At about the same time the bishop of Paris and nearly all other clergymen sitting in the Convention removed their crucifixes and renounced the priesthood. Celebrations in the ex-cathedral of Notre Dame were held in honor of a statue of liberty and a "goddess of reason." Soon thereafter sansculotte militants began knocking off the heads of the long rows of Gothic saints carved on the building's exterior....[157]*

Of Point 9 of the human rights charter:

> *As all persons are held innocent until they shall have been declared guilty, if arrest shall be deemed indispensable, all*

---

[156] Tackett, *Coming of Terror*, 196.
[157] Ibid., 316.

> harshness not essential to the securing of the prisoner's person shall be severely repressed by law....
>
> Most of those assaulted had already been suspected in recent months for a variety of pernicious activities, and now in a period of widespread fear it was all the easier to demonize them. Some were killed with extreme brutality, and decapitated heads and body parts were carried about town—just as in the most violent uprisings of the seventeenth century.[158]

As France was engaged in "revolutionary wars" with its neighbors, insurrections in her provinces, and mounting paranoia about alleged conspirators and traitors, it was decided that the "rights of man" only really applied to those committed to the revolution, and that important in "the institutionalization of the Terror":

> [W]as the infamous "law of suspects," passed by the Convention with very little debate on September 17 [1793]. The intention of the law was supposedly to give a more precise definition to the concept of "suspect." In fact, however, the text included a series of elastic clauses, targeting all those who "have shown themselves to be the partisans of tyranny or federalism or are enemies of liberty" or who could not produce evidence of civisme—a term signifying "public spiritedness" but whose meaning was never itself clearly defined. In any case, the actual designation of suspects was entirely in the hands of the local surveillance committees, which assumed the role often played earlier in the Revolution by the popular societies. Such committees would be all the more threatening, moreover, in that virtually no appeal was possible against their decisions and that they were now to be purged and to consist only of the most radical patriots. The previous June Barère[159] had attacked the activities of such surveillance committees for their violations of the Declaration of Rights. But since then the Committee of Public Safety had clearly changed its position. As Collot d'Herbois[160] explained it, "the rights of man were not made for counterrevolutionaries, but only for the sansculottes."[161]

---

[158] Ibid., 205.
[159] Bertrand Barère, a rival of Robespierre, was a prominent member of the Committee of Public Safety, and helped to inaugurate the Jacobin Terror.
[160] Deputy from Paris to the National Convention, and a member of the Committee of Public Safety.
[161] Tackett, *Coming of Terror*, 303.

De Sade's party was that of the most radical Jacobins. They were interested in depopulating France. They used the familiar rationale that there are too many people to sustain. The Abbé Barruel recounted of the Jacobins that they call out "by the mouth of the bloody Marat for 270,000 heads, declaring that before long it will count only by millions." Barruel commented that the Jacobins knew well that their doctrine of "Equality can only be accomplished in its full extent, by depopulating the world." Quoting a contemporary report he stated that when the inhabitants of Montauban were being starved they were met with the Jacobin response: "Fear not, France has sufficiency for twelve million of inhabitants; all the rest [the other twelve million] must be put to death, and then there will be no scarcity of bread."[162]

Under Jacobinism the Marxist concept of the "class enemy" manifested:

> *Whole categories of individuals were sent to the guillotine, not apparently on the basis of any specific crimes committed but because of the positions they held under the Old Regime. All of the former directors of the general tax farm who could be located; numerous members of the former Parlement of Paris; men and women from the greatest noble families of Paris: all were decimated in a manner of weeks. The proportion of nobles among those guillotined rose from about 8 to 20 percent. There were so many executions that in mid-June [1793] municipal leaders moved the guillotine to the eastern edge of the city, allowing a more efficient clean-up of the blood and the bodies.*[163]

Bolshevism Continues the Jacobin Process

The Jacobins set the precedent for Bolshevism, the Committee of Public Safety was the predecessor of the Bolshevik secret police, the Cheka, whose members were driven by a bloodlust that can only be explained by the convergence of psychotics. [164]

During the Russian Civil War between the White and the Red armies, after Denikin's White Army defeated the Bolsheviks at Odessa in August 1919, Rev. R. Courtier-Forster, Chaplain of the British forces at Odessa and the Black Sea ports, who had been held captive by the Bolsheviks, reported

---
[162] Barruel, *History of Jacobinism*, Part IV, Vol. IV, 443.
[163] Tackett, *Coming of Terror*, 33.
[164] Bolton, *Psychotic Left*.

the horrors of Bolshevism. He related that on the ship Sinope, the largest cruiser of the Black Sea Fleet, some of his personal friends had been chained to planks and slowly pushed into the ship's furnaces to be roasted alive. Others were scalded with steam from the ship's boilers. Mass rapes were committed, while the local Soviet press debated the possibilities of nationalizing women. The screams from women being raped and from other victims in what Rev. Courtier-Forster called the "Bolshevik's House of Torture" at Catherine Square, could be heard for blocks around, while at Catherine Square the Bolsheviks tried to muffle the screams with the noise of lorries thundering up and down the street.[165]

When the Rohrberg Commission of Enquiry entered Kiev after the Soviets had been driven out in August 1919, it described the "execution hall" of the Cheka:

> *All the cement floor of the great garage (the execution hall of the departmental Cheka of Kief) was flooded with blood. This blood was no longer flowing, it formed a layer of several inches: it was a horrible mixture of blood, brains, of pieces of skull, of tufts of hair and other human remains. All the walls were bespattered with blood; pieces of brains and scalps were sticking to them. A gutter twenty-five centimeters wide by twenty-five centimeters deep and about ten meters long ran from the center of the garage towards a subterranean drain. This gutter along its whole length was full to the top with blood.... Usually as soon as the massacre had taken place the bodies were conveyed out of the town in motor lorries and buried beside the grave about which we have spoken; we found in a corner of the garden another grave which was older and contained about eighty bodies. Here we discovered on the bodies traces of cruelties and mutilations the most varied and unimaginable. Some bodies were disemboweled, others had limbs chopped off, some were literally hacked to pieces. Some had their eyes put out and the head, face, neck and trunk covered with deep wounds. Further on we found a corpse with a wedge driven into the chest. Some had no tongues. In corner of the grave we discovered a certain quantity of arms and legs.*[166]

---

[165] Courtier-Forster, "Bolshevism," 2-4.
[166] Melgunov, *The Red Terror in Russia*, 161.

Jim Jones: Human Rights Folk Hero

Until his incident with Kool Aid, Rev. Jim Jones was feted by the liberal Establishment. When the Peoples Temple campaigned for George Mascone for Mayor of San Francisco and other liberal candidates for council, Mascone thanked Jones, writing:

> *Your contributions to the spiritual health and well-being of our community have been truly inestimable, and I am heartened by the fact that we can continue to expect such vigorous and creative leadership from the Peoples Temple in the future. By your tireless efforts on behalf of all San Franciscans, you have demonstrated that the unique powers of spiritual energy and civic commitment are virtually boundless, and that our lives would be sadly diminished without your continuing contributions.*[167]

During the 1976 presidential campaign, Jones met with Rosalynn Carter, wife of Democratic Party candidate Jimmy Carter, at the latter's urging. Jones also met vice-presidential candidate Walter Mondale in San Francisco. Jones was appointed by Mayor Mascone to the San Francisco Housing Committee, and became its chairman. City Supervisor Harvey Milk, the first open homosexual in office, enthused: *"Such greatness I have found in Jim Jones's Peoples Temple."* Dianne Feinstein and her colleagues on the San Francisco Board of Supervisors honored Jones "in recognition of his guidance and inspiration" in furthering "humanitarian programs." Jones was recipient of the Fourth Annual Martin Luther King, Jr. Humanitarian Award in 1977; and was named Humanitarian of the Year by the *Los Angeles Herald*.

Governor Jerry Brown spoke at the Peoples Temple in San Francisco. Willie Brown of the California Assembly; Lt. Governor Mervyn Dymally, and celebrity Bay Area reporter Paul Avery, praised Jones. Herb Caen, Pulitzer Prize-winning journalist for *The San Francisco Chronicle*, called Jones "the conscience" of San Francisco. Others who endorsed the Peoples Temple included: Senators Walter Mondale, Hubert Humphrey, Henry Jackson, Sam Ervin Jr., Warren Magnuson and Mike Gravel, Congressmen Philip Burton, Ron Dellums and Don Edwards, Congresswomen Bella Abzug and Patsy Mink.

---

[167] Abbott, *Politics and Jim Jones*.

The Peoples Temple was the fulfilment of the liberal utopia, honed to perfection as a social control mechanism; until the psychopathy of its "Dad" reached self-destruct mode.

The dispatching by Jones of around 900 zealots to an astral communist paradise, the Jacobin guillotine, the Bolshevik firing squad, or the fifty million annually aborted babies treated as "shit," in accordance with the Marquis de Sade's doctrine, all reduce to a common factor; what Malcolm Muggeridge called "the great liberal death wish."[168]

The Death Wish Against the Whites in Africa

Father Arthur Lewis, an Anglican minister who served in Rhodesia prior to its being flushed to oblivion, had referred to "Marxism and the Christian Death Wish."[169] This was at a time when the World Council of Churches (WCC) was at its height of influence, and taking a leading role in the destruction of the European remnant on the Dark Continent. The WCC pursued its foreign policy of human rights behind the facade of "Christianity." Father Lewis was one of the few traditional clergy remaining to resist.

In condemning the WCCs "Programme to Combat Racism" as a masquerade for the funding of savagery against Blacks and Whites alike in Southern Africa, Lewis turned to a 1977 Rhodesian newspaper file as representative of what was occurring:

> *Ten killed by mine: Scene of horror. A child's body hanging over a fence like a discarded doll, a decapitated woman's head hurled meters away from its mangled torso... The shattered bodies of women and children... Music as terrorist axes his victims.... Terror raid on murdered chief's funeral.... Mine blast kills fourteen: Fourteen Africans including two children, died on Saturday in the worst landmine incident since the war started.... Chief murdered by terrorists.... College gutted by attack... Terrorism wrecks schooling for 42,000. Schools razed by terrorists.... Pregnant wife died on terror march.... Terrorists murder sixteen, including a pregnant woman and two children.*[170]

---

[168] Muggeridge, *The Great Liberal Death Wish*.
[169] Lewis, *Christian Terror*, 11.
[170] Ibid., 57.

Lewis wrote of this:

These samples have been taken entirely at random, by thumbing through a file. White farmers have been and are being attacked and murdered.... Black children have been blown to smithereens with their ox-carts. There has been a case of burning at the stake. Old men are beaten to death, women raped and bayoneted. Men have had their ears and lips cut off, while their wives have been compelled to cook and eat them....

I myself visited the scene of the first Honde massacre in December 1976, where twenty-seven tea estate workers were bayonetted and shot before their families by followers of Robert Mugabe who crossed the Mozambique border and fled back again. They had dared to work for whites....[171]

On page 66 of Father Lewis' book is a picture of Natasha Glenny. I first saw Natasha's picture in 1977 in a magazine issued by the New Zealand-Rhodesia Society. I was twenty-one years old, and the image never left me. Father Lewis states of this:

What could be more ghastly than the bayoneting to death at the end of September, 1977, of the radiant six-months-old white baby Natasha Glenny, asleep in her cot at Chipinga? "She was lying face down," said her father. "Her back was a mass of lacerations and her flesh was white and pulpy. Before she was bayoneted she was thrown across the verandah." A tough security officer who saw the dead baby spent a sleepless night in tears.[172]

Whites worldwide are expected to "bend the knee" in homage to George Floyd, a cowardly Black criminal accidentally killed while resisting arrest. Who remembers Natasha Glenny? Robert Mugabe was rewarded with the presidency of Rhodesia and predictably reduced it to the sinkhole called Zimbabwe. What a travesty, what a sick joke that Rhodesia, orderly, prosperous, civilized, and run by those of British descent, was denied, in the name of "human rights" the independence that was routinely granted to every Black African tribal butcher in the process of European scuttle.

---

[171] Ibid., 58.
[172] Ibid., 61.

"Legacy of Enlightenment"

"Of all tyrannies, a tyranny sincerely exercised for the good of its victims may be the most oppressive. It would be better to live under robber barons than under omnipotent moral busybodies. The robber baron's cruelty may sometimes sleep, his cupidity may at some point be satiated; but those who torment us for our own good will torment us without end for they do so with the approval of their own conscience. They may be more likely to go to Heaven yet at the same time likelier to make a Hell of earth. This very kindness stings with intolerable insult. To be "cured" against one's will and cured of states which we may not regard as disease is to be put on a level of those who have not yet reached the age of reason or those who never will; to be classed with infants, imbeciles, and domestic animals."

C.S. Lewis (1948)[173]

The spectre of the "Enlightenment" hangs over several centuries of history like a giant funeral shroud embroidered with the term "human rights" over a mountain of corpses marked "liberated." Something of the origins and animating spirit of the "human rights" doctrine was explained by Ridrigo Salinas, of the Santiago branch of Huelen Freemasonry,[174] honoring the sixtieth anniversary of the United Nations Declaration of Human Rights. The commission drafting the Declaration was chaired by Eleanor Roosevelt, whose husband, the late president of the USA, Franklin Delano, was a 32nd Degree Mason.

On the 10th of December 1948, across the Seine from the Eiffel Tower—at the Palais Chaillot—the United Nations General

---

[173] Lewis, "The Humanitarian Theory of Punishment," in *God in the Dock: Essays on Theology and Ethics*, Chapter 4.
[174] The following year Salinas became Grand Master of the Santiago branch of Huelen Masonry, which had originated in Massachusetts in 1877.

> Assembly adopted the Universal Declaration of Human Rights. The Declaration had been written by a specially appointed Commission consisting of eight members...chaired by Eleanor Roosevelt and with the support of a secretariat....[175]

Salinas stated that the Declaration had been motivated by doctrines "going back generations," and this has served as the cornerstone of subsequent "human rights" laws. He alludes to "international enforcement":

> The Declaration...was inspired by a tradition of enlightenment going back generations, and by a morally fueled activism that had gained momentum during the preceding decades. Since then, a number of treaties, declarations and conventions, have shaped what today is understood as an international framework for the enforcement of Human Rights.[176]

Salinas specifically traces the origins:

> Human Rights, like Freemasonry, are a legacy of Enlightenment and a product of the eighteenth century. That period of history saw a deep moral transformation of society, through which human beings came to see themselves as autonomous, self-possessed creatures, recognizing other human beings as similarly autonomous creatures deserving equal respect.[177]

The individual is a "self-possessed, autonomous creature," which Salinas states is the doctrine of the Enlightenment epoch of which Freemasonry is a product. This "autonomous, self-possessed creature" was obliged by the "general will"—as determined by the Jacobin Assembly, and as enforced by Robespierre's Committee of Public Safety—to assume his role as "citizen" in the name of *liberty, equality, fraternity*, or face death. In the name of liberty, he was obliged to repudiate his faith, and offered instead the opportunity to worship in the cults of Reason and the Supreme Being. Again, this "self-possessed, autonomous creature" sounds precisely like the "free individuals" who have cut their bonds to the "primary ties" of family, faith, homeland, and ethnos, as described by Erich Fromm and the

---

[175] Salinas, "Human Rights."
[176] Ibid.
[177] Ibid.

critical theorists.[178] The century of Jacobinism is what Salinas calls the "deep moral transformation of society." It is the epoch George Washington—despite being a Freemason—and Alexander Hamilton feared would flood American in blood, as the Jeffersonians sought a second revolution on Jacobin lines.

Salinas refers to that messianic vision of "universal brotherhood," on the destruction of organic social and national bonds—again the "primary ties" condemned by the critical theorists—in the name of a nebulous equality for "all mankind." It is from that epoch that Reason was enthroned as the ultimate "authority," as Salinas calls it.

This profound psychological change created a new capacity of people to empathize across social boundaries, and a previously inexistent sense of universal brotherhood of all mankind. It was the period of human history in which Reason was advocated as the main source of authority.[179]

In was this "main source of authority"—*Reason*—that was elevated into a literal cult during the Jacobin regime. Established on November 10th, 1793, this cult of "enlightened rationalists" of the French Republic took over Notre Dame Cathedral and constructed a "mountain" inside Notre Dame, topped with a Grecian style "Temple of Reason." A flame burned on an altar. A column of young women dressed in white and adorned in tricolor sashes, holding torches, paraded up and down the hill, while the congregants sang André Chenier's hymn:

Thou, Holy Liberty, come dwell in this temple;
Be the Goddess of the French people.[180]

On November 24th, all churches in Paris were ordered to be turned into Temples of Reason. After its primary protagonists, Pierre Gaspard Chaumette and Jacques Hébert, were guillotined on March 24th the following year, it was replaced by the Cult of the Supreme Being in June,

---

[178] The title of Fromm's book *Escape from Freedom*, expresses his dismay that individuals would sooner have the security of "fascism"—"fascism" being defined as an attachment to the "primary ties" of family and homeland—than the freedom that requires severing those bonds and pursuing one's "self-actualization." The extent of one's intrinsic "Fascism" was later measured on an "F Scale" devised by sociologists (*The Authoritarian Personality*), according to one's affection for parents, one's nation, etc. For a detailed account of this movement see the author's book, *Perversion of Normality*.
[179] Salinas, "Human Rights."
[180] Kennedy, *French Revolution*, p. 343.

under the leadership of Robespierre. Another mountain was built, this time to the Supreme Being, in the National Gardens.[181]

How could the doctrine of equality *not* become a cult? Such an implicit fallacy cannot be erected and maintained without force of an increasingly tyrannical nature. Jacobinism was the beginning. Bolshevism followed. Jim Jones' People's Temple was nothing if not a cult of human rights. The cult of human rights, enshrined by the United Nations Declaration, uses whatever force is necessary where draconian laws are insufficient or cannot be imposed on a state. Can the "human rights" doctrine in the USA, Britain, New Zealand, Australia, or the EU be said to be any *less* pervasive than the doctrines of Jacobinism or Bolshevism, even if the methods of control are presently less violent, albeit with groups such as BLM or Antifa utilized as *de facto* Red Guards?

Salinas alludes to the cultic nature of "reason," seeing cultic symbolism in the UN Declaration:

> *It should not be seen, therefore, as mere coincidence that one of the members of the Commission in charge of drafting the Declaration, the French lawyer and philosopher André Cassin, compared the included rights to the portico of a temple. According to Cassin's view the first two articles of the declaration represent the courtyard steps of the portico and stand for human dignity, shared by all individuals regardless of their religion, ethnicity, or sex. The first pillar represents articles 3 to 11 and covers the rights of individuals to life and liberty. The second pillar, comprising articles 12 to 17, confers civil and property rights. The third, stretching from articles 18 to 21, alludes to political and social rights; and the fourth, from 22 to 27, encompasses economic and cultural rights.*[182]

The United Nations High Commission on Human Rights cites Cassin's (as above) description.[183]

Salinas next refers specifically to the slogan of Jacobinism as being the axiom of the present UN "human rights" ideology:

> *These courtyard and pillars support articles 28 and 30, the roof of the portico, stating that humans possess not only rights, but also duties to the community "in which alone the free and full*

---

[181] Ibid., 345.
[182] Salinas, "Human Rights."
[183] *Universal Declaration on Human Rights at 70.*

development of his personality is possible" and that everyone is entitled to a social and international order in which the rights and freedoms set forth in the Declaration can be fully realized. With an obvious enlightened—and French—inspiration Cassin identified these four pillars as representing dignity, liberty, equality, and fraternity.[184]

Salinas refers to an "international social order," "obviously" based on Jacobinism: "enlightened French inspiration," with its slogan of *liberty, equality, and fraternity;* the same slogan maintained by the Grand Orient de France as custodians of the Jacobin doctrine in the present-day: "The Freemasons of the Grand Orient de France are also intransigent defenders of republican ideals. They have taken as their own the French Republic's motto of 'Liberty-Equality-Fraternity' vital for solidarity and secularism."[185] They embrace "all beliefs...except those which are contrary to the values of the Republic and the Universal Declaration on Human Rights."[186]

---

[184] Ibid.
[185] "Grand Orient de France," 1.
[186] Ibid., 3.

In the Shadow of the Nuremberg Gallows: Raphael Lemkin and the Meaning of "Genocide"

The world in which we live, which is often referred by both advocates and antagonists as a "new world order," was formulated by globalist functionaries of the Roosevelt and Truman Administrations, blueprinting the details for the post-war world. The United Nations Organization was intended to be the infrastructure for a formalized, *de jure* world-government, where the USA would be able to buy a majority of the votes in the UN General Assembly, acting as a world parliament, through its Marshall Aid and other bribes to war-ravished, indebted, and decolonized states. Stalin stymied these plans for a post-war world-state via the UN, by (1) insisting that any one member of the UN Security Council is able to exercise a veto; and (2) rejecting the so-called Baruch Plan for the "internationalization of atomic energy," both plans regarded by Russia as having been designed to establish US global hegemony.[187] Nonetheless, a multitude of laws and treaties have emanated from the UN to secure its status as a *de facto* world-government, even if of a more shambolic variety than the global order envisaged by its founders.

The world war for what has been portrayed as a struggle against "nationalism" and "racism" provided moral justification for creating a legal edifice and doctrine to impose imprisonment and even the death penalty upon those who dissent, and are deemed as having committed "war crimes," "crimes of aggression," and crimes of "genocide." This would be well and good if the laws were applied equitably and justly. For centuries Western Christendom had been cultivating the virtues of "chivalry," at least in principle, and often in practice. Napoleon Bonaparte was, on defeat, exiled, not hanged as a "war criminal." The bodies of

---

[187] Bolton, *Stalin: The Enduring Legacy*, 125-134. The Soviet foreign minister of the time, Andrei A. Gromyko, confirms this in his memoires, Memories, 138-140. Ironically, conservatives, mainly in the USA, were preoccupied for decades about the UN being a "communist plot."

74 | *The Tyranny of Human Rights*

German and British airmen during World War I, when recovered behind enemy lines, were accorded a burial with full military honors. While the vengeance inflicted on Germany following World War I showed little of the chivalry of Western tradition, perhaps itself indicating a shift of power among elites, the aftermath of World War II betrayed a vengeance on the defeated devoid of any vestige of the Western ethos.

Nuremberg

The "international law" in the post-1945 world would be enforced by international tribunals and courts. The International Military Tribunal and other bodies created to jail or execute the statesmen and soldiers of the defeated Axis set the stage for the present plethora of laws and international courts. New laws and principles of law had to be created for the purpose, *expost facto*. At the time, the concept of an international military tribunal operating under contrived "international law" to try the defeated was widely condemned by judges, lawyers, scholars, diplomats, statesmen, and military officers throughout the world. For example:

> *It is my considered opinion that the Nuremberg Trials violated the reputation for justice so long held by the British and American peoples. Air Vice-Marshal Hugh Champion de Crespigny, Allied Military Governor, Schleswig-Holstein 1946–47.*[188]

> *The dangerous precedent set at Nuremberg must be removed. Rear Admiral Nils Wijkmark, Royal Swedish Navy.*[189]

> *...you are perfectly right in branding the Nuremberg "war crimes trials" in general as violating the common principles for civilized jurisdiction. General Olof Gerhard Thornell, Commander-in-Chief, Armed Forces of Sweden 1940–44.*[190]

> *As regards the War Crimes Trials...they were a grave mistake and illegal—an item of war hysteria such as happens in every*

---

[188] Thompson, *Doenitz at Nuremberg*, 10. Thompson compiled four hundred critical views on the Nuremberg Trials from eminent individuals throughout the world. The files were presented to Grand Admiral Doenitz on his release from prison, and collated into a book.
[189] Ibid., 15.
[190] Ibid., 16.

war. Maj. Gen. Henry V. Vaughan, Former Military Aide to President Truman.[191]

I would like to say that I regard the "war crimes trials" as a crime. Rev. Dr. John Haynes Holmes, Director, NAACP; Director, American Civil Liberties Union.[192]

The Nuremberg process is itself certainly not a juridical process, but an act of vengeance against the defeated.... Being a jurist myself and a Christian, I abhor the justice of Nuremberg. Most Rev. Bishop Vincetas Brizgys, Roman Catholic Bishop of Lithuania.[193]

My conclusion is that the entire program of war crimes trials either by International Courts...of by Military Courts...is basically without legal or moral authority. Hon. Edward Leroy van Roden, President Judge, Pennsylvania State Court; Secretary, US Army Commission to Investigate the Malmedy Case, 1948.[194]

The Charter of the Tribunal abolished the rules of evidence which in every civilized country has been introduced for the protection of accused persons against prejudiced and unreliable assertions. Hon. Charles Bewley, Irish jurist, Irish Minister to the Vatican and Germany.[195]

I thought at the time and still think that the Nuremberg trials were unprincipled. Law was created expost facto to suit the passion and clamor of the time. The concept of expost facto law is not congenial to the Anglo-American viewpoint on law. William O. Douglas, Professor of Law, Yale University 1928–39; Associate Justice, U. S. Supreme Court 1939–75.[196]

---

[191] Ibid., 23.
[192] Ibid., 27.
[193] Ibid., 33.
[194] Ibid., 67. The "Van Roden Commission" investigated the torture of German POWs under custody of the US Army in regard to the alleged "Malmedy massacre."
[195] Ibid., 131.
[196] Ibid., 194.

Even in the immediate aftermath of the world war and revenge, there were still many eminent figures who had the courage to condemn the post-war bloodlust. Today, such courage is rare.

Raphael Lemkin—Defining "Genocide"

The doctrine of the "crime of genocide" had been formulated as an *expost facto* law by an obscure Jewish lawyer from Poland. Raphael Lemkin (1900–1959) had already begun formulating the concept of "genocide" as a "war crime" during the 1920s and 1930s. Hence his original motive was not abhorrence of Hitlerism. What motivated Lemkin was opposition to European colonialism, an aspect of Europhobia since the European varieties were the only examples cited either before, during, or after the world war. It therefore becomes evident that those Lemkin sought to criminalize were not only the later Hitlerites, or other "fascists," but Europeans as "colonialists."

McDonnell and Moses, having studied Lemkin's unpublished papers, state that "the intellectual breakthrough that led to the concept of genocide occurred well before the Holocaust. Already in the 1920s and 1930s, Lemkin had begun formulating the concepts and laws that would culminate in his magnum opus, *Axis Rule in Occupied Europe* (1944), and in the United Nations Convention on Genocide four years later.[197] Although it seems that Lemkin was initially motivated by the Turkish genocide of Armenians, "central to his conception of genocide" was "early modern and modern colonialism."[198] Lemkin's anti-colonialism is implicit to his definition of "genocide," which was adopted by the UN and its international judicial bodies.

As cited by McDonnell and Moses, Lemkin defines "genocide" as having "two phases": "one, destruction of the national pattern of the oppressed group; the other, the imposition of the national pattern of the oppressor." The imposition might be on the oppressed group, who are allowed to remain in a territory, or on the territory, with the oppressed group being deported, and the land colonized. [199]

In fact, the intellectual breakthrough that led to the concept of genocide occurred well before the Holocaust. Already in the 1920s and early 1930s, he had begun formulating the concepts and laws that would

---

[197] Ibid., 501.
[198] Ibid.
[199] McDonnell citing Lemkin, *Axis Rule in Occupied Europe*, 79.

culminate in his founding text, *Axis Rule in Occupied Europe* (1944), and in the United Nations convention on genocide four years later.

It is noted that mass killings are not intrinsic to these definitions of "genocide." McDonnell and Moses state that Lemkin regarded the Holocaust as a continuation of the colonialism of Europe that had taken place for centuries, and which had not necessarily resulted in mass killings.[200]

Therefore, the European as a colonialist is indicted as "genocidal." Any form of European expansion is intrinsically "genocidal." "Apartheid" is "genocidal." Much of European history, including its Age of Discovery, is implicitly "genocidal." The suppression of *suttee* and *thuggee* by British imperialists in the *Raj* is imposing a "national pattern" and is therefore "genocidal."

Among Lemkin's unpublished projects is a history of genocide, in which he includes Germans in Africa, "Belgian Congo," genocide against North, Central, and South American Indians and the Tasmanian and other Aboriginals of Australia. That he includes "Genocide against the Maoris of New Zealand"[201] indicates the ignorance with which he applied what has become a reductionist dogma. Britain was requested by Maori tribes to assume jurisdiction over the country because the Maori tribes had long been committing "genocide" (in the form of mass killings, land invasions, cannibalism, and slavery) to the point of self-extinction.[202] This was no ruse by the Colonial Office to mark up another colony; there was reticence about extending Britain's imperial responsibilities by this time (1840). This apparently completely bypassed Lemkin's knowledge in his enthusiasm to apply his dogma universally.

Lemkin's Baseless Assumptions

Much the same can be said regarding genocidal conflicts among all the "oppressed groups" Lemkin cited, whether Amerindians, Africans, or Aborigines. While Lemkin might be excused for his lack of historical knowledge, the only excuses present academics have for perpetuating the same myths are a wilfully blind Europhobia, and the regressive maintenance of the doctrine of the noble savage.

---

[200] McDonnell, "Raphael Lemkin as historian," 502.
[201] Ibid.
[202] Robinson, *Unrestrained Slaughter*.

McDonnell and Moses allude to Lemkin's notes on the history of "genocide" as being "uneven, even anecdotal" and "drawn from a disparate and limited range of popular and scholarly sources."[203]

Let us take an example provided in Lemkin's notes, "Wounded Knee," an event that remains one of the great myths of Europhobia, analogous to the myth about Parihaka in colonial New Zealand,[204] or the Sharpeville Massacre in South Africa (1960). Wovoka, a prophet agitating the Lakota with promises of supernatural aid, stated that there would be something akin to a "rapture" where the Whites would be eliminated from America. The Ghost Dance invented by Wovoka became a widespread ceremony to fulfil his prophecies. Like other indigenous prophets, Wovoka stated that the Lakota would be impervious to bullets. In December 1870, as the 7th Cavalry sought to disarm the Lakota, a medicine man, Yellow Bird, started performing the Ghost Dance to remind the warriors that they are bullet-proof. When a struggle ensued with one of the warriors, Yellow Bird exhorted resistance. On a signal, warriors brought forth concealed weapons and began to fire.[205] The close quarter gun fight resulted in deaths on both sides, but this is portrayed as a great injustice to the Lakota by the White. The events indicate a planned confrontation schemed by Yellow Bird. Like Parihaka, where a Maori boy had his foot trodden on by a horse, Wounded Knee has entered the Holy Writ of Europhobia.

The alleged "extermination" of the Tasman Aborigines, supposedly hunted to oblivion by settlers, cited as an example of genocide by Lemkin, was challenged by Australian scholar Professor Keith Windshuttle, who showed that 118 Tasmanians died out of a total population of 2000.[206] In comparison 187 White settlers had been killed in skirmishes with the Tasmanian "Blackfellows."[207]

Of the "Genocide against the Aztecs," another chapter in Lemkin's intended history of genocide,[208] they had conquered the territory of a prior people, a rather predictable scenario. The hatred of the Aztecs by subjugated tribes enabled Cortez to form alliances, and there were many such tribes that regarded the Spaniards as liberators. One of these was the Tlaxcalans, who entered Tezcoco in 1520, and in the palace of the Aztec king burned the pictographic histories that celebrated the Aztec's bloody victories. Much of the knowledge that remained, however, was preserved by Spanish missionaries. So far from being an ordered empire, the Aztecs

---

[203] McDonell, op cit., 503.
[204] Bolton, *The Parihaka Cult*.
[205] Utley, *The Last Days of the Sioux Nation*, 210.
[206] Windshuttle, *The Fabrication of Australian History*, vol. I, 397.
[207] Ibid., 352.
[208] McDonnell, "Raphael Lemkin as historian," 502.

had by the time of Cortés degraded into a vast land of blood-sacrifice and cannibalism, for which wars were fought[209] and where religion, art, and architecture were dedicated to decay, death, and disease, where the whole region had degenerated into the celebration of one vast death-cult. Since Cortés and the Conquistadores are indicted as perpetrators of "genocide," what then should one make of the Aztecs, and why is it to be the Spaniards who are the eternal villains of history, rather than the Aztecs whose bloody hands they halted by the imposition of the Spanish "national pattern"?

How then does the UN become something other than "genocidal" when it imposes a "globalist pattern" over the entire world in the name of "human rights"? Does not the UN commit an immensely wider "genocide" of international "neocolonialism" than any traditional colonialist? Why do the British, French, Spanish, and other colonialists become slandered as perpetrators of "genocide" against indigenes, while the UN are celebrated for their "humanitarianism" when imposing their *transhumanism*[210] into every nook and cranny of the earth? Can the "national patterns" of British, French, and Spanish colonialism really be regarded as having been more intrusive than that of UN international meddling, and the corporate globalism that often sponsors it?

Methods of Genocide

Of the "methods and techniques of genocide," Lemkin included:

- *Physical: massacre, mutilation, deprivation of livelihood, (starvation, exposure, etc. often by deportation), slavery—exposure to death.*
- *Biological: separation of families, sterilization, destruction of foetus.*
- *Cultural: desecration and destruction of cultural symbols (books, objects of art, loot, religious relics, etc.), destruction of cultural leadership, destruction of cultural centers (cities, churches, monasteries, school, libraries) prohibition of cultural activities or codes of behaviour, forceful conversion, demoralization.*

---

[209] Kelley, *Blood-Drenched Altars*, 42.
[210] On the doctrine of *transhumanism* and the UN see: Bolton, *The Perversion of Normality*, 433-446.

- *Propaganda: rationalization of crime, appeal to popular beliefs and intolerance, sowing discord (divide and rule), misrepresentation and deceit, intimidation.*
- *Aftermath: cultural losses, population changes, economic dislocations, material and moral deterioration, political consequences, social and cultural changes.*[211]

Can these "methods and techniques of genocide" sketched by Lemkin accord any more precisely than with the *de fatco* and *de jure* policies and actions of the Allied occupation regime of Germany after World War II? The Morgenthau Plan, operative on a *de facto* and *ad hoc* basis for several years, resulted in the deaths of millions of civilians[212] and prisoners[213] after the war. Of "starvation, exposure, etc. often by deportation," ten to fifteen million ethnic Germans were deported from what had been their ancestral lands for seven hundred years. Millions died *en route* to Germany, while the Americans, British, and UN stood by. *Time* magazine stated:

> *In what was once eastern Germany, an anguished tide of humanity, one of the greatest mass movements of Germans in history, flowed towards the borders of the shrunken Reich. At least 10,000,000 hungry Germans were being uprooted from their old homes in East Prussia, Pomerania Silesia, Sudetenland by the new Polish, Czech and Russian owners.*
>
> *The wanderers choked the road in Russian-occupied Germany. Ragged, barefoot, with children in their arms, and the shabby remains of homes stacked on perambulators, carts and wheelbarrows. But they were barred from the British and US zones. No UNRRA was on hand to help, though their problem immediately outscaled that of Displaced Persons elsewhere in Europe.*[214]

Of the "desecration and destruction of cultural symbols" as a technique of genocide, the entirety of the *open city* of Dresden, one vast monument to Western high culture, was vaporized when two thousand bombers dropped three thousand tons of bombs, a fire-storm incinerating up to a

---

[211] McDonnell, "Raphael Lemkin as historian," 505.
[212] Bacque, *Crimes and Mercies*.
[213] Bacque, *Other Losses*.
[214] Quoted in App, *History's Most Terrifying Peace*, 42.

quarter-million individuals in a single night, February 13th, 1945, military reasons for which there were none.[215]

Of the destruction of "cultural leadership," "prohibition of cultural activities or codes of behaviour," and "demoralization," the award-winning post-war film-maker, social and cultural critic, and historian Hans-Jürgen Syberberg is instructive. He shows how the mythic status surrounding the world war culturally retarded and distorted European culture in general:

> *The central themes of our age are the collapse of the German Empire and its having been violated through liberation and re-education, in the middle of the continent and its consequences with the partition of Germany, and, therewith, of Europe, and the disappearance of one of the central states of culture, namely Prussia. Secondly, Auschwitz and the exodus of the European Jews to Israel and America. And thirdly, the expulsion of 15 million men from the eastern provinces of Germany to the west and its consequences and accompanying circumstances, which equates to a people's forced migration. Consequently, art from this cultural sphere must be measured accordingly; whether it is paintings, sculptures, films, books, theatre, history, or music...*[216]

The "taboos" that the post-1945 global regime imposed on European culture mean that:

> *...after Auschwitz no more poetry was possible.... No more poetry under the artistic commandment of intellectual beauty was a curse as a revenge for Auschwitz, acting, no matter how it was meant and came about, in vulgar reality as the highest law of post-war aesthetics coming out of Germany. It acted as a curse in the hands of vulgar authorities..."*[217]

Another "taboo" is against "agrarian culture," because of its suggestion of the Nazi "blood and soil" doctrine. This means, wrote Sybergberg, the suppression of the aesthetics that had "grown from an agrarian culture," which had been patronized by a landed aristocracy, "such as had determined European art through the aristocratic principles of hierarchies

---

[215] Estimates of the death toll range from the ridiculously low Russian number of 35,000 to 250,000. That there were 600,000 refugees crammed into Dresden at the time seems to make the maximum number the most likely. For various estimates see Irving, *The Destruction of Dresden*, 225-226.
[216] Syberberg, *On the Fortunes and Misfortunes*, 8.
[217] Ibid., 10-11.

of good and bad until the beginning of Modernism."[218] What has been imposed is the exaltation of "the small, the low, the crippled, the sick and dirt, as opposed to brilliance—for baseness is a strategy from below alongside the praise of cowardice, of betrayal, of criminals, of whores, of hate, of ugliness, of lies and crime, of unnaturalness, vulgarity, etc."[219]

The imposition of the "human rights" doctrine on the post-war world has been undertaken in the name of "combatting Hitler," and then of preventing a resurgence of what is considered intrinsically "Nazi," such as (for *Homo Europaeus*, that is) pride of race, of homeland, and even, according to the psychological survey invented by Critical Theorists, of one's own family. An attachment to any of these—race, home, nation, family—scores one high on the "F" scale of "Fascism," and is deemed as leading to a replay of Auschwitz.[220] The culture, aesthetics, morality, and ethos of the European has been thoroughly distorted, corrupted, and retarded, and it is in large measure undertaken by the pretext of expunging "Nazism," which is applied to any manifestation that is suspected of being at odds with globalization.

Lemkin was formulating his doctrine when Nazism was still embryonic, as far back as the 1920s. That his doctrine of "genocide" was adopted as a weapon firstly against Germany, then to generally impose a tyranny over the world in the name of "human rights" and of "preventing genocide" has enabled sundry treaties, international laws, and courts to be established for upholding the globalist system, usually under the auspices of the UN.

"Kindly" Aztecs; Genocidal Europeans

For Lemkin, the primary culprits of "world history" were the Europeans. McDonnell and Moses state that Lemkin's notes for his planned book on a world history of "genocide" lauded indigenous peoples. So for Lemkin, the Aztecs "despite tyranny," had a "fairly democratic government."[221] Spanish slavery is defined as a technique of genocide, yet Aztec slavery is not. Even the protective efforts of the Church towards the Indians is defined as a form of genocide, "since different techniques of genocide" need not be perpetrated "with the same motives."[222]

---

[218] Ibid., 14.
[219] Ibid.
[220] The "F scale" is not a spoof, but a very serious formulation by a team of Critical Theorists and published as Adorno, *The Authoritarian Personality* (1950).
[221] McDonnell, "Raphael Lemkin as historian," 505.
[222] Ibid., 511.

Hence, we might conclude that the suppression of the religious practice of human sacrifice, which became an obsession, and featured the cutting of the heart from the living victim, was a form of "cultural genocide." When Cortés reached the Gulf of Mexico in 1519, he told the "kindly Indians" (as Lemkin describes them) that they must stop sacrificing humans to their idols. An eyewitness account by Bernal Diaz de Castillo states:

> *Every day they sacrificed before our eyes three, four, or five Indians, whose hearts were offered to those idols, and whose blood was plastered on the walls. The feet, arms, and legs of their victims were cut off and eaten, just as we eat beef from the butcher's in our country. I even believe they sold it in the markets.*[223]

Of the method of human sacrifice, Diaz stated:

> *They strike open the wretched Indian's chest with flint knives and hastily tear out the palpitating heart which, with the blood, they present to the idols in whose name they have performed the sacrifice. Then they cut off the arms, thighs, and head, eating the arms and thighs at their ceremonial banquets. The head they hung up on a beam, and the body of the scarified man is not eaten but given to the beasts of prey.*[224]

Is this "religion" or is it psychosis? The Indians seem to have reached a degraded state long before the arrival of Europeans. The earlier religious cults centering on Viracocha and similar localized gods were of a different character. Of slavery, for which the Spanish are condemned by Lemkin, the Aztecs practiced this in plenitude, and slaves were sold at markets. And so we might proceed through most of the regions where European colonialism encountered similar practices, whether in Africa, the South Seas, or America.

However, Lemkin regarded such accounts of slavery, cannibalism, and human sacrifice as "rationalizations" for Spanish colonialism. He simply, did not believe them. McDonnell and Moses comment that Lemkin wanted

---

[223] Díaz, *The True History of the Conquest*, XXXV.
[224] Ibid.

his readers to believe that "the barbarians were the Spanish."[225] They call Lemkin's "research" "problematic."[226]

So long as a state can be termed "democratic," all is well, including the Aztec People's Democracy. The Jacobins were "democrats" *par excellence*; so too the Bolsheviks, and of course there is the Democratic People's Republic of Korea. Aztecs, Incas, and Mayas are portrayed as having possessed high cultures, until driven to degradation by European conquerors, the contrast of which Lemkin intended to describe in a chapter entitled "Aftermath."[227] Lemkin seems to have utilized the Enlightenment doctrine of the noble savage to slander Europeans while lauding natives. The Central and South American civilizations had reached their epochs of decay long prior to being discovered by the Spanish and Portuguese.[228] Yet, as we have previously noted, Lemkin acknowledged that the Spanish were able to easily defeat the Aztecs because such was their tyranny over other Indians that these oppressed Native Americans saw the Spanish as liberators. Lemkin however was apparently content to formulate his "history of genocide" on the basis of assumptions and clichés, so long as they accorded with his aim of denigrating European civilization as intrinsically genocidal.

When intra-Indian violence leads to the genocide of one "tribe" or "nation" by another, albeit of the same "race," does that mean this is *not* "genocide"? In New Zealand, the Maoris were on the verge of self-obliteration prior to the arrival of British colonialism. As the Kohimarama conference (1860) of hundreds of Maori chiefs indicates, most remained zealously loyal to the British Crown, which had ended cannibalism and the endless *utu* (blood feuds) that were leading to racial extirpation. It was with reluctance that in 1840, Britain extended her sovereignty over New Zealand at Maori request.[229] Why is European colonialism implicitly "genocidal" when suppressing indigenous bloodlust, but the wholesale intervention of the UN and its various agencies, often in partnership with global corporations that have a profit-motive behind the facade, lauded as "humanitarian work"? The only consistency, as usual, is that of Europhobia. Prior to European colonialism the "nations" of the Americas, Australia, New Guinea, New Zealand, Africa and other non-European lands, did not have any conception of race-unity, of themselves as a single ethnic bloc, but rather as tribes often contending to the death. Why does

---

[225] McDonnell, "Raphael Lemkin as historian," 512.
[226] Ibid., 515.
[227] Ibid., 505.
[228] See: Bolton, *The Decline and Fall of Civilisations*, 239-246.
[229] Proceedings of the Kohimarama Conference.

UN intervention in Africa become a humanitarian necessity that is somehow of higher morality than the intervention of European colonialism? The answer is that it serves a miscreant aim behind a moral facade.

The "Crime" of Being White

Of the Spanish in the America's Lemkin wrote in his notes that they "exhibited rapacity and ruthlessness against kindly natives."[230] McDonnell and Moses explain in a footnote that the aim of Lemkin's "activism" (sic) was to gain protection under international law of indigenous "civilizations."[231] Conversely, "indigenous civilizations" such as the British, Flemish, Afrikaner, Dutch, Swedish, Gallic are not only *not* included for protection from the many forms of "genocide," as defined by Lemkin and the UN, but they are specifically subjected to those aspects of "genocide." Furthermore, if any of these White indigenes object, *they* are accused of "racism," "neo-Nazism," and "White supremacy," for which there are prohibitive laws, again stemming from Lemkin and the UN.

The efforts of the Afrikaners to preserve their identity—that is, to protect themselves from "genocide" at multiple levels—is described by the UN in "double-think" manner as being a technique of "genocide." Of this the UN specifically states that "apartheid" is a "crime" that must be "suppressed" and "punished," citing the UN Genocide Convention.[232] When evidence is adduced that the Afrikaner is undergoing a process of genocide, this is dismissed as a "far right conspiracy theory."[233] The mass killing of a dispossessed and long-vilified White ethnicity is of no account; the killing of a single Black criminal draws world-wide outrage, elevated to the realm of eternal legend.

It is a small way from declaring that being White is a crime that must be punished for the sake of ending "genocide." Indeed, in this vein, when European indigenes object to "the great replacement" they are vilified and subjected to "human rights laws," yet the UN refers to the same process as "replacement migration." Under the category of "cultural" genocide, Lemkin defined this as

> ...desecration and destruction of cultural symbols (books, objects of art, loot, religious relics, etc.), destruction of cultural

---

[230] McDonnell, "Raphael Lemkin as historian," 506.
[231] Ibid., 525, footnote 23.
[232] United Nations, "International Convention on the Suppression."
[233] Wilson, "White farmers."

leadership, destruction of cultural centers (cities, churches, monasteries, school, libraries) prohibition of cultural activities or codes of behaviour, forceful conversion, demoralization.

What element of this "cultural genocide" is *not* being inflicted on *Homo Europaeus* the world over? Even the imperial tunes that are sung with gusto at the "Last Night of the Proms" were under threat of being purged,[234] and what of the process of demolishing European monuments and statues that is presently taking place to expurgate the memory of European culture and history? Even Western science is taught as an aspect of "colonialism," "racism," and "White supremacy," as we examine below.[235] The quandary is that Western science is a necessary predicate for the "growth economy" and globalization; it cannot be obliterated like a statue or a monument, so it must be presented in a way that ensures it does not encourage any feelings of "White pride," or conversely, any feelings of inadequacy from "persons of color." It is taught as a "necessary evil."

McDonnell and Moses point out that Lemkin was "part of a more general post-Second World War historiographic turn away from apologetic and pragmatic interpretations of colonialism and empire."[236] However, it is this post-war "turn," behind the facade of "human rights" and "anti-colonialism" that enabled the USA, much more than the Soviet-Russian Cold War bogeyman, to present itself as the champion of anti-colonialism. As Woodrow Wilson had proclaimed in the aftermath of World War I, and Franklin D. Roosevelt similarly during World War II with the Atlantic Charter, Truman and those following presented the USA, with its anti-colonial foundation, as the liberator of Africa and Asia from the empires of Europe. What transpired in the name of "liberation" was a neo-colonialism of faceless plutocrats, aligned with the UN and other "humanitarian" bodies such as USAID and the Africa-America Institute, which trained the leadership cadres of the "new Africa."[237]

---

[234] The BBC intended to delete "Rule, Britannia" and "Land of Hope & Glory" from the repertoire, but a rare success for public pressure stymied the intention. Nonetheless, this shows the mentality of those who form the modern "elite" of Western nations. See: BBC News, "Rule, Britannia! will be sung."
[235] See the chapter "Denigration of Western Science."
[236] McDonnell, "Raphael Lemkin as historian," 517.
[237] Bolton, *Babel Inc.*, 41-77.

Lemkin as Front-Man

Dr. James J. Martin opines that Lemkin was a front-man for a cabal of post-war policy-makers. Lemkin's book, *Axis Rule in Occupied Europe*, was published by Columbia University Press in 1944, with sponsorship by the Division of International Law Publications of the Carnegie Endowment for International Peace, which was "taking a leading position in the manufacture of post-war plans and schemes for rigging a world in harmony with and contributory to the interests of its prestigious sponsoring forces."[238]

Lemkin had been a member of the International Office for the Unification of Criminal Law,[239] an organ of the League of Nations, the precursor of the UN. His specialty was in laws governing the international movement of money, property and other assets.[240] On arrival to the USA in 1941 he rapidly gained influence as "head consultant" to the Foreign Economic Administration, focused on reassigning confiscated enemy assets after the war. He also became an advisor to the Bureau of Economic Warfare, the War Department, and State Department. As a lecturer at the School of Military Government, Virginia, he instructed future administrators for the Occupation government of conquered Germany.[241]

Dr. Martin, despite his eventual demonization as a "revisionist," was a scholar of repute and ideologically a libertarian. His view of Lemkin's *Axis Rule* indicates that it is no more impressive than Lemkin's previous research for his intended book on "genocide." Two-thirds of the large tome was not written by Lemkin but comprised a collection of German legal documents on the occupied states, regarding laws on property, money, exchange rates, etc., for the years 1940–1941.[242]

From Martin's analysis, 3 percent of the book dealt with "genocide legislation."[243] However, this was sufficient to introduce the Lemkin-coined word to the world: "genocide": from the Greek *genos* (tribe, race) and the Latin *cide*, where Lemkin uses as an analogy for definition the Latin *homocide* (sic).[244] In the short chapter entitled "Genocide" Lemkin draws on the ideas percolated from years previously, defining "genocide" as "the destruction of the national pattern of an oppressed group," and "the

---

[238] Martin, "Raphael Lemkin and the Invention of 'Genocide.'"
[239] Ibid., 20.
[240] Ibid., 22.
[241] Ibid., 20.
[242] Ibid., 23.
[243] Ibid., 25.
[244] Ibid., 28.

imposition of the national pattern of the oppressor." He states that "denationalization" was the word previously used for the processes.[245]

Martin points out that Lemkin only refers to "minority" groups. There is no mention of a "brief for the protection of a putative majority anywhere; as a consequence of the way he approached the subject philosophically and psychologically, he was unable to conceive of a situation where a majority group might be the one in grave danger of disappearance."[246]

Lemkin proceeded to avidly publicize the concept of "genocide" in periodicals, between 1945 and 1948.[247] After several years of debate, the UN General Assembly adopted the Genocide Convection in 1948.

Lemkin as Zionist

One would hope that Lemkin as the "father" of laws against "genocide," despite his Jewish background would have been, like the Israeli scholar Dr. Israel Shahak,[248] for example, an anti-Zionist, recognizing the genocidal character implicit in the Jewish colonization of Palestine. Lemkin was, however, a Zionist.

One might ask to what extent his opposition to European colonialism was motivated by his desire to see the European spheres of influence eliminated from not only the Middle East, but also from Africa. Israel, like the USA, sought to portray itself as the leader of the anti-colonialist movement, especially in Africa, as part of a geopolitical strategy.[249] Israel backed the bloody Mau Mau insurgency in Kenya against the British,[250] backed Idi Amin's coup in Uganda,[251] and portrayed its terrorist activities against the British mandate in Palestine as part of a broader anti-imperialist struggle. From the 1950s, in the wake of decolonization, Israel filled the void; in the Black states there were Israelis "aiding the military and civil systems," according to Israel Lior, military secretary to Prime Minister Eshkol.[252]

---

[245] Ibid., 29.
[246] Ibid., 30.
[247] Ibid., 31.
[248] Shahak, *Jewish Fundamentalism in Israel*.
[249] See: Carol, *From Jerusalem to the Lion*.
[250] Mau Mau leaders went to Israel for training in 1962, under the leadership of second-in-command "General China." Bolton, *Zionism, Islam and the West*, 116 and Carol, op cit., 68.
[251] Baruch Bar Lev, head of the Israeli military mission to Uganda referred to Amin as "our man" when he was still assistant chief of staff under President Obote. Bolton, op cit., 117. and Carol, op cit., 167.
[252] Bolton, *Zionism, Islam and the West*, 116.

It is therefore with dismay that Zionists saw Black Africa turn against Israel, identifying with the Palestinian cause, as did Black nationalist groups in the USA, despite the funds that Jews had given to Black civil rights movements such as the NAACP. Of this situation James Loeffler, associate professor of history at the University of Virginia, laments that Israel has been condemned for "apartheid" and "colonial occupation" by the UN General Assembly, and "Jewish student activists" have been spurned by "minority" "anti-racist" groups "because of their Israeli ties." Loeffler explains:

To those of us who follow the history of Zionism and the history of human rights, it is both strange and tragic to consider the current state of affairs. What the modern left has forgotten is the fact that Zionism and the modern human rights movement share a braided history. And 2018—70 years since Israel's founding, but also 70 years since the UN Universal Declaration of Human Rights—is the perfect moment to reconsider the notion that the two ideas are intrinsically in conflict.

Few today know that the Polish-born jurist Hersch Zvi Lauterpacht, widely regarded as the greatest international lawyer of the 20th century and the founding father of international human rights law, crafted influential drafts of the Israeli Declaration of Independence, and the Universal Declaration of Human Rights and the European Convention on Human Rights. He also advised Zionist leaders on their legal strategies for statehood at the same time that he advised the American prosecutors at Nuremberg. Oh, and he coined the term "crimes against humanity."[253]

Loeffler identifies an influential Zionist, Lauterpacht, as "the founding father of international human rights law," who coined the term "crimes against humanity." He also identifies Lemkin, somehow a "Holocaust survivor" (sic), as a Zionist since the 1920s:

Raphael Lemkin, the Polish-Jewish lawyer responsible for the word "genocide" and the UN Genocide Convention, was not only a Holocaust survivor but a Zionist activist who spent two

---

[253] Loeffler, "The Zionist Founders of the Human Rights Movement."

decades before the Holocaust fighting for Jewish legal rights in
Poland and a Jewish homeland in Palestine.[254]

Drawing from what Lemkin had written in Poland during the 1920s and 1930s, Loeffler states that:

> ...thus far no one has identified the precise political activities and affiliations that shaped Lemkin's concept of genocide.... Lemkin, far from being a Jewish Bundist,[255] a Polish nationalist or an apolitical cosmopolitan, was an active member of the interwar Polish Zionist movement, from which he drew the ideas that inspired his idea of the crime of genocide.[256]

According to Loeffler, Lemkin was motivated by Zionism in his conception of "genocide" and the formulation of international law. Yet, as we have seen, his primary target was European colonialism, while extolling a doctrine that could only have been achieved by the colonization of Palestine at the expense of the indigenes.

United Nations Genocide Convention

The UN Office on Genocide Prevention and the Responsibility to Protect states on their website of the Genocide Convention and Lemkin:

> The word "genocide" was first coined by Polish lawyer Raphäel Lemkin in 1944 in his book Axis Rule in Occupied Europe.... Lemkin developed the term partly in response to the Nazi policies of systematic murder of Jewish people during the Holocaust, but also in response to previous instances in history of targeted actions aimed at the destruction of particular groups of people. Later on, Raphäel Lemkin led the campaign to have genocide recognised and codified as an international crime.

As we have seen, this is not accurate. Lemkin did not focus on "the systematic murder of Jewish people," in *Axis Rule*, despite the role he was later assigned in the Holocaust narrative. Rather, as we have seen, the concept was one that he was developing as far back as the 1920s, and the

---

[254] Ibid.
[255] Jewish Bundist = Jewish socialist movement in Poland.
[256] Loeffler, "Becoming Cleopatra."

focus was on opposition to European colonialism as intrinsically "genocidal," with physical extermination only being one among numerous "techniques and methods of genocide." One might wonder that if it was not for his early fame in the Holocaust narrative, he might have been condemned, like the Jewish author John Sack,[257] or the Jewish scholar Norman Finkelstein,[258] for "relativizing the Holocaust," which seems to be a more horrendous heresy than "denying the Holocaust?"[259]

Nuremberg

The UN office states that "Genocide was first recognised as a crime under international law in 1946 by the United Nations General Assembly (A/RES/96-I)." This Resolution introduced the concept of post-war "international law" in conjunction with the Nuremberg Trials. Hence the Nuremberg Trials were the first post-war implementation of a projected "international law" of "genocide" which has since proliferated into a multitudinous web of laws, covenants, treaties, and agencies that impose a global tyranny in the name of "human rights." Here we see a reference to the "progressive development of international law and its codification":

> *The General Assembly, Recognizes the obligation laid upon it by Article 13, paragraph 1, sub-paragraph a, of the Charter, to initiate studies and make recommendations for the purpose of encouraging the progressive development of international law and its codification.*[260]

Next the resolution "takes note," in conjunction with this "progressive development of international law" of:

> *...the establishment of an International Military Tribunal for the prosecution and punishment of the major war criminals of the European Axis signed in London on 8 August 1945, and of the Charter annexed thereto, and of the fact that similar principles have been adopted in the Charter of the International Military*

---

[257] Sack, *An Eye for an Eye*.
[258] Finkelstein, *The Holocaust Industry*.
[259] Lipstadt, *Denying the Holocaust*. See especially Chapter 11, 209-222.
[260] UN General Assembly Resolution A/RES/96-I, 95 (I).

Tribunal for the trial of the major war criminals in the Far East, proclaimed at Tokyo on 19 January 1946.[261]

It is here in connection with the establishment of the Nuremberg Military Tribunal and the codification of its *expost facto* laws, that the word "genocide" is defined by the UN:

> *Genocide is a denial of the right of existence of entire human groups, as homicide is the denial of the right to live of individual human beings; such denial of the right of existence shocks the conscience of mankind, results in great losses to humanity in the form of cultural and other contributions represented by these human groups, and is contrary to moral law and to the spirit and aims of the United Nations. Many instances of such crimes of genocide have occurred when racial, religious, political and other groups have been destroyed, entirely or in part.*[262]

This new concept was to become punishable by the enacting of new laws and the establishment of new tribunals and courts on an international basis, the General Assembly affirming:

> *...that genocide is a crime under international law which the civilized world condemns, and for the commission of which principals and accomplices—whether private individuals, public officials or statesmen, and whether the crime is committed on religious, racial, political or any other grounds—are punishable; Invites the Member States to enact the necessary legislation for the prevention and punishment of this crime; Recommends that international co-operation be organized between States with a view to facilitating the speedy prevention and punishment of the crime of genocide...*[263]

The UN Economic and Social Council was requested to undertake studies for "drawing up a draft convention on the crime up genocide to be submitted to the next regular session of the General Assembly."[264]

The UN Office on Genocide Prevention states on their website that "Genocide" was "codified as a crime in the 1948 Convention on the

---

[261] Ibid.
[262] Ibid., "The Crime of Genocide," 96 (I).
[263] Ibid.
[264] Ibid.

Prevention and Punishment of the Crime of Genocide (the Genocide Convention). The Convention has been ratified by 149 States (as of January 2018)." Further:

> *The International Court of Justice (ICJ) has repeatedly stated that the Convention embodies principles that are part of general customary international law. This means that whether or not States have ratified the Genocide Convention, they are all bound as a matter of law by the principle that genocide is a crime prohibited under international law. The ICJ has also stated that the prohibition of genocide is a peremptory norm of international law (or ius cogens) and consequently, no derogation from it is allowed.*[265]

This means that intervention by the UN and affiliated organs such as the International Court of Justice and, where this fails, NATO/US/UN military action, can be initiated against not only any state, but any politician, deemed to be in breach of this law. State ratification of the law is not required for the UN to intervene.

The influence of Lemkin is seen from the Genocide Convention definition of "genocide":

> *In the present Convention, genocide means any of the following acts committed with intent to destroy, in whole or in part, a national, ethnical, racial or religious group, as such:*
> *a) Killing members of the group;*
> *b) Causing serious bodily or mental harm to members of the group;*
> *c) Deliberately inflicting on the group conditions of life calculated to bring about its physical destruction in whole or in part;*
> *d) Imposing measures intended to prevent births within the group;*
> *e) Forcibly transferring children of the group to another group.*[266]

It takes little or no evidence to allege that one is being "mentally harmed" by a government policy, collectively or individually, on "national, ethnical,

---
[265] Ibid.
[266] United Nations, *Convention on the Prevention*, Article II.

racial or religious" grounds. The acts that are punishable comprise: "(a) Genocide; (b) Conspiracy to commit genocide; (c) Direct and public incitement to commit genocide; (d) Attempt to commit genocide; (e) Complicity in genocide."[267]

For example, advocating or implementing policies for the restriction of immigration on racial, national, religious, or ethnical grounds, are liable to prosecution. This is the premise for "human rights," "hate speech," and "race relations" laws within states that can punish such advocates on an individual basis; and the formulation of laws such as the UN Global Compact on Migration, and a myriad of others. This is made unequivocal, and with a tone of threat: "Persons committing genocide or any of the other acts enumerated in Article III shall be punished, whether they are constitutionally responsible rulers, public officials or *private individuals*."[268] (Emphasis added).

"Public incitement to commit genocide" readily translates to any advocacy designed to protect a nation or ethnicity from threats, in other words, against their own "genocide," depending on whether the threatened group is in favor or out of favor with the UN, which generally means, whether the groups is of European descent. Therefore both state and international tribunals are established to exact punishment:

> *Persons charged with genocide or any of the other acts enumerated in article III shall be tried by a competent tribunal of the State in the territory of which the act was committed, or by such international penal tribunal as may have jurisdiction with respect to those Contracting Parties which shall have accepted its jurisdiction.*[269]

However, it is not necessary to even be a "contracting party" to be indicted by an international tribunal and punished. It is enough to be declared an enemy of "humanity" and to be militarily defeated. Yugoslavia is an example of this. Those deemed to be miscreant can be extradited.[270] The International Criminal Court has jurisdiction over the international legal processes.[271]

---

[267] Ibid., Article III.
[268] Ibid., Article IV.
[269] Ibid., Article VI.
[270] Ibid., Article VII.
[271] Ibid., Article IX.

Yugoslavia: War in the Name of "Human Rights"

The method by which the concept of "genocide" and associated "human rights" are used as a means of destroying any hindrances to the globalist agenda has been demonstrated as a warning to the world by the destruction of Yugoslavia. Here, through the allegation of "genocide," and the charging of Serbia's political and military leadership with "war crimes," was a war and its aftermath reminiscent of World War II and of Nuremberg.

As we have seen, there was very much more to the war against Yugoslavia, behind the facade of "human rights" and the allegation of "ethnic cleansing." The imposition of a "free market" economy, and the globalization of Kosovan mineral resources played a role which I contend was the actual reason. As with Nuremberg, only the military and political leaders of the defeated state were charged with "war crimes," while the one-sidedness was blatantly unjust, but obscured by the avalanche of media-manufactured "world opinion." The NATO spokesman Jamie Shea stated the manner by which Serbian "war criminals" would be prosecuted, while speaking of the Kosovo Liberation Army as a legitimate fighting unit:

> *For reconciliation it is essential that all criminals face justice, because until they do so the sense of vengeance, the sense of unrequited justice is extremely strong, as we found in Bosnia. When war criminals receive their just desserts people feel that some kind of retribution is unnecessary, because those responsible have faded their crimes, and then reconciliation can take place. So I can assure you no matter how difficult it is we have a duty to do our utmost to make sure that those who are responsible for these appalling acts do face justice. It is not only morally right, but it is also politically wise in that it does foster reconciliation. The Albanian community which suffered must know that those responsible brought to justice, and the Serb community has to also realize that terrible acts were committed in its name.*[272]

Shea blatantly stated that Serbians alone were responsible for "war crimes," that they alone would be punished. Serbians would be made to realize the criminal nature of their fight against their own "genocide," that

---

[272] US Information Agency, "TRANSCRIPT: Jamie Shea Talks."

had for years been perpetrated by what the US State Department had previously cited as Albanian narco-criminals and terrorists seeking a Greater Albania.

In 2010 Wesley Clark, who had been NATO commander during the war against Serbia, reiterated that the war had been justified in the name of "human rights," stating in an interview:

> *Well, in 1999 action was taken because we could see the beginning of a replay of a familiar pattern of ethnic cleansing in the Balkans. And it was that replay which prompted NATO to act. It wasn't just that it was a humanitarian action, it was an action to prevent a humanitarian catastrophe that was unfolding in front of us.*[273]

Yet the year before the NATO attack, the Kosovo Liberation Army (KLA) was describe by Robert Gelbard, US Special Envoy to Bosnia, as "terrorists." A few months later he was talking with KLA representatives.[274]

Prior to the intervention of Serbia the KLA had both Albanian and Serb ethnics in a state of terror. US official sources stated that Albanians were fleeing their homes en masse because of KLA threats. The association of the KLA with organized crime in Europe and Turkey was well-known by US and European police agencies. The KLA aim was a "Greater Albania," incorporating large parts of Serbia, most of Macedonia, and parts of Greece and Montenegro. Chris Hedges, then Balkan Bureau chief for the *New York Times* (1995–1998), wrote in *Foreign Affairs* of his finding a map in a destroyed KLA compound based on the territorial claims of 1878 by the League for the Defense of the Albanian Nation.[275] This nineteenth century dream of a Greater Albania motivated the KLA in its "ethnic cleansing" of Serbs from what they regarded as Albanian territory. Hedges wrote that, "Between 1966 and 1989 an estimated 130,000 Serbs left the province because of frequent harassment and discrimination by the Kosovar Albanian community." Few reports reached the "world community," however. One was a KLA attack that killed fourteen Serbian farmers involved in harvest:

> *Gracko, Yugoslavia, July 24—Fourteen Serbian farmers harvesting hay were killed in bursts of automatic gunfire Friday*

---

[273] RFE/RL. "Wesley Clark: We did the right thing in 1999."
[274] Sebak, "The KLA—terrorists or freedom fighters?"
[275] Hedges, "Kosovo's Next Masters."

night within earshot of British peacekeeping troops in the worst single attack against Kosovo's beleaguered Serbian civilians since NATO forces entered the province six weeks ago.... The killings provoked outrage among the few hundred Serbian villagers in Gracko, and defiance from Yugoslav President Slobodan Milosevic, who called for the return of the Yugoslav Army and Serbian police to Kosovo, a province of Serbia, the dominant republic of Yugoslavia. In condemning the killings, NATO and United Nations officials urged Serbs in Kosovo not to join an exodus that has already slashed by three-quarters the province's prewar population of 200,000 Serbs, about a tenth of the total population.[276]

The UN offered platitudes and apologies for their failure:

"I see your tears. Your pain. And I beg your pardon," said Bernard Kouchner, the UN administrator for Kosovo, who visited Gracko this afternoon with Bishop Artemije of the Serbian Orthodox Church in an attempt to persuade the villagers to remain. "We failed to protect you."[277]

The following month a mortar attack on a mainly Serb village, Klokot, killed a fourteen-year-old girl and a sixteen-year-old boy and wounded five others.[278]

Nearly a decade (1987) prior to the NATO war against Serbia *The New York Times* reported that Kosovo was on the verge of civil war due to the ethnic cleansing by Albanian Kosovars against Serbians. The Yugoslav army had uncovered hundreds of KLA cells within its ranks. *The Times* report stated that "Ethnic Albanians" in the Yugoslav government had "manipulated public funds and regulations to take over land belonging to Serbs."

Slavic Orthodox churches have been attacked, and flags have been torn down. Wells have been poisoned and crops burned. Slavic boys have been knifed, and some young ethnic Albanians have been told by their elders to rape Serbian girls. Ethnic Albanians comprise the fastest growing nationality in

---

[276] Finn, "Serbs Killed Within Earshot."
[277] Ibid.
[278] Associated Press. "Mortars kill Serb 2 teens."

> *Yugoslavia and are expected soon to become its third largest, after the Serbs and Croats.*[279]

This was the situation that had been unfolding for years when Yugoslav president Slobodan Milosevic ordered the army into Kosovo to restore order.

Milosevic's Serbia was an anachronism. In that respect, Serbia shared an identity with the Afrikaners, and ironically with certain Muslims (Syria, Iran) who are fighting US-backed *Wahhab-jihadism*.

Milosevic and his military and government officials were tried by a reconstructed War Crimes Tribunal, Nuremberg style. Their offense had been to defend their people against genocide, for which they were accused of genocide: the Orwellian double-think of the dialectical method. The UN established an "International Criminal Tribunal for the Former Yugoslavia" in 1993, in the name of "international humanitarian law."[280] The term "ethnic cleansing" was used in the UN resolution forming the tribunal, but the word "genocide" was also used in the indictments against the defendants, of which there were 111. For example, Radovan Karadzic, sentenced to forty years jail, was "convicted of genocide [2 counts], crimes against humanity and violations of the laws or customs of war." Milosevic died in 2006 while in the process of being tried.

Serbia was a small, isolated state; hence a comparatively easy mark for elimination. Theoretically, former President Donald Trump, Viktor Orbán of Hungary, and Vladimir Putin of Russia are as "guilty" of offending the "new world order" as Milosevic. Should they have been as vulnerable, the gallows would await.

---

[279] Binder, "In Yugoslavia, rising ethnic strife."
[280] UN Security Council, "Report of the Secretary General."

"Human Rights" as a Social Control Mechanism

"Now, there is no such thing as 'man' in this world. In my life I have seen Frenchmen, Italians, Russians, and so on. I even know, thanks to Montesquieu, that one can be Persian. But as for man, I declare I've never encountered him."

Joseph de Maistre (1797)

When the Bolsheviks erected their bloody edifice in Russia, the Constitution of the Union of Soviet Socialist Republics (USSR) assured its citizens all manner of rights, one scholar writing:

> *The first Soviet Constitution, adopted by the Russian Republic in 1918, contained a section on fundamental rights in which freedom of speech, association, assembly, press, conscience, unions and access to knowledge, as well as equality of civil rights and the right to asylum were explicitly mentioned.*[281]

The piggish oligarchy at Orwell's *Animal Farm* put it this way in their declaration on "rights": "all animals are equal, but some animals are more equal than others." The drafters of "human rights proposals" assure us, in Soviet manner, that our freedoms are not under threat—unless you challenge their dogma. Conform, and all is well.

Role of United Nations Organization

The United Nations continued this legacy, proclaiming a multiplicity of "universal rights" that are supposedly applicable to every nation, people,

---

[281] Towe, "Fundamental Rights," 1252.

culture, and race across time and space. With every "human right'" comes a new set of laws, and the extension of United Nations authority to oversee those laws, the preamble of the UN Charter (1945) stating the aim to be, "to reaffirm faith in fundamental human rights, in the dignity and worth of the human person, in the equal rights of men and women and of nations large and small..."

The UN issued its Universal Declaration of Human Rights in 1948. John Humphrey, Professor of International Law at McGill University, who had served as director of the UN Human Rights Division (1946–1966), described the process in drafting the declaration, in an article celebrating the UN International Year for Human Rights in 1968:

> *The history of human rights in the United Nations extends, of course, beyond the two decades which followed the adoption of the Declaration. The Charter was adopted twenty-three years ago, and it is twenty-one years since Eleanor Roosevelt presided over the first session of the Commission on Human Rights. The period before the adoption of the Declaration is very important, for it was then that the foundation was laid for everything that has happened since. An essential part of this foundation was the Charter itself. One of the most revolutionary innovations of the Charter and what distinguishes it most sharply from any previous international constitution was its attitude towards human rights. The Dumbarton Oaks Proposals recommended that their promotion should be included in the chapter on economic and social co-operation, 'with a view to the creation of conditions of stability and well-being which are necessary for peaceful and friendly relations among nations'. At San Francisco, the promotion of human rights became one of the four or five stated purposes of the Organization, as enunciated in Article 1 of the Charter; and other articles dealing with human rights were included, the most important being Articles 55, 56 and 68.* **This was due chiefly to energetic lobbying carried on by certain non-governmental organizations**, *to the attitude of certain small countries and to the imaginative leadership of the United States' delegation which, once it had been impelled to act by the voluntary organizations, was able to obtain the agreement of the other sponsoring powers, without which the articles would never have been adopted.*[282]

---

[282] Humphrey, "Human Right, UN, and 1968," 1-2. Emphasis added.

Humphrey alludes to the focus on "human rights" at the UN founding conference being "due chiefly to energetic lobbying carried on by certain non-governmental organizations." This was the presence of the American Jewish Committee (AJC) as a consultant to the US delegation. Gaer writes of the AJC role in a recent report that:

> *The representatives of the American Jewish Committee (AJC), present in San Francisco as consultants to the US delegation, played a major role in insisting that the safeguarding of human rights for all persons must be a part of any future world order.*[283]

The identity of the NGO referred to by Humphrey is made known in the report:

> *AJC's commitment to the idea of universal human rights and to promoting American leadership in pursuit of their realization, and the skill employed by its representatives in realizing these goals, were noted by observers of the San Francisco Conference. Columbia University Professor James Shotwell, America's foremost expert on international organizations at the time and a participant in the San Francisco Conference, later recalled that AJC leaders did "the major and strenuous part of the thinking"*[284] *that led to the human rights provisions in the UN Charter. Author William Korey concluded that the "historic breakthrough" of the inclusion of human rights in the UN Charter "never would have taken place without the commitment, determination and pressure of a group of American NGOs," citing Judge Joseph Proskauer and Jacob Blaustein as the "sparkplugs" whose initiative was decisive.*[285]

The AJC report is clear in stating that when their leaders met with President Franklin D. Roosevelt to lobby for the inclusion of "human rights" laws in the UN Charter, the actual motive was to secure the interests of Jewry behind the facade of concern for "humanity":

> *On March 21st, 1945, Joseph Proskauer and Jacob Blaustein, respectively President and Chair of AJC's Executive Committee, met with President Franklin D. Roosevelt and pressed for the*

---

[283] Gaer, "AJC's Advocacy."
[284] Shotwell, "Tribute."
[285] Korey, *NGO's and Human Rights*, 29, 33.

*United States to take a leadership role in advancing the idea of human rights in the new world organization. Proskauer was a lawyer, had served as a judge in New York State, and was an eloquent speaker. Blaustein was a businessman, the founder of Amoco Oil, and known for being practical and outcome oriented. Both were committed to seeing incorporation of human rights for all in a **new world order**, and they wanted the international organization to draft an International Bill of Rights to provide protection to all people. As Blaustein put it, "**A fundamental tenet for the Committee has been the conviction that equality and security cannot be assured for Jews unless ensured for all.**"*[286]

Gaer refers to the 1968 Humphrey article as alluding to the NGOs lobbying for the "human rights" focus, and reveals that he was alluding to the AJC:

As John Humphrey, the first head of the UN's human rights office pointed out: "NGOs played a pivotal role in securing the inclusion of human rights language in the final UN charter…. [They] conducted a lobby in favor of human rights for which there is no parallel in the history of international relations, and which was largely responsible for the human rights provisions of the Charter." Truly, if not for the coordination, engagement, and persuasive advocacy by the consultants at the San Francisco conference, and by AJC's representatives in particular, it seems clear that the UN Charter would not have enshrined human rights as the preeminent multilateral organization's "Third Pillar" (alongside international peace and security and development) or laid the institutional groundwork for the subsequent development of international human rights law. Their timely and influential advocacy demanding that the new world body incorporate more about human rights and fundamental freedoms changed the views of the US delegation and the assembled diplomats, and indeed, changed history.[287]

Humphrey affirms that the "human rights" doctrine adopted by the UN has had "as radical a development as has ever taken place in the history of international law and international relations." Its affect is to subvert the

---

[286] Gaer, "AJC's Advocacy," 2.
[287] Ibid., 8.

sovereignty of states and peoples, providing a moral rationalization for the elimination of "rogue states," having laid the foundations of a *de facto* world state that is now becoming *de jure*, and increasingly invasive, in the name of "global governance," referring to "the fact that the United Nations was endowed with a constitutional and institutional base on which it could build."[288]

> *The Charter reflected, of course, the reaction of people everywhere to the indescribable violations of the most fundamental rights which had taken place in certain countries during and immediately before the Second World War. Their effect was to make the promotion of human rights a matter of international concern, whereas they had traditionally been considered as coming within a State's domestic jurisdiction.* **This has been as radical a development as has ever taken place in the history of international law and international relations***. It is enough to compare the Charter with the Covenant of the League [of Nations] to realize its revolutionary character.*[289]

The declaration enables the UN to interfere in the sovereignty of states and peoples to the extent of armed intervention via the so-called "UN policing operations." It states:

> *Everyone is entitled to all the rights and freedoms set forth in this Declaration, without distinction of any kind, such as race, colour, sex, language, religion, political or other opinion, national or social origin, property, birth or other status. Furthermore, no distinction shall be made on the basis of the political, jurisdictional or international status of the country or territory to which a person belongs, whether it be independent, trust, non-self-governing or under any other limitation of sovereignty.*

The way these "universal human rights" are granted, then subjected to qualification—*Animal Farm* style—can be deduced by comparing two articles (19 and 29) within the *Universal Declaration of Human Rights*:

---

[288] Humphrey,"Human Rights, UN, and 1968," 4.
[289] Humphrey, "Human Rights, UN, and 1968," 1-2. Emphasis added.

Everyone has the right to freedom of opinion and expression; this right includes freedom to hold opinions without interference and to seek, receive and impart information and ideas through any media and regardless of frontiers. (Article 19)

But...

In the exercise of his rights and freedoms, everyone shall be subject only to such limitations as are determined by law solely for the purpose of securing due recognition and respect for the rights and freedoms of others and of meeting the just requirements of morality, public order and the general welfare in a democratic society. (Article 29)

Here in the manner of the Jacobins and the Bolsheviks, we have the creation of a tyranny behind the facade of "human rights." The way this is intended to be imposed as an "international order" is explicitly stated: *"Everyone is entitled to a social and international order in which the rights and freedoms set forth in this Declaration can be fully realized."*[290]

United Nations Authority Usurps National Sovereignty

For this "international order" to be established and enforced, the UN has created a global edifice of authority based on ever increasing declarations and "covenants," which are in turn ratified as laws by member states. Among these is the UN Declaration of Human Rights, from which proceed many other declarations.

In conformity with these United Nations declarations, in 1972 New Zealand enacted the Race Relations Act. In 1993 this was extended by the Human Rights Commission Act that created a Human Rights bureaucracy under which the Office of the Race Relations Conciliator was subsumed. The jurisdiction was widened to include disabilities, gender and marital status. When some questions were raised as to the authority vested in the United Nations when New Zealand ratified the UN Global Compact for Migration, it was denied that such laws give the UN any legal jurisdiction over New Zealand, and that criticism was alarmist and even the creation of the "far right."[291] Yet

---

[290] Ibid., 28.
[291] It is notable that the assurances were given by then Minister of Foreign Affairs, New Zealand First Party leader Winston Peters, a critic of immigration when it suited his purpose,

the New Zealand Department of Justice plainly states regarding UN declarations:

> New Zealand is party to 7 core international human rights treaties of the United Nations. **By signing up to these instruments, New Zealand has assumed obligations under international law.**[292]

The Justice Department plainly states that laws have been enacted to put into effect these UN declarations, and that the nation's sovereignty can be usurped by UN authorities:

> New Zealand has also undertaken to **put into place domestic measures and legislation compatible with its obligations under the treaties**, and has agreed to **submit periodic reports** on the measures taken to give effect to its treaty obligations. Where domestic legal proceedings fail to address unjustified limitations on human rights, mechanisms and procedures for individual complaints are available at the international level to help ensure that **international standards are indeed respected, implemented, and enforced.**[293]

"The Universal Periodic Review Process" examines the "human rights situation in all Member States of the United Nations," which is "reviewed by the Human Rights Council once every four to five years."[294] The declarations emanating from the UN Declaration of Human Rights, which New Zealand ratified, are listed:

- International Covenant on Civil and Political Rights (ICCPR)
- International Covenant on Economic, Social and Cultural Rights (ICESCR)
- International Convention on the Elimination of All Forms of Racial Discrimination (CERD)
- Convention on the Elimination of All Forms of Discrimination against Women (CEDAW)

---

who said that the Compact does not undermine sovereignty when, like other UN declarations and treaties, it clearly does. See: Devlin, "New Zealand Votes."
[292] "Constitutional Issues."
[293] Ibid.
[294] Ibid., International Human Rights Legislation, Core Human Rights Instruments.

- Convention on the Rights of the Child (CRC)
- Convention against Torture and other Cruel, Inhuman or Degrading Treatment or Punishment (CAT)
- Convention on the Rights of Persons with Disabilities (CRPD)[295]

While no sane person would object to the protection of the welfare of children, women, and the disabled, it is the "universal human rights" ideology that has premised the implementation of a veritable revolution that is designed to impose a neo-Jacobin dogma. In particular this body of doctrine provides the foundation for measures designed to denigrate, dispossess, and to make passé the very existence of the New Zealand European which—and of course Whites worldwide—despite being an officially designated ethnic group for the purposes of census counting, is the only ethnicity to be denied the "human rights" that are assumed for all other ethnicities and races.

UN Declaration on the Rights of Indigenous Peoples

Hence, the UN Declaration on Human Rights premised the UN Declaration on the Rights of Indigenous Peoples (UNDRIP),[296] as the New Zealand Justice Department states: "Instruments such as the Declaration on the Rights of Indigenous Peoples are extremely important in promoting and protecting the rights of indigenous peoples."[297]

UNDRIP in turn has premised in New Zealand *He Puapua*, a government policy discussion document that is intended to convey sovereignty to the Maori. That UNDRIP is the basis of *He Puapua* is stated in the subtitle of the document: "report of the working group of a plan to realise the UN Declaration on the Rights of Indigenous Peoples in Aotearoa/New Zealand."[298] What can be clearer?

He Puapua has recommendations for an Upper House or Senate that could veto Parliament, and wants to grant privileges to the Maori that the New Zealand European has never held at any time in New Zealand history, including the colonial epoch. The European settler never had rights and privileges that were not also granted to the Maori. That was enshrined in

---

[295] Ibid., International Human Rights Legislation, Universal Periodic Review.
[296] *The United Nations Declarantion on the Rights of Indigenous Peoples.*
[297] "Constitutional Issues."
[298] *He Puapua.*

the Treaty of Waitangi in 1840, granting the Maori the same rights and privileges as all other Crown subjects.[299]

Now that treaty, which is being touted as the founding document of New Zealand (increasingly referred to as *Aotearoa*) is being reinterpreted as having granted the Maori chiefs "partnership" with the Crown in the "co-governance" (sic) of New Zealand. However, even this bogus interpretation of "co-governance" does not suffice for the Europhobes; the aim is Maori sovereignty over the entirety of New Zealand, sustained with European largesse and capital, despite Maori assets totaling $69 billion (in 2018),[300] thanks to repeated treaty "full and final settlements" (sic). The aim is for another Rhodesia/Zimbabwe, where the European is dispossessed.

The dispossession of the New Zealand European is of no concern to the deracinated global oligarchy, which already works in partnership with Maori enterprises—built up with the capital of New Zealand Europeans—through the treaty process. In fact, the emerging Maori oligarchy has already served as a bridge between New Zealand resources and economic globalization.[301] International capital was active in the de-Europeanization of Rhodesia and South Africa and in the decolonization of Africa, to open up for neo-colonialism.[302]

When a "failed state" ensues, the European, albeit now powerless, will nonetheless be blamed because of the "legacy of colonialism." The European is the eternal scapegoat. The European in whatever part of the world he resides, whether as a migrant or an indigene, will always be placed in a no-win situation. As for the UN Declaration on the Rights of Indigenous Peoples, when will these "rights of indigenous peoples" ever be granted to the Afrikaners, indigenous to South Africa, or the White indigenes of Britain and the European continent, facing colonization through immigration?

He Puapua: "Breaking" the New Zealand European

He Puapua is defined as a "break" in Maori and is interpreted by the working group drafting the document as meaning to "break political and

---

[299] See the ongoing series by Bolton, in answer to the Ministry of Education's proposed Europhobic school "histories" curriculum starting in 2022: "Aotearoa New Zealand Histories."
[300] "Kimihia te mea."
[301] For a study on the potential for the "internationalization" of Maori business see: Warriner, "Internationalisation of Maori."
[302] Bolton, *Babel Inc.*, 79-95.

societal norms," from which New Zealand will re-emerge as Aotearoa, based on UNDRIP and a re-interpreted Treaty of Waitangi.[303] It is proposed that the plan be effected by 2040. The proposals include "the restructure of governance"[304] and "a sometimes dominant voice" in resource management.[305] "All New Zealanders will embrace and respect Maori culture," and the state services will be imbued with that culture.[306]

Where the New Zealand European is envisaged to fit into this new order is as the provider of financial largesse, where there is "dedicated funding for Maori governance development."[307] This will presumably be based on continually expanding Treaty of Waitangi commitments, as a bizarrely defined "living document."

There is a strong basis for indoctrination or re-education involved to ensure the complicity of the New Zealand European, from kindergarten toddler to public servant. That this process has started is evident from the Critical Race Theory programs that are being taught to teachers, and have entered the classrooms.[308]

The "groundwork for constitutional change" involves continuing to develop the New Zealand history curriculum in schools. This is a reference to the new "school histories curriculum" starting in 2022, which is premised on the denigration of the New Zealand European, and the portrayal of the Maori as a victim of colonization.[309] A "public education programme" will imbue New Zealand Europeans with the Treaty of Waitangi and "human rights" (sic) as the basis for "constitutional matters" (sic).[310] The creation of an "Upper House" is proposed for this Maori-Crown "power-sharing."[311] By 2023–2025 the aim is to bring all legislation into line with UNDRIP and Treaty provisions.[312]

While the Government insists that *He Puapua* is not being implemented, the inauguration of Critical Race Theory courses, and the "new histories curriculum" indicates otherwise. The first stage is indoctrination. The strengthening of the race relations and "human rights" laws is intended to prohibit criticism.

---

[303] *He Puapua*, i. See: Robinson, *He Puapua*.
[304] Ibid., iii, (5).
[305] Ibid., v. (2).
[306] Ibid., (4).
[307] Ibid., 37, Groundwork for Constitutional Change.
[308] This will be discussed further.
[309] *"Aotearoa New Zealand's."*
[310] *He Puapua*, Groundwork for Constitutional Change.
[311] *He Puapua*, 38.
[312] Ibid., 89.

Hate Speech Proposals

Given the changes that are sought by the Government, which are nothing short of revolutionary, it becomes evident why the government is eager to enhance the Human Rights Act with "hate speech laws" that increase punishments to a crippling extent. Behind the facade of "human rights" a tyranny is being created to outlaw resistance to the government's far-reaching agendas. Since the government is also aiming to introduce legislation that will outlaw criticism of "gender fluidity," to the point of criminalizing parents and health professionals by *dishonestly* calling *all counseling* critical of gender change faith-based "conversion therapy"; the "hate speech" proposals are extended to this as well. The promotion of transgenderism is also a feature of the "school histories curriculum." The hate speech laws are intended to stifle criticism of:

1. UN Global Compact for Migration
2. New school histories curriculum
3. *He Puapua*
4. Prohibition of Conversion Therapy Bill[313]
5. All criticism of multiculturalism, Maori intransigence, and the denigration of the New Zealand European.

Considering that the opposition to globalism and multiculturalism is sporadic, muted, and without resources, the state must be very paranoid, as tyrants generally are, to consider it necessary to strengthen "human rights" laws, using the pretext that a lone gunman from Australia, Brenton Tarrant, was motivated to kill Muslims in Christchurch in 2019 because he had been radicalized by "far right" extremism on social media. He had been radicalized by seeing the migrant impact on Europe, and a feeling of powerlessness produced his psychosis. Scapegoating the "far right" serves the globalist agenda.

It is the "far right" that is the sole "enemy of the state," that must be purged through imprisonment and crippling fines, when smearing by the state's bought news media is insufficient. The news media has been made into a *de facto* government propaganda agency through state subsidies. It is a "bought" news media in a literal sense, and hence a state media or propaganda outlet. The Public Interest Journalism Fund was established by the government to subsidize news media for the purposes of

---

[313] "Prohibition of Conversion."

propagating the party line.[314] This at least partly explains why there has been a sudden and sustained amount of Maori words and phrases from the news media.

Yet even Wally Hirsh, a Zionist,[315] when Race Relations Conciliator, stated in 1986 that:

> [R]ace assimilation is immoral.... that New Zealand must move away from assimilation where differences between races were removed and aim for cultural maintenance. It is everybody's right to be strengthened by knowing where they came from, being strong in their own traditions, values, customs, language and so on. A strength of a harmonious society is one which not only enables but encourages people to be strong in their own identity.[316]

Paradoxically, this is also the view of the "far right," while those *neo-whigs* who favor "one nation, one people" melting pot assimilation are mistakenly described by media and academia as "right-wing."[317] The problem arises because the multicultural edifice is *imposed* from the top down, and denies identity to the European while demanding it for all others.

Where there should be accord between the dissident right and Maori there is difference because Maori will not accept self-assessment, but rather insist on scapegoating New Zealand Europeans, while demanding

---

[314] A statement by the Ministry of Culture and Heritage explains, with the euphemism being the propagation of a "healthy democracy":

> The $55 million Public Interest Journalism Fund will support New Zealand's media to continue to produce stories that keep New Zealanders informed and engaged and support a healthy democracy. The $55 million package will be made up of $10 million in 2020/21, $25 million in 2021/22 and $20 million in 2022/23.

The condition for receiving the subsidies is a commitment to the Treaty of Waitangi and multiculturalism. "Public Interest Journalism: General Guidelines."

[315] "Pro-Palestine Group Slates New Conciliator": The Wellington Palestine Group objected to Hirsh's appointment as Race Relations Conciliator on the grounds that he is a Zionist, and that Zionism was described in 1979 by the UN General Assembly as a "form of racism and racial discrimination."

[316] "Policy Immoral."

[317] See Hobson's Pledge as an example of this. Here liberal capitalists such as ex-Reserve Bank Governor Don Brash promote the assimilationist, melting-pot, "one people" doctrine. Although routinely called "right-wing" by the media and academia, the pseudo-right condemns "separatism" as analogous to South African Apartheid, which it regards with as much anathema as the left, and cannot differentiate between leftist "identity politics" and rightist "identitarianism." Any group identity is rejected as "socialism," and an encroachment on the sovereignty of the individual.

that New Zealand Europeans fund their own denigration, dispossession, and demise. Worse still, while Maori are rejecting the assimilationism that was fostered by nineteenth century English liberalism, with the famous dictum spoken by Governor Hobson to the Maori chiefs when they signed the Treaty of Waitangi in 1840 ("We are one people") they demand that the New Zealand European assimilate into a new Maori dispensation. This is clearly stated in *He Puapua* and in the "new school histories curriculum." The English liberalism of the eighteenth and nineteenth centuries sought to create brown-skinned "Englishmen"; today the aim is to create something nebulous called a "Kiwi" with some Maori cultural trappings, since "New Zealander" is implicitly European and colonial, while "Kiwi" is becoming increasingly common in state and media parlance.

It is not so much that the laws will even need to be enforced, but that they enhance the already toxic atmosphere. This atmosphere of repression recently manifested when a first place award for a New Zealand Defence Forces essay competition[318] was withdrawn because the writer had deviated from the party line: *deviationism* as the communists call it. The author, N. Dell, presciently opened his essay with the hope that it would not be suppressed on the altar of liberal conformity:

> *I write this essay fully aware of the backlash and, at times, real world consequences afforded to the authors of similar documents in the current socio-political climate. Nevertheless, I would invoke the NZ Army ethos "3CI"—particularly "Courage" and "Integrity"—in defence of the opinion I will express herein. The open discussion of any issue must be possible without fear of repercussions on both sides of the debate if the best outcome is ever to be reached. That is the fundamental value of free speech that permits the free enquiry, self-reflection, self-criticism and peer review that underpin our scientific and academic edifices and, in fact, our entire civilisation.*[319]

Dell foresaw that he had just signed his own death warrant for promotion prospects, unless he has shown the necessary remorse. His theme is that preoccupation with ideological agendas in shaping the military is both wasteful and diversionary:

---

[318] "Writing Competition Winner."
[319] Dell, "Can Army Afford?"

The "Woke" culture that has led to the popular preoccupation with Diversity and inclusion is antithetical to the Army's ethos and values. It is built on the notion that feelings are more important than facts. It asserts that everyone is the same while promoting the merits of Diversity. It shuns notions of excellence and meritocracy. It diminishes personal responsibility and erodes resilience, even rejecting the notion that resilience is a virtue. Social media has been the vector for this intellectual contagion and evidence has even surfaced that this has been cynically aided and abetted by belligerent foreign governments with the explicit goal of weakening western democracy. We must not capitulate to our enemies' efforts.

The primary threat of any effort to be more "Diverse" and "inclusive" is opportunity cost. Put simply, every resource that we divert toward programmes aimed at improving Diversity and Inclusion is a resource that is not available to be used for the Army's only responsibility: to protect New Zealand. Whether that is in preparing for wars or fighting them (or civil defence). Every man-hour that is spent on "cultural awareness training" or similar programmes is a man-hour that is not spent training for combat or monitoring our enemies. How are they spending their man-hours?[320]

Seeds of Self-Destruction

The whole edifice and ideology serves to marginalize, denigrate, and dispossess New Zealand Europeans; this is the only consistency that is required. The Race Relations and Human Rights laws have never been applied equitably, and are not intended to be so.

The anti-White intent of the "human rights" regime was clarified in 1988 when Walter Hirsh stated of complaints to the Race Relations Office that "the majority of people who complain are offended and hurt White people. This was never the intention of the [Race Relations] Act; it was drafted for the protection of minority groups." [321]

The following year (April 1989) Alister Grant resigned from the Equal Opportunities Tribunal,[322] stating that the Race Relations Office and the

---

[320] Ibid.
[321] *Sunday Times*, 1988.
[322] The Tribunal has wide ranging powers to try those accused of breaching the Act, and impose fines and prohibitions on speaking and writing. The Tribunal was empowered to

Human Rights Commission practiced "reverse racism." Grant had observed that "people of color," to use a present social construct, were considered by those offices as always right regardless of the facts.

We see the implicit *Europhobia* in the reactions from the news media when anyone so much as chalks up "it's okay to be White," the implication being that *it is not okay to be White*. Even stating "White lives matter" is objectionable; hence clearly for those who object, *"White lives do not matter."* Double-think must be employed to describe such slogans as "it's okay to be White," and "all lives matter" as "hate speech." For example, the Human Rights Commission opined in 2019 in regard to items adorned with "it's okay to be White" being sold on Trade Me that, "it seems likely that the stickers and T-shirts are intended to convey a message of intolerance, racism and division. There is no place for that in New Zealand." The same article refers to outrage in 2017 from the Napier mayor when "it's okay to be White" posters appeared in the city.[323]

Brainwashing Techniques

An effective tyranny cannot be maintained with laws alone. Indoctrination plays a key role. We have already seen the "new school histories curriculum," which is designed to indoctrinate children and youths, based on the denigration of the European heritage as nothing more than rapacious colonialism, while the Maori and all other ethnicities are to be lauded in sanitized form. Pride and self-confidence will be inculcated into Maori and all other ethnicities, except for the European child who will be taught self-loathing.

Teachers are being re-educated to instruct children in *Critical Race Theory*. The Ministry of Education announced:

> *On 29 March, around fifty of our staff were privileged to attend a workshop with Glenn Singleton and Dr Matthew Farry, who represent the Institute for Courageous Conversations About Race—an organisation committed to achieving racial equity in education.*
>
> *A Courageous Conversation is an award-winning protocol for effectively engaging, sustaining and deepening interracial dialogue. Some of you will be familiar with this work, as this*

---

prohibit the reporting of proceedings, thereby making proceedings tantamount to a secret court. This writer was witness to such proceedings in the 1980s.
[323] NZ Herald, "Trade Me defends selling."

workshop has also been delivered to a number of schools and Kāhui Ako.

Our staff were also joined by Daniel Pepper, Principal of St Dominic's Catholic Primary School and Kāhui Ako Lead for the Auckland Central Catholic Kāhui Ako. Daniel shared with our staff his own engagement with Courageous Conversations and why the Kāhui Ako have embarked on the Courageous Conversations journey.[324]

What "courage" is supposedly required to denigrate the New Zealand European is best left to the imagination of self-loathing Pakeha-Maori.[325] There is no faster way to ingratiate oneself to those in authority than to be a self-abasing European. No "courage" is required to conform.

The Institute for Courageous Conversations About Race that runs the program is part of the lucrative global human relations industry, a United States' edifice run mostly by "persons of color," according to their website's "About" page. New Zealand is the first country outside of the USA to be blessed with a branch of the Institute, established in 2016. This has serviced the Pacific region since 2018, when the Institute was partnered with Unitec.[326] In New Zealand its workshops are based on the Treaty of Waitangi "governance model." Certified "facilitators" run the workshops. In May 2021 David Seymour, leader of the Act Party, exposed the existence and character of the program:

> The people in charge of our education system are having to ask themselves, "What is my white privilege score"? and "What is my relationship to white fragility"?
>
> The Courageous Conversations programme makes a number of claims about so-called "white privilege":
>
> "'Whiteism'—not recognizing White as a dominating color nor the unearned power and privileges associated with having white skin; having a sense of (White) entitlement…is a condition that more White people must begin to recognize, understand and acknowledge."

---

[324] Ministry of Education, *Ministry Bulletin for Scool Leaders,* 15-16.
[325] Early whalers and escaped criminals who subjected themselves to the authority of Maori chiefs and attached themselves to tribes were referred to as *Pakeha-Maori*. Today, this manifests in the widespread tendency by nominal "Whites," especially those in government, media, churches, schools, and academia, to try to immerse themselves in the Maori world and detach from any link to their actual heritage. It most commonly manifests in their sporadic use of Maori words and phrases, to speak a type of New Zealand Pidgin English.
[326] Unitec Institute of Technology, Auckland.

> "...entitled white men do not appreciate the power of their entitlement because they have never experienced the absence of power."
>
> "Power, as manifested in the form of privilege, or entitlement, is part of the history, tradition and economic status of white men."

The program suggests that even people who aren't overtly racist perpetuate racism:

> *We are taught that racism must be intentional and that only bad people commit it. Thus a common white reasoning in crossracial conflicts is that as long as we are good people and don't intend to perpetuate racism, then our actions don't count as racism.*

It also claims that the role of teachers is to end oppression:

> *When history is taught by culturally competent teachers, our society will be much more conscious of the entitlement of some groups, and much more proactive in ending oppression.*[327]

Teachers, public servants, and schoolchildren are obliged in the workshops to acknowledge their "white privilege." Seymour cited an example of "A student in Whangārei [who] recently had to stand up in front of their classroom and say what they had done to acknowledge their white privilege." [328]

From what little can be discerned, and the institutes are not forthcoming as to the content of their workshops (while the Ministry of Education has taken down a link to the program), they are based on the *self-criticism* model. This has been used as a method of establishing group conformity and social control by, for example Jim Jones, and by the human relations industry, where it is called "team building." Those who resist become pariahs, whether in the cult, the Soviet state, or the business enterprise. The aim is that of brainwashing: to deconstruct the individual then reconstruct him in the desired image, as a "team player."

An example of a letter to Reverend Jim, "Dad" Jones, from one of his followers at the apocalyptic Jonestown settlement, is typical of the way the *self-criticism* process operates:

---

[327] "Govt Departments Teaching."
[328] "Govt's Denials."

February 21, 1978

Dad,

I feel I don't work as hard as I should and I feel I am lazy compared to others here that I've seen work. I feel as a supervisor I ain't shit. I see alot of shit go on and I fail to write it or report it because I want to look good and I want people to like me. I value friendship too highly that's why I never make any complaints on the people I associate with. I feel that I am to [sic] family oriented.

Thank you Dad,
Shirley Baisy[329]

In Cambodia under the Khmer Rouge, an observer described a *self-criticism* session at the end of the day among the guards of a prison camp:

"Comrades," began the eldest, "let us appraise the day that has passed, in order to correct our faults. We must cleanse ourselves of the repeated sins that accumulate and slow down our beloved revolution. Do not be surprised at this!"[330]

While Bolshevik Russia, Mao's China (Russian: Самокритика, samokritika; Chinese: 自我批评, zìwǒ pīpíng) and Pol Pot's Khmer Rouge used *self-criticism*, in the West "sensitivity training" was formulated by the Tavistock Institute, which had begun as a psychological warfare department in Britain during World War II. It is used in what is at times called "group therapy." "Sensitivity training" became a fad in the USA by the 1960s and continues to be widely used in the public and private sectors.

In 1968 the process was applied to race relations by two Black psychiatrists, Price M. Cobbs and William H. Grier, who co-authored the influential book *Black Rage*. With the book becoming a bestseller, Cobbs initiated "diversity training seminars," which utilized *group therapy*. Through Pacific Management Systems, a consulting firm which he founded in 1967, Cobbs conducted workshops on race relations in schools, police departments, social service agencies, community organizations, and the business world. These were called "racial confrontation groups." The basis of the "therapy" was that the USA was infused "with the idea of white supremacy," and that this was causing widespread mental illness among

---

[329] Bolton, *Psychotic Left*, 195-198.
[330] Bizot, *The Gate*, 52.

Blacks. These programs have proliferated through the USA and beyond.[331] These are the origins of enterprises such as the Institute for Courageous Conversations About Race.

Facade for Tyranny

In the aftermath of the defeat of Hitlerism lofty ideals were proclaimed that are said to be universally and perpetually valid. Where UN treaties applied locally as prohibitive laws do not work, bombs are the ultimate guarantee: Iraq, Libya, Serbia, Syria. "Color revolutions" throughout the former Soviet bloc and elsewhere have been another consequence. While the Jacobins stated that their revolutionary wars would liberate Europe, and while the communists thought that they had a similar formula to "liberate" all of humanity, today the foreign policy and geopolitical designs of the USA utilize "human rights" to justify the elimination of "rogue states."

The US State Department maintains a "human rights ranking index" that serves as a hit-list for "regime change," based on the *UN Universal Declaration of Human Rights*. Wherever the USA seeks "regime change," whether through war, or through economic embargoes, or well-planned "spontaneous" (sic) "color revolutions," through a global network of public and private organizations (National Endowment for Democracy, Freedom House, USAID, Open Society Institute), that state is first declared to be in breach of "human rights."[332] The so-called "world community" is assured that such states are a threat to "democracy" and must be eliminated to ensure "world peace." That sets the stage for the process of elimination. For example, as one should expect, Russia, the primary globalist bugbear, is placed poorly on the "human rights' index."[333]

---

[331] This method of brainwashing is explained in Bolton, *The Perversion of Normality: From the Marquis de Sade to Cyborgs*.
[332] For a history of the globalist networks see: Bolton, *Revolution from Above*.
[333] "2020 Country Reports."

The Role of the Oligarchs: The Rockefeller Foundation and Black Riots

"Monopolistic capitalism has no colour and no country."

William Lane, Australian Labour leader (1888).

"Cursed be the gold that gilds the straiten'd forehead of the fool!"

Alfred Tennyson (1835)

The election to the presidency of Donald Trump, the accidental death of George Floyd, and the killing of fifty-one Muslims by a lone-wolf gunman in Christchurch, New Zealand, provided the pretext to loosen upon the White world forces that had been under varying degrees of self-constraint in what has been a process of *gradualism*. Restraints were cut, Fenris was unleashed, and the events have been used to justify far-ranging changes that are striking at the very root of the existence of *Homo Europaeus* and what remnants exist of his culture. The funding by the Rockefeller Foundation of the Black Lives Matter movement is a primary present day example of the manner by which the global oligarchy uses race relations and "human rights" to advance their agendas.

It is fashionable, even among rightist intelligentsia, to dismiss "conspiracy theories." In doing so, one overlooks the covert forces that are funding—and always have funded—the forces of pseudo-revolt. These oligarchic sponsors are not fools or dupes, whose funds have been "taken over" by their anti-capitalist enemies, as was assumed by conservatives during the Cold War. Since the establishment of the tax exempt foundations over a century ago, the aims have been to promote what is now called a globalized "inclusive economy." As even Dr. Noam Chomsky, a leftist icon, has stated, concepts of race and ethnicity are hindrances to such a world economy, stating that, "Capitalism basically wants people to be interchangeable cogs, and differences among them, such as on the basis of race, usually are not functional…"[334]

None of the left, Antifa, or Black Lives Matter are capable of understanding this, any more than their frenetic predecessors circa 1968; any more than the legions of the naive who marched against the Afrikaners understood it, despite the globalization of South Africa's economy being plain to see.

Whether one calls it a "conspiracy," "corporate planning and strategy," or taking advantage of organically unfolding circumstances, it amounts to the same end.

The misinformation that is being published by the Establishment news media, which has been uniformly on the side of the rioters, had the groundwork prepared by think tanks that rationalized the rioting. For example, the Sentencing Project, which focuses on "racism" among police and justice departments, is funded by the Ford Foundation, Open Society Foundations, and the David Rockefeller Fund, among others.[335] One might think that there are those among the far-left, who imagine the revolution is at hand, who would give pause to reflect on why the Establishment media are so unanimously in favor of the rioters if it is an anti-Establishment revolt? However, that would necessitate the existence of critical faculties that have long since been etiolated by the media, the education system, and the entertainment industry. The production line zombie-left is the result. The phenomenon known in psychology as "cognitive dissonance" is widespread among them.

Rockefeller Foundation President Issues Inflammatory Statement

Amidst the rioting, looting, and burning, the Rockefeller Foundation declared its support. The Rockefeller Foundation is as connected with international capitalism as it ever was.

The Chairman of the Board is Richard D. Parsons, Senior Advisor of Providence Equity Partners LLC. Historically, Rockefeller trusts have always had among their boards those who have come up through Rockefeller enterprises. Parsons has been Chairman of Citigroup. Prior to

---

[334] Chomsky, *Understanding Power*, 88. The Chomsky passage is given more fully in this author's Parliamentary submission on the hate speech proposals, appended below.
[335] Refer to: "Annual Reports," Sentencing Project.

that, he was CEO of Time Warner. "Prior to that, he held various positions in state and federal government, as counsel for Nelson Rockefeller [when New York Governor, and when Vice President] and as a senior White House aide under President Gerald Ford." He is also a Board member for the Lazard bank, and others. Other Board members are from Morgan Stanley, Solomon Bros., GIC Singapore, African Development Bank, Man Group China, International Chamber of Commerce, The Carlyle Group, et al. The Rockefeller family is represented by Sharon Percy Rockefeller, formerly a member of the Steering Committee of the Bilderberg Group, the reclusive globalist think tank.

Hence when the president of the Board, Dr. Rajiv J. Shah, issues a public statement on behalf of the Rockefeller Foundation, one can assume that it has the endorsement of a cabal representing the top echelons of global capitalism. Shah was the director of USAID during the Obama Administration. USAID is a vanguard for American globalization. He also served on the National Security Council and other government departments. He was the founder of Latitude Capital, an international investment firm. The tone of Shah's statement is inflammatory:

> *Dear Foundation Friends and Colleagues,*
>
> *The past eight days have been a time of extreme pain, heartbreak, and reflection for our country.*
> *My wife and I are both children of immigrants from India, and like every person of color, we each know the exact moment when we first realized we weren't like everyone else. And even though we have both experienced racism and discrimination in different forms, the systemic racism and extraordinary violence African-Americans have lived with and continue to experience is unique in its history and depth.*[336]

The allegation that "every person of color" has "experienced racism and discrimination" and recalls the "exact moment," is intended as a swipe at every White American. Shah has lived a life of privilege, as have few Americans, and so have other "persons of color" on the Rockefeller Foundation Board. Eight of the thirteen Board members are "persons of color," most of whom are high in the echelons of global capitalism. Shah proceeds:

---

[336] Shah, "Reflecting on Violence."

> *As I said earlier this week, the recent murders of Ahmaud Arbery, George Floyd, Tony McDade, Sean Reed, and Breonna Taylor leave me angry and heartbroken. These acts of violence and police brutality are despicable. Yet again, innocent men and women were killed for no other reason than the color of their skin.*[337]

Shah repeats the misrepresentation that Blacks are disproportionately represented as victims of police brutality. Pointing out that Whites are victims, too—and disproportionately so—does not serve any oligarchic interest for the restructuring of the USA. Hence when Shah and others intone the names of Ahmaud Arbery, George Floyd, Tony McDade, Sean Reed, and Breonna Taylor as the martyrs in the service of pseudo-revolt, they will never be heard mentioning the names of Justine Damond, or Tony Timpa, both killed by police after making 911 calls, or the savage, prolonged beatings of Robert Leone (one of whose police assailants broke his wrist while punching Leone's head, for which Leone was prosecuted!); or college student James King, mugged and seriously beaten without reason by two plainclothes police thugs.

While it is stated that the number of deaths is disproportionate among Blacks in terms of the American population, this is a skewered way of looking at statistics: the amount of criminal behavior committed by Blacks is far ahead of that of Whites, proportionately. The number of Black deaths is *underrepresented* in comparison to Whites. Yet White victims, regardless of how one interprets statistics, are non-persons. Shah continues:

> *Enough is enough. How many more African-American men and women, boys and girls will die before we finally stamp out the racism, bigotry, and hatred that plagues our society? It's time for this to end. And yet I know we've said "Enough is enough" and "it's time for this to en" so many times before. We said it after Philando Castile, after Sandra Bland, after Tamir Rice, after Michael Brown, after Eric Garner, after Trayvon Martin, and many more. We've been saying it years. For decades. For centuries.*[338]

---

[337] Ibid.
[338] Ibid.

The rhetoric of Shah is no different from that of a histrionic ghetto Black about to loot a shop. Shah proceeded to allude to discussions about the current situation among the "Rockefeller team":

> *I'm grateful to our entire team at the Rockefeller Foundation for their thoughtful engagement in multiple dialogues we've had over the last week. Our team—global, diverse, and driven by the fundamental desire to serve others and particularly the most vulnerable amongst us—understands this is a moment when we can say "enough is enough" and through our actions help make that statement real.*[339]

This last allusion indicates that, as has been assumed, oligarchic funding and direction would be applied to the rioting. Rationalizing the posturing expressions of camaraderie of these privileged "persons of color" with the ghetto Black, this is explained as a matter of racial solidarity:

> *It's painful that our African-American colleagues have to relive the trauma of watching someone who looks like them be killed, and once again feel the incomprehensible worry about whether they or someone they love might be next.*[340]

Sheer demagogic cant. Excuse me, but where is there any identity between the rioting and looting Soul Brothers and Sisters with Mellody Hobson or Niddi Nwuneli on the RF Board? Of course, there are those who are blacker on the Board, and perhaps they are placed there to justify this great alliance between the oppressed and the oppressors? But trying to establish some type of race bond between the RF trustees and ghetto Blacks, rather than the money nexus that exists between those on the Board regardless of race, seems to be a cynical attempt at oligarchic manipulation. The Board, like that of every board of global capital, forms its own ethnos; what G. Pascal Zachary lauded as the "Global Me" in his book of that name.[341]

Shah attempted to create an image of the Rockefeller eminences being neighbors to the rioting ghetto Blacks:

> *It's painful to see police vehicles charging into groups of unarmed protesters in broad daylight just a few minutes' walk from the*

---
[339] Ibid.
[340] Ibid.
[341] Zachary, *Global Me.*

homes and neighborhoods where our colleagues live and raise their families.[342]

After James Fields seems to have accidentally killed Heather Heyer while he was trying to get away from a crazed mob, he was sentenced to jail with life plus 149 years. Where was the justice for Fields? Did Rockefeller assist with young Fields' defense on the basis of color-blind justice? What of the thuggish manner by which the police attacked the lawful and law-abiding Unite the Right Rally at Charlottesville in 2017? Conversely to the media praise for the present savagery, the victims in 2017, because they were White, were portrayed as the villains.

Black Riots in Rockefeller's New York

When Nelson Rockefeller, as Governor of New York, ordered the State troopers to occupy Attica Prison in 1971, killing twenty-nine inmates and ten hostages, he remarked to Nixon that it was a "beautiful job." "You can't have sharpshooters picking off the prisoners when the hostages are there with them, at a distance with tear gas, without maybe having a few accidents."[343] Between 2000 and 2005, families of those shot received state settlements. In 1964, in Rochester, New York, weeks of rioting after a police altercation with youths at a street dance was quelled when Rockefeller called out the National Guard. It is nothing but a hypocritical facade for the RF to present the Rockefellers as paragons of virtue, even though Nelson Rockefeller carved his political career out of being a liberal, especially when running against Barry Goldwater—portrayed as a new Hitler—for the Republican presidential nomination.

"Not enough can ever be said of the unique pain, suffering, and injustice..." stated Shah. This implies that the collective guilt complex among Whites should be maintained in perpetuity. But if this is "unique pain," is it "relativizing the Holocaust"? Perhaps it is something for the Anti-Defamation League and the Southern Poverty Law Center to consider.

---

[342] Shah, "Reflecting on Violence."
[343] Roberts, "Rockefeller on Attica."

Thank You, Massa

The second part of Shah's appeal for support to the Black rioters and looters outlined the wonderful Rockefeller legacy to Blacks over a hundred years:

For more than 100 years, The Rockefeller Foundation has worked to advance racial equality in America because it is core to our values. We are proud to have stood for and fought for racial justice for decades, and we're proud of our team members, grantees, and partners that are on the front lines today. Many have been in this fight for a long time.[344]

Note that the oligarchic fund regards the matter as a "fight" with allusions to "front lines." The terminology is inflammatory, amidst an inflamed situation. Shah proceeds:

Going back more than a century our organization has been an imperfect yet consistent supporter of the cause. In fact, the Rockefeller tradition of supporting racial equity started before this Foundation existed. Our founder, John D. Rockefeller, Sr. supported historically black colleges and universities (HBCUs) when they were one of the only avenues for young African American women and men to pursue higher learning; Spelman College is named after his wife Laura Spelman and her parents, who were among its earliest benefactors in the 1880s. And The Rockefeller Foundation has carried forward this banner.[345]

Up until a few decades before, the Southern plantation owners were housing and feeding Blacks who had been sold by other Blacks from amidst wretched conditions in Africa. As two liberal academics showed by studying plantation records, much to their amazement, many of the myths surrounding plantation slavery in the South are precisely that—myths, on which perpetual hatred can feed.[346] The situation was hardly ideal for Southern White workers. In such an oligarchy, there was no concept of racial kinship, no "White privilege" from which subsequent generations of Whites supposedly profit at the expense of the Black. As Hinton Rowan

---

[344] Shah, "Reflecting onViolence."
[345] Ibid.
[346] Fogel and Stanley, *Time on the Cross*.

Helper showed at the time, with extensive documentation, the Southern White laborers lived in abject poverty, but did not have any influential zealots of the Abolitionist type to speak for them.[347] In Britain, the condition of the working class was far below that of Black slaves. The preoccupation of White liberals with Blacks so embittered the *Chartists* that they broke up Abolitionist meetings, and William Cobbett was scathing of Wilberforce's preoccupations about Black slavery, while the British worker was left to rot.[348]

Friedrich Engels published a detailed study on the conditions of laborers in Britain, during the epoch in which our forefathers were supposedly the beneficiaries of "White privilege" and "White supremeacy."[349] As one should expect, the left has long since put such history down the Memory Hole in their quest to ingratiate themselves to non-Whites, due to their utter failure to recruit the proletariat. Besides which, such White working class misery is an important part of the process of dialectical materialism, and efforts at amelioration were considered by Karl Marx to be a "reactionist" spanner in the "wheel of history." Shah continues:

> *When modern medicine was in its infancy in the early 20th century, and schools refused to admit African-Americans, we helped create medical schools at HBCUs to train generations of African-American doctors and nurses. They had early insights into what we now know to be true: that HBCUs have been essential to creating upward mobility for low-income students of color.*
>
> *When Jim Crow prevented seven-in-ten African-Americans in the South from voting in the 1960s, we supported the Southern Regional Council to create the groundbreaking Voter Education Project, led at the time by civil rights icon (now-Congressman) John Lewis. It helped register more than 300,000 new voters, who regained their right to participate in our democracy's most sacred practice. And we helped the NAACP Legal Defense Fund expand beyond litigation to develop a division that supports the basic rights of the poor and victims of discrimination.*
>
> *When black mothers who relied on America's social safety net came under attack in the early 1980s, we partnered with community-based organizations to help provide job training,*

---

[347] Helper, *Impending Crisis*.
[348] Searle, *Morality and Market*, 65.
[349] Engels, *Condition of Working Class*.

placement, and childcare support to thousands of low income single mothers. More than ninety-five percent were women of color. And building on that work in the early 1990s, we helped launch Living Cities, a partnership of foundations and financial institutions originally focused on affordable housing, and now focuses on community and economic mobility for people of color in thirty cities.[350]

Since all Whites intrinsically benefit from the historical legacy of "White privilege" and "White supremacy," White poverty cannot be acknowledged to exist, but it does, as this report shows:

A fact sheet released today by the National Center for Children in Poverty (NCCP) shows that, contrary to some common stereotypes about America's poor, at least one-third of the thirteen million children living in poverty are White.

"Poverty affects children of all colors, contrary to stereotypes. The notion held by many Americans that poverty is not a white problem is simply false," says Jane Knitzer, EdD, director of NCCP, a research center at Columbia University's Mailman School of Public Health. "The sooner all Americans realize these facts about poverty, the better chance we have of eradicating it."

The NCCP fact sheet shows that among America's poor children, 4.2 million are white, 4 million are Latino, 3.6 million are African American, 400,000 are Asian, and 200,000 are American Indian.[351]

Interestingly, the RF was "quiet" in its support for the destruction of Southern monuments in 2017, and attacks on other elements of the Southern heritage:

Because we know this work is still unfinished, we've continued to stand against racism and hatred in our current era: When the city of New Orleans needed a financial guarantor so it could take down Confederate statues in 2017, ***we quietly stepped forward to help them remove those reprehensible***

---

[350] Shah, "Statement on Violence."
[351] "Supurb Excellence."

symbols that glorified violence against African Americans.[352]

Shah heralds the role oligarchic wealth can take in funding, organizing, and directing what amounts to a pseudo-revolt reminiscent of the New Left during the 1960s,[353] which was promoted by the same interests:

> *Our actions speak to the unique role philanthropy can play in driving social change.... And we can bring together different parts of society—serving as a bridge between public and private, between non-profits and investors, between communities and government officials, bringing everyone to the table to help solve some of the biggest problems we face—to create plans, programs, and innovations that others can follow.*
>
> *Now is unquestionably a time when we must all join together to say "enough"—but would an end to racist violence be enough?*[354]

Shah proceeds with the usual litany about Black poverty and discrimination. The premise is that this can only be ended when there is an "inclusive economy"; not the overthrow of plutocracy, but its extension so that all sections within a common landmass can become integral parts of the production and consumption process, united through the money nexus. It was what stood behind the same process for the dispossession of the Afrikaner; what Harry Oppenheimer, South Africa's leading oligarch, wanted was "a vast new consuming public," which apartheid was preventing.[355]

The declared goal of RF is "promoting the well-being of humanity throughout the world," by a "specific goal of promoting inclusive economies." A specific example of the need and manner of change is given as that of South Africa, where apartheid was an obstacle to this "inclusive economy," and change was attained "through conflict and bargaining," via the "anti-apartheid movement."[356] The key to understanding such movements as feminism, transgenderism, and racial integration is to think in terms of an "inclusive economy," where women, for example, are not

---

[352] Shah, "Reflecting on Violence." Emphasis added. See following chapter.
[353] As one example of the funding of the 1960s and 1970s New Left pseudo-revolt, the Rockefeller Foundation funded the iconic "community organiser" Saul Alinsky's Industrial Areas Foundation training program. See: "President's Review," 131.
[354] Shah, "Reflecting on Violence."
[355] For more on Oppenheimer, see the following chapter.
[356] Benner and Pastor,"Economy Indicators," 30.

held back from full integration into the production process through the bonds of home and children. Hence, why feminism is as assiduously promoted by RF, Soros, Ford, and a multitude of others along with the array of causes now called "identity politics."[357]

No declaration of this type would be complete without referring to Martin Luther King:

> *In 1967, Dr. Martin Luther King, Jr. gave a speech titled "Where do we go from here?"—a question that many of us are asking today. He described the structural foundations of racism, poverty, and inequality—rooted in "a system that still oppresses" today as it did then, a system still in dire need of reform. He declared the need to massively assert "dignity and worth," with the ultimate objective of "restructuring the whole of American society."*[358]

Martin Luther King was a good *house nigra*. He was backed by the oligarchs, as were from the start the NAACP and Urban League, to thwart Black separatism. Even militant Blacks during the Civil Rights era were often paid off with good jobs and funding. King was particularly close to Nelson Rockefeller, who had been giving the Southern Christian Leadership Conference checks since 1961.

Why do individuals who have been on the boards of Citigroup, Lazard, Morgan Stanley, Salomon Bros., GIC Singapore, Man Group, the International Chamber of Commerce, The Carlyle Group, et al. declare themselves for "restructuring the whole of American society"? Are they mental retards or psychotics? Do they really not understand what they are doing? No. They understand exactly what they are doing. This is not a sudden radical and transformative realization from wealthy people with a social conscience. It is part of a long-term process. Shah writes:

> *We go forward. We stay focused. We stand tall, together. We listen, and learn, and help our family and friends do the same. We rededicate ourselves to fighting racism, bigotry, and hatred everywhere it exists—using our voice and our privilege and our resources and our capacity to be moral leaders, both personally and professionally.*[359]

---

[357] For detailed documentation on this process see: Bolton, *Perversion of Normality*.
[358] Shah, "Reflecting on Violence."
[359] Brinkley, "The Man Who Kept."

"Our privilege," Shah states. It is the privilege of oligarchs, the real privilege of exploitation that hides behind demagogic rhetoric about "White privilege" and "White supremacy," deflecting responsibility from their system onto those who are subjected to it.

Lessons from 1790

Quite remarkably the great Conservative thinker Edmund Burke perceived during his time that behind the revolutionary tumult unfolding in France there stood the hidden factor of money and new wealth; the *nouveau riche*. He described what had occurred in France in terms of a new oligarchy having arisen against a nobility (albeit itself having become increasingly debased by money) aligned with the uprooted and the alienated among both the proletariat and intelligentsia. The alignment of destructive forces that Burke described in 1790 pertains with exactitude today. In the tax-exempt foundations and think tanks, so-called "civil society," sponsored by the wealth of oligarchs, the intelligentsia are employed to mobilize the rabble behind the banner of "human rights" and "social justice." Burke stated of the same situation 230 years ago:

> *The monied property was long looked on with rather an evil eye by the people. They saw it connected with their distresses, and aggravating them. It was no less envied by the old landed interests, partly for the same reasons that rendered it obnoxious to the people, but much more so as it eclipsed, by the splendour of an ostentatious luxury, the unendowed pedigrees and naked titles of several among the nobility.*
>
> *Even when the nobility which represented the more permanent landed interest united themselves by marriage (which sometimes was the case) with the other description, the wealth which saved the family from ruin was supposed to contaminate and degrade it. Thus the enmities and heartburnings of these parties were increased even by the usual means by which discord is made to cease and quarrels are turned into friendship.*
>
> ***In the meantime, the pride of the wealthy men, not noble or newly noble, increased with its cause. They felt with resentment an inferiority, the grounds of which they did not acknowledge. There was no measure to which they were not willing to lend themselves in order***

to be revenged of the outrages of this rival pride and to exalt their wealth to what they considered as its natural rank and estimation. They struck at the nobility through the crown and the church. They attacked them particularly on the side on which they thought them the most vulnerable, that is, the possessions of the church, which, through the patronage of the crown, generally devolved upon the nobility. The bishoprics and the great commendatory abbeys were, with few exceptions, held by that order.

In this state of real, though not always perceived, warfare between the noble ancient landed interest and the new monied interest, the greatest, because the most applicable, strength was in the hands of the latter. *The monied interest is in its nature more ready for any adventure, and its possessors more disposed to new enterprises of any kind. Being of a recent acquisition, it falls in more naturally with any novelties.* **It is therefore the kind of wealth which will be resorted to by all who wish for change.**

Along with the monied interest, a new description of men had grown up with whom that interest soon formed a close and marked union—I mean the political men of letters. *Men of letters, fond of distinguishing themselves, are rarely averse to innovation. Since the decline of the life and greatness of Louis the Fourteenth, they were not so much cultivated, either by him or by the regent or the successors to the crown, nor were they engaged to the court by favours and emoluments so systematically as during the splendid period of that ostentatious and not impolitic reign. What they lost in the old court protection, they endeavoured to make up by joining in a sort of incorporation of their own; to which the two academies of France, and afterwards the vast undertaking of the Encyclopedia,*[360] *carried on by a society of these gentlemen, did not a little contribute.*[361]

---

[360] The *Encyclopaedia* was a vast undertaking of philosophers led by Diderot, to expound the sciences and by so doing undermine religion. Its influence contributed to the inculcation of revolutionary ideas among the bourgeoisie, new rich and debased nobility who sought novelty in salon philosophizing.
[361] Burke, *Reflections*, 91-92. Emphasis added.

Edmund Burke discerned 130 years before Oswald Spengler[362] and other twentieth century historians that behind revolution stands plutocracy.[363]

---

[362] Spengler wrote in the second volume of his *magnum opus* (1926) that "the concepts of Liberalism and Socialism are set in effective motion only by money." He traced the phenomenon as far back as Tiberius Gracchus's revolt that had the backing of the *Equites*, "the big-money party." Spengler, *The Decline of The West*, Vol. 2, 402. See also: Bolton, *Revolution from Above*, passim; *The Perversion of Normality*, passim. For the most documented book on the funding of revolutions in Russia, see: Spence, *Wall Street and the Russian Revolution*.

[363] Burke points out that one immediate gain for the new rich who backed the Jacobins was that confiscated Church property—rather than their money—would be used to redeem the national debt.

The Place of BLM: Funds from the Oligarchs

"Writing about the Ford Foundation's work on urban community action, school decentralization, and the arts in the 1960s and 1970s, scholar Karen Ferguson[364] argues that 'the critical national project for the American liberal establishment was to domesticate black power and its challenge to liberalism.'"

Rachel Wimpee, "Funding a Social Movement."

At the time of the George Floyd killing, Black Lives Matter was already positioned to exploit the situation, and as in prior decades, mobilize masses in the desired direction. The funding of Black Lives Matter shows the role that has historically been played by plutocracy in promoting what is today called an "inclusive economy."

As Harry Oppenheimer showed in his address at the founding of the business lobby, the South Africa Foundation, plutocracy uses a two-pronged assault, one on the streets and one in the echelons of power; pressure from above and pressure from below, squeezing the life out of any obstacles. Their representatives then come forward with what seems to be a "moderate" alternative, and the whole of society is pushed a step further leftward. Hence the likes of Martin King or Nelson Mandela are seen as the "moderate" options to the violence of Black and New Left street thugs, and a crisis is averted through "compromise." That is how the Afrikaners gave up their homeland.

Oppenheimer in explaining his strategy to the assembled businessmen, stated that "the white electorate must be persuaded that, under my

---

[364] Ferguson, *Top Down*.

system, all the things that the White man really cherishes will be preserved."365 He next held forth his vision:

> *Picture the industrial revolution that will take place in Africa if the Black man's economic fetters are struck from him. Think of the millions of skilled men who will enter the labour market. Think of the vast new consuming public! And if we arrange our political affairs carefully, we can achieve all this and still retain effective political power in the hand of the white man.*366

He alluded to his corporation, Anglo-American, becoming *"an ally of the African National Congress."*367 The result was the dispossession, increasing destitution and outright genocide of the Afrikaner, while those "White men" who not only retained power, but vastly extended it when the ANC Government privatized the state utilities and resources that had been built up by the nationalists, preserved what *they* "really cherish"—money-power: *plutocracy*. Like the mine workers on the Rand whose strike against the Oppenheimer dynasty in 1922 was brutally suppressed by the Smuts Government, the Afrikaners have always been regarded with contempt by the oligarchy. Their nationalist government, and especially Prime Minister Verwoerd, often called "the architect of apartheid," hated by the oligarchs, could not be removed by the ballot box. An electoral challenge would be "utterly futile." The tactic was "the merger of moderates," while continuing to support the opposition Progressive Party was "imperative,"368 as their White faces would be needed one day to reassure the Afrikaners.

The US oligarchs have operated this strategy for a century, funding the NAACP, Urban League, Martin Luther King, and the Southern Christian Leadership Conference, etc. The funding of BLM constitutes this legacy, which brings the Whites across the world to their knees—literally—in remorse for the "Whiteness."

In a frank statement, the Black radical Malcolm X alluded to his own role in selling Martin King to the American mainstream as a moderate alternative:

> *I want Dr. King to know that I didn't come to Selma to make his job difficult. I really did come thinking that I could make it*

---
365 Oppenheimer, "Portrait of a Millionaire," 16.
366 Ibid.
367 Ibid., 13.
368 Ibid., 16.

easier. If white people realize what the alternative is, perhaps they'll be more willing to hear Dr. King.[369]

Here we have Malcom X, regarded as one of the most extreme Black nationalists, stating that he served to make King the acceptable alternative to Black violence. Nelson Mandela served the same purpose. The New Left rioters during the 1960s and 1970s were also being backed by their supposed "Establishment enemies" for the same reason: to make what would otherwise be regarded as unacceptably radical, seem moderate. The aim and outcome is explained by an article on funding for Black organizations carried by the Rockefeller Archive Center:

In the case of African-American civil rights groups, Haines[370] *documents how media coverage of increasingly militant action led to an overall increase in financial support (from all donor sources), and that support was especially targeted to moderate groups.*

This was as true for large scale philanthropy as it was for individual donors: the groups garnering the most foundation support were the most long-standing ones. Ford Foundation staff admitted that these organizations were considered "old hat" but the long-standing reputation, infrastructure, and networks made them logical nodes of foundation activity.[371]

Note, the more violent the Black nationalists, the more the media publicity, the more the funding for the "moderates"; that is, those such as King, the NAACP, and Urban League who were demanding not separatism, but integration: that Blacks take their place as *Homo Economicus* in "the inclusive economy." Hence, the left did its part—as it still does—not in liberating Blacks or any other from capitalism, but in extending plutocracy over all races is the name of equality and human rights. The same process played out in South Africa, guided by Harry Oppenheimer, with Mandela playing the lead role.

That is now precisely the same role as BLM. In Baltimore a leading Black Lives Matter activist DeRay Mckesson, raised $222,000 for his mayoralty campaign,[372] which included six thousand dollars each donated by Netflix CEO Reed Hastings and Twitter Executive Chairman Omid

---

[369] Quoted in Herbert Haines, 1995.
[370] Haines, author of *Black Radicals and the Civil Rights Mainstream*, quoted above.
[371] Wimpee, "Funding Social Movement."
[372] Mckesson came 6th in the Democratic primaries in April 2016.

Kordestani. Another corporate donor was Stewart Butterfield, founder of Slack.[373]

BLM has been compared to "Arab Spring" and other "color revolutions" because of the pivotal use made of social media for mobilization. David Z. Morris writing for *Fortune* commented on this:

> *Technology has played a major role in McKesson's career as an activist. He first rose to prominence in 2014, when he began live tweeting events in Furgeson, Missouri following the police shooting of eighteen year old Michael Brown. He now has more than 323,000 followers on Twitter.*[374]

Morris points out what is apparent when one looks at the sponsoring of "human rights" movements by the likes of Walmart whose own treatment of Latino workers leaves a lot to be desired.[375] The sponsorship can be seen as a PR gimmick, or as a means of expanding their own markets via the promotion of "ethnic diversity":

> *Aside from execs' personal politics, tech company support for Mckesson makes sense for two reasons. First, he's a sterling example of the influence of platforms like Twitter, which benefits from serving as the home of any important national conversations. And second, Silicon Valley has a widely discussed and continuing diversity problem. Support for minority influencers like Mckesson could help shore up those shortcomings, at least from a PR perspective.*[376]

George Soros and the Democracy Alliance

Of significance is the omnipresent hand of George Soros via the Democracy Alliance (DA), a "club" of plutocrats aligned with the Democratic Party, who fund leftist causes. In November 2015 BLM leaders met with the billionaire leftists at the DA annual conference. The DA states on their "About" page that it was formed in 2005 to:

---

[373] Morris, "Netflix and Twitter."
[374] Ibid.
[375] Bolton, *Babel Inc.*, 253-257.
[376] Morris, op cit.

...play a leading role in fostering the infrastructure necessary to advance a progressive agenda for America. We invest in every aspect of progressive power-building—from policymaking to organizing grassroots communities to winning state and national issue and electoral campaigns. We address the most pressing challenges of our day through investments in three connected areas: a just democracy, a fair economy and an environmentally sustainable future.... In our collaborative giving strategy, an informed and engaged body of donors comes together to aggregate resources for focused investment, for which we have marshaled as much as $60 million per year.

Sixty million dollars per year granted to colored, feminist, and immigrant groups constitutes a formidable movement of change towards what DA and its oligarchs call "progressive." Something of the elitist and secretive character of the DA was seen at its annual conference in 2014, when several journalists were roughed up by security guards:

Security was tight at the Democracy Alliance conference last week at the chic Ritz Carlton in Chicago. Politico reporter Ken Vogel was manhandled by security when he tried to interview an attendee. Other conference-goers ripped off their nametags when a Washington Free Beacon reporter approached.[377]

While the involvement of labor unions with a left wing cause is hardly surprising, only those unfamiliar with the alliance that has often existed between oligarchs and the left would also be surprised by the association between unions and big money at DA.

The Washington Post reported that Soros was among those who initiated DA, and it would be surprising if he had not. Others include insurance magnate Peter Lewis, San Francisco hedge fund manager Tom Steyer, and software entrepreneur Tim Gill.[378]

What was discussed between BLM leaders and their oligarchic friends at the DA 2015 conference does not seem to have been reported. However, Soros had already given a staggering thirty-three million dollars to Black radical groups in Ferguson, Missouri during 2014, coalescing into the BLM movement. *The Washington Times* reported:

---

[377] Markay, "Confidential Document."
[378] Gold, "Wealthy Donors."

> Mr. Soros spurred the Ferguson protest movement through years of funding and mobilizing groups across the US, according to interviews with key players and financial records reviewed by The Washington Times. In all, Mr. Soros gave at least $33 million in one year to support already established groups that emboldened the grass-roots, on-the-ground activists in Ferguson, according to the most recent tax filings of his non-profit Open Society Foundations. The financial tether from Mr. Soros to the activist groups gave rise to a combustible protest movement that transformed a one-day criminal event in Missouri into a 24-hour-a-day national cause celebre.[379]

The *Washington Times* report stated: "Soros-sponsored organizations helped mobilize protests in Ferguson, building grassroots coalitions on the ground backed by a nationwide online and social media campaign."[380] This is the same strategy that was used to instigate "color revolutions" by Soros, USAID, National Endowment for Democracy, and a myriad of other NGOs, across the former Soviet bloc and North Africa, prompting President Vladimir Putin to give them their marching orders out of Russia. The scenario is explained in further detail; the parallels with the "color revolutions" become apparent:

> Buses of activists from the Samuel Dewitt Proctor Conference in Chicago; from the Drug Policy Alliance, Make the Road New York and Equal Justice USA from New York; from Sojourners, the Advancement Project and Center for Community Change in Washington; and networks from the Gamaliel Foundation—all funded in part by Mr Soros—descended on Ferguson starting in August and later organized protests and gatherings in the city until late last month.[381]

Groundwork from Soros-Funded Lobbies

Among the throng was Kassandra Frederique, policy manager at the Drug Policy Alliance. DPA is yet another organization initiated by Soros. What this has to do with BLM might be explained by Soros' drug reform

---

[379] Riddell, "Soros Funds Ferguson."
[380] Ibid.
[381] Ibid.

movement being part of an international movement to reshape the world. Frederique provided the rationalization:

> *We recognized this movement is similar to the work we're doing at DPA. The war on drugs has always been to operationalize, institutionalize and criminalize people of color. Protecting personal sovereignty is a cornerstone of the work we do and what this movement is all about.*[382]

The DPA is a lobby for marijuana legalization. Why are Soros and other oligarchs interested in this? As Frederique explained, it is part of a broader front, and each aspect happens to be directed at undermining the foundations of cultural, national, and ethnic cohesion, ultimately in the interests of economic globalization, behind the facade of "human rights." Hence, DPA lauds the BLM rampage, posting on its blog site an article by Asha Bandele, where she remarks, in response to "yet another police killing": "I am stunned. And grieving. And enraged." Bandele is the senior director of Grants, Partnerships and Special Projects of DPA.[383]

BLM was co-founded by Opal Tometi,[384] executive director of the Black Alliance for Just Immigration (BAJI), a group to which Soros' Open Society Foundation gave a hundred thousand dollars in 2011, according to their "About Programs" page on their website. Feted by *Cosmopolitan* and *The Los Angeles Times*, and invited to the White House, Tometi is an example of what life is like for a left wing radical in a plutocratic state. Another patron of BAJI is Unbound Philanthropy, established by William Reeves. Reeves is director and founder of BlueCrest Capital Management (London). Previously Reeves had been with J.P. Morgan in London and New York, and with Salomon Brothers Asset Management.

Alicia Garza, another of the three BLM co-founders, is director of the National Domestic Workers Alliance, also funded by Unbound Philanthropy. NDWA has also been funded by the Open Society Foundation, according to their website.

A scholarly facade for BLM was provided by the Open Society Foundation, which sponsored via the Center for Policing Equity a conference of *"the nation's top law enforcement executives, researchers, civil rights advocates, and community groups to discuss accountability, transparency, data collection,"* at the US Department of Justice. Two reports with Soros funding were prepared by the National Justice

---

[382] Ibid.
[383] Bandele, "A Message From Our Partners."
[384] Dalton, "Three Women."

Database, a branch of the Center for Policing Equity, and the Urban Institute.385 The Center for Policing Equity works with law enforcement agencies to emasculate the police in the face of Black violence, or in their words on their website, *"We use data to create levers for social, cultural and policy change."* The founder of the Center, Dr. Philip Atiba Goff, Associate Professor of Social Psychology at UCLA, was sponsored in this initiative by the Open Society Institutes, and the Ford Foundation, among others.

The above named Urban Institute was founded in 1968 at the initiative of President Lyndon Johnson. This Establishment think tank includes a board of trustees drawn from those who have served with the World Bank, J.P. Morgan, Charlotte Investment Bank, National Security Council, CityView Investments, Hudson Institute, J.P. Morgan Chase Institute, Bank of America, Promontory Financial Group LLC, Federal Reserve Bank, et al. The presence of Brookings Institution, a globalist strategic think tank in which state, business, and academia converge, is particularly evident. Funding for the Urban Institute is provided by the Ford Foundation, J.P. Morgan Chase, Rockefeller Foundation, Bank of America, Rockefeller Philanthropic Advisors, Open Society Foundations, World Bank, Packard Foundation, PepsiCo., Heinz Endowments, along with many other corporations and US state agencies. The Establishment revolutionists at the U.I. have jumped on the BLM bandwagon, headlining with *"What can we do to prevent the next killing?"*386

Support for BLM is provided by The Sentencing Project. This is funded by the Ford Foundation, Open Society Foundations, David Rockefeller Fund, et al.387 However, a paper for the National Bureau of Economic Research, "which examined thousands of incidents at ten large police departments in California, Florida and Texas, concluded that police were no more likely to shoot non-Whites than Whites after factoring in extenuating circumstances." "On the most extreme use of force—officer involved shootings—we find no racial differences in either the raw data or when contextual factors are taken into account," according to Harvard economics professor Roland G. Fryer Jr.388

Stephen E. Broden, a Black pastor who had worked among poor Blacks in Dallas for thirty years, commented:

---

385 Goff, "Documenting Racial Disparities."
386 Brown, "What Can We Do."
387 Ghandnoosh, "Black Lives Matter."
388 Richardson, "No Racial Bias."

Whatever legitimacy the "Black Lives Matter" movement may have is lost in its funding from one George Soros. Mr. Soros is the major financial source responsible for funding the leftist movement in America.... These left-wing groups supported by Soros have one thing in common: to transform America.[389]

Role of Social Media

Social media kick-started BLM, just as it has played a prominent role in instigating and co-coordinating the "color revolutions" across the former Soviet bloc and North Africa. Alicia Garza commented, "Twitter can be a vehicle that connects us and helps bring us together to strategize around how we're going to build the kind of power that we need to transform the world that we live in."[390]

As stated above, Twitter Chairman Kordestani donated to BLM mayoral candidate DeRay Mckesson' campaign. Twitter CEO Jack Dorsey, claiming personal friendship with Mckesson, shared a question-and-answer platform. While both agreed very broadmindedly that all views should get a hearing, this contradicts Twitter's avid censorship of anything regarded as illiberal and conservative.[391]

A BLM sign was painted on Twitter's San Francisco headquarters, and at the Facebook headquarters. Facebook CEO Mark Zuckerberg called employees who had replaced BLM with a sign reading "all lives matter" "unacceptable" and "malicious."[392] Google tweeted "Black lives matter" in revolutionary solidarity. This is more than rhetorical: Facebook and Google were among the founders of an international movement promoting "color revolutions" by mobilizing youth through social media. The Alliance of Youth Movements, also called Movements.org was founded by Howcast CEO Jason Liebman and Google director Jared Cohen. Movements.org played a key role in the "Arab Spring" across North Africa. Liebman said of social media and Movements.org:

> *We tell people, you can use Tweet-to-Speak, which Google rolled out during the Egypt uprising, to dial in from a landline and tweet. We're trying to provide the resources for activists to do*

---

[389] Broden, "Real Power and Purpose."
[390] Dalton, "Three Women."
[391] Breitbart Tech, "Jack Dorsey, BLM's DeRay Mckesson."
[392] Mercury News, "Facebook hangs 'Black Lives Matter' sign."

what they've been doing for a while, but more effectively and faster.[393]

When Liebman conceived the idea, he was employed by the US State Department, so the character of the revolutions he and his corporate comrades are advocating should be in no doubt. Sponsors in addition to Google and Facebook included MTV, CBS News, Pepsi, YouTube, the US State Department, and others.[394]

---

[393] Boyd, "Liebman on Creating Space."
[394] Bolton, *Revolution from Above*, 237.

Martin King and Nelson Rockefeller

"These two, Exeter Hall philanthropy and the Dismal Science,[395] led by any sacred cause of black emancipation, or the like, to fall in love and make a wedding of it—will give birth to progenies and prodigies: dark extensive moon-calves, unnameable abortions, wide-coiled monstrousities, such as the world has not seen hitherto!

Alas, in many other provinces, beside the West Indian, that unhappy wedlock of philanthropic liberalism and the Dismal Science, has engendered such all-enveloping delusions, of the moon-calf sort—and wrought huge woe for us, and for the poor, civilized world, in these days! And sore will be the battle with said moon-calves; and terrible the struggle to return out of our delusions, floating rapidly on which, not the West Indies alone, but Europe generally, is nearing the Niagara Falls.

My philanthropic friends, can you discern no fixed headlands in this wide-weltering deluge of benevolent twaddle and revolutionary grapeshot that has burst forth on us—no sure bearings at all? Fact and nature, it seems to me, say a few words to us, if, happily, we have still an ear for fact and nature. Let us listen a little, and try."

Thomas Carlyle, (1849).

Every year, the third Monday of January is designated Martin Luther King Day, and the much-lauded paragon of "passive resistance and equality" is praised to high heaven with the aura of sainthood, or even godhood, perhaps only equaled by his South African counterpart, Nelson Mandela, and more latterly by the sanctification of George Floyd.

Repeating the South African scenario, where Harry Oppenheimer and other oligarchs pushed for the dismantling of apartheid, the Black civil rights movement in the United States was created to integrate and expand

---

[395] Carlyle's name for Economics, or Political Economy as it was then called.

the labor and consumer markets. Both the "moderates" of the King variety and the rabid rioters of the New Left played their roles.

So how it is that King overcame such seemingly insurmountable odds against Southern "White supremacy" to achieve the status of an American saint? Beaten, jailed, and condemned as "communists," King and his colleagues underwent much hardship on the "long march to freedom," as Nelson Mandela termed his odyssey. King spawned the '68 Generation in many ways. Their goals were achieved, but only because they converged with those of plutocracy.

The ideological seeding had been planted decades earlier. In 1937, the Swedish sociologist and economist Gunnar Myrdal was invited to the USA to prepare a study on race relations that would be published as *An American Dilemma*. This was funded by the Carnegie Corporation.[396] It seems likely that Myrdal, a Social Democrat, had become enamored with the utopian possibilities of American liberalism while visiting the country in 1929–30 on a Rockefeller Foundation fellowship. *An American Dilemma* became the scientific rationalization for the Supreme Court's desegregation rulings during the 1950s.

Andrew Carnegie's essay "The Gospel of Wealth" (1889) is described as the founding document of philanthropy. Carnegie was perhaps an entrepreneur with genuine social ideals, but nonetheless, his doctrine for a wider redistribution of wealth lacks both the advocacy of fundamental reforms, and enhances the power of the oligarchy through philanthropy. In the name of social justice, the doctrine of philanthropy as outlined in 1889 justifies an oligarchy on the basis of paternalism towards the lower classes:

> *Thus is the problem of Rich and Poor to be solved. The laws of accumulation will be left free; the laws of distribution free. Individualism will continue, but the millionaire will be but a trustee for the poor; intrusted for a season with a great part of the increased wealth of the community, but administering it for the community far better than it could or would have done for itself.*[397]

The "millionaire"—read billionaire today—will continue to operate in a free market, individualism will continue as the doctrine, and most of all the oligarchy will maintain control over the distribution of wealth,

---

[396] Myrdahl, *American Dilemma*.
[397] Carnegie, "Gospel of Wealth."

administering it "far better" than the community could. This remains the ideology and goal of the oligarchs who use their wealth to reshape society in the name of "equality," "human rights," and "democracy."

"Black Civil Rights" a Precursor of the American New Left

Oligarchs had established the National Association for the Advancement of Colored People (NAACP) in 1909.[398] The idea came from no less than Jacob Schiff of Kuhn Loeb & Co., Wall Street, who had in 1905 poured money into funding the writer George Kennan to organize socialist revolutionary cells among Russian POWs of the Japanese (from the Russo-Japanese War of 1904–1905), which became the nucleus of the revolutionary movement in Russia.[399] Another eminence was Herbert Lehman, head of Lehman Brothers, future Senator and Governor of New York, who decades later played a lead role in the destruction of Senator Joseph McCarthy.[400] Other contributors during the 1930s who sustained the NAACP were William Rosenwald, Samuel Fels, Felix Warburg, and Edsel Ford.[401]

On another front, as part of a Cold War strategy for recruiting leftists against the USSR, the CIA funded the National Student Association (NSA), from which the New Left emerged.[402]

Key figures of the New Left, including Abbie Hoffman (of the *Yippies*) and Tom Hayden of the Students for a Democratic Society (SDS), the primary New Left organization, began their revolutionary careers in the "Black civil rights" protests that took place just prior to the emergence of the New Left. The primary organization for this apprenticeship was the Student Nonviolent Coordinating Committee (SNCC), founded in 1960. Martin Luther King's Southern Christian Leadership Conference (SCLC) was founded in 1957. Ella Baker, who had been with the NAACP during 1938–46 and again in 1952, and was an official of the SCLC, is credited with conceiving the idea of the SNCC. In 1957 she had co-founded In Friendship, which supported agitation in the South. The other co-founders were Bayard Rustin and Stanley Levison.[403]

Stanley Levison combined realty investment with fundraising for the Communist Party USA and the American Jewish Congress (AJC). Levison

---

[398] Trachtenberg, "Philanthropy That Worked."
[399] Spence, *Wall Street and the Russian Revolution*.
[400] Lehman led Senate censure of McCarthy. See: Bolton, *Revolution from Above*, 40-41.
[401] Lau, *Democracy Rising*, 73-74.
[402] Stern, "Short Account."
[403] "Baker, Ella Josephine."

arranged for AJC financial patronage to King.[404] An FBI report on King a month prior to his death described Levison as a "shrewd, dedicated communist," as a principal aide to King, and as a strategist, speechwriter, and fundraiser. The book *Where do we go from here? Chaos or Community*, supposedly authored by King, was regarded to have been co-written with Levison. Levison has been cited as stating to Clarence Jones, King's other primary aide and his liaison with the New York oligarchs, that King was such a "slow thinker" who should not be permitted to say anything without first clearing it with Levison or Jones.[405] In 1961, Levison became a treasurer of the SCLC.[406] In 1964, King asked Levison and Jones to submit speeches that he could use when accepting the Nobel Peace Prize.[407]

Tom Hayden, who wrote *The Port Huron Statement*, the manifesto of the SDS, started his career as New Left agitator in the NSA, unaware of its CIA and State Department connections despite vague suspicions among some leftists, until the full exposure by *Ramparts* in 1967. In his autobiography, Hayden wrote that, with ties to US government agencies, the older NSA leaders tended to be "quite liberal," inspired by the revolutionary upheavals throughout the world. Among these was Allard Lowenstein, an NSA founder who "welcomed the civil rights movement in the South, as did most NSA leaders."[408] Several years before his death, Hayden wrote of the NSA's CIA connections, including Lowenstein, who had been a key adviser to the SNCC:

> *Another figure I met at the turn of the 1960s was Allard Lowenstein, who had attended every NSA conference since the group's inception and had obscure but real connections to State Department and CIA powers behind the scenes. Lowenstein courageously helped smuggle black South Africans into the West, was an adviser to the Student Nonviolent Coordinating Committee during the Mississippi Summer in 1964, led the national "Dump Johnson" campaign in 1967 and 1968, was elected to Congress in 1968, and eventually was murdered in 1980 by a disturbed protégé, Dennis Sweeney . . .*[409]

---

[404] "American Jewish Congress."
[405] "Martin Luther King," 3.
[406] Ibid., 5.
[407] Ibid., 7.
[408] Hayden, *Reunion: A Memoir*, 6.
[409] Hayden, "CIA's Student Activism."

Hayden wrote, based on the research in Karen Paget's book *Patriotic Betrayal*[410] and his talks with her, that although Lowenstein was not a CIA agent, he knew about the CIA penetration of the NSA, was an ardent anti-Soviet Cold War liberal (of the type that was going over to the CIA in numbers, via the NSA and the Congress for Cultural Freedom), and that:

> *Lowenstein went out of his way to block the Ramparts story from being published, joining a 1967 meeting of CIA and NSA officials considering how to manage the story if it was leaked.... Paget writes that "[t]oday none of the NSA officers who were present can explain Lowenstein's involvement." Lowenstein, she says, also went to the White House, where he was asked by Walt Rostow, Lyndon B. Johnson's national security adviser, to draft a reply to the Ramparts story if it came out.*[411]

Black civil rights, the SCLC and SNCC, preceded the Vietnam War issue, and hence, writes Hayden, the efforts of the SNCC were "the real catalyst to change."[412] The SNCC drive into Mississippi to register Black voters was the start not just of a movement, "but a revolution," wrote Hayden.[413]

Birmingham: Rockefeller Money Bails King Out

In April 1963, "the focus shifted dramatically to Birmingham, Alabama," where the SNCC and SCLC were agitating against segregation.[414] Birmingham was a "turning point" in terms of worldwide publicity. It was here that King was arrested. Bombs exploded at King's hotel and at the home of a local Black leader. The result was eight hundred demonstrations and fourteen thousand arrests in seventy-five Southern cities. It was the catalyst for the passing of new civil rights legislation in Congress.[415]

Hayden states that King's bail was arranged through Attorney General Robert Kennedy.[416] What Hayden did not know is that the bail money was put up personally by Nelson Rockefeller. In 2006 Clarence Jones, King's lawyer and close adviser from 1960 until 1968, gave an interview to *Vanity*

---

[410] Paget, *Patriotic Betrayal*.
[411] Ibid.
[412] Hayden, *Reunion*, 61.
[413] Ibid., 55.
[414] Ibid., 111.
[415] Ibid., 111-112.
[416] Ibid., 112.

Fair in which Jones is described as having "circulated easily among the rich of New York and L.A., [finding] willing donors to fuel King's frenetic activities with the Southern Christian Leadership Conference (SCLC) which King co-founded. Jones was, in essence, the moneyman of the movement."[417] Here we get a hint of King's funding by the New York oligarchy and from further afield. King's iconic "Letter From a Birmingham Jail," has become part of the United States' Holy Writ, but:

It wasn't the moral clarity of the letter, however, that freed King from his tiny cell. Money did. With no bail bond funds available, King and the others were facing the prospect of spending weeks or months behind bars. But an unexpected angel arrived, courtesy of a telephone call from [Harry] Belafonte. Jones remembers Belafonte saying in an excited tone, "'I was discussing [the Birmingham problem] with Nelson Rockefeller's speechwriter. It's a fellow named Hugh Morrow—he used to work for The Saturday Evening Post—who you'll be hearing from.' Next thing I know I got a call from Morrow—'How can I help?'"[418] *Jones replied, 'Well, I'm coming back [to New York] tonight. Let's meet.'"*

Since 1961, Nelson Rockefeller had been writing occasional checks to the SCLC, usually in the range of $5,000 to $10,000. This time, they would need much, much more. "I arrived in New York late," Jones recounts. "Morrow lived on Sutton Place. I called him at one o'clock in the morning. Half asleep, he says, 'We want you to be at the Chase Manhattan Bank tomorrow, even though it's Saturday. We want to help Martin.'"

"I walk in at the [appointed] time and there is Rockefeller, Morrow, a bank official, and a couple of security guards. They open the huge vault. There was a big circular door with a driver's-wheel-like handle on it. Lo and behold there was money stacked floor to ceiling! Rockefeller walks in and takes $100,000 in cash and puts it in a satchel, a briefcase-like thing. And one of the Chase Manhattan Bank officers says, 'Mr. Jones, can you sit down for a moment?' I sit down and he says, 'Your name is Clarence B. Jones, right? We've got to have a note for this.'

Jones hesitated, flabbergasted. "This man filled out a promissory note: Clarence B. Jones, $100,000 payable on

---
[417] Brinkley, "The Man Who Kept."
[418] Ibid.

demand," Jones recalls. "Now, I wasn't stupid. I said, 'Payable on demand?! I don't have $100,000!' And the bank official...said, 'No, we'll take care of it, but we've got to have it for banking regulations.'"

Worried that he was being impudent, Jones signed the document. "I took the money and got on a plane headed back to Alabam," Jones says. "I am a hero. All the kids are bailed out."

"Everybody around Martin knew that I had somehow magically raised bail," he contends, citing others who deserve more credit than he: especially Belafonte, along with Morrow, Walker, and Birmingham minister Fred Shuttlesworth. "I stayed mum all these years about the donor. I didn't tell the story I'm telling you—except to King, who was ecstatic. I had a firm 'Don't Ask' policy."[419]

The Black civil rights movement was not rebelling against the "Establishment" any more than the New Left. The civil rights movement was promoted and funded by the Establishment in a war against the South, segregation, like apartheid, being an anachronism in a modern capitalist economy. The aim was and remains an integrated workforce and a standardized consumer market. Martin King was backed by the Federal government via Attorney General Robert Kennedy, and Nelson Rockefeller against the beleaguered Birmingham authorities. The ensuing violence enabled the passage of desegregation legislation.

Despite all the cant around King's pacifism, and "White police brutality" against the Blacks in Birmingham and elsewhere, what seems to be overlooked in King's famous letter is the blatantly obvious: he sought to provoke the police to violence for the martyrdom that it would give his cause; his was a "strategy of tension," as he put it. King was annoyed by the leniency of the police in Birmingham; by their lack of violence:

> It is true that the police have exercised a degree of discipline in handling the demonstrators. In this sense they have conducted themselves rather "non-violently" in public. But for what purpose? To preserve the evil system of segregation. Over the past few years I have consistently preached that nonviolence demands that the means we use must be as pure as the ends we seek. I have tried to make clear that it is wrong to use immoral means to attain moral ends. But now I must affirm that it is just

---

[419] Brinkley, "The Man Who Kept."

as wrong, or perhaps even more so, to use moral means to preserve immoral ends. Perhaps Mr. Connor and his policemen have been rather nonviolent in public, as was Chief Pritchett in Albany, Georgia, but they have used the moral means of nonviolence to maintain the immoral end of racial injustice.[420]

FBI Assessment

There has been much comment regarding the FBI's surveillance of King. While the left is portrayed as a victim of government surveillance, even middle-class, anti-communist organizations such as The John Birch Society were ongoing subjects of FBI investigations.[421] Yet the most important elements have been overlooked or ignored, even by King's detractors. The main interest seems to be whether or not he was a communist, and to what extent communists were involved in the SCLC.[422] The FBI analysis of King a month prior to his death centers, as one would expect, on communist influences in the SCLC, as well as King's sexual permissiveness relative to his public moral posturing.

The FBI's real interest, however, was in the source of King's funding. The FBI reports in "Funds from firms and foundations" during February 1967 that the stockbrokerage firm Merrill, Lynch, Pierce, and Fenner & Smith had contributed fifteen thousand dollars to the SCLC. In August, the Edward Lamb Foundation of Ohio contributed stock worth six thousand dollars. In November, the Ford Foundation was slated to give $230,000 for leadership training. In October 1965 Nelson Rockefeller, Governor of New York, gave twenty-five thousand dollars to the Gandhi Society for Human Rights, a fundraising adjunct of the SCLC.[423] With the money that King had received from the Ford Foundation for leadership training for "Negro ministers," two workshops were held in Miami in February 1968. One attendee was dismayed at the "drinking, fornication, and homosexuality" that took place, as well as an all-night sex orgy with White and Black prostitutes.[424]

Also of interest is the Federal Government funding that the SCLC received for joint projects. In 1966, the SCLC received a four million dollars loan from the Federal Housing Administration for projects in

---

[420] King, "Letter From Birmingham."
[421] See the voluminous FBI files on The John Birch Society at the Ernie Lazar FOIA Collection.
[422] "Martin Luther King."
[423] Ibid., 17.
[424] Ibid.

Chicago, from which it would gain a four hundred thousand dollars profit. In November 1967, the Department of Labor contracted with the SCLC for sixty-one thousand dollars to train Blacks in Atlanta.[425]

In February 1968, sixty wealthy individuals were invited to a fundraising gathering for the SCLC at a thousand dollars per head at the home of entertainer Harry Belafonte. Among those invited were Governor and Mrs. Nelson Rockefeller, as well as Mary and Stephen Rockefeller.[426]

"In Some Mysterious Way"

Shortly prior to King's assassination there was a resurgence of Black separatism, which took over the SNCC, and its White members were expelled.[427] There had long been a Black separatist tradition, distinct from the integrationism promoted by the NAACP, King, et al. Marcus Garvey had established a trained and disciplined Black Nationalist movement, the Universal Negro Improvement Association, during the 1920s. W. E. B. Du Bois resigned from the NAACP in 1934 in favor of Black Nationalism, although he returned during the 1940s. In 1967, H. Rap Brown was elected chairman of the SNCC, stating that "violence is as American as apple pie." The call now was for Black Power.

Hayden recalls that the assassinations of Martin Luther King and Robert Kennedy:

> ...led to a meltdown of the system's core. The breakdown happened not only in Chicago, not only in America; in some mysterious way, it was a global phenomenon. Perhaps history is random and the search for logical meaning a fruitless illusion. But why did so many forces flow toward a climax in this one particular year, the watershed year for a generation? Surely there has been no other quite like it in American history?[428]

King's death in 1968 instigated the Days of Rage in New York City, where the SDS rampaged, "trashing store windows in Time Square."[429] As a consequence, even more civil right laws were passed by Congress. At Columbia University, Mark Rudd, an SDS eminence, staged a protest. It

---

[425] Ibid.
[426] Ibid., 17-18.
[427] Hayden, *Reunion*, 164.
[428] Ibid., 254-255.
[429] Ibid., 269.

was the beginning of the New Left riots of '68 that spread to Europe in May, almost toppling President Charles de Gaulle, who happened to be the only European statesman resisting American global hegemony and the supremacy of the dollar. The New Left riots even extended into the Soviet bloc.

Hayden was puzzled by the seemingly spontaneous outburst that wracked the world in 1968. He had a hint of that "mysterious way" when referring to the CIA connections with the NSA, and through that organization to the Black civil rights movement and the New Left. The CIA and an array of oligarchic foundations had been funding the ultra-liberal causes, from which the New Left emerged for decades. The mayhem of the era resulted in a paradigm shift leftward. In comparison to the Black Panther militias and New Left rioting, the options demanded by the Establishment looked mild, even "conservative," by comparison. If King and the integrationist movement had represented an actual rebellion against the Establishment, they would have been crushed as completely as Marcus Garvey. They served a dialectical purpose.

Prelude to the Fall of Africa: Haiti and America

"What are the true relations between negro and white, their mutual duties under the sight of the Maker of them both; what human laws will assist both to comply more and more with these? The solution, only to be gained by earnest endeavor and sincere experience, such as have never yet been bestowed on it, is not yet here; the solution is perhaps still distant; but some approximation to it, various real approximations, could be made, and must be made; this of declaring that negro and white are unrelated, loose from one another, on a footing of perfect equality, and subject to no law but that of supply and demand according to the Dismal Science; this which contradicts the palpablest facts, is clearly no solution, but a cutting of the knot asunder; and every hour we persist in this is leading us toward dissolution instead of solution."

Thomas Carlyle (1849)

The story of the eclipse of White rule in Africa, as with the European colonies of Indo-China and elsewhere, is one of calculated world power-politics, behind the facade of "human rights." As referred to previously, the process started when British-based mining interests sought to capture the wealth of the Transvaal from the Afrikaners with the pretext of intervening on behalf of the *Uitlanders* whom it was said, were being denied their democratic rights by the boorish Boers. Those who have ultimate responsibility for bringing ruin to White Africa were not primarily, as is commonly supposed, Moscow-trained communists and terrorists, but the "Money Power" centered in Washington and New York.

Background: The French Revolution on San Domingo

Ideologically, the "Black liberation" movements originate in the Enlightenment doctrine of egalitarianism, despite Rousseau claiming that the races shaped by hot climates were not suited for living in a free society. Such an outlook, which would have him tried under "human rights" laws today,[430] was overtaken by the revolutionary ferment of Jacobinism; and the Whig clamor for the "Abolition" of slavery, albeit such "humanitarianism" not generally extending to the conditions endured by the White proletariat.

Lothrop Stoddard refers to the first of the Black revolts against colonialism as the "French Revolution in San Domingo" (Haiti), "the gem of the West Indies," in 1789, the year of the Jacobin revolt in France.[431] Stoddard states that when the new regime in France questioned the "color line" that maintained order between Whites, Black slaves, and free and often wealthy Creoles, the White colonists resisted change,[432] seeing it as opening the way for dispossession and even extermination.

The colonial representatives at the National Assembly in Paris warned on August 12th, that "people here are trying to raise a revolt,"[433] while Mirabeau in particular forcefully demanded that Jacobinism be brought to San Domingo.[434] In France the Friends of the Blacks was formed (*Amis des Noirs*) to agitate for the Blacks and mulattos. Wealthy mulattos in Paris formed the *Colon Américains* to demand full citizenship on San Domingo.

The year of the revolution there were Black uprisings at Guadeloupe and Martinique,[435] and mulatto uprisings at the West Province in 1790 and 1791.[436] On May 15th, 1791, the National Assembly granted citizenship to "free people of color."[437] On August 23rd, Blacks revolted at the North Plain, burning plantations and massacring owners and their families.[438] In France, the Jacobin, Mirabeau, declared that the White colonists "slept on

---

[430] As would Karl Marx, who ridiculed Ferdinand Lassalle as a "Jewish Nigger," (Marx to Engels, July 30th, 1862) and considered colonialism to be a necessary part of the dialectical process (Marx, "The Future Results of British Rule in India."), and Friedrich Engels, who regarded the Slavs as devoid of history who could only attain civilization through foreign domination. Engels, "Democratic Pan-Slavism." See: Bolton, "Karl Marx: Profile and Assessment" in Southgate, *The Dialectics of Dictatorship*, 28-41.
[431] Lothrop Stoddard, *The French Revolution in San Domingo*, 7.
[432] Ibid., 39.
[433] Ibid., 82.
[434] Ibid., 78.
[435] Ibid., 95.
[436] Ibid., 112.
[437] Ibid., 122.
[438] Ibid., 129.

the edge of Vesuvius."[439] Stoddard referred to the influence of voodou cults in risings in July.[440] A revolt on the North Plain on August 22nd, led by Boukman, a priest of voodou, was preceded by bloody rituals. Scattered plantations were raided, the men tortured and killed, and women raped.[441] On the North Plain the National Guard confronted Black insurgents who carried as their standard the impaled body of a White child.[442] Within a few days "the whole of the North Plain was to be only a waste of blood and ashes." By August 23rd, the whole Plain was ablaze.[443] A contemporary report refers to the earth being blackened, and the air becoming pestilential from the masses of dead.[444] The Blacks built a stockade whose palisades were topped with the skulls of prisoners.[445] In September a mulatto militia mutinied and massacred its officers.[446] Meanwhile, the National Assembly decreed political equality for mulattos and freed Blacks, and a Jacobin commission was sent to impose the law.[447]

In February 1792, the Colonial Assembly appealed to France for troops. But the Jacobins were now dominant in the National Assembly, and stymied all appeals from the colonists. The representatives of the Colonial Assembly issued a statement on June 7th, that after being "slaughtered, burned, ruined, by the monsters we must now take them to our hearts like beloved brothers. We are then to be forced by bayonets to sign our death warrants. This is the climax of horror, tyranny and despair."[448]

The Jacobin commission arrived with six thousand troops, not to protect the colonists but to enforce the decree.[449] This was the Commission Intermédiaire, composed of six White Jacobins, five mulattos, and one Black.[450] In June 1793, under threat from Britain and Spain, the Commission promised "liberty to all Negro warriors who fight for the Republic."[451] The Blacks were thus armed. In August, Léger-Félicité Sonthonax, a member of the *Amis de Noir*, arriving as Civil Commissioner of San Domingo, decreed the freeing of the slaves in the North Province. This prompted Toussaint Louverture with his army of ex-slaves to join the

---

[439] Ibid., 130.
[440] Ibid., 129.
[441] Ibid., 130.
[442] Ibid., 131.
[443] Ibid.
[444] Ibid., 135.
[445] Ibid., 136.
[446] Ibid., 137.
[447] Ibid., 174.
[448] Ibid., 175.
[449] Ibid., 180.
[450] Ibid., 190.
[451] Ibid., 225.

French forces against Britain and Spain. He declared himself Governor General in 1801, regardless of Napoleon's opposition. He also invaded the Spanish territory of San Domingo, in defiance of Napoleon.

After Louverture was deported to France on suspicion of planning a coup, he was replaced by Jean-Jacques Dessalines in 1803, who defeated the French army, two-thirds of whose soldiers had died from yellow fever. The French withdrew, leaving around six thousand colonists. In 1804, a race war ensued between Black and mulatto brigands. Dessalines proclaimed himself Emperor and renamed the island Haiti.

In November 1803, Dessalines had promised protection to all White civilians who chose to remain, and invited those Whites who had fled from the island to safely return. With a false sense of security among the Whites, on April 25th, 1805, Dessalines issued a proclamation for the extermination of all White residents. A French officer at Port-au-Prince, escaping to Jamaica and to the safety of an English jail, wrote of events:

> *The murder of the whites in detail began at Port-au-Prince in the first days of January, but on the 17th and 18th March they were finished off en mass. All, without exception, have been massacred, down to the very women and children. Madame de Boynes was killed in a peculiarly horrible manner. A young mulatto named Fifi Pariset ranged the town like a madman searching the houses to kill the little children. Many of the men and women were hewn down by sappers, who hacked off their arms and smashed in their chests. Some were poniarded, others mutilated, others "passed on the bayonet," others disemboweled with knives or sabers, still others stuck like pigs. At the beginning, a great number were drowned. The same general massacre has taken place all over the colony, and as I write you these lines I believe that there are not twenty whites still alive—and these not for long.*[452]

Stoddard concludes: "This estimate was, indeed, scarcely exaggerated. The white race had perished utterly out of the land, French San Domingo had vanished forever, and the black State of Haiti had begun its troubled history."[453]

Dessalines was killed in 1806, his body dismembered and mutilated by a mob, and a civil war ensued.

---

[452] Private letter from Kingston, Jamaica, to a friend in France, June 1, 1805, Arch. Nat., AF-iv, 1213, cited by Stoddard, 350.
[453] Stoddard, ibid.

What was begun in San Domingo, with the way opened by Jacobinism and the "Rights of Man," proceeded to Africa, following the same pattern: Kenya, Congo, Mozambique, Angola, and still in the process of enactment ex-Rhodesia and South Africa. But today any suggestion that the Afrikaners are being systemically exterminated is described as a "far right conspiracy theory," as the heirs of Saint Nelson could not possibly be so inclined.

As the custodian of the Enlightenment revolution, in the service of its own brand of internationalism, albeit antithetical to the warnings of George Washington and Alexander Hamilton, the USA became the center of opposition to the Whites in Africa, and indeed to any remnant of European colonial influence after 1945.

Reconstructing the Old South

Americans had looked warily on the slave revolt and bloodbath in San Domingo. Yet in the aftermath of the civil war between the Unionists and the Confederacy American Jacobinism, aligned with puritan zealots, breathed fire and brimstone against the defeated South, demanding that the Southern Whites figuratively and collectively "bend the knee" before former slaves.

What was imposed on the South was the prelude for what is now demanded for the entirety of *Homo Europaeus*, in the USA, Europe, and indeed wherever the *genus* can still be found. However, those who had been particularly resistant to liberal pathogens, the Southerners and the Afrikaners, are especially targeted, while there remains a residual paranoia in regard to Germans, no matter how subdued they are.

The "Reconstruction" of the former Confederacy established a precedent as to how a defeated enemy might be kept in subjugation, while also showing how Blacks and other "people of color" can be manipulated in the service of oligarchic interests; in this case the Northern industrial and financial oligarchy, that had brought ruin to the Southern agricultural oligarchy, with the White proletariat and middle class caught in the middle and reduced to destitution and a level far lower than that of slavery.[454] One is also reminded of how the Germans fared under Allied occupation after World War II. All such matters, one should keep in mind, are justified in the name of "the rights of man," or "human rights," as the same doctrine

---

[454] For how poor Whites fared under Southern slavery, see: Helper, *The Impending Crisis of the South*. For a summary see: Bolton, *Perversion of Morality*, 371-375.

is now more succinctly called. As Thomas Carlyle pointed out, there was a class of "philanthropist" who postured most zealously about the condition of the Blacks, but treated poor Whites, at best, as though they did not exist. The situation remains.

The "Reconstruction" of the South is a subject that one is not likely to hear much of, even in the South. However, in 1941, Colonel Winfield Jones, a notable Northern journalist, wrote an account of the "era" that shows an aspect of White suffering, like the Afrikaners, or the Germans in the aftermath of both world wars, that has been put down the memory hole, because *Homo Europaeus*, as an endangered *genus*, cannot be allowed to remember his suppressed history, lest he stop "bending the knee," and rebel against his plutocratic overlords.

The Southern Whites had accepted defeat and assumed that, with government returned to Southerners and able representatives, the shouts of a few Northern fanatics for Old Testament vengeance would go unheeded. With much of the South in ruin, peace prevailed for over a year, until the demands, especially in New England, for the chastisement of the Southerner increased in tempo, "[F]rom pulpits rostrums and public halls enemies of the South preached a crusade of extermination against the Southern people."[455]

The nature of the anti-South crusade can be discerned from a speech by Wendell Phillips, like some foreboding of Henry Morgenthau Jr. speaking of Germany 1945, from the pulpit of Henry Ward Beecher's[456] church:

> *I do not believe in battles ending this war. You may plant a fort in every district of the South, you may take possession of her capitals and hold them with your armies, but you have not begun to subdue her people. I know it means something like absolute barbarian conquest, I allow it, but I do not believe there will be any peace until 347,000 men of the South are either hanged or exiled.*[457]

As Colonel Jones remarked, this "tirade" was made *after* the war. Phillips, a Puritan who believed in racial amalgamation, had been called

---

[455] Jones, *The South Occupied*.
[456] Beecher was a Congregationalist minister. His sister, Harriet, wrote *Uncle Tom's Cabin*. Prior to the Civil War he raised funds for the purchase of guns for Abolitionists fighting in Kansas. President Lincoln sent him on a speaking tour of Europe, agitating against the Confederacy. Col. Jones quotes Beecher that Blacks are "superior" to Whites, and that the latter will only survive if they breed with the healthier Negro.
[457] Quoted in Jones, *The South Occupied*.

"abolition's golden trumpet" for his oratory. In 1859, he had given the eulogy at the funeral of the unbalanced John Brown, who had sought to incite a slave revolt. Phillips demanded the year prior to the war's end that once the South was defeated only those states enfranchising the freed slaves should be readmitted to the Union.[458]

The lunatic rhetoric is reminiscent of today's BLM, Antifa, politicians, ministers, tenured professors, social workers, human relations facilitators, think tank CEOs, Afro-American reverends, et al. In high gear, William "Parson" Brownlow, Methodist minister, newspaper publisher, Whig Party Senator, Governor of Tennessee (1865–69),[459] and originally avidly pro-slavery, stated at a convention in New York:

> *If I had the power I would arm every wolf, panther, catamount and bear in the mountains of America, every crocodile in the swamps of Florida, every Negro in the South, every devil in hell, clothe them in the uniform of the Federal army and turn them loose on the rebels of the South and exterminate every man, woman and child south of the Mason and Dixon's line. I would like to see Negro troops...crowd every rebel into the Gulf of Mexico and drown them as the devil did the hogs in the Sea of Galilee.*

That is the type of politician imposed on the South after the Civil War. Parson Brownlow stated that the war had ended "too soon," and that the South had not been "whipped" enough. He referred to the Reconstruction regime as a "second war." He said that the South would be occupied and become "without form and void."

Colonel Jones wrote that with the anti-South agitation having been successful in hardening Northern attitudes, the Reconstruction Act passed Congress after radical Congressmen defeated President Andrew Johnson's vetoes. Southern Congressmen and Senators were sent packing, and in the South "the negro was placed in power in every department, state and national."

The Freedmen's Bureau was established in 1866 by Congressional act, and under the jurisdiction of the War Department, with the backing of Federal troops and armed Negroes, was given control over all issues relating to the freed slaves. *Habeas corpus*, the right of appeal and trial by jury were eliminated; the bureau agents were given autocratic powers.

---

[458] Phillips, "Wendel Phillips on Reconstruction."
[459] As a Reconstruction era governor, Brownlow disenfranchised Confederate supporters and imposed his rule by calling in Federal troops.

Most of the Southern states were divided into military districts and placed under martial law. Veterans and anyone who had supported the Confederacy (most Whites), were disenfranchised and could not hold any office. Again, there are parallels to post-1945 occupied Germany.

> Elections in the South were carried out at the point of the bayonet, white men of the South were forced away from the polls and negroes and conscienceless carpetbaggers[460] from the North, who had been in the South only a few weeks, were allowed to cast ballots and were elected to office...

Behind the illiterate Negroes who dominated the local and state legislatures stood the "carpetbaggers"; analogous to the present where oligarchs fund and direct organizations in the name of Black "civil rights" and "liberation." Land taxes became so excessive, that the farms and plantations were either deserted and became waste, or were given to Negroes, in a situation which might remind one of today's South Africa and "Zimbabwe."

Into this situation Confederate veterans formed guerrilla militias, the so-called "White leagues,"[461] and Southern states were gradually taken back. With an agreement from Southern Democrats to support Rutherford Hayes as Republican president, the "Compromise of 1877" ended Reconstruction, which by then, due to the resistance of the "White leagues," only had three states (Florida, South Carolina, Louisiana) remaining with Reconstruction regimes.

The "Jim Crow" segregation laws based on the principle of "separate but equal," were upheld as constitutional by the Supreme Court in 1896,[462] but were ruled to be unconstitutional by the Supreme Court in a landmark school desegregation suite in 1954. However, it would be a mistake to assume that the freed Blacks were left helpless after the overthrow of the Reconstruction tyranny and the inauguration of state "Jim Crow" laws, as much as it would be naive to assume that the White proletariat had gained anything but destitution from slavery.

---

[460] Agents of the Freedmen's Bureau, who usually traveled down from North with their possession in carpetbags.
[461] The first "White league" was formed in Louisiana in 1874.
[462] *Plessy v. Ferguson*, US Supreme Court, May 18, 1896. Homer A. Plessy, who was barely Negroid, acted on behalf of the Comité des Citoyens, under Creole leadership, by seating himself in a "Whites only" rail carriage in Louisiana. In race laws more restrictive than the Third Reich's Nuremberg Laws, or Afrikaner apartheid, many Southern states had the "one drop" law that defined anyone with a single Black forebear as colored.

From 1867, with the establishment of the Peabody Fund, a course was set for the sponsorship of American Blacks that does not seem to have been accorded to the sons of the White *lumpen proletariat* of the defeated South. The Fund was established specifically for freed Blacks, and was augmented with state taxes:

> By the second decade of the Twentieth Century a large number of southern communities had been able to build schools because of efforts by the Peabody Fund joined by others such as the Slater Fund, the Jeanes Fund and the giant General Education Board, established by John D. Rockefeller, Sr.[463]

The Julius Rosenwald Fund, set up by the owner of Sears Roebuck in 1917:

> ...was used primarily to fund projects to enhance education for blacks, especially in the South.... When the program ceased in 1932, over 5,300 schools, homes, and shops had been constructed. North Carolina had the largest number of Rosenwald Fund schools with a total of 787.[464]

The General Education Board was established by John D. Rockefeller Jr. in 1902, to fund schools in the South supposedly without regard to race, which was a facade for funding Black schools while trying to avoid White resentment:

> Ultimately, the GEB would spend $325 million (roughly $28.4 billion in 2020 dollars) between 1903 and 1964, the year it ended its operations. This included more than $60 million (more than $500 million in 2020 dollars) spent specifically on African American education.[465]

Behind the philanthropic facade the purpose might be discerned from a comment by Leo M. Favrot, GEB supervisor of County Training Schools:

> Under the industrial system that prevailed in slavery times the Negroes were not left in ignorance, but were carefully trained

---

[463] "Peabody Fund."
[464] Roose, "Rosenwald Fund Schools."
[465] Goldberg and Shubinski, "Black Education and Rockefeller Philanthropy."

along industrial lines[466]... *In those days it was to the interest of the slaveholder to train the slave Negro to become efficient. It is no less to the interest of the South today to train the Negro for efficiency.*[467]

In 1954 the Supreme Court ruled that school segregation was unconstitutional in *Brown v. Board of Education of Topeka*. This inaugurated Reconstruction II over the South, as Southerners fought to maintain their schools. The most dramatic resistance began at Arkansas when nine Black students enrolled at Little Rock Central High School in 1957. President Eisenhower responded by placing the National Guard under Federal control and augmenting them with a thousand paratroopers from the 101st Airborne Division. With the Federal Government enforcing the "general will" Jacobin and Bolshevik style, students returning to the high school were obliged to literally walk past troops with bayonets drawn.

In 1962, mass resistance was re-sparked when bayonet-ready Federal troops enforced the desegregation of the University of Mississippi. Leading the resistance was retired General Edwin Walker, who was arrested for inciting sedition and insurrection. While awaiting bond, Walker was taken by military aircraft to the facility for the criminally insane at Springfield, Missouri. Due to his high profile he was saved from an extended confinement and torture at what was a hellhole used by the Federal government against right-wing dissidents.[468]

Enacting "human rights," Arkansas 1957

---

[466] It was such training of the slaves, referred to by Hinton Rowen Helper, that placed the Southern White proletariat in a position of impoverishment.
[467] Goldberg and Shubinski, "Black Education and Rockefeller Philanthropy."
[468] Szasz, "The Shame of Medicine." Dr. Szasz was an expert adviser for the Walker defense team.

The Curtain Falls on White Africa

"We believe as much in the purity of race as we think they do.... We believe also that the white race of South Africa should be the predominating race."

Gandhi, (1903)[469]

Although the Portuguese had established their colonies in Africa since the sixteenth century, the Congress of Berlin (1884–1885) brought the European colonial powers together to delineate spheres of interest to allow the harmonious development of the continent. Even here, however, the USA was a signatory, showing that it had wider interests in the world than suggested by the Monroe Doctrine, and had already departed from the Washington-Hamilton doctrine of non-intervention overseas.

World War I had shown the "colored world" fracture and weakness in the White world, about which Oswald Spengler wrote:

> *This war was a defeat of the white races, and the Peace of 1918 was the first great triumph of the colored world: symbolized by the fact that today it is allowed to have a say in the disputes of the white states among themselves in the Geneva League of Nations—which is nothing but a miserable symbol of shameful things.*[470]

This was a harbinger of the more acute crisis for the White world wrought by World War II.

---

[469] Gandhi, *The Collected Works,* Vol. 3, 255-256.
[470] Spengler, *Hour of Decision,* 209.

The Anglo-American Breach

President Woodrow Wilson's "Fourteen Points" for the reorganization of the post-war world promised on internationalism and free trade, gave the colored world the assurance of American support for the destruction of the European empires:

> *In regard to these essential rectifications of wrong and assertions of right we feel ourselves to be intimate partners of all the governments and peoples associated together against the Imperialists. We cannot be separated in interest or divided in purpose. We stand together until the end.*[471]

It is from this time that a misconception arises that British imperialists from the old Cecil Rhodes "Round Table" network at Oxford, and the internationalists around Wilson, who formed the Council on Foreign Relations, established an Anglo-American conspiratorial network to rule the world. This misconception came from a conspiratorial rendering[472] of several dozen pages from American historian Dr. Carroll Quigley's *Tragedy and Hope*.[473] Quigley, however, got the facts uncharacteristically wrong, and they have since spawned a lot of theorizing.

So far from there being a longstanding accord between Anglophile elitists in the USA and Britain to rule the world, when the empires had become too restrictive for High Finance, an anti-imperialist, internationalist agenda centered on Washington and New York became the new paradigm. As Quigley stated, this did indeed center around the foreign policy think tank, the Council on Foreign Relations (CFR), but the mooted alliance between the Americans and British did not eventuate.

In fact, the British imperialists of the Round Table Group and the Wall Street internationalists who were represented by Colonel Edward House's[474] think tank, The Inquiry,[475] had a falling out over post-war aims. The intentions of these internationalist bankers, industrialists, and intellectuals were to unite with the British Round Table Group (which became the Royal Institute of International Affairs). This had been

---

[471] Wilson, *Fourteen Points*.
[472] Skousen, *Naked Capitalist*.
[473] Quigley, *Tragedy and Hope*.
[474] Colonel House, President Wilson's *alter ego*.
[475] After World War I The Inquiry became the Council on Foreign Relations, originating for the purposes of advising President Wilson on post-war foreign policy. See: K. R. Bolton, *Revolution from Above*, 30-47.

discussed at the Versailles Peace Conference in 1918. The aim had been to create an American Institute of International Affairs. However, it soon transpired that neither the British nor the Americans were eager to continue with a joint project.[476] CFR historian Peter Grose confirms this early Anglo-US breach, writing in the official CFR history:

> To Shepardson fell the task of informing the British colleagues of this unfortunate reality. Crossing to London, he recalled thinking that "it might be quite unpleasant to have to say for the first time that the Paris Group of British colleagues could not be members" of the American branch. The explanation to the British was begun (shall we say?) haltingly. However, instead of the frigid look which had been feared, the faces of the British governing body showed slightly red and very happy. They had reached the same conclusion in reverse, but had not yet found a good way of getting word to the other side of the Atlantic![477]

The Atlantic Charter

World War II had brought the imperial powers to exhaustion, and the USA and the USSR emerged as the dominant powers in the midst of European ruin. What Wilson had failed to do with the "Fourteen Points," and the abortive League of Nations, President Franklin D. Roosevelt succeeded in doing after World War II with the "Atlantic Charter" and the UN, establishing the foundations of the post-1945 world under which we continue to endure. It was a victory for the Jacobin faction of US politics that had emerged since the days of Thomas Jefferson, and a defeat for the "America first" vision of George Washington. A "world revolution" would proceed not under the auspices of the USSR, which remained a convenient bogeyman and red-herring, but under the inspiration of the Jeffersonian-Wilsonian *Democratic Internationale*.

The Atlantic Charter had established the US vision for the post-World War II era with the same internationalist, anti-imperial agenda as the Wilsonian manifesto, phrased in what would become the familiar "human rights" doctrine. Point four stated that Britain and the USA would "endeavor, with due respect for their existing obligations, to further the enjoyment by all States, great or small, victor or vanquished, of access, on

---

[476] Burnett and Games, *Who Runs the World*, 102.
[477] Grose, *Continuing the Inquiry*.

equal terms, to the trade and to the raw materials of the world which are needed for their economic prosperity."[478]

Churchill was alarmed by Roosevelt's intentions, as evident from the account of proceedings given by the President's son, Elliott. The USA's post-war agenda would include the dismantling of the empires for the purpose of creating an American neo-colonialism in the name of free trade and democracy. Roosevelt said to Churchill:

> *Of course, after the war, one of the preconditions of any lasting peace will have to be the greatest possible freedom of trade. No artificial barriers. As few favoured economic agreements as possible. Opportunities for expansion. Markets open for healthy competition.*[479]

When Churchill raised the question of the empire trade agreements Roosevelt interjected:

> *Those Empire trade agreements are a case in point. ...The peace cannot include any continued despotism. The structure of the peace demands and will get equality of peoples. Equality of peoples involves the utmost freedom of competitive trade. Will anyone suggest that Germany's attempt to dominate trade in central Europe was not a major contributing factor to war?*[480]

Note that Roosevelt stated a major factor in the war against Germany was the Reich's success in negotiating what had become a self-sufficient trading bloc based on barter, thereby undermining the international trade and financial system. Roosevelt aimed for the domination of this predatory system, by the elimination not only of the Reich, but also of all the allied empires that he equated with the German system.

The following day, Churchill spoke in despair, knowing that Britain could not survive the war without US support: "Mr. President, I believe you are trying to do away with the British Empire. Every idea you entertain about the structure of the post-war world demonstrates it."[481]

---

[478] Roosevelt and Churchill, *Atlantic Charter*.
[479] Roosevelt, *As He Saw It*, 35.
[480] Ibid.
[481] Ibid., 31.

Cold War

The Roosevelt policy shows that the USA aimed to achieve global hegemony on the ruins of the European empires. In place of these empires there was to emerge a United Nations World Government, which would operate as a facade for plutocracy. The plan was based on:

1. Vesting nominal authority in the UN General Assembly which would function as a world parliament on the basis of majority vote. Decolonization would mean that votes would be packed in favor of the USA, which would easily buy off the new states with loans and aid.
2. The so-called "internationalization" of atomic energy through the UN Atomic Energy Agency, under the terms of the Baruch Plan, which would mean *de facto* control by the USA.

The USSR would be expected to be a junior partner and rebuffed the US agenda. Hence, the USSR stymied a world state, and the Cold War resulted. This is more than hypothesis. The Foreign Minister of the time, Andrei Gromyko, reminisced decades later that the USSR regarded the US plans for the UN and the Baruch Plan as the means by which the USA would dominate the world.[482]

However, the bogeyman of world communism provided a pretext for the USA to extend its hegemony over the world, under the guise of "protection from communism," and advancing freedom, democracy, and human rights. This was the policy pursued in Africa at the expense of the European settlers.

Decolonization of Africa

While the USA pursued a decolonization agenda throughout the world, being able to point to its own relinquishing of the Philippines as the evidence of its good faith, it is in Africa that the Europeans were left to their fate with the Mau Mau in Kenya, Holden Roberto's butchers in Angola, and the terror that continues today in former Rhodesia and South Africa. When conservatives throughout the world looked with alarm at the prospect of the USSR controlling the former colonies and especially the mineral wealth, this served as a convenient sleight-of-hand for the USA to

---

[482] Bolton, *Stalin*, 137-140.

advance its neo-colonialist agenda on the pretext of thwarting communism by handing power over to "moderate Blacks." Hence while the USSR trained Black leaders at Patrice Lumumba University,[483] the USA was training and funding its own Black cadres to establish puppet governments.

The first imperial powers to be targeted by the USA were France and Britain in West Africa. America gave 94.7 million dollars to West Africa.[484] The intention of such aid in displacing the European administrations was clear. In 1955, the US House of Representatives stated "that the United States should administer its foreign policies and programs and exercise its influence so as to support other peoples in their efforts to achieve self-government or independence."[485]

Creating the Post-Colonial Bureaucracy

In 1953 the Africa-America Institute (AAI) was established to fund and train the leadership of decolonized Africa. The purpose was stated to be to enable the USA to "build relationships with the new African leadership," after the White administrators were ousted. Debbie Meyer, an AAI director, stated that over the course of fifty years twenty-two thousand Africans have received their postgraduate education in the USA, many having returned to Africa "to play leading roles in developing their countries and in linking them to the global economy."

As stated on the AAI "About" page on their website, its "work is made possible through funds provided by the US government, African governments, private foundations, corporate donors, multilateral institutions, and individuals."

Among its first major programs was the establishment of the US–South Africa Leader Exchange Program in 1958, according to their website site page on 1950s history. According to their "Past Programs" page, the AAI's Guinea Scholarship Program 1960–1969, provided the training for the new leadership of "post-independence Guinea," with funding from the American government agency, USAID. The Southern African Student Program 1961–1983 was funded by the US State Department, as "an effort to provide educational training to students from South Africa, Namibia, Angola, Mozambique and Zimbabwe, to provide a cadre of leadership in these countries which were transitioning into independent nations." The

---

[483] Germani, "Moscow's Academic Nightmare."
[484] Pedler, *Main Currents*, 96.
[485] Ibid., 267.

African Training Program 1964–1969 was directed toward Africans in the French colonies, with funding from USAID.

In 1975, a year following the Portuguese scuttle of its territories, the AAI established the Development Training Program for Portuguese-Speaking Africa (DTPSA) to establish the post-colonial leadership for the former colonies of Angola, Mozambique, Guinea-Bissau, Cape Verde and Sao Tome and Principe. This program was funded by USAID.

The Portuguese had been tough to crack, and the regular army had uprooted FRELIMO in Mozambique in 1970 with Operation Gordian Knot. FRELIMO received largesse from the Ford Foundation via the Mozambique Institute,[486] so the Portuguese soldiers were up against more than jungle terrorists, as were their counterparts in Rhodesia.

In what was presumably training for fleeing terrorists the AAI operated training programs for "refugees" including the East Africa Refugee Program (1962–1971) and the Southern African Training Program (1971–1976). The initial program was for the training of personnel "in anticipation of independence." The latter program—once Portugal had scuttled from Africa—was then directed towards the remaining White states of Southern Africa: "Namibia, South Africa and Zimbabwe, for employment in their countries of asylum with a later focus on the repatriation of trainees." This program was continued through 1976–1981, with funds from USAID.

After the Portuguese fled Mozambique for their lives, the money power moved in, unperturbed by noises about "nationalization." Millions in aid money came in from the West, and the very day that President Machel announced his nationalization program, General Mining, linked with the Oppenheimer Anglo-American Corporation, negotiated with the new regime a deal for bulk handling chrome loading equipment.[487] The same pattern followed the other decolonized states. In Zambia, when Kenneth Kaunda took a fifty-one percent share in the Anglo-American owned copper industry, Oppenheimer regarded "government participation" as a welcome move.[488]

The AAI is not some Marxist lobby, or a group of naive, wealthy liberals who have been tricked into funding communistic causes. It has since its foundation been a nexus between the US government and big business in shaping post-colonial Africa and providing the personnel for the bureaucracies.

---

[486] Whitaker, *The Foundations*, 24.
[487] Benson, *Struggle for Africa*, 54.
[488] Ibid., 47.

The president and CEO of the AAI board, Kofi Appenteng, is also the Chair of the Board of the Ford Foundation, previously served as Senior Counsel at Dentons, a global law firm, "is a Senior Advisor to The Rock Creek Group, a global investment and advisory firm," and is a lifetime member of the Council on Foreign Relations (CFR) according to their website's "Membership Roster," where the Chair of AAI Steven B. Pfeiffer is described as:

> [A]partner in the Washington, D.C. office of Norton Rose Fulbright LLP. He served as the Chair of the Executive Committee of Fulbright & Jaworski L.L.P. from 2003 until 2013, having been elected by his partners on three occasions. Mr. Pfeiffer previously served as Partner-in-Charge of Fulbright & Jaworski's Washington and London offices and as head of the firm-wide International Department. In his law practice, he has had principal responsibility for a wide variety of corporate and commercial transactions involving United Kingdom, African, Middle Eastern and European-based banks, corporations and individuals investing in the United States. Mr. Pfeiffer has been responsible for the firm's representation of certain sovereign entities, including the U.K., Canada and several African governments.... Mr. Pfeiffer is a member of the Council on Foreign Relations in New York and the International Institute of Strategic Studies in London...

The AAI provides some profiles of the twenty-three thousand Africans they have trained, such as: Joy Phumaphi, Botswana, Vice President and Head of the World Bank Human Development Network; Dr. Mbuyamu I Matungulu, Congo, Mission Chief to Benin, International Monetary Fund; Charles Boamah, Controller and Director, African Development Bank; H.E. Nahas Angula, Prime Minister, Republic of Namibia; Mamadou Dia (Senegal) Country Director for Cote d'Ivoire and Guinea, Africa Region, World Bank; Dr. Renosi Mokate, Deputy Governor, South African Reserve Bank, et al.

Belgian Congo

The former Belgian colony of the Congo represents a special story in the incursions of neo-colonialism, the civil war between the central authority and the breakaway province of Katanga, reflecting rivalry between two factions of monopoly capital. US Congressman Donald Bruce exposed the forces at work in a speech before Congress in 1960. When Katanga attempted to secede, United Nations troops invaded. Congressman Bruce showed that the reason for the UN invasion of Katanga was to secure for the American Anaconda group the copper mining interests owned by Union Miniere du Haute Congo.

A consortium had been formed by American and Swedish companies, and was directed by Bo Hammarskjoeld, brother of the UN Secretary-General. Sture Linner, UN representative in the Congo, had been the chief engineer of the Liberian-American Mining Company (LAMCO), one of the consortium. UN Congo "experts" Sven Schwartz and Borj Hjortsberg-Nordlund, were both also part of LAMCO. From the US Fowler Hamilton, the State Department official responsible for implementing US policy through USAID in Africa, was part of the US-Swedish consortium. Congressman Bruce's investigation found that prior to the UN invasion, Schwartz had been sent to the Congo by the UN to undertake a study of mining. His recommendation was that Union Miniere interests should be nationalized.[489]

US policy operated through the United Nations, with the aim of undermining the Katanga secessionist government of Tshombe, where Belgian mining interests were maintained, and which had the support of Rhodesia and of Belgian interests. The UN invasion aroused much ill will in Europe against the US-UN action.[490] The UN went on a rampage through Katanga, where ambulances were strafed and bombed and civilians were shot.[491]

In 1974 what was now called Zaire served notice on fifty thousand non-Blacks that their properties and businesses had been nationalized.[492] Conversely, American big business was described as "a financial power in the country."[493]

Portuguese Territories

Portugal held Africa for so long because the Portuguese state itself had a unique social order that had been functioning on Catholic social principles since the 1920s and had subordinated money to the interests of the state. Hence Portugal was one of the few states in the world that could not be controlled by international finance. It fell in 1974 through the coup

---

[489] Benson, *Struggle for Africa*, 51-53.
[490] US Dept. of State, "Congo Crisis."
[491] Griffin, *Fearful Master*.
[492] Benson, *Struggle for Africa*, 49.
[493] Ibid.

by leftist junior army officers who soon dismantled the empire. Like the South African government up to the time of Dr. Verwoerd, the Portuguese leaders knew that they faced more than communist terrorists. Ivor Benson, who lived in Africa and knew the situation intimately, having been an adviser to the Rhodesian government, commented that "in Portugal politics has remained in power and has not become subordinate to economics... they have not made the Gross National Product their God. Therefore, in Portugal economics is the servant, not the master."[494]

Dr. Franco Nogueira, Portuguese Foreign Minister, exposed the forces at work in Africa, stating:

> *Africa has been subjected to a regime that excludes European interests and African interests as well, neither being sufficiently strong to impose themselves. A form of autonomy and independence has been created which ensures the destruction of the old forms of sovereignty and permits the setting up of new forms of sovereignty so precarious and so artificial that it is an easy matter to dominate them. The result has been that the real autonomy and the real control are to be found outside the frontiers of the new political units. The aim is to dominate Angola and Mozambique and to include them in the spheres of foreign influences, to utilise their economic and strategic positions for the benefit of other Powers.*[495]

Andresen Fernando Guimarães stated that the USA gave support at an early stage to the murderous Holden Roberto:

> *The Kennedy administration also acted beyond the United Nations and sought directly to support an anti-colonial movement against the Portuguese. Holden Roberto, the UPA (and later FNLA leader) had by the end of the 1950s established a wide range of contacts in the United States. Due to its prominent role in the anti-colonial uprising in northern Angola in 1961, the UPA was the Angolan nationalist movement with the most international exposure. Washington authorized the CIA to extend support to Roberto and UPA.*[496]

---

[494] Benson, *Worldwide Conspiracy*, 73.
[495] Quoted in ibid., 70-73.
[496] Guimarães, "The United States."

In 1959 Roberto traveled to Washington, where he met Kennedy and remained appreciative of the US support. Guimarães wrote of this:

> *A university scholarship program had been established for African students from the Portuguese colonies; the military assistance program for Portugal was cut back from the original US$ 25 million to US$ 3 million; a ban on commercial sales of arms to Portugal was imposed in mid-1961; and the US supported the prohibition on the use of NATO war materiel in Africa.*[497]

Guimarães focuses on Washington's fear of alienating Portugal during the Cold War, yet it is also evident that high level contacts with Roberto continued. Roberto's adviser was John Marcum, an adviser to Averell Harriman[498] on the Portuguese colonies. Already in 1964 there was a close association between Americans in Leopoldville linked to the US Embassy and the CIA, Congolese political circles, and Holden Roberto. "Later in 1975, this triangle was to be instrumental in formulating the context for the US decision to provide covert support for the FNLA."[499]

However, US support to Roberto was more significant than indicated by Guimarães. Since 1969, Roberto had been on a ten thousand dollars-a-year retainer from the CIA.[500]

What is not stated in such analyses is that international power politics and Cold War rivalries were being played out over the corpses of the White settlers. Roberto, as the "moderate" option to the Soviet-backed MPLA, was later to recall that when his gang invaded from their base in the Congo in 1961, over-running farms, government outposts, and trading centers, "this time the slaves did not cower. They massacred everything."[501] The subsequent twenty-seven year civil war between the FNLA and the MPLA resulted in five hundred thousand deaths in what became just one more "liberated Black state."

---

[497] Ibid.
[498] Harriman was a US Establishment luminary, serving in numerous ambassadorial roles, and as assistant and Under Secretary of State, chairman of the Business Council, member of the internationalist Club of Rome, and the CFR, and an initiate Yale fraternity, Lodge 322.
[499] Guimarães, "The United States."
[500] Gelb, "U. S., Soviet, China."
[501] "Holden Roberto Dies at 84."

Rhodesia and South Africa

The destruction of White rule in the Portuguese Territories was the beginning of the end for the White geopolitical bloc of Southern Africa. Rhodesia was targeted next. In 1965, R. D. McClelland, US Consul-General in Rhodesia, gave the American green light to the terrorists when he stated that:

> [T]here is as much legitimacy in revolution as there is in government. To be other than a revolutionary is to defend the status quo, and the status quo was colonialism. It is the innate role of the revolutionary, and this applies a fortiori to the still white-dominated southern part of the Continent, to change an existing and unsatisfactory order."[502]

Pressure began to be applied on Rhodesia when Henry Kissinger met with South Africa's Vorster to lay down the law on the northern neighbor, while simultaneously "South Africa suddenly found the money taps of America and Europe inexplicably turned off," according to G. Sutton, editor of the *South African Financial Mail*. The strategy to destroy White rule in Rhodesia followed a familiar tactic: a pincer movement of terrorism from below and economic pressure from above. These names stand out in the elimination of White rule:

- Lord Soames, last Governor of Rhodesia, installed for the purpose of handing over political power, was a director of N M Rothschilds and the National Westminster Bank;
- "Tiny" Rowland, CEO of Lonhro, involved in brokering the Lancaster House talks of 1979, which settled the political future of Rhodesia;
- British Foreign Minister Lord Carrington, a director of Hambros Bank, Chairman of ANZ Bank, and a member of the Rockefeller globalist think tank The Trilateral Commission; chairman of the globalist Bilderberg Group, and a member of Kissinger Associates, the global consultancy firm of omnipresent former US Secretary of State Henry Kissinger.

South Africa, the final redoubt of White rule anywhere in the world, lost its vision after the assassination of Verwoerd. Like the Portuguese under

---

[502] Quoted in Benson, *This Worldwide Conspiracy*, 69.

Salazar and Caetano, Verwoerd knew precisely what the forces were at work against White authority.

Legacy

In 1959 J. G. van der Meersch of the international banks J. H. Whitney and Dillon Reed & Co. formed the American-Eurafrican Development Corporation, "with the object of meeting the financial needs of emerging African nations when the former colonial powers left,"[503] Mr. van der Meersch stated with exactitude what lay behind the facade of "human rights," equality, decolonization, "opposition to apartheid," and the other facile slogans that were used to remove White rule from Africa.

In human terms, since "liberation" in 1994, over three thousand White farmers have been killed.[504] The old ANC slogan is again popular: "One settler, one bullet!"; "Kill the Boer, kill the farmer!"; *Maak dood die wit man* (Kill the White man).

In former Rhodesia four thousand farmers have been driven from their land.[505] However, it would be an error to think that the Blacks are the sole benefactors of the lunatic land policy. The biggest landowner in Zimbabwe is Nicholas Hoogstraten who, along with the late "Tiny" Rowland of Lonhro Corporation, were the main patrons of rival terrorist leaders Mugabe and Nkomo respectively. Hoogstraten first purchased land in Rhodesia in 1963, where he met Rowland, and they agreed to each back the two terrorist leaders, but Hoogstraten "like any canny businessman did a bit of betting on both sides."[506]

At the time when Hoogstraten was serving a ten years jail sentence for the contract killing of a debtor, Claire David wrote that he is "one of Britain's richest sons...best known as an unscrupulous landlord."

> *In his property business, Hoogstraten was always clear that it was the buildings that concerned him not the people in them; he was well known for hounding out sitting tenants by whatever means possible. He once said: "Tenants are filth, by their very nature. What kind of person is a tenant? A person with no self-respect. I don't look after tenants. Why should I look after tenants? One looks after the building, looks after one's asset."*[507]

---

[503] Chesterton, *Candour*.
[504] McDougall, "White Farmers."
[505] Ibid.
[506] Block, "An Aristocrat of Africa."
[507] Davies, "Downfall of the Devil's."

His view of British tenants as "filth" echoes his opinion of Zimbabwe farmers as "White trash."[508]

In 2006 Hoogstraten, obviously with much political clout in Zimbabwe, had a British television crew from Channel 4 put under house arrest when he learned they were to make a documentary critical of Mugabe, and retorted that "if they stepped out of line I would deal with them personally." A 2006 report stated that he had become "Mugabe's most prominent friend in international business," after John Bredenkamp fled, having backed a losing Zanu-PF faction. "Mr. van Hoogstraten, who has a vast ranch in central Zimbabwe which has not been seized by the president's supporters, has spoken frequently of his friendship with Mr. Mugabe, and said recently that he had lent him $10m, although Mr. Mugabe's spokesman later denied it."[509]

In 2005 Hoogstraten, following the same pattern as big money in other African "socialist" states, became "the majority shareholder in Zimbabwe's leading coal producing company…and has a controlling stake in the National Merchant Bank,"[510] and has numerous other important investments.[511]

> *The Daily Mail (Australia) commented in 2013 that Mugabe, notoriously drove the country's white farmers—often of British descent—off their land in a prolonged campaign of terror, and is now introducing laws banning whites from owning businesses.*
>
> *Yet, curiously, one British man is flourishing under Mugabe's murderous regime. While his fellow white farmers have been murdered in their hundreds, and their land given to the despot's cronies, this slight grey-haired individual has become Zimbabwe's biggest landowner.*
>
> *As well as owning a staggering 1,600 square miles of prime land in the heart of the country the British exile also owns two sprawling homes replete with tennis courts, swimming pools and garish chrome architecture, with grounds patrolled by Mugabe's secret police.*[512]

---

[508] Peta, "Van Hoogstraten to take over."
[509] Meldrum, "Tycoon Flees Zimbabwe."
[510] Peta, "Van Hoogstraten to take over."
[511] Ndlela, "Zimbabwe: Hwange Crisis."
[512] Malone, "Mugabe's Henchman."

South Africa's Road to Hell

"Envy wears the mask of love, and, laughing sober fact to scorn,
Cries to weakest as to strongest, 'Ye are equals, equal born,'
Equal-born! Oh yes, if yonder hill be level with the flat.
Charm us, orator, till the lion look no larger than the cat:
Till the cat, through that mirage of overheated language, loom
Larger than the lion Demo—end in working its own doom.
Tumble Nature heel o'er head, and, yelling with the yelling street,
Set the feet above the brain, and swear the brain is in the feet.
Bring the old dark ages back, without the faith, without the hope
Beneath the State, the Church, the Throne, and roll their ruins down the
    slope."

Alfred Tennyson (1886)

South Africa is a particularly valuable case study in how the "human rights" doctrine facilitates ethnocide. Total, unconditional warfare was declared on the Afrikaner from the day gold and diamonds were discovered. "Human rights" sloganeering from streets and rostrums made the Afrikaner a pariah.

The UN declared 1968 the International Year for Human Rights. In Montreal an Assembly for Human Rights was convened:

> ...as a group of private individuals from many areas of the world representing different disciplines and ideologies, to express profound concern about the condition of human rights in this year of international crisis and to explore the ways in which mankind's shared aspirations to human dignity can become a reality.[513]

---

[513] "Montreal Statement," 94.

The assembly issued a declaration affirming the UN and UN Charter as the foundation of "human rights" to which member states were bound: "The Charter of the United Nations, the constitutional document of the world community, creates binding obligations for Members of the United Nations with respect to human rights."[514] "The Universal Declaration of Human Rights constitutes an authoritative interpretation of the Charter of the highest order, and has over the years become a part of customary international law."[515] Note that it is plainly stated even by 1968, by this international convention that the UN Declaration of Human Rights had become international law. This had been "enshrined in the national constitutions of many States."[516] The assembly referred to further UN declarations that had extended the UN declaration into "international law":

> *The Covenant on Economic, Social and Cultural Rights; the Covenant on Civil and Political Rights and various conventions adopted by the United Nations and the specialized agencies further clarify the obligations of the Members of the United Nations.*[517]

Since that time, we might look aghast at the way UN treaties, declarations, and covenants have proliferated, and become the basis of state laws. On the issue, specifically of "human rights," these covenants were already proliferating:

> *The rule of non-discrimination has in the last twenty years been reaffirmed in numerous international declarations and conventions, notably the International Convention on the Elimination of All Forms of Racial Discrimination, the Discrimination (Employment and Occupation) Convention of the International Labor Organization, the UNESCO Convention against Discrimination in Education, the ILO Convention Concerning Equal Remuneration for Men and Women Workers, and the United Nations Declaration on the Elimination of Discrimination against Women.*[518]

---

[514] Ibid., I. Areas of Progress.
[515] Ibid., 95.
[516] Ibid.
[517] Ibid.
[518] Ibid., 96. II. Non-Discrimination.

Although stating "yet discrimination in all its internationally outlawed forms is rampant in all parts of the world," only South Africa was specified: "Particular attention must be drawn to southern Africa, where apartheid stands as a shocking reminder to mankind everywhere of the international lawlessness that still remains to be eradicated."[519] This meant that lip-service could be given to "human rights" in theory, but in practice only South Africa was targeted:

> *The most flagrant violation of human rights today is the abhorrent practice of apartheid enforced as official policy in the Republic of South Africa and in some other parts of southern Africa. Apartheid constitutes a gross denial of the most basic civil and political rights of non-white South Africans, and their most fundamental economic, social and cultural rights. The Assembly joined in the universal condemnation of this repugnant practice and the daily shocking violations associated with it. The Assembly was particularly concerned that the governments involved have thus far totally ignored and defied all requests and demands on the part of the international community for remedial action in this regard. International efforts to bring about a solution to this problem should continue to receive particular attention by all organs of the United Nations family of organizations in the context of their concern with all human rights. Steps should be taken to increase the effectiveness of the measures required to bring about a prompt and just solution of this vital problem.*[520]

Specifying what states were in violation of UN laws on slavery and the like would have shown that by comparison to the rest of Africa, South Africa (and Rhodesia) were lights unto the world. Yet, the assembly of "human rights experts" went on to state:

> *Persons belonging to ethnic, religious or linguistic minorities must not be denied the right, in community with other members of their group, to enjoy their own culture, to profess and practice their own religion, or to use their own language. At the same time minority groups have a duty to contribute to the development of the State in which they are settled and to join in the mainstream*

---

[519] Ibid.
[520] Ibid., 97. III. Apartheid.

of its life. The Assembly noted in this connection that it is necessary to give further study to methods of assuring to each person belonging to a group the opportunity to fully exercise his individual rights.[521]

This was precisely what *apartheid* was intended to achieve. South Africa, and no other, was attempting to fulfil these aims. Now that the Afrikaner obstacle and associated White obstacles in Angola, Mozambique and Rhodesia, have been eliminated, all nominally "White" states, including the most liberal, are targeted for ethnic and cultural cleansing under the guise of advancing "ethnic, religious or linguistic minorities." The UN Declaration on the Rights of Indigenous Peoples (UINDRIP) is the latest measure to serve this purpose, while of course not applying to "White" indigenes such as Afrikaners, Britons, Slavs, Germanics, Franks, et al.

While half of Europe was occupied by troops from the USSR, and the "experts on human rights" talked of concern for world peace, only South Africa was singled out for condemnation for retaining its mandate over South West Africa, and the assembly alluded to the need for the intervention of international law:

The Assembly noted a suggestion that the unique status of the Territory of South West Africa which, by virtue of the actions taken by the United Nations General Assembly, is under direct United Nations jurisdiction, provides a special opportunity to experiment with further implementation procedures. Criminal courts and procedures might be established for dealing with gross violations of human rights in that Territory.[522]

The assembly recommended—in regard to South Africa—support for the violent overthrow of the state, euphemistically referred to as "the legitimacy of the struggle of the peoples of southern Africa."

With Respect to Apartheid:
6. *The international community should confirm the legitimacy of the struggle of the peoples of southern Africa toward the achievement of their inalienable right to equality, freedom and independence in accordance with the Purposes and Principles of the United Nations Charter.*

---

[521] Ibid., 99. VIII. New Areas of Concern, Rights of Groups.
[522] Ibid., 107. XI. International Implementation Measures, South West Africa.

7. *All States and organizations should provide appropriate moral, political and material assistance to the people of southern Africa in their just struggle for the rights recognized in the Charter of the United Nations and the Universal Declaration of Human Rights.*
8. *All States should facilitate effective action, under the auspices of the United Nations, to secure self-determination and enjoyment of human rights and fundamental freedoms for all the inhabitants of southern Africa.*[523]

The UN in lauding its role in the ethnocide of the Afrikaner, lists "Key dates in the UN campaign against apartheid" on their website:

- *2 December 1950—The General Assembly declared that "a policy of 'racial segregation' (apartheid) is necessarily based on doctrines of racial discrimination.'" (Resolution 395(V))*
- *1 April 1960—The Security Council, in its first action on South Africa, adopted Resolution 134 deploring the policies and actions of the South African government in the wake of the killing of 69 peaceful African protesters in Sharpeville by the police on 21 March. The Council called upon the government to abandon its policies of apartheid and racial discrimination.*
- *2 April 1963—First meeting of the Special Committee on the Policies of Apartheid of the Government of the Republic of South Africa, It was later renamed the "Special Committee against Apartheid."*
- *7 August 1963—The Security Council adopted Resolution 181 calling upon all States to cease the sale and shipment of arms, ammunition, and military vehicles to South Africa. The arms embargo was made mandatory on 4 November 1977.*
- *13 November 1963—The General Assembly, in Resolution 1899 (XVIII) on the question of Namibia [South West Africa], urged all States to refrain from supplying petroleum to South Africa. It was the first of many efforts by the UN to enact effective oil sanctions against apartheid.*
- *23 August–4 September 1966—International Seminar on Apartheid, Brasilia, organized by the UN Division of Human*

---

[523] Ibid., 111. Proposals for Action.

Rights, the Special Committee against Apartheid and the government of Brazil – the first of scores of conferences and seminars on apartheid organized or co-sponsored by the United Nations.

- 2 December 1968—The General Assembly requested all States and organizations "to suspend cultural, educational, sporting and other exchanges with the racist regime and with organizations or institutions in South Africa which practice apartheid."
- 30 November 1973—International Convention on the Suppression and Punishment of the Crime of Apartheid approved by the General Assembly (Resolution 3068(XXVIII)). The convention came into force on 18 July 1976.
- 1 January 1976—The UN Centre Against Apartheid was established.
- 17 August 1984—In Resolution 554 the Security Council declared null and void the new racist constitution of South Africa.
- 16–20 June 1986—World Conference on Sanctions against Racist South Africa, organized by the United Nations in cooperation with the OAU and the Movement of Non-aligned Countries.
- 14 December 1989—The General Assembly adopted by consensus the "Declaration on Apartheid and its Destructive Consequences in Southern Africa," calling for negotiations to end apartheid and establish a non-racial democracy (Resolution A/RES/S-16/1).
- 22 June 1990—Nelson Mandela addressed the Special Committee against Apartheid in New York—his first appearance before the Organization.
- 30 July 1992—With political violence escalating and negotiations at risk, Nelson Mandela requested the United Nations to send observers to South Africa. On the following day the Secretary-General announced that he would send a small group of UN monitors. The United Nations Observer Mission in South Africa was established by the Security Council on 17 August 1992.
- 8 October 1993—The General Assembly requested States to restore economic relations with South Africa immediately, and terminate the oil embargo when the Transitional

Executive Council in South Africa became operational (Resolution 48/1).

- *10 May 1994—South Africa's first democratically elected non-racial government took office following the general elections of 26–29 April.*
- *23 June 1994—The General Assembly approved the credentials of the South African delegation and removed the item of apartheid from its agenda. The Security Council removed the question of South Africa from its agenda on 27 June.*

The UN states that its position on apartheid was declared soon after its inception, with India introducing the first motion. One might suspect that India, newly independent, was attempting to posture on the world stage, and present itself as the leader of the emerging de-colonialized states; a position for which a number of states were vying, the most notable being the USA and the USSR. From the UN website:

The elimination of South Africa's system of legalized racial discrimination known as apartheid ("apart-ness" in the Afrikaans language of the descendants of the first Dutch settlers) was on the agenda of the United Nations from its inception. On 22 June 1946, the Indian government requested that the discriminatory treatment of Indians in the Union of South Africa be included on the agenda of the very first session of the General Assembly.

In the decades that followed the world body would contribute to the global struggle against apartheid by drawing world attention to the inhumanity of the system, legitimizing popular resistance, promoting anti-apartheid actions by governmental and non-governmental organizations, instituting an arms embargo, and supporting an oil embargo and boycotts of apartheid in many fields.

"Legitimizing popular resistance, promoting anti-apartheid actions by governmental and non-governmental organizations," is euphemistic terminology for the support of terrorism, the symbol of which was "Necklacing," an ANC practice of placing gasoline filled tires around the necks of recalcitrant Blacks and setting them alight.

In 1994 "the Security Council removed the question of South Africa from its agenda" because the situation of the Whites did not matter.

A particularly notable event in the UN's litany of Europhobia in South Africa is Resolution 134 (April 1st, 1960), otherwise known as "April Fool's Day," with the Security Council "deploring the policies and actions of the South African government in the wake of the killing of 69 peaceful African protesters in Sharpeville by the police on 21 March." It is another of those events that have taken on mythic status in the liturgy of worldwide Europhobia.

The so called "Sharpeville Massacre" of March 21st, 1960, is popularly described as the shooting of sixty-nine peaceful Black demonstrators protesting the "pass laws." These laws were designed to protect jobs for indigenous Blacks from illegal immigrants, since Black migrants seemed eager to get into South Africa to endure the alleged oppression of apartheid, rather than the freedom of their home states. The "pass laws" nonetheless became a *cause celebre* against apartheid. Twenty thousand demonstrators organized by the African National Congress (ANC) and the Pan Africanist Congress (PAC) surrounded the 150-manned police station at Sharpeville, demanding that they be arrested for destroying their passes. Two months previously nine policemen (four White, five Black) had been stoned and hacked to death by drunken partygoers when they were on a routine patrol in Cato Manor, Durban.[524]

The Sharpeville rioters cut telegraph lines to isolate the police station. Armed with poles and *pangas* (homemade machetes)—the preferred weapon of the PAC—and throwing rocks, they converged on a line of police. Demonstrators elsewhere had been dispersed, mainly peacefully, but low flying jets had failed to have an effect at Sharpeville. The PAC officials had presented themselves inside the police station, demanding that they be arrested for breaking the "pass laws," but the police had refused to respond to these attempts to cause confrontation. Since the PAC had cut the phone lines, emergency services were slow to arrive to tend to casualties.

March 21st is officially designated Human Rights Day in South Africa in honor of the rioters. Sharpeville is heralded as an example of "passive resistance."[525] According to a PAC speech appended by Gerhart and Glaser,[526] Sharpeville is heralded as the beginning of "armed resistance" and a maneuver that had been carefully planned by this breakaway faction of the ANC.

---

[524] Goodson, *Hendrik Vervoerd*, 43.
[525] An account of the Sharpeville riot and background events can be found at: "The Road to Sharpeville."
[526] Gerhart and Glaser, *From Protest to Challenge*, 557.

"White Workers of the World Unite for a White South Africa"

How many of those who were committed to the dispossession of the Afrikaner "exploiters" have heard of the epochal 1922 revolt on the Rand? This Afrikaner revolt against the mining interests was the catalyst for the victory of a Nationalist-Labor alliance that inaugurated the first steps towards apartheid. The same mostly monopolists who had opposed the Afrikaner from start to finish intended to use Black labor to undermine the White miners.

In late 1922 the Chamber of Mines announced that twenty-five semi-skilled job levels reserved for Whites would be given to Blacks, and that there would be thousands of White redundancies. At the same time coal mine owners announced wage cuts. The Mineworkers Union called a general strike. While the Communist Party was involved, the main influences were the Afrikaner Mynwerkersbond; mostly former Boer farmers, and war veterans who had been left destitute by the British scorched earth policy during the Anglo-Boer War, and allied Labour Party supporters.

When the mineworkers raised their banners proclaiming "Keep South Africa White" and "White Workers of the World Unite for a White South Africa," the communists were in no position to object. The coal miners, gold miners, engineers, and power workers on the Rand voted to strike and had the backing of both the Labour Party and the National Party. Prime Minister Jan Smuts urged the Chamber of Mines to negotiate, but they refused, and instead viciously announced a new labor ratio of two Whites to twenty-one Blacks, meaning many more redundancies.

The South African Industrial Federation created a "strike commando" to resist Black scab labor, although resisting calls for a general strike. Smuts relented to the demands of the mine owners and ordered the miners back to work. In response, the Miner Councils of Action deployed commandos throughout the Rand. Smuts responded with force and three Whites were killed by police at Boksburg. The National Party demanded a parliamentary enquiry.

The Industrial Federation wanted to negotiate but the Chamber refused. Only then was a general strike called. Armed commandos seized Johannesburg and proclaimed a "White Workers' Republic." Mine officials, bosses, and Black scabs were executed. Government forces attacked. The air force leveled the miners' quarters. On March 14th, 1922, the strike headquarters was overtaken, and the strike leaders were killed. The last resistance was put down on March 16th.

Such was the outrage against Smuts that in 1924 the Afrikaner Nationalists, in alliance with the Labour Party, assumed office, and with the enactment of labor laws, the foundations of apartheid began to be laid.

Plutocratic Crusade Against Afrikaners

As in 1922 the primary enemy of the Afrikaner was the Oppenheimer mining, industrial and media empire, which includes the Anglo-American Corporation and DeBeers. The head of the dynasty during most of the apartheid era was Harry F. Oppenheimer. He became a Member of Parliament for the United Party when that party was the main opposition to the nationalists. When anti-nationalist veterans founded the militant Torch commando in 1950, Oppenheimer provided the funding.[527] When the Progressive Party was formed by a breakaway from United in 1959, Oppenheimer became the financial patron of the party. When the progressives first contested the Coloured seats in 1965, Oppenheimer funded all the campaigns then and subsequently, with forty thousand rand annually. In 1966 he funded the Progressive General Election campaign with fifty thousand rand.[528]

We have already seen Oppenheimer's motives and plans that he explained at the founding of the business lobby, the South Africa Foundation in 1960.[529] Nearly two decades later he reiterated: "Nationalist politics have made it impossible to make use of Black labor."[530] Perhaps "the good and the righteous" should contemplate that, the next time they pontificate about how they "marched against apartheid"?

Up until the assassination of Prime Minister Dr. Hendrik Verwoerd on September 6th, 1966, the Nationalists remained acutely aware of the identity of their real adversaries, Prime Minister Malan stating: "What we have against us is money power, principally under the leadership of Oppenheimer."[531]

Verwoerd, a statesman of immense stature who had the respect of Black Africa, provided the philosophical basis for separate development and the defense of the European in Africa.[532] After his assassination in 1966, his successors lacked the ideological coherence and a comprehen-

---

[527] Pallister, *South Africa Inc.*, 78-80.
[528] Ibid., 91.
[529] Oppenheimer, "Portrait of Millionaire."
[530] Oppenheimer interview cited in Pallister, op cit., 87.
[531] Pallister, op cit., 80.
[532] For example, read: Verwoerd, *Verwoerd Speaks*.

sion of the forces working against them. In 1962, Verwoerd stated of these anti-Afrikaner forces in a speech before Parliament:

The directors, when they meet, hold private discussions. In the case of such a powerful body there is also a central body which lays down basic policy. The influence of that central body, to say the least, must be great in our economic life. Nobody knows, however, what they discuss there. In the course of his speeches, Mr. Oppenheimer, the leader, makes political statements; he discusses political policy, he tries to exercise political influence. He even supports a political party...In other words he has political aims; he wants to steer things in a certain direction. He can secretly cause a great many things to happen. In other words, he can pull strings. With all that money power and with his powerful machine which is spread over the whole country, he can, if he so chooses, exercise enormous interference against the Government and against the state.[533]

In 1953, even Mandela stated of the Oppenheimer empire:

Rather than attempt the costly, dubious and dangerous task of crushing the non-European mass movements by force, they would seek to divert it with fine words and promises and divide it by giving concessions and bribes to a privileged minority.[534]

Yet when Oppenheimer died in 2000 Mandela eulogized: "His contribution to building a partnership between big business and the new democratic government in the first period of democratic rule can never be appreciated too much."[535]

The Long Road to Capitalist Serfdom

While journalists, politicians, clerics, academics, etc. worship Mandela as the Risen Christ, South Africa has descended into a hell on earth. What has been the outcome for post-apartheid South Africa? The answer is that the "anti-apartheid struggle" ushered a regime of privatization and globalization on the ruins of the state-directed economic structure that the

---

[533] Pallister, *South Africa Inc*, 98.
[534] Mandela, "The Shifting Sands of Time."
[535] Mandela, "Eulogy: Harry Oppenheimer."

Afrikaners created. So far from being exploitive capitalists, beating old Darkie with the *sjambok*, as stereotyped by Marxist propaganda and the democratic press, the Afrikaners were an anomaly in the world economy: the last of a traditional European peasantry bonded to faith, blood, and land. The industrial structure included the parastatals, state-owned or partly owned corporations. With the advent of Mandela's ANC/Communist Party coalition, the "comrades" set about delivering South Africa to international capitalism. In 1996 Mandela, despite once having supported nationalization, stated: "Privatisation is the fundamental policy of the ANC and will remain so."[536]

ANC economics adviser C. Mostert has detailed the history and ideology of privatization in South Africa, stating that the nationalists introduced state supervision of the economy in 1948; a policy which began to be dismantled by the (corrupted) National Party in 1987, and which has been continued by the ANC government.[537] Mostert stated that the ANC has embarked on a policy recommended by the International Monetary Fund; that the word "privatization" is not generally used, but rather it is the phrase "restructuring of state asset." The Government Communication and Information Service (GCIS) uses the two phrases interchangeably when it describes economic developments and policy.[538] He writes:

> *These privatization initiatives have taken different forms and include:*
> - *The complete sale of companies, like Sun Air and seven radio stations to consortiums;*
> - *Build, Operate and Transfer arrangements for the building of roads;*
> - *The opening of private-public partnerships at local government level for the provision of services like water;*
> - *Selling a partial stake (30%) in Telkom to combined American-Malaysian consortium; and*
> - *The proposed sale of a 25%-30% stake of South African Airways*

The ANC has stated: "Eskom is one of a host of government owned parastatals created during the apartheid era which the democratically elected government has set out to privatize in a bid to raise money."[539]

---

[536] Quoted in Barnett, "The Limits of media democratization," 655.
[537] Mostert, "Reflections on South Africa," 13.
[538] Ibid., 18.
[539] ANC Daily News Briefing, June 27, 2001.

Why does a country that had hitherto been so prosperous now need to raise capital by selling off its assets? The answer lies in South Africa having been quickly reduced to a basket case, a bottomless economic sinkhole, like every other "decolonize" state on the Dark Continent. There are big profits to be made due to such incompetence.

Mandela: Another False God

"A Master had a Colored Servant. Thinking the skin was dirty from his former master's abuse, Master subjected the servant to constant washing. No change. Moral: Some things you cannot change."

Aesop (600BC)

Nelson Mandela's name cannot be spoken of by television and radio journalists other than with tones of utmost reverence. I recall when he was released from jail and women radio hosts were imparting the news while hardly holding back cries of joy. He has long been treated as godlike. As I am writing this (December 2013), I am listening to television news stating that he is in deteriorating condition, and making the invariable references to having brought "freedom to the rainbow nation." I see his visage portrayed on the colored glass of a church in South Africa while a Black congregation sings his praises.

How many times hell on earth has been created in the name of "democracy" and "human rights"? The *Mujahideen* were funded and armed by the USA in the name of "human rights" to instigate the Soviet scuttle in Afghanistan. Now the chickens have come home to roost (2021).

The People's Republic of China brought deaths to some eighty million. More millions died in the name of the "people's democracy" in Bolshevik Russia and Cambodia. Every state claims to be a "democracy." The word, with associated clichés such as "human rights" and "freedom," means little or nothing in substance. It is a propaganda ploy that can be used either for or against a state. The South Africa that was delivered up to Mandela has set about its onslaught of Whites, especially farmers, and over three thousand have been murdered since 1990, while the murder rate generally is one of the highest in the world.[540] However, the media claims that the

---

[540] Conway-Smith, "South African Farmers."

genocide of the Afrikaner is a "far right conspiracy theory," because the image of the Rainbow Nation ethnically cleansing its Boers does not accord with the holy status assigned to post-apartheid South Africa.

For South Africa, "the long road to freedom" has meant hell's pandemonium. So long as the Black has the vote, all else is permitted.

What has the post-apartheid regime ushered by Mandela offered the Blacks? Not only has life not improved, it has become much worse, and public services and utilities are barely functional. Crime is rampant, slums persist. Such is the existence of South Africa after the abdication of the Afrikaner that John Minto, perennial protester and a leader in the antiapartheid protests in New Zealand during the 1980s, declined to accept the Steve Biko Award for his services in helping to wreck South Africa because even he could not see any sign of the new Black utopia. In January 2008 Minto wrote to President Mbeki: "Receiving an award would inevitably associate myself and the movement here with ANC government policies. At one time this may have been a source of pride but it would now be a source of personal embarrassment which I am not prepared to endure."[541] How or why Minto believed that post-apartheid South Africa would be any different than any other Black state is a mystery that might never be solved, even by Minto.

As we have seen, like the image of Martin King, who talked peace but practiced a strategy of tension,[542] Mandela's image is humbug. Mandela was committed to violence. It is assumed that Mandela was unjustly convicted and imprisoned, for standing up for "freedom," as a "prisoner of conscience." He was convicted for his involvement in a planned terror campaign.

A plan to unleash a terrorist campaign on South Africa had been hatched on the Rivonia farm near Johannesburg. The South African authorities had received information that leaders of the militant wing of the African National Congress, *Umkhonto we Sizwe* (Spear of the Nation), were ensconced at the farm, which was owned by Arthur Goldreich. On July 11th, 1963, police raided the farm where they discovered another decidedly non-African "Black" leader, Denis Goldberg, and outside in a thatched roofed building "two whites and one Bantu." Eight suspects were caught during the raid: Goldberg, Rusty Bernstein, Raymond Mhlaba, Bob Hepple, Govan Mbeki, Arthur Goldreich, Ahmed Kathrada, and ANC leader Walter Sisulu.[543]

---

[541] "John Minto to Visit Abahlali baseMjondolo."
[542] King, "Letter From Birmingham."
[543] Linder, "Nelson Mandela Trial."

The raid discovered a plan for the terrorist campaign known as Operation Mayibuye, drafted by the ANC National High Command. The defendants contended that Operation Mayibuye had not been formally adopted by the High Command and was only under consideration. Mandela, who was already in jail, insisted that it was a "draft document" which he did not consider realistic. However, Mandela always also insisted on not being a communist, a lie that has only recently been exposed by documents proving that Mandela was indeed a senior member of the Communist Party.

It is significant that the plan was designed to cause such chaos as to motivate military intervention from the United Nations, through South West Africa.[544]

Mandela had been jailed in 1962 for inciting a general strike in 1960. This had met with less support than expected. The failure prompted him to state that "the days of non-violent struggle were over." Mandela was among the first to urge the ANC to take a violent course. It was Mandela's prompting that persuaded the ANC to establish the guerrilla organization, *Umkhonto we Sizwe*. Douglas Linder states of this:

> *In June 1961, Mandela sent to South African newspapers a letter warning that a new campaign would be launched unless the government agreed to call for a national constitutional convention. Knowing that no such call would be forthcoming, Mandela retreated to the Rivonia hideout to begin planning, with other supporters, a sabotage campaign. The campaign began on December 16, 1961 when Umkhonto we Sizwe saboteurs lit explosives at an electricity sub-station. Dozens of other acts of sabotage followed over the next eighteen months. (Indeed, the government would allege the defendants committed 235 separate acts of sabotage.) It is significant that the sabotage included attacks on government posts, machines, and power facilities, as well as deliberate crop burning.*[545]

In February 1962, Mandela left South Africa to gather support from states, including six months training in guerrilla warfare in Ethiopia. He was arrested shortly after his return to South Africa.

In July 1963, Mandela was called into a Pretoria prison office where he met ten others. He and these others became known as the "Rivonia 11."

---

[544] "Operation Mayibuye."
[545] Ibid.

They included seven captured at Rivonia, two who were previously detained (Andrew Mlangeni and Elias Motsoaledi), and James Kantor, an attorney.[546] ANC lawyer, Harold Wolpe, and Arthur Goldreich had evaded arrest.

Mandela's statement from the dock is a declaration of violent intent:

> *At the beginning of June 1961, after a long and anxious assessment of the South African situation, I, and some colleagues, came to the conclusion that as violence in this country was inevitable, it would be unrealistic and wrong for African leaders to continue preaching peace and non-violence at a time when the Government met our peaceful demands with force. This conclusion was not easily arrived at. It was only when all else had failed, when all channels of peaceful protest had been barred to us, that the decision was made to embark on violent forms of political struggle, and to form Umkhonto we Sizwe.*[547]

ANC chief Sisulu testified that Operation Mayibuye was formulated by Arthur Goldreich, a member of the High Command and a veteran of the Zionist terrorist underground in Palestine during the British Mandate. Sisulu stated that sabotage would be needed but that there was no intention to kill anybody. The judge pointed out that a passerby had been killed by an explosion at a post office, but Sisulu was content to say what amounts to "shit happens."

Justice de Wet concluded that "beyond doubt Nelson Mandela had been the leading spirit behind the creation of *Umkhonto we Sizwe*," and that "Operation Mayibuye comprised a detailed plan for waging guerrilla war intended to culminate in full scale revolt against the Government of South Africa."[548]

It was because of international pressure that the defendants were sentenced to life imprisonment rather than hanged, Justice de Wet stating that he "decided not to impose the supreme penalty," although it was "the proper penalty for the crime...The sentence in the case of all of the accused will be one of life imprisonment."[549] Of course such leniency did not do South Africa a jot of good, and one has heard nothing other than how Mandela was wronged. All the defendants broke into smiles, and Mandela

---

[546] Ibid.
[547] Ibid.
[548] Ibid.
[549] Ibid.

gave the thumbs up to his supporters.⁵⁵⁰ As the police wagon drove from the Court house, Mandela gave a clenched fist salute to his chanting supporters.

In 1985, having already released Denis Goldberg, Prime Minister Botha offered Mandela his release if he renounced violence. He refused. The same year the government entered into secret negotiations with Mandela to scuttle their own existence. By 1990, with negotiations ongoing, Mandela was living in a bungalow at Victor Verster Prison. Released that year, he was elected president in 1994.

The myth of Mandela has grown with time, as do many myths about figures acclaimed as gods. Mandela the liar is not so well known. He always denied being a member of the Communist Party. While this writer does not care whether he was a party member, it is part of the myth that Mandela was not a communist but just a sincere democrat who believed in justice for everyone. His denial also means that he was a liar, and if he lied about that, should his protestations about anything else, including those during the Rivonia trial, where he insisted he was not a party member, be trusted? The defendants in the Rivonia trial were very cagey in regard to their association with the Communist Party. In was only in 2012 that the minutes to a 1982 meeting of the Communist Party were found in the private archives of a party official deposited at the University of Cape Town. These papers discuss Mandela's party membership. Membership was kept secret so as not to jeopardize the ANC's relationship with the West.

Umkhonto we Sizwe was established in 1961 after ANC leaders had gone to China and the USSR and obtained support for a guerrilla war. The first attacks were launched on December 16th, 1961. Its campaign of sabotage and bombings over the subsequent three decades claimed the lives of dozens of civilians, and led to the organization being classed as a terrorist group by the USA.

Professor Stephen Ellis, a former researcher for Amnesty International, who is now at the Free University of Amsterdam, having discovered the archives revealing Mandela's senior position in the Communist Party, wrote of "how the ANC's military wing had bomb-making lessons from the IRA, and intelligence training from the East German Stasi, which it used to carry out brutal interrogations of suspected 'spies' at secret prison camps." Ellis writes that:

---

[550] Ibid.

I think most people who supported the anti-apartheid movement just didn't want to know that much about his background. Apartheid was seen as a moral issue and that was that. But if real proof had been produced at the time, some might have thought differently.[551]

"The ANC's campaign of sabotage and bombings over the subsequent three decades claimed the lives of dozens of civilians, and led to the organization being classed as a terrorist group by the U.S,"[552] states *The Telegraph* report on Ellis' book. However, such a designation by the State Department means little or nothing, and such an organization might nonetheless receive backing from the USA. Such a designation can quickly change should the organization become useful to US foreign policy or commercial interests.

In Angola the ANC had a notorious detention center, Quatro, where dozens of the movement's own supporters were tortured and sometimes killed as suspected spies by agents from their internal security service, some of whom were "barely teenagers." East German instructors taught the internal security agents that anyone who challenged official ANC dogma should be viewed as a potential spy or traitor.[553]

If anyone would be startled and perplexed that the ANC could do such things, it is only because generations have been reared on the fantasy that real angels have black faces—the blackest of all being Nelson Mandela[554]—and the color of the Devil is white.

The Nelson Mandela Foundation went into denial mode when confronted with the evidence:

On Friday night, a spokesman for the Nelson Mandela Foundation said: "We do not believe that there is proof that Madiba (Mandela's clan name) was a Party member...The evidence that has been identified is comparatively weak in relation to the evidence against, not least Madiba's consistent denial of the fact over nearly 50 years. It is conceivable that Madiba might indulge in legalistic casuistry, but not that he would make an entirely false statement."[555]

---

[551] Freeman, "Nelson Mandela Proven."
[552] Ibid.
[553] Ibid.
[554] Only in a metaphorical sense, as Mandela is "high yellow" with a mongoloid eyefold indicating Hottentot descent.
[555] Freeman, "Nelson Mandela Proven."

Whether Mandela was a communist is largely an irrelevant point, however, in comparison to Mandela's legacy of helping to bring ruin to the Afrikaners, who have spent most of their four centuries of existence fighting persecution, while South Africa was pushed onto the path of globalization. While conservatives in the West fretted that South Africa might go communist, that the resources and geopolitical position of South Africa would be brought within the orbit of the Eastern bloc, something far worse eventuated: the Afrikaner was sacrificed on the altar of globalization. Far from the economy being nationalized, it was thrown open to a rapacious global oligarchy. Communism had fulfilled its historic mission as the handmaiden of international capitalism is it has so often.

Multiculturalism and Social Trust: The Social Consequences of Ethnic Diversity

> *"The stranger within my gate,*
> *He may be true or kind,*
> *But he does not talk my talk—*
> *I cannot feel his mind.*
> *I see his face and the eyes and the mouth,*
> *But not the soul behind.*
> *The men of my own stock,*
> *They may do ill or well,*
> *But they tell the lies I am wonted to,*
> *They are used to the lies I tell;*
> *And we do not need interpreters*
> *When we go to buy or sell...."*
>
> Rudyard Kipling (1908)

Apartheid was the Afrikaner means of dealing with deep problems of racial and ethnic difference. While the slogan of "majority rule" became a cliché shouted through the streets and from the UN and other rostrums, saying that a "White minority" was lauding over a "Black" majority is a typical simplification. There was no simple "Black majority." There were 3,600,000 "Whites" of Afrikaner and mainly British descent. There were an equal number of Xhosa. There follows: 3,400,000 Zulu; 1,500,000 South Sotho; 1,400,000 Tswana; 1,200,000 North Sotho; 600,000 Shangaan; 400,000 Swazi; 400,000 Ndebele; 300,000 Venda; 300,000 Bantu groups; 1,900,000 Coloureds; 600,000 Asians.[556]

---

[556] de Villiers, *Case for South Africa*, 23.

To claim that these groups were all "Blacks" is not simply in error but maliciously dishonest. Not only are these races and ethnicities different each from the other, but they have a deep hostility or distrust, and no great desire to mix. The apartheid doctrine sought to achieve maximum "separate development" based on the creation of territorial homelands. This policy was successfully fulfilled in the creation in 1963 of the Xhosa states, the Transkei, and the Ciskei. The reaction of the UN General Assembly was a resolution calling the Transkei a "sham."[557] The other autonomous homelands were: Bophuthatswana, Venda, KwaZulu, Lebowa, QwaQwa; and in South West Africa: Ovamboland, Kavangoland, and East Caprivi. These were abolished by the ANC regime in 1994.

Kaiser Matanzima, Prime Minister of the Transkei, stated in the Xhosa Parliament:

We are busy implementing as system of government in South Africa founded on this policy of separate development. We wholeheartedly endorse this as being the only policy whereby the different races in South Africa can live side by side in peace and harmony.[558]

In 1969 the Transkei Minister of the Interior, Curnick Ndamse, a scholar of anthropology, stated, *"Without apartheid, with a general multi-racial free-for-all, we would be lost within a decade as a people, and our territory would be gone."*[559]

Dr. Verwoerd had lectured as a professor of sociology and psychology at the University of Stellenbosch. He applied his training to the problems of South Africa. He sought to build a state on the basis of sociological and anthropological realities. His unfilled long-term aim had been to build separate homelands of sufficient viability to enable the halting of migratory labor to the cities;[560] precisely the situation that Oppenheimer and the oligarchy opposed while they posed as the friends of the Blacks.

"Diversity is strength," "Unity in diversity"; such clichéd terms have become the slogans for social revolution. They are regurgitated with the backing of press, pulpit, and parliament, and protected from questioning with draconian laws; hence they become part of a secular unholy writ. Yet history, sociology, and ethnography do not support the dogmatic

---

[557] "U. N. General Assembly, Resolution A/RES/31/6 A."
[558] Quoted by de Villiers, 57.
[559] Ibid.
[560] Goodson, "Hendrik Verwoerd," 28.

assertions.[561] In this chapter we consider a meta-analysis that has been recently undertaken of all of the primary studies on ethnic diversity. The analysis finds that ethnic diversity, far from strengthening a society, increases social distrust. The reply of the Establishment will be increasingly repressive laws, and perhaps even the compulsory mediation of irredeemable racists.

An extensive "meta-analytical review" of hundreds of studies on the impact of ethnic diversity on "social trust" indicates that there is something gravely amiss about the sloganeering of politicians and academics and their plutocratic sponsors on the supposed benefits of multiculturalism and ethnic diversity. Plain sense, whether by instinct or intuition or anecdotal observation, obliges many to look in askance when experiences contradict dogma. However, the plebs are assured that this is only due to their innate racism, which is supposedly indicative of a psychological imbalance, that can be fixed by a variety of methods such as self-criticism, indoctrination, "education," and for the unreconstructed, jail terms, public humiliation, and even medication.

Of the latter alarming possibilities, a group of scientists at Oxford University found that implicit racial bias can be reduced by the use of the heart medication propranolol, which blocks "activation in the peripheral 'autonomic' nervous system." 'Professor Julian Savulescu of Oxford University's Faculty of Philosophy, a co-author, added: "Such research raises the tantalizing possibility that our unconscious racial attitudes could be modulated using drugs, a possibility that requires careful ethical analysis."[562]

What seems to be discarded as irrelevant by these scientists is the possibility that such "implicit racial bias," existing at an unconscious level, is likely to be a *survival mechanism* descended over millennia. But if such possibilities confound modern dogma on equality multiculturalism, human oneness, and the imagined efficiency of a global market place, such "racism" is an impediment that should be eliminated in neo-Jacobin style, and like the sociopathic Jacobin and Bolshevik intelligentsia of 1789 and 1917, methods become increasingly extreme when the dogma does not accord with the reality.

What the Oxford tests do indicate (albeit the number of subjects was small) is that "implicit racism" is biologically innate, and hence the widespread and persistent phenomena of "social distrust" in multicultural societies is likely to be an innate part of the "autonomic nervous system."

---

[561] For the consequences of multiculturalism on civilizations see: Bolton, *The Decline and Fall of Civilisations*.
[562] "Drug Reduces Implicit Racial Bias."

It could be that this persistent and congenital illness might be cured by placing huge amounts of propranolol in public water supplies along with fluoride and chloride, as a means of compulsory mass medication. Since "racism" is regarded to be pathogenic it would be justifiable as a public health issue.

The meta-analytical review of hundreds of studies on "social trust" in multicultural societies shows the sociological manifestation of what the Oxford scientists have discerned biologically. The study is called "Ethnic Diversity and Social Trust: A Narrative and Meta-Analytical Review." It has been published online as a preliminary to being published in the *Annual Review of Political Science* (Volume 23, 2020).[563] The authors are Peter Thirsted Dinesen, Professor, Department of Political Science, University of Copenhagen; Merlin Schaeffer, Associate Professor of Sociology, University of Copenhagen; and Kim Mannemar Sønderskov, Professor of Political Science at Aarhus University.

The paper is written from a sociological perspective, without an input from other disciplines, such as the biological or psychological, but unlike many such studies from the social sciences we are spared gratuitous moralizing from the authors.

Some Preliminary Thoughts

Of the many studies cited by the meta-analytical review one of the most significant and earliest, because the study was based on forty communities and thirty thousand individuals in the USA, is by Dr. Robert D. Putnam, political scientist at Harvard University.

Putnam's 2007 study found that ethnic diversity causes a decrease in community trust, engendering feelings of powerlessness and alienation, but Putnam seeks to show that nonetheless in the long-term assimilation of immigrants and ethnic groups will pay good dividends.[564] When Putnam and other social scientists do not get the result they wish for from empirical studies, they nonetheless claim to remain optimistic that ethnic diversity can be made to work. They often do so by looking for examples in contrived situations, where common interests might be created that can at least temporarily or partially circumvent the outcomes of normal circumstances. Hence, domesticated cats and dogs raised under special circumstances in a household might "prove" that there can be a future

---

[563] Dinesen, Schaeffer, and Sønderskov, "Ethnic Diversity."
[564] Putnam,"E Pluribus Unum," 137-174.

world where cats and dogs can not only tolerate each other, but can become "friends" and overcome their primal "implicit *specism*"; a world moreover where one day the lamb might lay down with the lion. Putnam gave an optimistic view (from the liberal perspective) that his study on social fragmentation caused by ethnic diversity among thirty thousand individuals across forty communities, can nevertheless be circumvented by the very limited and specific examples of such contrived situations as military and religious institutions. He wrote:

> *In the long run, however, successful immigrant societies have overcome such fragmentation by creating new, cross-cutting forms of social solidarity and more encompassing identities. Illustrations of becoming comfortable with diversity are drawn from the US military, religious institutions, and earlier waves of American immigration.*[565]

Putnam is using what amounts to *associative theory* to conjure the prospect of intentional communities that can override ethnic division, such as the accord that might exist in a multi-ethnic sports team. But *associative theory* is based on the dictum, *like attracts like*, and ethnicity remains a constant, and one might question the costs when attempts are made to forcibly remove such constants not only from the human conscious but also from the unconscious. That is to say, what is the cost of trying to reshape what has been innate to *homo sapiens* for tens of millennia? It will become the same type of cost that has expended the blood of around hundred million in the quest to perfect communism, and is should be kept in mind that communism and liberalism are premised on the same belief in the perfectibility of humanity through the manipulation of social forces.

Putnam's hope that situations will unfold for inter-ethnic harmony contrary to his own findings, can reasonably be expected to be the hope of social scientists in general. The paper by Dinesen, et al., however, refreshingly does not attempt to draw moral conclusions from their analysis of data.

Putnam cites situational communities such as "religious institutions" and the military. Such situational communities might in themselves take on the traits on an ethnic community. The situation for the forming of the institution, group, or community itself creates "in-group" solidarity and identity relative to an out-group, and such traits of an ethnos might indeed

---

[565] Ibid., Abstract.

transcend a biological "race." Hence, the Marine Corps has its own ethos, mythos, structure, history, and purpose regardless of its racial composition, relative to non-Marines. The same situation pertains to monastic monks, or college fraternities. A "nation" and society might indeed be built up by an amalgam of ethnicities, into a new ethnos, if the nation and state building processes are strong enough, and in particular if they can find a common in-group ethos relative to a perceived out-group. Jews and Judaism are an obvious and particularly strong example. A corporation might develop a similar in-group ethos among its employees, cutting across other bonds. Nation-states might also be built and maintained by developing a sufficiently strong *symbiotic* bond through the symbiosis of otherwise separate ethnicities.

Singapore: Multi-Ethnic Symbiosis Through Separation

Singapore is an example of this, where different ethnicities are given a large degree of autonomy. Singapore is a "multiracial nation" that maintains separate identities in an organic relationship, as South Africa attempted to do in its own way under apartheid. Singapore has an ethos that is far from liberal, nor is it the "one nation" melting pot policy that has become a mainstay of some parties regarded as "conservative." It is ironic that the very justification that many prominent advocates of "ethnic diversity" use in regard to its being beneficial to a powerful economy, are rejected by an economy that is particularly successful. A Singaporean news report stated on the Prime Minister's remarks on the state's policy:

> *Singapore is not a melting pot, but a society where each race is encouraged to preserve its unique culture and traditions, and appreciate and respect that of others, Prime Minister Lee Hsien Loong said on Friday (May 19). No race or culture is coerced into conforming with other identities, let alone that of the majority, he added. In fostering such an approach for a multiracial, multireligious society rooted in its Asian cultures, Singaporeans also need the arts and culture "to nourish our souls," Mr. Lee said. "We certainly don't wish Singapore to be a first-world economy but a third-rate society, with a people who are well off but uncouth," he said. "We want to be a society rich in spirit, a gracious society where people are considerate and kind to one*

another, and as Mencius said, where we treat all elders as we treat our own parents, and other children as our own."[566]

This is not to say that Singapore offers a universal template for ethnic relations, but that is exactly the point: there is no universal template, but liberal social scientists, politicians, and businessmen generally start from the predicate of the desirability of a melting-pot within the context of globalization, held together by production and consumption; what a real conservative, Thomas Carlyle critiqued in Britain under free trade as the cash nexus and the rule of *Mammon*.[567] Books such as *The Global Me*[568] are written by economic commentators for popular consumption, showing that the rootless individual who can be transplanted across the world according to the requirements of global business, is the wave of the future, and the guarantee for individual, national, and corporate prosperity: *Homo Economicus*.

Singapore is remarkable in many ways, and is the antithesis of the universal model upheld by liberal academic, politicians, and plutocrats. In particular, the Singaporean state upholds that strong, authoritarian sense of identity and culture that is antithetical to liberal and globalist ideology, by ensuring that material wealth does not erode a national spirit. As *The Straits Times* article goes on to state of Mr. Lee, within the context of Chinese, Malay, and Eurasian cultures, each are developing their own Singaporean distinctiveness, within the broader context of the Singaporean national identity. However, Singapore's experience is unique, as was the Afrikaners' in trying to maintain their identity while faced with the double-headed hydra of communism and plutocracy.

Additionally, when under tension are the situational communities referred to by Putnam necessarily able to maintain their stability as well as those who are not forced into such a heterogeneous relationship? The loyalty of a military under tension when drawn from disparate sources has always been a matter of concern for rulers. A paper on the Black experience in Vietnam states:

> *One of the least known but most important chapters in the history of America's encounter with Vietnam was the internal rebellion that wracked the US military. From the Long Binh jail*

---

[566] "Singapore's Approach To Diversity."
[567] Thomas Carlyle, *Past and Present*. "One thing I do know," wrote Carlyle, *"Never, on this Earth, was the relation of man to man long carried on by Cash-payment alone."* (Chapter X, 258). Those who today imagine that Whig-liberalism and the defence of free trade capitalism is conservatism, should read Carlyle.
[568] Zachary, *The Global Me*.

in Vietnam, to Travis Air Force Base in California, to aircraft carriers in the South China Sea, the armed forces faced widespread resistance and unrest. Throughout the military morale and discipline sank to record lows. Antiwar committee and underground newspapers appeared everywhere. Unauthorized absence rates reached unprecedented levels: in the Army in 1971 there were seventeen AWOLs and seven desertions for every one hundred soldiers. Harsher forms of rebellion also occurred— drug abuse, violent uprisings, refusal of orders, even attacks against superiors. The cumulative result of this resistance within the ranks was a severe breakdown in military effectiveness and combat capability. By 1969 the Army had ceased to function as an effective fighting force and was rapidly disintegrating. The armed forces had to be withdrawn from Indochina for their very survival. The strongest and most militant resisters were black GIs. Of all the soldiers of the Vietnam era, black and other minority GIs were consistently the most active in their opposition to the war and military injustice. Blacks faced greater oppression than whites, and they fought back with greater determination and anger. The rebellions that shook American cities like Watts, Newark, and Detroit erupted at major military installations just a few years later. The result was a military torn by racial rebellion.[569]

The "Black experience" in the USA was far removed from being capable of inculcating in Black GIs a kinship with one's comrades against the ostensible "outer." Indeed, the outer to the Black GI was the White GI, and there was a kinship with the Vietcong. The sense of what it meant to be an "American" was and remains too nebulous to give any sense of common meaning even in as tightly controlled structure as the military. If the authority, hierarchy, and discipline of the military, even when confronted by a hostile "out-group" is insufficient in shaping an in-group with the broad attributes of an ethnos, to what extent will social scientists, politicians, and plutocrats resort [to a leveling tyranny] to achieve their aims? Today's social engineers in academia, politics, and business are the heirs of the Jacobin and the Bolshevik doctrines that have spilled more blood in the pursuit of a global utopia in the name of equality, than any other creed.

---

[569] Cortrwright, "Black GI Resistance."

The Review

The question posed by the review of Dinesen, et al., is: "Does ethnic diversity erode social trust"?[570] It is stated that there have been many studies on the question over twenty-five years, with a plethora of different findings. The meta-analysis aims to find common patterns by analyzing data from the literature covering 1001 estimates from eighty-seven studies.[571]

There are several definitions of social trust examined: (1) generalized social trust (strangers); (2) out-group trust; (3) in-group trust; (4) trust in neighbors.[572]

The "key debates in the literature" involve:

Debate 1. Why does ethnic diversity erode trust? The question posed is why the closer the proximity of out-groups the more consequential it is for social trust?

A 2015 study by two of the review's authors, Dinesen and Sønderskov, had found that "mere exposure to people of different ethnic backgrounds erodes social trust." This is related to the concept of out-group aversion. "Shared norms" and other factors impact on this,[573] and it is shared norms that are a distinctive feature of what defines an ethnos.

One might question the clichés large businesses and governmental agencies like to purvey about being "inclusive," "diverse," and the strength that these provide to corporate structures. If a high-tech corporation in the USA employs a significant number of high-tech specialists from say India and then lauds the benefits such "diversity" has brought to the corporation, can it really be said that this has been the benefit of ethnic diversity, or that it has been the benefit of employing those who are especially advanced in the particular areas of expertise required by the business? Rather than there being "diversity," there will be a common corporate culture, with shared corporate values and aims. Where Pascal Zachary's "global me" comes into such situations, is through the ease by which individuals with the needed qualifications can be transplanted around the world in accordance with the requirements of global capital and technology. As is normally the case when dealing with the predicament of the modern era the criterion for "success" is that of money. Any notion of what it is to be an "American" for example was and remains

---

[570] Dinesen, "Ethnic Diversity," op. cit., 1.
[571] Ibid., Abstract.
[572] Ibid., 1-2.
[573] Ibid., 3.

too nebulous to assure a sense of camaraderie among Black and White GI's even in times of war, and indeed especially in times of war, when added stresses are placed upon a diverse population. Where then is there the oft-proclaimed "unity in diversity"? The Black predation upon Whites during catastrophes such as Hurricane Katrina shows the fragility of grandiose liberal notions. In such circumstances what the study refers to as "conflict theory" and "group competition"[574] is liable to shatter the fragile facade of civility that might exist under normal circumstances.

The authors also refer to "in-group trust" increasing when there is a perception of being "surrounded by more ethnic out-groups."[575] There might also arise feelings of isolation or alienation—"constrict theory"[576]—as one becomes increasingly surrounded by ethnic aliens, some studies referring to "people's inherent preference to interact with people like themselves."[577]

Debate 2: Can contact alleviate the negative effect of ethnic diversity? Here "contact theory"[578] postulates that we could all get along in a multicultural utopia if we all just sought our friends from different races, and that the positive experiences would destroy any prejudices inherited from the biased generation of our parents and grandparents. "Positive intergroup relations" might be built thereby and "negative stereotypes" reduced.[579] It is here where the propagandists for multiculturalism can be at their most fervent, producing streams of entertainment depicting the joys of having ethnically diverse pools of friends and work colleagues; where the power of friendship overcomes small town bigotry etc.

Interestingly, the authors pose the question as to whether "out-group trust" might conversely reduce "in-group trust."[580] The implication is that ethnic diversity can subvert in-group solidarity.

---

[574] Dinesen, op. cit., 3.
[575] Ibid.
[576] Ibid.
[577] Ibid.
[578] Ibid., 4.
[579] Ibid.
[580] Ibid., 5.

The Sociology of Snowflake Liberalism

"Revenge sits within your soul: a black scab grows wherever you bite; with revenge your poison makes the soul giddy!
 Thus do I speak to you in parables, you who make the soul giddy, you preachers of equality! You are tarantulas and dealers in hidden revengefulness!
 You preachers of equality, thus from you the tyrant-madness of impotence cries for 'equality': thus your most secret tyrant-appetite disguises itself in words of virtue."

Friedrich Nietzsche (1969)[581]

Is liberal sensitivity a neurotic syndrome based on rationalized narcissism, rather than a laudable trait that creates a tolerant and inclusive society? The histrionic character of liberals, which is so easily triggered, suggests an intolerance and bigotry that they project onto others. The syndrome might become aggravated to the point of psychosis of the type that, in the name of social justice, leads Jim Jones to dish out the Kool Aid, Pol Pot to fertilize the Killing Fields with the blood of class enemies, and Robespierre to crank up the guillotines. Is there a little Pol Pot or Jim Jones in every snowflake liberal, awaiting the opportunity to manifest?

A recent empirical analysis, the first of its type, examines what the study's author, Professor Jeremy Bernerth, Department of Management, San Diego State University, terms the *Proclivity to Be Offended* (PTBO).[582] Bernerth examines the consequences of this syndrome from the perspective of how it impacts on business efficiency and personnel relations.

---

[581] Nietzsche, "Of the Tarantulas," *Thus Spoke Zarathustra*, 123.
[582] Bernerth, "You're Offended, I'm Offended."

While it can easily and widely be observed that what is popularly called the "Snowflake" syndrome often manifests as *histrionic personality disorder* (seeking attention through excessive emotional reactions), PTBO acts more subtlety and pervasively.

Paving the Way for De-Normalization

Narcissism, hysteria, sociopathy, and other mental disorders tend to cluster around adherents to leftist ideologies including liberalism.[583] Certain notables of the Frankfurt School of Critical Theory and other neo- and post-Marxists such as Louis Althusser, rationalized their *Oedipal* anxieties into ideologies of social conflict, for example. The Marquis de Sade placed an ideological facade over his sociopathic manias and was heralded by Jacobin France.[584]

Several generations have been mentally reprogrammed to respond with degrees of offence like Pavlovian dogs, to stressor words such as "racism." On a basic, grassroots level, this widespread mental disturbance is often perceived as "political correctness," and when manifested histrionically the term "Snowflake" has come into the popular lexicon to describe bizarre phenomena that became increasingly apparent after the Trump election.

A human relations industry has grown around the associated area of "unconscious bias." Corporations expend time, energy, and money attempting to address what are regarded not only as conscious, but even as unconscious prejudices in the name of "good corporate citizenship." The human relations industry emerged from the "sensitivity training" and "group therapy" ideas that become popular during the 1960s and 1970s as a new form of psychotherapy, as forms of mind manipulation. Generations have been inculcated with a culture of grievance, as victims or as perpetrators, the latter mostly being termed "unconscious bias," resulting in self-censorship, self-recrimination, and what would otherwise be regarded by psychiatrists as self-negating, self-destructive thinking. There is a term for it that was used by communist China and Bolshevik Russia: *self-criticism*. The same techniques entered the West decades ago as "human relations."[585]

Although Bernerth does not address the matter, it would seem that PTBO might be the result of several generations of the reinforcement of

---

[583] Bolton, *The Psychotic Left*.
[584] Ibid., 64. For de Sade, Critical Theorists et al, see Bolton, *The Perversion of Normality*.
[585] Zelevansky, "The Big Business."

beliefs of entitlement and protection from hitherto common factors of life that once toughened the individual physically and psychologically.

An assault on normality was initiated by the Frankfurt School of neo-Marxist and post-Marxist social scientists who produced well-funded studies intended to show that the *cause* of mass psychosis, including "fascism," which could be measured on an "F scale," is the *White patriarchal family*.[586] Note that it was only the family institution that was "White" that was the "problem." Margaret Mead was sent by her mentor, Franz Boas, dean of cultural anthropology at Columbia University, whose protégés came to dominate cultural anthropology, to Samoa to prepare a study that would show how vastly superior Samoan society was to the Western, because its youth supposedly grew up free of authoritarian patriarchy, in the bliss of the carefree noble savage.[587] Since then, we in New Zealand for example, are often told how much *Pakeha* can learn from the Maori concept of *whanau* (extended family), despite the high rates of child abuse and family breakdown among Maoris, which is blamed on "colonialism" and "neo-colonialism."

There were many others such as Gunnar Myrdal's *American Dilemma* (1944) on race and Alfred Kinsey's sexology; deeply flawed studies intended to subvert what remained of Western traditions. So far from being sidelined as the preoccupations of a few eccentrics, such ideas percolated within institutions such as Columbia University, which received influential patronage from the Ford, Carnegie, and Rockefeller Foundations, and became the mainstream discourse throughout all levels of society.

White self-doubt became White self-loathing, White repentance, and White self-abnegation. There is none that becomes so outraged as a self-loathing White liberal. These are the psychological types who will become the pervasive network of informers at your workplace, bar, or café, who will report to state bureaucrats on overheard jokes or comments that might be deemed "hate speech."

PTBO Survey

Bernerth's concern is the impact this hyper sensitivity has on business relations. A survey was completed by 395 individuals, with an average age of 25.9 years and an average job tenure of 3.6 years. Of the whole group,

---

[586] Adorno., *Authoritarian Personality*.
[587] Mead, *Coming of Age*.

54.6 percent indicated they were male; 70 percent indicated they were White; 10.9 percent Black, 9 percent Hispanic; 6.5 percent Asian; 3.6 percent other. Questions involved job satisfaction and employee engagement to the job. The aim was to measure the degree of dissatisfaction from feelings of "offence" that interfered with full commitment to one's job. This includes cognitive *interference theory*. As the name suggests, *cognitive interference* involves the intrusion of unconscious thoughts into consciousness, diminishing ability to focus on an immediate task. The survey sought to measure not moral outrage towards a specific event, but a more generalized attitude.

1= Not at all offensive
2= Indifferent or neutral
3= Somewhat offensive
4= Offensive
5= Extremely offensive

These were measured against reaction to events/topics on a scale of 1 to 5:

1. The term Washington "Redskins"
2. Wearing a shirt that has an American flag on Cinco de Mayo
3. Telling someone to "man up"
4. Dressing up as an American Indian for Halloween
5. Saying "God bless you" after someone sneezes
6. The playing of the USA National Anthem
7. Believing that individuals who do not have legal status to be in a country should be deported
8. Using the term Islamic terrorist[588]

Bernerth in introducing his paper writes that the problem considered is that:

Managers are increasingly working in politically charged contexts. Polls show citizens of many countries are more polarized today than ever before and that these political divisions increasingly arise in and affect the workplace. As political divisions grow, so too do reports of people taking offense to politically or socially sensitive events and issues.[589]

---

[588] Bernerth, "You're Offended, I'm Offended."
[589] Ibid., 314.

Corporations want to be "inclusive" within the context of a global economy where profit maximization is hampered by vestiges of customs and traditions hindering the development of the global marketplace. Bernerth's study looks at the way the broader agendas of "political correctness" seem to have induced and reinforced neurotic attitudes among individuals towards issues that were until recently regarded as trivial.

Political Correctness

Bernerth continues:

> *Whereas acquiescing to these sensitivities is lauded by some as "a force for promoting positive social outcomes," others call into question the altruistic portrayal of outrage over perceived social injustices. This divergence of views translates into two contrasting perspectives regarding the implications for employees and organizations: one perspective holds that proactively limiting perceived injustices and offenses may benefit both employees and organizations as it helps employees to adaptively respond to the environment and thus advance their careers, while organizations likewise benefit as they send a message to the public that they are concerned with redressing historical injustices and thus attract better applicants and a larger proportion of the market. The other perspective suggests individuals and organizations are overly sensitive, and that "politically correct" stances and behaviors stifle communication and distract the individual and organization from developing competencies.*[590]

Bernerth finds that—like the Dinesen study on social trust and diversity—liberal theories do not achieve the assumed results. By pandering to the neuroses of the perpetually offended, despite the amount of time, energy and money, there is a lack of evidence that the "capital expenditures are necessary or beneficial."[591] The result has been to reinforce and to multiply feelings of grievance, "including the increasingly common tendency to be offended by a vast array of events and traditions."[592]

---

[590] Ibid.
[591] Ibid.
[592] Ibid.

Bernerth's concern is to examine how PTBO as a hitherto unexplored form of *cognitive interference* intrudes on and disrupts employee performance. So far, the tendency has been to attempt to eliminate *cognitive interference* with the use of, "team building" (*sensitivity training*), by eliminating both conscious and "unconscious bias" while pandering to the perceptions of the offended.

That such coercive and accusatory techniques might cause *cognitive interference* among those being subjected to mental, moral, and even religious deconstruction does not seem to be considered. In other words, is a backlash of resentment being created among those who are unjustly accused of "unconscious bias"? Presumably the political and economic interests intent on eliminating "unconscious bias" are confident that a combination of repressive laws and indoctrination at all levels of society will eliminate residual dissent, and become "thought crime."

What must be exorcised from every employee is any discernible vestige—including especially that of the "unconscious" variety—of bias at which someone might take offence, on the condition that the target will always be someone holding hitherto normal values, usually referred to as "White," "male," and "patriarchal," or anyone retaining a traditional outlook; such customs and values having long been deemed as high on the "F scale" (Adorno, et al.) and in need of elimination.

Offended by Trivia

The empirical study of PTBO specifically examines the "tendency to be sensitive to customarily innocuous societal events and traditions." Bernerth gives the example of the playing of the US National Anthem; once a source of pride, but now a symbol of "oppression" for an increasing number. It is important to note that PTBO is not considering any single tradition or event but such examples as part of a syndrome of offence towards an array of issues and differs from "moral outrage" (feelings of anger directed at third party transgressors).[593]

PTBO resides permanently as an intrusive element of the unconscious intruding on the consciousness, and triggered by an array of individually perceived issues. Hence institutions including workplaces might be perceived as intrinsically unjust and pervaded with "unconscious bias." As a form of *cognitive interference*, "off-task thoughts interfere with concentration and performance by drawing limited processing and sense-

---

[593] Ibid, 315.

making resources away from task-relevant stimuli to task-irrelevant stimuli."594 PTBO is both a *stressor* and a *task-irrelevant stimuli*, interfering with "reasoning abilities and memory retrieval processes." "Additional research indicates worrisome thoughts have a peremptory power, taking precedence over other areas and priming one to focus on aspects of the stimuli not perceived or felt by other."595 It is with the latter, that of stressors and stimuli "not perceived or felt by others," that such concepts as "unconscious bias" and "White privilege" or the "patriarchy" are part of the itinerary of the thought control techniques used by "human relations experts."

Might it not then be asked whether such measures are *reinforcing* the syndrome and are having an adverse impact on those with PTBO who are supposedly being helped, while creating resentment or self-loathing and even alienation among those who are being scapegoated and accused?

Bernerth writes of this *cognitive interference* in the workplace:

*The proclivity to see offense in ordinarily innocuous events, as a result, likely gets in the way of effective task performance as being offended diverts attentional resources away from task-relevant cues and requirements towards the processing of peripheral or secondary cues. The offensive event competes with and impairs task-relevant thoughts and actions by reducing the amount of accessible cognitive resources. Rather than focusing on task requirements, those high in PTBO are distracted by perceived offenses that seem unjust; moreover, existing research indicates being distracted by worrisome thoughts creates a feeling of helplessness as divided attention prohibits resolving actions.*596

Bernerth concludes that those with PTBO make poor employees. Perhaps this is among the variables that account for areas where women and "ethnics" are said to be underrepresented, rather than being a result of "unconscious bias," "discrimination," "White patriarchy" etc. PTBO can be so obsessive that a "woman of color" for example might be offended if she is asked for her opinion as a "black woman," while also being offended if her uniqueness is *not* recognized. This is the type of scenario that is described among the human relations industry. Hence, a "damned if you do, damned if you don't" pattern emerges not only for employers but at

---
594 Ibid.
595 Ibid.
596 Ibid., 315-316.

least as much for employees who are White generally, and White males particularly.

Teambuilding and Citizenship

As seen with the study of the data on social trust and multiculturalism (Dinesen, et al), the supposed "unity in diversity" that is lauded is also shown by studies on PTBO to impact negatively on workplace team building. Might it not therefore be stated that what applies to the sociology of a business also applies to society generally? When agitated this seething PTBO can erupt into mass violence, as seen by the George Floyd/BLM riots. When Bernerth writes of the "citizenship" standards required for a successful workplace "team," we might apply that to the requirements for the building of a nation as a "team." The team spirit whether in a business or in a nation is undermined by widespread PTBO. One might see how a society could be deliberately undermined by encouraging PTBO among suggestible elements.

Bernerth makes such an analogy between corporate and social teambuilding and the requirements of reciprocation:

> *As individually-aimed citizenship behavior requires an awareness of the needs of others, it seems those with a proclivity to be offended may not pick up cues suggesting help is needed and/or not have the available resources needed to help. Citizenship behaviors may also (and frequently are) aimed at the broader organization. Sportsmanship, for instance, represents an employee's tolerance or willingness to overlook problematic work characteristics and maintain a focus on resolving task demands. Other key sporting behaviors include avoiding complaints about trivial matters and "making mountains out of molehills." Recent media reports suggest those who take offense to social issues and events are increasingly vocal—a pattern likely repeated within organizations.*[597]

Where such team building is sought by a corporation or a state or local government department, via "human relations seminars," for example, the assumption is that behavior modification is required not for those with PTBO but to the contrary for those who are deemed to be showing insufficient deference (including "unconsciously") towards the perpetually

---

[597] Ibid., 316.

offended. The syndrome is thereby reinforced, not dissipated. Where it is undertaken on a nationwide scale, we see laws and campaigns to reinforce PTBO. The current Human Rights Commission campaign "Voices of Racism" serves this purpose, normalizing PTBO by reinforcing neurotic notions about events and comments that would normally be considered harmless, well-intentioned, or insignificant.

So far from placating those with PTBO being helpful Bernerth states that, "both anecdotal and objective data suggests giving in to those individuals expressing the most outrage is not an advisable strategy."[598] Again, one is confronted with the prospect of reinforcing abnormal behavior by accommodation and appeasement. Bernerth suggests that both narcissism and neuroticism are involved.[599]

Repressive Agendas

Bernerth notes a study that suggests "those with a tendency to monitor and scan the environment for threatening information do not live a 'happy-go-lucky' lifestyle."[600] One might say that preoccupation with *finding* events or traditions that can reinforce one's feeling of being offended leads to neurosis; when sufficiently agitated, psychosis, and in the right milieu mass psychosis. Yet, is this not what is encouraged by the Human Rights Commission, or by the government advocating the need for a "hate speech" law?

Bernerth alludes to PTBO being analogous "to a threat of sorts," with those high in PTBO taking more time "processing and making sense of stimuli overlooked or disregarded by many."[601] One is tempted to see this as the mentality behind Human Rights Commissioner Dr. Paul Hunt's melodramatic report on supposed hate crimes in New Zealand, "It Happened Here," based mostly on media accounts, devoid of context.[602]

---

[598] Ibid., 321.
[599] Ibid.
[600] Ibid., 316.
[601] Ibid., 316
[602] Hunt, "It Happened Here."

Behavioral Problems

Bernerth states that:

> The most fundamental implication of this research is the finding that the current trend of taking offense to an array of events and traditions represents an underlying phenomenon and not isolated reactions. Moreover, this state correlates with some of the most important work-related outcomes and in ways one might not expect or predict. For example, **one might assume those who display PTBO are the most helpful in the organization as their prescriptive morality dictates helping and providing for others but study results indicate a negative relationship between PTBO and two different forms of citizenship behavior**. Moreover, PTBO negatively correlated with task performance and positively correlated with counterproductive work behaviors, suggesting not only that these individuals engage in fewer citizenship behaviors but also engage in behaviors managers and organizations want their employees to avoid.[603]

Applying the findings of Bernerth to broader sociological questions, at the most extreme posturing on social issues in the name of "liberty, equality fraternity," "human rights," or "all power to the soviets," has resulted in mass psychosis and social collapse.[604]

---

[603] Bernerth, 320. Emphasis added.
[604] Bolton, *Psychotic Left*.

Pied Pipers

"The Mayor was dumb, and the Council stood
As if they were changed into blocks of wood,
Unable to move a step, or cry
To the children merrily skipping by—
Could only follow with the eye
That joyous crowd at the Piper's back.
But how the Mayor was on the rack,
And the wretched Council's bosoms beat,
As the Piper turned from the High Street
To where the Weser rolled its waters
Right in the way of their sons and daughters!
However he turned from South to West,
And to Coppelburg Hill his steps addressed,
And after him the children pressed;
Great was the joy in every breast.
He never can cross that mighty top!
He's forced to let the piping drop,
And we shall see our children stop!
When, lo, as they reached the mountain's side,
A wondrous portal opened wide,
As if a cavern was suddenly hollowed;
And the Piper advanced and the children follow'd,
And when all were in to the very last,
The door in the mountain side shut fast."

Robert Browning (1842)

Marching beside the Snowflake Syndrome is the new and sudden realization by increasing numbers of young people, and in many cases very young people, that they are not really the gender that has been "assigned" to them by society. While transgenderism has been percolating as a movement since sexology institutes were set up in Weimer Germany a century ago with Marxist affiliations,[605] in the midst of the post-war social and moral breakdown, this has been portrayed as a reasonable extension of the "rights of the child." Like other movements subverting tradition that have been discussed here, the transgender movement has received increasing backing from both the left and the oligarchy as a further means of destroying the primary bond that maintains and advances a cohesive social organism.

The family and traditional gender roles as targets of the plutocratic left nexus have been documented in two previous works by this author: *Revolution from Above*, and *The Perversion of Normality*. In these I have shown how the left and plutocracy are in accord in regarding the family and traditional genders as obstacles to the economic production process, and what plutocratic think tanks today call the "inclusive economy." They both also see the traditional family as an obstacle to total control. I shall not recapitulate here what is explained in detail in those two books. We shall here deal with the movement against the traditional family and gender roles as they relate to the bogus concept of "human rights." This is what gives these movements ideological foundations.

UNICEF—Your Child's "Guardian"

The global moral and legalistic impetus is enshrined in the United Nations Convention on the Rights of the Child.[606] It is concomitant with the broad general worldwide movement against *Homo Europaeus*. UNCIEF's New Zealand branch now focuses on Maoris in keeping with the radical changes that have been taking place in New Zealand at an accelerated rate to obliterate the New Zealand European legacy. Hence, as in so many other sectors of society the name, imagery, and terminology have been changed to reflect the Maori focus of UNDRIP and *He Puapua*:

> *Our role as UNICEF Aotearoa is to be kaitiaki o ngā uri o āpōpō. Guardians of the generations of tomorrow.*

---

[605] Magnus Hirschfield established the Institute for Sexual Science in Berlin in 1919. For an examination of this and its ramifications see: Bolton, *Perversion of Normality*.
[606] "Convention on the Rights of the Child."

> *We support te reo Māori[607] revitalisation and want to ensure that te reo Māori is more visible, particularly for our tamariki and rangatahi (young people). We also value the importance of a Tikanga based approach in how we engage with Māori; and appreciate the significant role and connection Māori share within whānau, hapū and Iwi[608] systems.*
>
> *Our goal is to convey in a powerful and unique way, what UNICEF Aotearoa stands for. We're standing up for children's rights in everything we do. It's about equality, inclusion and recognising that culture is a taonga (treasure) to be cherished.*
>
> *We are committed to honouring Te Tiriti o Waitangi (the Treaty of Waitangi) and recognise the status of Māori as Tangata whenua, as well as the need for organisations such as ours (Tangata Tiriti) to work together with Māori in partnership for outcomes in the participation, potential and, protection of all Tamariki and Rangatahi throughout Aotearoa.*
>
> *In Aotearoa, you'll now see us using our new name UNICEF Aotearoa | mo nga tamariki katoa.*
>
> *We are proud to unveil a new name and brand identity, reflecting the mahi we do every day to protect tamariki in Aotearoa, the Pacific and around the world.[609]*

The absence of images of European children signals that they have become non-persons according to UNICEF Aotearoa. Yet it is the Maoris who have an intricate social-political-economic-cultural network from family to tribe, nationally and locally organized from marae (meeting ground) upward, with representation at every level, corporate assets of over sixty-nine billon, and the advantage of racial quotas in the professions. Nonetheless, Maoris remain at the lowest strata of the social indices, their failings in a Western *growth economy* blamed on "White privilege" and "colonization," rather than the flawed doctrine of global liberal hegemony that victimizes all peoples.

In 2003 the Green Party Member of Parliament, Sue Bradford, whose relationship with communism began as a teenage member of the Progressive Youth Movement,[610] introduced the "anti-smacking bill," which was passed in 2007. It was yet another means of social revolution in the guise of humane welfare, aimed at subverting parental authority in

---

[607] The use of Maori language.
[608] Family, group of families, and tribe.
[609] "UNICEF Aotearoa."
[610] The PYM was the youth front of the Communist Party of New Zealand, aligned with China.

the name of child protection. The Green Party was open in its stating the origins of the bill when alluding to "UN demands":

> *The Greens are designing a bill that will stop parents physically punishing their children, in line with United Nations demands.*
>
> *Green MP Sue Bradford says her bill will repeal Section 59 of the Crimes Act, the provision that condones the use of physical force by parents against children.*
>
> *"We want to end the situation where there is a legal defence to striking a child."*
>
> *A new report from the UN Committee on the Rights of the Child says it is deeply concerned New Zealand has not changed the law which allows parents to use so-called "reasonable" force against their children.*[611]

As with all such rhetoric on "human rights" from Jacobinism onwards, the UN Convention on the Rights of the Child guarantees all manner of protection. Parenthood and family are even the central focus. However, the social revolutionary character of Bradford's bill was barely realized by most, although she hinted at the ramifications as part of the left's culture war. The specter of parents imposing their authority with the use of violence, the institution of the traditional family as violent and authoritarian, the insinuations about parenthood predicated on brutality, and the need for draconian laws to place the state as the guardians of the child vis-à-vis the parents, are implicit in Bradford's justifications for the bill:

> *Ms. Bradford said today parents have used Section 59 to get away with, not only smacking their children, but also whacking them with bits of wood and other objects.*
>
> *"I can't understand why the Government is delaying doing anything about Section 59 until the next election year. The safety and welfare of our children is too important to put on hold."*
>
> *"Parents are supposed to be protectors, not attackers, and children should feel totally safe at home. Section 59 adds to the whole culture of abuse of children that is still so rampant in New Zealand society."*[612]

---

[611] "Greens Draw Up Their Own Anti-Smacking Bill."
[612] Ibid.

What the Green Party avoided stating, and what the news media now states they will stop reporting, is that "the whole culture of abuse of children that is still so rampant in New Zealand society" is overwhelmingly a problem within Maori families, yet here too the blame is put on "White privilege" and "colonization," while New Zealand Europeans are even told that they can "learn" from Maori family relationships.

Bradford had however been clear on the motives, albeit largely forgotten or overlooked. In a comment during an interview with *The Waikato Times*, reported in the *Dominion Post*, she stated: "It's a choice between an old psychology which says children are our property.... Old New Zealand versus New Zealand."[613]

Here Bradford stated that the motive behind her bill was based on ideological concepts of power relationships, and of property relationships. Her explanation reflects Marxist and post-Marxist (critical theory) reductionism, defining social institutions and traditions as reflecting economic relations based on whatever class possesses the power.

In this context, there appears to be a more than coincidental similarity between Bradford's statement to *The Waikato Times*, and the outlook of classical Marxism towards the family, Marx having stated in *The Communist Manifesto*:

> *On what foundation is the present family, the bourgeois family based? On capital, on private gain... The bourgeois family will vanish when its complement vanishes, and both will vanish when capital vanishes.... Do you charge us with wanting to stop the exploitation of children by their parents? To this crime we plead guilty.*[614]

Where Marx used the term "bourgeois," Bradford used the term "Old New Zealand." Bradford described the familial bond of "Old New Zealand" as a "power relationship" and as a "property relationship," while Marx called it the "bourgeois family's exploitation of its children." Both strike at the root of the traditional family using similar terminology and the same ideological premises.

Given what Bradford stated about power and property relationships in connection with her "anti-smacking amendment," and the Marxist aim of eliminating the traditional family against the contemporary background of "identity politics" and "intersectionality," it might be asked whether the

---

[613] Taylor, "Feeling the strain of the front line."
[614] Marx and Engels, Proletarians and Communists, *Communist Manifesto*, 68.

Bradford bill was not also intended as a method of undermining traditional parental roles. The implication is that children have become a component of "identity politics" in the same manner as gays, women, refugees, immigrants, and sundry ethnicities, and these new alliances that have replaced the left's failed appeal to the proletariat are what is termed "intersectionality"—the "intersection" of sundry disparate causes that are used as a strategy by cultural Marxism, and its oligarchic allies.

Queerest Parliament in the World

New Zealand's Parliament is being lauded by those whom one would expect to be celebrating, as the queerest in the world. The term used is "rainbow." We are a "rainbow nation," sharing that term with the chaotic mess still known as South Africa. "Rainbow" apparently can be applied to any foul-up that accords with a liberal-globalist agenda. *The Auckland Herald* states:

> *The overall rainbow representation will be at 10 per cent—providing the Green Party is successful holding on to its preliminary 11 seats—bypassing the UK which holds the current title of the most rainbow Parliament with a 7 per cent representation.*
>
> *Meanwhile the openly rainbow MPs in New Zealand's recently elected Parliament include Labour's incumbents Grant Robertson, Louisa Wall, Meka Whaitiri, Tamati Coffey and Kiri Allan and newcomers Ayesha Verrall, Shanan Halbert and Glen Bennett.*
>
> *They will be joined by openly LGBTQIA+ Green Party member and spokeswoman for Rainbow issues Jan Logie, Chloe Swarbrick, Elizabeth Kerekere and Ricardo Menendez. About 40 per cent of the Green Party MPs are also from the rainbow community.*[615]

Inside Out managing director Tabby Besley stated that with the Green Party's Elizabeth Kerekere having campaigned on "rainbow issues":

> *I think for our communities a lot of us know she will be waving the flag as one of her main priorities whereas I guess many MPs*

---

[615] Preston, "World Record, New Zealand."

might have other portfolios or some people may not want their rainbow identity to be the main thing they talk about because they are just doing their job like other people. At least with her position we know she's not going to be shy around raising these issues so that is quite exciting.[616]

What Besley is referring to is a state within a state, with allusions to the way the so-called "community" sees "queer issues" as of paramount importance. Raising the "rainbow flag" is both literally and figuratively a declaration of separate identity while exclaiming that "inclusion" is the aim. "Inclusion" and "diversity" are two words that are used in conjunction as a type of *double think*. What is meant is the destruction of traditional, organic, authentic identities with the use of social constructs. From out of the bedlam will emerge not "diversity" but the alchemical amalgamation of all the uprooted elements into one nebulous mass of automatons: *Homo Economicus*.

The campaign for transgender identity confusion is part of an ideological agenda, where, as is more often than not the case, the left and oligarchy converge. Prior to the New Zealand general election Labour Party leader Jacinda Ardern alluded to the need to criminalize criticism and opposition to such agendas as part of the proposed "hate speech law." Besley also mentioned *"their"* (sic) hope that the "rainbow" parliament would result in "a swift ban of *conversion therapy*"; a term used to discredit several therapies used by medical specialists for those who have become confused as to their gender identity; perhaps not such a surprising quandary in this *epoch of decay*. A private Member's Bill was drafted which states:

Conversion therapy is a flawed and abhorrent practice that continues to happen in New Zealand. This practice tells people that, due to their sexuality or gender, there is something fundamentally wrong with who they are and they should be changed. It has no basis in modern science or psychology, goes against every ethical requirement for practitioners, is demonstrably harmful, and has no place in New Zealand.

...It is opposed by numerous organisations, including the United Nations Committee Against Torture, the Royal College of Psychiatrists London, the Canadian Psychological Association, and the Australian Medical Association.

---

[616] Ibid.

> ...This Bill creates an offence for any person who advertises, offers, or performs conversion therapy on another person. Under this Bill, any person is guilty of an offence if they remove another person from New Zealand for the purposes of conversion therapy. No one should, or even can, have their sexual orientation, gender identity, or gender expression changed through the pseudo-psychology of conversion therapy.[617]

Clauses include a ten thousand dollars fine or one year jail for professionals (doctors, social workers, and teachers) who assist in the process. Parents are liable to prosecution because, *"Every person is a party to and commits an offence who aids, abets, counsels, procures, or incites"...* under the definitions of the bill.[618] Therefore, professional advice would only be available if intended to *reinforce* gender identity confusion, while contrary advice and alternatives would be illegal. The bill was submitted for draw by Labour List MP Marja Lubeck, who was rejected by the electorate by more than 4,400 voted in the 2020 elections but returned on the Labour List.

Indoctrination in the Schools

As one would expect, in order to push this agenda it is most important to target children, because they are still going through stages of socio-psychological development and are therefore most susceptible to social engineering. More significant than parliamentary electoral shadow boxing are the entrenched bureaucrats and advisers who devise state policies.

In 2020 the Ministry of Education issued to primary schools a document touted as an expert study, *Relationships and Sexuality Education: A Guide for Teachers, Leaders and Boards of Trustees—Years 1-8*.[619]

The guide is designed for indoctrinating five to twelve-year olds with a transgender or *gender fluid* bias. As with such ideologically driven agendas, there must be a core reference to the Treaty of Waitangi and the customs of sundry ethnic communities, which makes necessary some type of semantic double-dealing for acceptance by those who might not be as acquiescent as White parents. For example, in Britain militant protests against such "rainbow" agendas in schools have come from Muslim

---

[617] "Prohibition for Conversion Therapy Bill," general policy statement.
[618] Ibid., 10.
[619] Note: the guide for years 9-13 mostly mirrors that of Years 1-8.

parents. It is one of many examples of "diversity" conflicting with the West's secular liberal humanism.[620]

Another predicament is that many feminists regard such *gender fluidity* as an outrage against womanhood. This has caused vitriolic conflict between more traditional feminists (called TERFS: Trans-Exclusionary Radical Feminists) and those who see political mileage in *intersectionality*, where the left becomes an amorphous combination (rainbow) of ethnic and LGBT+++++++ issues, with scant regard for old time class war.

Globalist Agenda

United Nations intrusion is acknowledged, albeit when such matters are addressed critically, they are condemned as "Far Right conspiracy theories" and "false news." In regard to *Relationships and Sexuality Education* (RSE):

> *These guidelines also acknowledge Aotearoa New Zealand's international legal commitments to the United Nations Sustainable Development Goals (2015), the United Nations Convention on the Rights of the Child (1989), and the United Nations Convention on the Rights of Persons with Disabilities (2006).*[621]

What is RSE?

The "guide" is deemed a necessary update to previous "guides" (2002, updated 2015) to keep pace with change: "shifting social norms in relation to gender and sexuality"; "global shifts, including trends towards earlier puberty and changing family structures"; "continued societal concerns about child protection and abuse prevention"; "increasing calls for social inclusion," and so forth.[622] Changing social norms and global shifts are regarded as primary justifications for imposing those changes onto New Zealand children. It is imposed conformity to globalist ideological agendas, constructed and promoted by vested interests behind a bogus facade of recognizing "differences."

What is implemented is not "sex education," but "relationships and sexuality education" (RSE). The former no longer suffices; indeed, it must

---
[620] Parveen, "Birmingham School Stops LGBT."
[621] Smith, *Relationships and Sexuality Education*, 8.
[622] Ibid.

now be eliminated as reactionary and antithetical to the new "sexuality," as the former sex education was predicated on *binary gender,* now an affront to "progressives." The whole edifice is underpinned by the use of Maori terms, in what is surely a manipulation of that culture for an ideology that is derived from Western liberal modernism.

Throughout, it is claimed that RSE accords with the insights of new scientific evidence.[623] Rather, the reason why children are targeted so early is because that is when attitudes can be conditioned like Pavlov's dogs, with rewards and punishments, at an age range that lacks developed critical faculties. They are regarded as *tabula rasa,* a blank slate, susceptible to any form of indoctrination. Yet the "guide" states that children will be taught to exercise critical judgment. Nonsense. They will be told how to think. They will not be able to critically evaluate the supposed "new evidence" that is presented to them by RSE, nor would the Ministry wish them to do so. They are led along a course that conforms to liberal globalist doctrines emanating from the UN and elsewhere, so that they are molded into "world citizens" of the type required by globalization.

The "guide" links RSE with environmental and other agendas tantamount to leftist *intersectionality,* and then claims that RSE proceeds from questions posed by children, rather than as imposed indoctrination, despite the "guide" having previously identified the UN as the originating body:

> *Families are now more diverse than ever before, and children and young people are questioning gender norms and binaries. Climate change continues to impact how young people view their worlds and their relationship with others and with the environment.*[624]

One such source is identified as the UN Convention on the Rights of the Child, where the "guide" states, "Children and young people have the right to engage in critical inquiry about relationships, gender, and sexuality as part of meaningful learning."[625] This is hypocritical cant. What youngster of the age range being targeted has the ability to "engage in critical inquiry"? The youngster is under the thrall of the teacher's authority as a substitute parent figure. If a child does have the genuine independence and courage to reject what is being imposed, he or she will be regarded as a problem to be corrected. The parents will be called by the school and

---

[623] Ibid., 12.
[624] Ibid.
[625] Ibid.

questioned as to the attitudes they have imparted to their child. There is no room for nonconformity. According to Freudian-Marxian critical theory parents are the first of the *primary ties* from which the individual must be "liberated"[626] and the traditional family is the germ-cell of fascism. [627] A large corpus of literature has arisen over the decades, written by critical theorists to destroy the foundations of Western tradition, which is the basis for what our current mind-manipulators call the "latest research."[628]

Revolution in Morals

Just how far-ranging RSE is, can be gauged from the aims:

> *Quality RSE policies and programmes enable young people to:*
> - *challenge homophobia, transphobia, sexism, and gender-based violence*
> - *interrogate the ongoing effects of colonisation*
> - *study the environmental impacts of changes in population growth and of related issues such as people's use and disposal of menstrual products*
> - *engage with mātauranga Māori*
> - *gain knowledge about the diversity of cultures in Aotearoa New Zealand—including religious diversity*
> - *gain understandings about the strengths of sexual and gender diversity. This learning is vital for children and young people's individual development and overall wellbeing, so it contributes to their academic success. It also enables us to develop more inclusive and positive societies.*[629]

Again, the *intersectional* doctrine of the left is the basis, with key words such as homophobia, transphobia, and sexism conjoined with "ongoing colonization," demographics, multiculturalism, and religious diversity.

While traditional Christian attitudes of one's parents can be routinely ridiculed and disposed of, how does one dispose of the traditional attitudes of Muslim parents? Will this conflict with the diversity utopia, as it did at the first "hui" on "hate speech," where the Israeli-Arab conflict took a bow?

---

[626] Fromm, *Escape From Freedom*.
[627] Adorno., *Authoritarian Personality*.
[628] See Bolton, *Perversion of Normality*, passim.
[629] Smith (ed)., "Relationships and Sexual Education," 12.

There is an assurance, however, that RSE accords with Maori custom and that "Maori models of sexuality" will be a premise:

> Sexuality is an element of hauora.[630] Ākonga[631] who are supported in regard to their sexuality are likely to have better overall health, which in turn supports their educational success and strengthens their relationships with whānau[632] and friends.[633]

Analogous to the hijacking of the American Psychiatric Association in 1973 and the redefinition of homosexuality by a militant lobby,[634] in recent years a long forgotten Maori word, *Takatāpui*, meaning a close bond between males, was augmented by a few other obscure cultural remnants and "reclaimed by Māori in lesbian, gay and trans communities in the 80s. In recent years its definition has expanded to encompass all tāngata whenua[635] with diverse gender identities, sexualities, and sex characteristics—similar to the way the word 'queer' is used now," according to Maori queer lobbyist Ngahuia Awekotuku.[636] Hence, the social engineers are able to inculcate their ideology by recourse to indigenous custom redefined with modernist interpretations.

A sanitized version of the Maori and Polynesian precolonial societies is required, which amounts to a return of the eighteenth century Western liberal salon doctrine of the noble savage.

Deconstruction of Language

To facilitate and encourage "gender fluidity" whether among staff or children, the prescription includes:

- ākonga and staff are known, and addressed at school, by their name of choice[637]
- [One day Mister Smith might show up to class and declare that "they" is (sic) now Ms. Smith. God help the child who is caught sniggering;

---

[630] Health, well-being.
[631] Students.
[632] Family.
[633] Smith (ed)., "Relationships and Sexual Education," 13.
[634] Socarides, "Sexual Politics."
[635] Original inhabitants.
[636] Thomas, "Early Maori View."
[637] Smith (ed)., "Relationships and Sexual Education," 19.

that might impact on "their" "academic success" unless confession and penance are shown].
- School rolls and records use each person's name, gender, and pronoun of choice
- [Johnny decides "they" is now a girl and is to be called Joanna]
- all school forms allow for genders in addition to male or female (e.g., gender diverse, nonbinary, *takatāpui*)
- [Given that there are now more than 120 "genders" and counting this will be an ever-expanding task]
- the school has clear and safe procedures for disclosures and complaints
- [Encourage anonymous informants, with all the abuse and suspicion that entails]
- school uniform policies are reviewed so that all the school's uniforms are inclusive and don't reinforce outdated, Eurocentric, and exclusionary notions of gender
- [All children, no matter what discomfort this causes, will be obliged to wear a uniform that is so nebulous as to obliterate authentic identities]
- procedures for sports are inclusive so that all *ākonga* can take part, whatever their sexual or gender identities.
- [Striving for excellence is passé and reactionary; inclusion is the sole aim]

Imposed and Enforced

For all the cant about consulting the diverse ethnic communities, the Ministry of Education unequivocally states that the RSE agenda will be imposed from on high; not subject to reform or rejection by any such community:

> *The school culture is very powerful. Whether or not they plan to do so, all schools give ākonga and their families messages about what is acceptable and what is not, in terms of gender and sexuality. Values are inherent in the practices, policies, and language used by teachers and school leaders.*
>
> *The New Zealand Curriculum recognises human rights and the values of diversity, equity, and respect. These values ensure the rights of all ākonga to self-expression, self-identification, and support. RSE acknowledges and supports diversity among ākonga. It is crucial that schools establish and maintain cultures*

of inclusivity. Schools are encouraged to question gender stereotypes and assumptions about sexuality, including:
- *gender norms*
- *gender binaries*
- *gender stereotypes*
- *sex norms, for example, the assumption that sex characteristics at birth are always male or female. School cultures should acknowledge the sexual diversity of Aotearoa New Zealand communities.*

The culture should recognise and actively support the rights of those who identify as:
- *takatāpui, lesbian, gay, bisexual, queer, intersex, transgender*
- *whakawāhine, tāngata ira tāne*
- *māhū (Tahiti and Hawai'i)*
- *vakasalewalewa (Fiji)*
- *palopa (Papua New Guinea)*
- *fa'afafine (Sāmoa and American Sāmoa)*
- *'akava'ine (Cook Islands)*
- *fakaleitī or leitī (Tonga)*
- *fakafifine (Niue and Tokelau)*
- *other sexual and gender identities.*[638]

Freedom of opinion of the left liberal type is called "repressive tolerance," coined by New Left guru Herbert Marcuse, where freedom of opinion is encouraged, *but only for those who agree with the left agenda,* while any opposition is "repressed." That is, it is blatant, undisguised Orwellian *double-think*. Hence: "Ākonga should be free to challenge school practices (such as rules about uniforms). School leaders and teachers need to be open and provide spaces for student voices and feedback."[639] If Johnny or Mary signify that they are less than comfortable being forced into participating in these intrusive programs they and their parents will be given corrective treatment in short order. There is no room provided for challenging this RSE program, despite supposed assurances under the Education Act.

Manipulative techniques to alter the psyche include the obliteration of traditional binary gender roles:

---

[638] Smith (ed)., "Relationships and Sexual Education," 19.
[639] Ibid., 20.

During play and discovery times, encourage children to engage with a wide range of equipment, toys, and play materials. These times offer opportunities to discuss and challenge unhelpful stereotypes about girls and boys (for example, if ākonga suggest that only girls play dress-ups or that only boys play with trucks).[640]

Here again we might discern implicit coercion. Previously we are assured that children must be listened to; now it is that if a child does not conform to *gender fluid* role-play *"they"* is (sic) to be corrected for being *"unhelpful."*

Awareness Raising

If a child comments or laughs when *"they" finds* (sic) it funny that Johnny is playing dress-up with dolls, this will become an issue of major consequence, for child, parents, and the entire school, if not further:

When specific issues arise in the school (for example, an incident of homophobic bullying), specific discussions or programmes (in classes, assemblies, or parent and whānau meetings) can **raise awareness** *of the school's related support systems and policies. When the whole school community is aware of the issue, all can work together to address it.*[641]

Making an example of such a child for not conforming to the agenda is called an opportunity by the social engineers to "raise awareness." *"Awareness raising"* is a concept long the basis of Marxism. It is also called "consciousness raising." While originally applied to "class consciousness" among the proletariat, the post-Marxist critical theorists extended the concept to what is popularly called *political correctness*. Where Marxism was established as a dictatorship, "raising awareness" was maintained by frequent political indoctrination sessions in factory and field. Jim Jones operated a pervasive system to "raise awareness" at Jonestown, where the aim was to build a communist utopia. The method involves public confession of guilt, renunciation of one's "errors," and humiliation for lack of conformity; the method was called "self-criticism," discussed previously.

---

[640] Ibid., 21.
[641] Ibid., 22, emphasis added.

One might readily envisage a classroom scenario where a child is embarrassed and uncomfortable being forced to perform roles which call for the class to "consider plays and role plays that critically investigate gender stereotypes." The term being "outside one's comfort zone" has been employed often enough by liberals. What of the child being pushed outside "their" (sic) "comfort zone" as part of RSE enforced indoctrination? "They" will presumably be subjected to humiliation, and a process of *"awareness raising,"* and possibly permanent psychological damage for the sake of imposing a fallacious ideology that the Ministry of Education "experts" dogmatically insist is proven by the latest science. One might be reminded that for many years the USSR persisted with Lysenko's theories as the "latest science" applied to agriculture, and geneticists who objected were eliminated, professionally if not physically.

Remolding Generations

The aim of RSE is to remold children into new, but amorphous beings who will conform to a brave new world, behind the facade of pseudo-identity. Modes of thinking will be re-engineered to conform:

> *Ākonga will make sense of information about growth and development, sexuality, relationships, pubertal change, and societal issues. They will:*
> - *reflect critically on that information*
> - *examine their own and others' attitudes, values, beliefs, rights, and responsibilities with regard to development, gender, sexuality, and relationships*
> - *consider how to solve problems in social situations.*[642]

Every aspect of education will conform to RSE. For example, when learning about technology: "explore symbols linked to the gay and transgender rights movements."

- *challenge gender stereotypes in relation to design and materials*
- *explore symbols linked to the gay and transgender rights movements*

---

[642] Ibid., 24.

- *identify how gender expectations are embedded in technology, for example, in the design and style of power tools and other tools, the range of colours, textures, and designs available for clothing*
- *explore the way toys, apps, and online games and activities are designed for a gendered audience*
- *engage in a gender-neutral design challenge.*[643]

Here we arrive at the actual aim, behind the *double-think* dialectics: "engage in a gender-neutral design challenge," as with "gender neutral" language, "gender neutral" clothing... The aim is not to champion identities, but rather to obliterate authentic identities, and to manufacture a *transhuman* (as Julian Huxley, and UNESCO called it), a nebulous being that can be slotted into any circumstance desired by a *Brave New World* (as his brother Aldous warned).[644]

How can an identity be *"neutral"*? How can an identity be *"fluid"*? Identity is premised on duration, passed down through generations; not transience based on whim and fashion as defined by social engineers and corporate planners.

No Choice

Parents are reassured that according to the *Education & Training Act* (Section 51) they are able to remove their child from a particular program, if they present their case in writing, although the school is not required to first seek permission from parents.[645] However, RSE is intended to permeate the entirety of the curriculum, and not just "health education," as with the previous "sex education." RSE is implemented in technology, mathematics, art, science, English, and sports; that is to say, "RSE across the curriculum."[646] The reassurances to parents are dishonest. A list of suggestions for teachers to use on parents who express concern is provided with such examples as, *"Connect back to The New Zealand Curriculum and the established place of relationships and sexuality in the context of the curriculum key competencies."*[647] Hence if parents object then they are told that RSE is an intrinsic part of the curriculum, and that their child's learning will suffer unless there is participation.

---

[643] Ibid., 29.
[644] See Bolton, *Perversion of Normality*.
[645] Smith (ed)., "Relationships and Sexual Education," 43.
[646] Ibid., 28-29.
[647] Ibid., 46.

"Aotearoa-New Zealand New Histories Curriculum"

As pervasive and mind-bending as the curricula on gender relations is, the new curriculum for teaching the "histories" (sic) of "Aotearoa/New Zealand"[648] is intended to have a similar impact. To control the future, one must reinterpret the past. The instilling of a guilt-complex, a "bend the knee" mentality in New Zealand European children and youths is based on a reconstruction of the colonial heritage. It is analogous to the situation *vis-a-vis* Americans with "slavery" and "Jim Crow"; Afrikaners with *Apartheid*; Germans with the Holocaust; and Britons, French, Dutch, and other Europeans with their imperial pasts.

In regard to New Zealand, the manner by which these "histories" will be taught will be at the expense of the Euro-New Zealander and particularly the Anglo-Saxon-Celtic heritage. Hence there is a denial to this element of what is being avidly promoted among all non-European elements: a sense of place and identity. This double standard is rationalized on the premise of "White privilege,"[649] and that the notion that White identity in New Zealand cannot exist as anything other than one of colonial invasion and exploitation. What this assumes is that Whites can be lumped into an indistinguishable mass who have all profited from the legacy of colonialism. In order to right this alleged historical wrong it is necessary to deny Whites any form of consciousness other than that of collective shame and guilt.

Those most open to this *psychowar* are of course children.

When several generations of White children have been inculcated with the feeling that their heritage is of no account in the future of Aotearoa (the days of "New Zealand" are surely numbered[650]) then they will be *passé* as an ethnic component and exist as nothing other than to serve the economic system. It is a paradox that while there is such a commitment to the demise of White heritage and identity, what will remain is the exploitive system under which *most people of all races suffer, and from which a very few of all races, benefit*.

---

[648] The Maori name for New Zealand is supposed to have been Aotearoa: "Land of the Long White Cloud." The name does not seem to have been widely used among the numerous, conflicting Maori tribes prior to the romanticization of it by colonials, the first mention possibly being in 1839. It was not used at the national conference of several hundred Maori chiefs at Kohimarama in 1860. See: "Proceedings of Kohimarama Conference."
[649] On "The Myth of White Privilege," see: Bolton, *The Perversion of Normality*, 365-375.
[650] Over the past few years, the use of the name "New Zealand" is being gradually but increasingly replaced with Aotearoa, without any consultation or referendum, particularly by commercial advertising, state bureaucracies and news media.

Education Department Proposals

Planned for implantation in 2022, the premise of the "new histories curriculum," interlaced with Maori words and phrases, as is the fashion among commercial advertisers, media, and bureaucracy, in the process of developing a localized pidgin-English, is introduced:

> *Through the Education Conversation / Kōrero Mātauranga and wider public discussion New Zealanders have made it clear that the current gaps in knowledge of our histories are not okay. We have heard a strong call for Aotearoa New Zealand's histories to be taught to all students and ākonga at all schools. We want the next generation to be able to apply lessons from the past as they shape our future.*
>
> *Given the calls from New Zealanders for this to change, we will be updating the National Curriculum, to make explicit the expectation that Aotearoa New Zealand's histories will be part of the local curriculum and marau ā kura in every school and kura.*[651]

What is being described are the demands of Maori supremacists being adopted by the state and pushed by "progressives" in academia and bureaucracy, in an alliance that is cynically called "wider public discussion." It is notable that there is reference to the "new histories curriculum" being locally adapted. That is to say, there will be focus on local tribal grievances against some aspect of colonial history perceived as injustice. This will mean that pupils in Hamilton schools for example, will focus historical studies on the besmirching of Captain John Hamilton and that of the bravery of the colonial soldiers who fought at Gate Pa.

Multiply this example throughout every school and one begins to get an image of what will be taught, and the feelings of guilt and shame that will be imparted on White children. Have the liberal ideologues that are so eager to obliterate all things European given any thought to the consequences of what really amounts to "hate speech" on children, or do they just not care, or is a Zimbabwe-type situation of dispossession the aim of a hidden agenda? Anti-White race hate will proceed from the present *de facto* situation to that of *de jure*. Such a situation is what Orwell called

---

[651] "Aotearoa New Zealand's Histories in Schools and Kura."

"double-think"; simultaneously holding contradictory views: race-hate in the name of "human rights," to atone for the alleged misdeeds of the past.

Draft Premises

The Education Department began to look at drafting proposals for the "new histories curriculum" in 2019, when Marielle Hawkes prepared a "briefing note" to Associate Minister of Education Kelvin Davis, and Education Minister Chris Hipkins, summarizing discussions with department officials on the Treaty of Waitangi as the predicate for teaching history. Since it was decided a few decades ago that the treaty is a "living document," this means that it can be interpreted and extended in any manner deemed necessary by *Europhobes* of whatever hue, whether dark or self-loathing White. According to Hawkes it was decided that all pupils, "across all year levels," must have access to "facts" (sic) in accordance with the "living" treaty, and that these "facts" should be applied to local areas. What these "facts" are would be determined by consultation with local tribes. A White input is not mentioned.[652]

The type of individual drafting these premises for the curriculum might be discerned by the background of Hakwes. According to her account on social media she witnessed a 2017 "White supremacist" activity that made it clear that "the time for meaningful dialogue has passed there." The implication is that she once thought "meaningful dialogue" with those New Zealand Europeans who had not a succumbed to self-hate, was possible, which is of course nonsense. To her any expression of dissent can be relegated to that of a few dozen (peaceably and lawfully assembled) adherents of what was probably the National Front or right-wing Resistance, facing the frenetic, histrionic rage of self-loathing "Whites" and possibly a few token "persons of color," instigated by ultra-left grouplets, whose significance is maintained by the Establishment news media and some Establishment politicians. However, all is permitted in the name of "human rights," "democracy," and "equality," especially given that these "White supremacists," states Hawkes, represent views against which "millions died fighting." This is the regurgitation of Herbert Marcuse's "Repressive Tolerance" doctrine, which provides the ideological rationalization for the "heckler's veto" against anyone who dissents from the liberal and leftist notions of the "social contract." Whether Hawkes was herself part of an Antifa mob she does not say. Never mind the "millions

---

[652] Hawkes, "Briefing Note: Teaching of Te Tiriti o Waitangi."

upon millions" who have died in the name of "human rights." Her and her "well-educated, White, liberal, able-bodied" (sic) friends pontificated about Aotearoa's future in their own mini "*hui*," (sic)[653] using a set of guidelines, which she calls "kiwi values" (all expressed in Maori terms) provided by a far-left website/lobby called *Action Station*. [654]

A "briefing note," as the basis for discussion, alludes to the "new histories curriculum" as being part of the "continuity and change strand," for compulsory implementation.[655] Here students shall learn about past events and how interpretations change and how to "imagine possible futures." The aim will be to pervade the "strand" with the Waitangi Treaty as a "living document." Therefore, the pupil will learn how to interpret history and "imagine" its future as a "living" treaty. Schools will develop their programs according to both national and local situations, including historical trends and movements, from "the Maori perspective." It will be interesting to see what the "Maori perspective" is on cannibalism, slavery, endless *utu*,[656] precolonial despoliation of the flora and fauna, and precolonial land wars.

Incorporated into this grand historical narrative will be, it is stated, the history of leftist protest movements, including anti-Apartheid protests and the LGBT movement, the latter reflecting the parallel compulsory "strand" on "gender fluidity." Pupils will be instructed on how to be "good and active citizens for change," (sic) enabling them to be mobilized to support some part of the state's agenda under the delusion that they are

---

[653] *Hui* = Maori name for a meeting.
[654] Hawkes, "Kai & Korero."
[655] Boast, "Briefing Note: Aotearoa New Zealand's History."
[656] *Utu* = blood feuds, which resulted in a perpetual cycle of self-annihilation that prompted Maoris to plea for British colonial intervention and the rule of British law. The result was the Treaty of Waitangi signed between the Crown and Maori chiefs in 1840. In return for protection as "British subjects," the Maori chiefs ceded their sovereignty to the Crown.
  In recent decades a revised interpretation of the Treaty insists that the chiefs did not cede their sovereignty. This reinterpretation is the basis of Maori grievances against the Crown. That the chiefly sovereignty was ceded to the Crown was recognised by the 1860 Kohimarama conference of several hundred Maori chiefs, who continuously referred to their having ceded their *mana* to the Crown in return for their rights as British subjects. *Mana* is a term that reflects very much more than any other Maori name for "governorship" or "sovereignty." The present interpretation claims that this was not a surrendering of sovereignty but a "partnership" between the Crown and the chiefs. It is a nonsense that nonetheless serves as one of the primary weapons in the denigration and dispossession of the New Zealand European.
  The Treaty is the product of English social contract theory, based on the assumption that a nation could be forged by the signing of a contract (Treaty), Governor Hobson stating to each signatory, "We are one people." That the Maoris would become "brown-skinned English" was also a widespread assumption not only among colonial administrators, educators, and settlers, but very much among the Maori chiefs. The proceedings of the Kohimarama conference make this abundantly clear. Here also we see the doctrine of *tabula rasa*, the "blank slate," of John Locke and eighteenth and nineteenth century liberalism.

exercising their individuality, reminiscent of a prior generation that was befuddled into thinking they were helping to attain "freedom" for Blacks in South Africa rather than globalist servitude. The churning out of such indoctrinated zombies by the state education system will ensure a ready supply of liberal state bureaucrats, and a continual supply of street fodder for the Aotearoan equivalent of Red Guards, having been instructed on being "good and active citizens for change."

An "education report" of August 2019, misdated 2018, refers to the new curriculum being an extension of existing programs on the Treaty of Waitangi.[657] It is said, cynically, that students "develop an understanding of their own identity" through what has "shaped New Zealand," and that this is "woven through all the strands" of the "treaty principles," that premise the social sciences curriculum. The new curriculum will update these "strands," incorporating local and national histories based on local Maori input.

What does this say about developing a sense of "identity" for Euro-New Zealand pupils? Will the new curriculum impart anything at all to the Euro-New Zealand pupil other than that his forefathers were colonial invaders and exploiters and that he continues to live in a position of "White privilege" thanks to this legacy, for which he must beg forgiveness and make amends? *At a time when we hear much about enhancing a child's self-esteem and not doing or saying anything that supposedly undermines that, to the point of dis-empowering parents thanks to another neo-Marxist agenda, what is this other than inflicting on children an inherited collective guilt complex? What seeds of self-loathing, alienation, and pointlessness are being sowed in White children that will surface in dysfunctional and self-destructive ways?*

In an "aide memoire" to Chris Hipkins, the Minister is reminded that "it is not okay" that children are not being sufficiently taught the historical events that have shaped New Zealand.[658] Although there has been such instruction, it has been "left to chance," and to local school decisions. Such an *ad hoc* approach is unacceptable. "Every" student is required to learn about "New Zealand histories." The "new histories curriculum" will be developed between the Ministry of Education, "experts," Maori, Pacific and ethnic communities, teachers, students, parents, *whanau*,[659] and "other groups with a strong interest in shaping how New Zealand's histories are taught." This, of course, is pure *cant*. Will White parents be

---

[657] McHardie, "Education Report: Including NZ History."
[658] Cleaver, "Aide Memoire: New Zealand's Histories in Schools and Kura."
[659] *Whanau* = family. This word is increasingly used as part of New Zealand parlance in place of "family."

widely consulted at local and national levels? Will actual "experts" be consulted, such as Dr. David Round[660] and Dr. Paul Moon, whose perspective, despite being a Maori academic, does not always square with liberal agendas?[661]

In an "aide memoire" to Kelvin Davis from the Education Department's Pauline Cleaver and Kiritina Johnstone the first point is that people's lives are today strongly influenced by history.[662] Sure enough, but the interpretation of history is the crucial point. Point 2 states that "we have an opportunity to ensure students have their history, and their place in Aotearoa New Zealand, acknowledged at their kura or school." More cant. What will be the history imparted to White students; what will be their place? Will they learn of the hardships of their forebears before they even reached New Zealand,[663] let alone what they faced in a strange land which had been promoted as a South Seas idyll by New Zealand Company land agents?

Cleaver and Johnstone state in their "aide paper" to government that to build a "treaty-based nation" everyone must understand the perspectives of the "diverse people" who keep the treaty alive "as treaty partners." Again, liberal *social contract* theory, reanimated from eighteenth and nineteenth century theoretical assumptions. Point 4 states that *tangata whenua*[664] and *iwi* have their own unique histories and experiences, as do other ethnicities who have migrated here. This is a means of enabling a multiplicity of ethnic communities to have their input as vital contributors to the "treaty-based nation." This will enable Chinese and Polynesians to enhance their identities and feeling of place[665] at the expense of Whites. The aim is said to be to build "empathy and connections" between people. It has all the meaning of an Orwellian paradox from *Animal Farm*. Included in this are Maori, women, "gender diverse people," and "people with disabilities." The disabled are given their own identity construct. Whites *per se* are non-beings *vis-à-vis* building a positive identity. The common factor for them all will be the discrimination they have suffered. Hence identities are constructed by negativity; feelings of grievance, and as for the rest, the Whites, they will be rendered peripheral by feelings of collective guilt and self-loathing. Disabled and transgender Whites are enabled to establish an identity by

---

[660] Round, *Truth or Treaty*.
[661] Moon, *Fatal Frontiers*.
[662] Cleaver and Johnstone, "Aide Memoire: New Zealand's Histories."
[663] McLean, *Voyages of the Pioneers*.
[664] *Tangata whenua* = "people of the land"; the Maoris as the indigenes.
[665] "Cabinet Paper Material," Point 21.

means of what the left calls *intersectionality*,[666] whereby sundry incongruous categories are constructed into an alliance against whatever remains of traditional Western norms.

Future "Red Guards" of Globalization

The detachment of children from the family bond and the replacement of parental authority with that of globalist, agenda-driven bureaucrats is the primary aim of the globalization process. The organic bond of family is the mainstay of an organic society (*Gemeinschaft*) and its destruction cannot proceed until that bond is eliminated. That is why the critical theory of the Frankfurt School that condemns the "primary ties" of family as being "repressive" and inherently "Fascist" has been of so much benefit to the oligarchs who are patronizing this social and moral world revolution.[667] The Marquis de Sade, on the extreme wing of the Jacobin faction, behind the facade of "human rights," had condemned the "repressive" role of parents in protecting their daughters (one suspects form predatory psychopaths such as himself).[668] As mentioned above, Marx condemned the family for this reason, and the Bradford so-called "anti-smacking" law was introduced in New Zealand for the primary purpose of changing the traditional relationship between parents and children. When Trotsky condemned Stalin for having "betrayed the revolution," he was particularly outraged that Stalin had been restoring traditional family relationships, in contrast to the original Bolshevik policy of replacing the family and parental bonds with the factory crèche and communal dining in the factory canteen, abortion prohibited in 1936, and motherhood honored in a manner suggesting "Fascism." [669]

Of education the Jacobin mentality was declared by Mirabeau: "In order to reconstruct everything, it was necessary to destroy everything." [670] That could well be the axiom of education departments and ministries throughout much of the world, and of the institutions that promote "progressive education," globally, without regard to local customs, communities, religions, traditions, and morality; whether as UNICEF or the oligarchic foundations and think tanks. For the common ideological, whether of the plutocracy or left-socialism, is universal and cosmopolitan;

---

[666] Bolton, *The Perversion of Normality*, 353-364.
[667] Ibid., passim.
[668] Ibid. 13.
[669] Trotsky, *The Revolution Betrayed*, Chapter 7, Family, Youth and Culture, cited in Bolton, *Stalin: The Enduring Legacy*, 13-20.
[670] Quoted in Kennedy, *Cultural History of the French Revolution*, 157.

a "one size fits all" world-hegemony, whether for education or for political institutions, economics, or moral outlook; all in the name of a *universal* "human rights," imposed by *universal* laws, and *universal* tribunals, and deemed to be as equally applicable to Hottentot and Swede.

Again, turning to the French revolutionary epoch, as analogous to our present situation, predicated on the same ideology.

The Bouquier Law (1793) established a new system of universal primary education. In the name of the "liberty of teaching," teachers were nonetheless obliged to obtain a "certificate of civicism,"[671] attesting to their subservience to the "social contract." The result was a shambles. By the following year, Paris, for example, had one teacher per four hundred pupils.[672]

Of the doctrinaire character of education, "History was thought to be a dangerous subject laden with errors that had to be expunged before it could enter the students' minds. It was the historian's duty to draw moral lessons from the past, eschewing its "prejudices" and errors."[673] This could just as well be describing the demands on teachers and historians, obliged to teach the "new histories" of the 2022 "histories curriculum," and the "new morality" of *Relationships and Sexuality Education*. However, unlike France, where there had been a strong religious tradition, in New Zealand generations of teachers have already come through an indoctrination process and are craven and zealous servants of the state dogma. Bizarrely, although the Republic was eager enough to enforce the "general will," and as per the recommendations of Rousseau, to execute those who breached the "social contract," students were given "liberty" reminiscent of today's abjuring of "authority" in the classrooms, perhaps because it might seem analogous to the authority of parents, which is deemed an affront to "progress." Of the French students, "nobody seemed to take charge of these boys who drifted in and out of class at will."[674] Teachers lacked the authority to expel unruly students, "who might appeal this action to the departmental authorities."[675] One might recall here how any disciplining of students now becomes a matter of controversy, and the subject of legal appeals. "[T]he reluctance to give teachers sufficient sanctions to assure discipline was symptomatic of the revolutionary critique of authority."[676] It took Napoleon to end the nonsense and restore order. The Revolution bore the seeds of its own destruction, as do the

---

[671] Ibid., 160.
[672] Ibid., 161.
[673] Ibid., 165.
[674] Ibid.
[675] Ibid.
[676] Ibid.

present manifestations. The horror of the "progressives" is that a new authoritarianism, or a new populism, (Putin, Orban, Trump), will triumph during the transition phase towards a *new world order*.

So, what is it that the globalists want in their reconstruction of youth? Like the bogus "youth revolt" of the New Left during the 1960s, they seek to create an easily manipulated mob that, divorced from the "primary ties" (organic bonds) that are condemned as "Fascist" by the "progressives," will become the compliant *global citizens* of a *universal general will*. During the Cultural Revolution, Mao Zedong used the youth to destroy "class enemies," and unleashed anarchy as a prelude to greater tyranny. In 1966, Mao established the Cultural Revolution small Group, headed by his wife. This Cultural Revolution was analogous to the Jacobin Reign of Terror, but on a far more colossal scale.

> *[Mao] picked as his first instrument of terror young people in schools and universities, the natural hotbeds for activists. These students were told to condemn their teachers and those in charge of education for poisonings their heads with "bourgeois ideas"— and for persecuting them with exams, which henceforth were abolished. The message was splashed in outsize characters on the front page of People's Daily, and declaimed in strident voices on the radio, carried by loudspeakers that had been rigged up everywhere, creating an atmosphere that was both blood-boiling and blood-curdling. Teachers as administrators in education were selected as the first victims because they were people instilling culture, and because they were the groups most conveniently placed to offer up to the youthful mobs, being right there to hand.*[677]

The young were told that their role was to "safeguard" Mao, although it was not explained where the danger was to him. However, after years of repression, mobs were let loose. Lessons were stopped to enable the students to mobilize. The first to be targeted was Peking University, where teachers were dragged through the streets, beaten, publicly humiliated, and adorned with dunce's hats. The rampages escalated throughout China, triggering many suicides.[678] In June the "Red Guards" were created, as a prelude to "Red August." High officials, many not realizing they were on Mao's blacklist, encouraged their children to create Red Guard groups.

---

[677] Chang and Halliday, *Mao: The Unknown Story*, 534.
[678] Ibid., 535.

> *Learning from their fathers and friends that Mao was encouraging violence, the Red Guards immediately embarked on atrocities. On 5 August, in a Peking girl's school packed with high officials" children (which Mao's two daughters had attended) the first known death by torture took place. The headmistress, a fifty year old mother of four, was kicked and trampled by the girls, and boiling water was poured over her. She was ordered to carry heavy bricks back and forth; as she stumbled past, she was thrashed with heavy army belts with brass buckles, and with wooden sticks studded with nails. She soon collapsed and died. Afterwards, leading activists reported to the new authorities...*[679]

On August 18th, in military uniform, Mao stood on Tiananmen Gate to review hundreds of thousands of Red Guard youngsters. A leader of the fatal torture of the headmistress at the Peking girls' school was given the honor of putting a Red Guard armband on Mao. After some brief banter, Mao advised the girl: "be violent"; the girl changed her name to Be Violent, and her school became "The Red Violent School."[680]

Families were targeted for coming from the wrong social background. An axiom of the Red Guards was that "a reactionary father produces nothing but a bastard." In the girls' school where the first torture and killing had occurred, pupils from the wrong type of family had ropes tied around their necks, were beaten, and forced to say: "I'm the bastard of a bitch. I deserve to die."[681]

Those who were deemed to represent "old culture" (sic) were targeted. The Peking Writers' Association premises was attacked by Red Guards, and several dozens of China's best known writers were beaten, while placards were hung around their necks. These together with opera singers and artists, were taken to an old Confucian temple, where they knelt before a bonfire of opera costumes and props and were beaten.[682]

The police chief Xie Fu-zhi advised his subordinates: "Don't be bound by rules set in the past... If you detain those who beat people to death... you will be making a big mistake."[683]

This "revolt of the underman," to paraphrase Lothrop Stoddard, that received official sanction in China, seems in many ways analogous to the Antifa and BLM riots that have occurred in the West, where the state turns

---

[679] Ibid., 537.
[680] Ibid.
[681] Ibid., 538.
[682] Ibid., 539.
[683] Ibid., 540.

a blind eye to leftist violence and vandalism, and the news media, rather than condemning leftist violence vitriotically, damns and smears Andy Ngo who accurately reports on it.[684] Think of the Charlottesville riot where the police were told to stand down and allow a peaceful and legally permitted rally to be attacked by Antifa and BLM mobs, and where the media condemned and smeared the victims. The spectre of Xie Fu-zhi seems to have haunted Charlottesville's police and City Hall. The major news media took the same position that *People's Daily* had taken. Antifa and BLM had served as the Establishment's Red Guards. Just as the Cultural Revolution had wrought destruction on China's Confucian traditions, so too the present West is undergoing a cultural revolution, with the backing of those in power, to destroy any vestige of the cultures, traditions, and heritage, on *Homo Europaeus*.

---

[684] Ngo, *Unmasked*.

UNICEF "Playbook":
Manual for Globalizing Children

"But whoever causes one of these little ones who believe in me to sin, it would be better for him to have a great millstone fastened around his neck and to be drowned in the depth of the sea."

Matthew 18:6

We have considered something of the role of the United Nations International Children's Emergency Fund (UNICEF) in the previous chapter, "Pied Pipers." UNICEF was established as an organ of the United Nations Organization in 1946, to focus on the re-shaping of the world's children as global citizens, imbued with the *transhumanist* values, morals, and ethics of the UN.[685]

It is surely evident that any goal of world control rests on the manipulation of the young. Without the conquest of the minds of children, all that the oligarchy and their fellow-travelers have striven for, for generations, is gone within a generation, and has to be rebuilt, perhaps from the beginning. There is much indignation about the overt control of youth by totalitarian regimes, whether Fascist or Communist (with Jesuits also often cited) and the efforts expended in indoctrinating the young. Yet Liberalism has been indoctrinating the young and its cultural syphilis is done, as usual, in the name of "human rights," "equality," and today in the name of the "inclusion" that rings forth from corporation boardrooms.

---

[685] For the "transhumanist" ideology of the UN, as formulated by Dr. Julian Huxley, see: Bolton, *Pervasion of Normality*, 433-442.

Karl Marx's dream, and his nightmare

The globalist oligarchs and their technocratic and managerial functionaries usually—but not invariably—rely on "soft power" of the type so well described by UNESCO founding-director Julian Huxley's brother Aldous, in *Brave New World*. Today we might say, to paraphrase Marx, that *consumerism* is the "opiate of the people." The notable US strategist Ralph Peters wrote of this "soft power" as the real measure of the USA's success in dominating the world:

> [T]raditional intellectual elites are of shrinking relevance, replaced by cognitive practical elites—figures such as Bill Gates, Steven Spielberg, Madonna, or our most successful politicians—human beings who can recognize or create popular appetites, recreating themselves as necessary. Contemporary American culture is the most powerful in history, and the most destructive of competitor cultures. The genius, the secret weapon, of American culture is the essence that the [traditional] elites despise: ours is the first genuine people's culture. It stresses comfort and convenience—ease—and it generates pleasure for the masses. We are Karl Marx's dream, and his nightmare.... Our cultural empire has the addicted—men and women everywhere—clamoring for more. And they pay for the privilege of their disillusionment.[686]

Peters wrote of how the masses throughout the world succumb to control through the distractions of what amount to "play," to fatuous entertainments and consumer trinkets, which he states rely on their transience, and are devoid of permanence. That, he sees as the USA's "strength" and meaning. Hence, in this state of narcosis, few among the masses are sufficiently perceptive to realize their own chains in a world-expansive system that is portrayed as the epitome of "progress." According to the globalist theorists we are at the "end of history," as the ultimate of all prior human striving, with the universal triumph of "democracy" and "human rights." Here, "life, liberty, and the pursuit of happiness" are enshrined as sacred principles across a borderless world; upheld by whatever means necessary. Peters describes this mass universal culture as

---

[686] Peters, "Constant Conflict."

one that "includes" rather than "excludes."[687] It is the "inclusive society" and the "inclusive economy" that have become premises of the era. It is a culture of "equality" that relies on *leveling* rather than a continual striving towards the sublime, that defined both Hellenic and Western High Cultures each in their own unique ways. It is the pseudo-culture of universal democracy, for which the USA has claimed to be the champion since the days of Thomas Jefferson. It is what Ezra Pound, T. S. Eliot, W. B. Yeats, et al., saw would destroy the will-to-excellence in the name of "democracy," and the commodification of culture, creating and supplying transient mass markets: culture as trend and fashion; culture as "democratic" and universally "inclusive."

Globalization in the Name of the Child

This world vision is upheld as the most precious legacy we can leave to our children, in a world of universal *brother/sister/other-hood*. UNICEF was created for the purpose of guiding the indoctrination of children throughout the world. The globalized economy is the *Great Moloch* to which children are fed. Towards this end, UNICEF has published a guide—a "playbook"—on how commerce can be used as a means for both indoctrination and profit.

It was Edward Bernays, the nephew of Sigmund Freud, who, as the acknowledged father of the advertising and public relations industries, showed how advertising can be used to increase profits behind the facade of idealism, and how mind manipulation can be achieved through such slogans as "liberty." He called the process "engineering consent." Employed by the American tobacco industry to extend their product to a hitherto large, untapped market, cigarettes were promoted as "torches of freedom" among women. Smoking became a symbol of the "liberated, modern woman."[688]

There is another large market to be exploited—that of children, including toddlers, as "consumers." Like much else we have been considering, this is undertaken behind the facade of "human rights" or in this case, more specifically, "the rights of the child," divorced from the "rights of parents," despite the rhetoric in UN documents about upholding the "family," which is itself being redefined.

---

[687] Ibid., 129.
[688] Bolton, *The Perversion of Normality*, 40-41.

UNICEF Playbook

UNICEF calls the program "promoting diversity and inclusion in advertising," in a blueprint that it calls a "UNICEF playbook." The opening paragraph cogently explains the premise, referring to "the power to influence" that "advertising and marketing" have over "individual and community beliefs" in their "ways of thinking and behaviours." It is the doctrine of Bernays. The reference is to how "constantly" children and families are "exposed to advertising and media." Hence, the importance of "diversity and inclusion in marketing messages," impacting on "children and youth." [689]

In the name of "diversity and inclusion," the dialectical move is to destroy organic, authentic identities and to reconstruct children for the *brave new world*. Gender, racial and ethnic "stereotypes" are seen as negatives that need to be eliminated in advertising and manufacturing directed towards children. UNICEF advises corporations on marketing and advertising products and content to achieve their agendas, to create "more diverse and equal worlds of play."[690] The innocent play of children is a means of indoctrination. The purpose of the "playbook" is to outline a "strategy" for business; particularly those involved with "toys, gaming, publishing, film and TV, and children's clothing and accessories."[691]

The doctrinal foundations include the UN Convention on the Rights of the Child, Convention on the Elimination of All Forms of Discrimination Against Women, Convention on the Rights of Persons with Disabilities, Declaration on the Elimination of All Forms of Racial Discrimination, and the 2030 Agenda for Sustainable Development.[692]

Among the aims is to eliminate the stereotyped idealization of body images.[693] Hence, in the name of "equality' and inclusion" traditional aesthetics of beauty, the Hellenic legacy of form and ratio, must be eliminated. No longer should there be an idealized aesthetic to elevate, and inspire, even if not achievable by most. Liberals can only see with envious eyes, with "ressentiment," as Nietzsche called it, and they will-to-destroy in the name of "equality," "democracy," and "human rights," where the healthy see nobility and the expression of the Godhead.

---

[689] Rutgers, *Promoting diversity and inclusion*, 4.
[690] Ibid.
[691] Ibid.
[692] Ibid., 7.
[693] Ibid.

In the *brave new world* form, order and proportion are eliminated from aesthetics, as "unrealistic beauty norms."[694]

Also, the "sexual orientation" of parents and caregivers is relevant.[695] Hence, we might expect Barbie, Ken and friends portrayed as 120+ variations on the scale of gender fluidity. The variety of marketing possibilities becomes endless—once the child consumer is reconditioned to want such products.

When identities are multiplied *ad infinitum* they become so nebulous, so amorphous as to make any identity meaningless. An amoebic existence is reached in the name of "inclusion," because all criteria are discarded, and culture-nihilism proceeds.

UNICEF's Social Constructs

UNICEF lists four categories to be addressed: (1) Gender; (2) race, ethnicity, and culture; (3) disability; (4) family and caregivers. [696]

For "Gender" we see how the elimination of "stereotypes," that is, binary gender, contributes to the "inclusive economy," to which every major corporation is committed. This now includes "gender expression;"[697] that is to say, the rights of children to determine their own gender, on the sliding scale. "Transgender" becomes a UNICEF model for children. Therefore traditional gender roles must be eliminated from marketing and advertising, by "gender-equal representation." "Masculinities and male roles are harmful for boys."[698]

The role of advertisers and manufacturers is to eliminate any notion of organic binary-genders, causing confusion, uncertainty and normalizing pathologies at the earliest stages of childhood development. This, UNICEF affirms, is done in the interests of mental health. Yet how does this respect authentic "diversity"? It necessitates the suppression of all traditional societies, religions, customs, ethics, and morals; from the Amazon to the Sahara. Such "inclusion" imposes a universal system of values based on a doctrine that arose within the late epoch of Western civilization. It is a system of global conformity and ideological hegemony, cynically undertaken in the name of "diversity."

---

[694] Ibid., 9.
[695] Ibid., 7.
[696] Ibid.
[697] Ibid., 9.
[698] Ibid.

"Race" is defined as a "social construct" invented as a "tool of oppression" to justify inequalities in the name of "science."[699] This reflects the UN doctrine on "race" which had been defined by UNESCO in *The Race Concept: Results of an Inquiry* published in 1952, and in its *Statement on Race* published in 1950. "Racism" is the means by which domination is used through the use of "race" as a "social construct" by a dominant group. It is a factor in lowering self-esteem and in obstructing the providing of positive role models to children.[700]

"Ethnicity" and "culture" are however defined by UNICEF as legitimate forms of identity, once they are divorced from "race." An ethnicity is a group identity "based on ancestry, language, clothing, religion and other characteristics."[701]

"Culture," defined in the UNESCO Universal Declaration on Cultural Diversity, is "the set of distinctive spiritual, material, intellectual and emotional features of a society or social group… encompassing art and literature, lifestyles, ways of living together, value systems, traditions and beliefs."[702]

Families are redefined according to new social constructs. Like "race," since gender is also a "social construct" it can be deconstructed and reconstructed according to an ideological agenda. Other than "single parent," "nuclear," "blended" and "extended" families, there are "LGBTIQ+ families" where parents are "lesbian, gay, bisexual, transgender, non-binary or queer;" and "mixed race or multicultural families." "Parenting" is any process of "nurturing."[703] Among the "stereotypes" that are condemned are that happy families are achieved when the mother stays at home to look after children—i.e., rather than becoming part of the production process.[704] This is where feminism has played its role, and the notion of "women's liberation," from out of the home and into the factory and office. It is the equivalent of Bernays' "torches of freedom." Here the UN plays its part in what the corporations, oligarchic think tanks and foundations call the "inclusive economy."

Another stereotype considered harmful by UNICEF is that "parents control their children's fate."[705] As we have seen, the "rights of the child" and such measures as New Zealand's so-called "anti-smacking law" are

---

[699] Ibid., 10.
[700] Rutgers, *Promoting diversity and inclusion*, 11.
[701] Ibid., 10.
[702] Ibid.
[703] Ibid., 14.
[704] Ibid.
[705] Ibid.

used to subvert traditional parental authority, which can then be replaced by authority outside the home.

In the early years of Bolshevik Russia parents were "liberated" from the home so that they could focus entirely on the production process, while children were "nurtured" by factory crèches. Lev Trotsky, in lamenting the "betrayal" of Bolshevism by Stalin, stated that:

> *The revolution had made a heroic effort to destroy the so-called "family hearth"—that archaic, stuffy and stagnant institution in which the women of the toiling classes perform galley labor from childhood to death. The place of the family as a shut-in petty enterprise was to be occupied, according to the plans, by a finished system of social care and accommodation...the complete absorption of the housekeeping functions of the family by institutions of the socialist society...*[706]

The "housekeeping functions" are replaced by the functions of economic productivity. "Galley labor" is replaced by factory labor. The home was replaced by the factory, and it was called "liberation." The same processes proceed under centralized and globalized capitalism, which becomes indistinguishable from Communism.

Another "harmful stereotype" in need of eradication, is that "The 'normal' family is racially, ethnically and culturally homogenous."[707] The implication is that the family as a unit should have no common bond. What then is the purpose of the "family" under the UNICEF doctrine? What is its identity? Family, like race, and gender becomes so nebulous it ceases to exist in any meaningful sense.

Another "harmful stereotype" to be eliminated is any notion that "families live in detached houses" with gardens.[708] That was once regarded as a worthy ideal and in New Zealand in was largely achieved. The New Zealand vision was for the widest possible ownership of a quarter acre section with a garden. Speculative capitalism has made that dream impossible. High rise buildings and in-filling have produced a cramped and overpopulated urbanization.

The aim is for corporations to produce toys and games that do not suggest that the child of the ghetto or the high-rise tenement building are living in a lesser condition than the child who lives on a property with a yard, or that such a yard might be a preferable place of play than on a

---

[706] Trotsky, *The Revolution Betrayed*, "The Thermidor in the Family."
[707] Rutgers, *Promoting diversity and inclusion*, 14.
[708] Ibid.

street? That at least was suggested by Mattel with the presentation stand for its "Flavas" dolls being a graffitied wall as the backdrop to a "place to hang out."

Global Hegemony

The question is to determine what forms of culture and identity are acceptable in the world-view of the UN. For example, how does one eliminate morals, religions, customs and taboos that reject homosexuality, let alone the new normal of transgenderism; or maintain that women are firstly *mothers*? The whole push towards "human rights" and "universal equality" can only be implemented by a universal leveling in which differences, far from being celebrated, are eliminated. What is this other than *cultural imperialism*, constructed from a doctrine that derives from the Late West, and from no other? It is ironic that those Europeans who resist such globalization are accused of "White supremacy" by those whose doctrine comes from Europe.

As will be shown, manufactured, artificial youth subcultures such as Hip-Hop are ideal for creating a global cultural melting pot that embraces everything in general but stands for nothing in particular. All is nebulous. Culture becomes synthetic. As the UNICEF playbook shows, toys and play are essential in molding children into a new synthetic being; a melting-pot generation produced in the name of "inclusion."

"Transformative Model"

In order for this dystopia to be constructed children must be reconditioned and this can be done by detaching them from traditional identities of ethnicity, gender, and family, so that they become "fluid" units in the world economic process.

For the guidance of manufacturers and advertisers UNICEF has developed a "transformative model" to "avoid stereotypes in design and marketing." Within this are three categories: (1) "discriminatory," (2) "aware" and (3) "transformative."

Discriminatory perpetuates binary gender stereotypes where only "majority children" [i.e. White] are represented in advertising, marketing and communications; the disabled are not represented; heterosexual "nuclear families" are presented as the norm.

Aware acknowledges gender inequality, but it is not "robustly" addressed; *tokenism*; disabled are represented, but "not all types;"

acknowledgement of "different family models" such as grandparents and solo-mothers—but this is inadequate because of lack of LGBT+. Perhaps one could also raise awareness on the "underrepresentation" of brother/sister incestuous parents and retarded offspring? What of their inclusion?

Transformative is the holy grail of advertising and marketing as all variations of gender fluidity; "racial" (despite being an oppressive social construct), ethnic and cultural backgrounds (cannibals, head-hunters) are represented as "capable, intelligent, and independent; disabled are "meaningfully engaged;" "consistently portrayed varied family types," (crack-head parents and kids); "extended," (Muslim *harem*); "blended," (human father, bitch-mother, hybrid child-pup); gender fluid, and economically diverse.[709]

"Key performance indicators" are set to assure that a corporation is pervaded at every level with the UNICEF doctrine. Here the corporation itself must show the extent of its "diversity" and "inclusion." The three "transformative" categories are applied to the internal policies of the corporation.[710] Here the use of "group therapy" and "sensitivity training," euphemistically called "team building" by the "human relations" corporations, is implemented as a means of bullying any dissident into submission, which includes the acknowledgement of one's "unconscious bias." That process is part of the "transformative" phase where "there are honest discussions about challenges" faced on this "journey."[711] There should be "regular" "internal workshops and training sessions" "to raise awareness about unconscious bias and how the issue of diversity, equity and inclusion can impact content and product development and marketing."[712] At this point the nomenclature sounds communistic, but as oligarchy proceeds to global hegemony capitalism and communism become increasingly convergent.

"Product marketing and brand communication" are the means of influencing children through toys, books, and games, where children "learn through play." Children's views of "themselves, of family members and of the outside world," are shaped. UNICEF talks of keeping "child consumers" "loyal" through brands, television shows, apps, films, and magazine.[713] UNICEF is open in its agenda: the globalization of child consumers. If the reader can interpret this any other way, by all means do

---

[709] Ibid., 15.
[710] Ibid., 18.
[711] Ibid.
[712] Ibid., 20.
[713] Ibid., 21.

so. The child becomes enchained to the production and consumption process on a global scale, in the name of "diversity" and "inclusion," and what the UN calls "the rights of the child."

UNICEF Favorites

The UNICEF "playbook" provides examples of companies that are perpetrating the globalist agenda among children worldwide:

Netflix comes in first. A study is cited which examined "on-screen talent (based on gender, race/ethnicity, LGBTIQ+ or disability identity) and storylines;" as well as the "creators, producers, writers and directors for 126 films and 180 series released during 2018–2019."[714]

Pixar Animation Studios. UNICEF lauds the company's employees' annual "Inclusion Summit," where stories of diversity and inclusion are shared. Pixar's "film soul" is especially lauded for its diversity of voices and Black consultants.[715] I invite the reader to think of a single animated movie that has *not* featured at least one primary character with wise-cracking Black "attitude."

Toca Boca digital game company (Sweden). Founded in 2011, the company manufactures digital toys for children aged six to eleven. Each product must include diversity of race/ethnicity, including skin, eye and hair color and tone; respectful portrayal of cultures (headhunting, cannibalism, scalping, human sacrifice, female circumcision?) without "cultural appropriation;" "functional diversity" without making disability a defining trait (retardation, spasticity?); body shape, including "tall, short, wide and thin" (what about morbid obesity or *anorexia nervosa*?); gender, where children choose; family, including single parent, multicultural, and grandparents;[716] and children who are "bold and have their own style and personality;" that is to say, kids who are targeted as consumers of fashion and trend. Toca Boca employs a "Diversity Advisory Board."[717]

Lottie Dolls. Manufactured in 2012, after eighteen months of research, including consulting with child psychologists and nutritionists, the aim

---

[714] Ibid., 27.
[715] Ibid., 28.
[716] The elderly should be depicted as still being at the workplace grindstone, as evidence of their continuing worth to the production process. Late capitalism wants to postpone the retirement age, and this, of course, is promoted as the "rights of the aged" or the "dignity of the elderly," rather than as being chained to the economic treadmill until one drops, or has few years left for retirement.
[717] Rutgers, *Promoting diversity and inclusion*, 28.

was "to bring inclusivity, gender neutrality and representation into the toy industry." With such a task, one would expect that the most accurate depiction would be that of a nebulous blob: *homo blobicus*. "Lottie and her friends" are designed to be "non-stereotypical" in their "activities and costumes," "with different types of hair and skin tones." "Lottie dolls do not mention the differences on the packaging;" children are supposed to figure out what they are "from the literature provided inside the box." They represent the "playmates" that one might have, with a diversity of race, gender and disability. The toys are sold in thirty-five countries, and have received awards.[718]

Goodnight Stories for Rebel Girls. They have sold seven million books, in fifty-one languages, with podcasts downloaded fourteen million times. One book is subheaded "journal to start revolutions."[719] The artists are not solely female, but also "nonbinary." Volume 4: "Black Lives Matter and Women Power," includes Meghan Markle (comment would be superfluous); and Winnie Mandela, whose corruption, opulent lifestyle, and direction of "hits" on rival Blacks are presumably features for girls to admire and emulate.[720]

Salam Sisters. Five "culturally diverse" Muslim dolls, with diverse interests, passions and careers[721]; none of which *seem* to be as a Wahhabi suicide bomber.

Crayola. There are now forty skin tones, allowing children to see the wide range of skin colors in the world. This enables the child to draw his "true selfie."[722]

Aboriginal Peoples Television Network (APTN), a Canada based corporation that broadcasts on indigenous peoples throughout the world, with a focus on Canadian indigenes.[723] Laudable, but I am not aware whether the APTN is also "inclusive" of the indigenous—and generally beleaguered—peoples of Europe or South Africa (i.e., Afrikaners).

---

[718] Ibid., 30.
[719] Ibid., 31.
[720] In 2003 "the mother of the nation" was convicted of sixty charges of fraud and twenty-five of theft from the ANC Women's League. Staff and agencies, "Winnie Mandela found guilty of fraud." Reuters reporting on her death in 2018, referred to her use of the Mandela United Football Club, which served as her "enforcers" in Soweto. Sowetan Africans referred to her as "The Mugger of the Nation." In 1991 she was convicted of ordering the cut-throat murder of a fouteen year old suspected of being an informer. Her "punishment" was a fine. The ANC later sought to distance itself from her for her murderous and corrupt actions (a case of the "pot calling the kettle black"). Cropley, "Winnie Mandela, tarnished 'Mother.'"
[721] Rutgers, *Promoting diversity and inclusion*, 32. I detect implicit anti-Semitism in the lack of Jewish Sisters, which might include a gun-toting "Settler," a crassly bejewelled banker's wife; and a screeching feminist harridan of the Bella Abzug type.
[722] Ibid., 33.
[723] Ibid., 34.

Microsoft Adaptive Controller (for disabled children).[724]

Flamingo Rampant: Celebrating all kinds of families. This offers children an alternative to being confronted with "heteronormative family" situations. Flamingo Rampant produces books on "racial justice, disability pride, children taking action, and loving, positive LGBTIQ+ families and communities."[725]

Alfabantu: teaching African history to children around the world. Digital games and storytelling in Bantu. Founded in Brazil, there is a focus on the Afro-Brazilian connection.

Dora the explorer. The series on a Latina girl, debuted on Nickelodeon cable network in 1999; now translated into twenty-two languages. "The show includes linguistic and cultural elements..." Dora is also marketed as clothes, toys, bed linen, and games. Bottom line: "Sales of Dora merchandise have totaled $11 billion since being introduced in 2002."[726]

Doc McStuffins: showing children engaged with compelling characters of all backgrounds. (Disney Junior Worldwide). The first US preschool show to "feature a Black girl as the lead character." But since "race" is only a social construct, how do we know she is a "Black girl," and what precisely is a "Black girl," and what is "Black" and what is a "girl"? Her mother is a doctor, and her father is a "stay-at-home dad."

Any half-decent program promoting "diversity and inclusion" would portray the parents as gender fluid, or at least depict the parents as lesbian or gay. The social background seems thoroughly bourgeois. What about the mother as whore and the father as pimp?

Bottom line: as a toy line this sold more than $500,000,000 in 2014 alone.[727]

Nike: levelling the playing field for black women and girls. UNICEF lauds Nike for its stand on "controversial issues," including sponsoring the NFL quarterback Colin Kaepernick, who "took the knee," during the US national anthem. In 2021 Nike released an advertisement celebrating Black women athletes for International Women's Day.[728]

Barbie. (Mattel). She was "reinvented" as she became increasingly side-lined by "diversity" among toys, and caregivers started steering children away from a doll based on "Eurocentric beauty" (sic). In 2016 Mattel launched the "Fashionista Barbie" line which includes "different skin tones, facial features and hair textures. One doll is bald; another has

---

[724] Ibid., 35.
[725] Ibid., 36.
[726] Ibid., 38.
[727] Ibid., 39.
[728] Ibid., 41.

a prosthetic limb. One has curly dark hair that is swept away from her face to show she has vitiligo (a skin condition that causes pigment loss); another is in a wheelchair."729 In a civilization that is in terminal decay, it seems apt that sickness is celebrated. I await Syphilitic Barbie, and Leprous Barbie.

More than half the dolls sold by Mattel represent "diversity." In 2019 the bestselling doll was a "black Barbie with an Afro."730

"Bratz" and "Flavas"

Mattel, manufacturer of Barbie, began a "diverse" line prior to "Fashionista Barbie in 2016." This was the "Flavas" line of dolls and accessories, inspired by Hip-Hop, a genre that is promoted by the US State Department.731

"Flavas" was launched by Mattel in 2003. It was Mattel's answer to MGA Entertainment's "Bratz," launched in 2001 of what appears to be a multicultural collection of child prostitutes, which was outselling Barbie.

The term is derived from Hip-Hop. The product, manufactured in China, was marketed to girls from age eight. The line promotes the whole gamut of ghetto subculture in speech, fashion, and "attitude." It promotes the idea of forming a "crew." The display stands were backgrounded with walls daubed with graffiti. The instructions stated that the "street stands" were places to "hang out." The Hispanic, White and Black figures sported bling, stick-on "tattoos," and ghetto blasters. The Television commercial for "Flavas" was aired to the sound of rapper Craig David's "What's Your Flava?" "Flavas" was rolled out in conjunction with Mattel's sponsorship of Christina Aguerila's 2003 summer tour. In Britain they were launched by Hip-Hop group Mis-Teeq.

"Flavas" flopped and were discontinued the following year. *Newsweek*, describing the dolls as "ghetto fabulous," reported:

> Some think these Flavas leave a bad taste. "When I saw the dolls I was in shock," says Raquel Wilson, editor in chief of hip-hop e-zine Verbalisms. "They completely misrepresent the culture." She takes issue with the superficial treatment of the movement, and notes that the term "flava," which means personal style, is no longer commonly used. But Bossick [a Mattel senior vice

---

729 Ibid., 40.
730 Ibid.
731 What the State Department refers to as "Hip-Hop Diplomacy."

president], who says Mattel didn't hire hip-hop consultants, stands behind the line. "Fearless self-expression and individuality are very positive messages for girls." The vandalized street wall's just a side effect.[732]

Ironically, Mattel spokeswoman Julia Jensen said that "Flavas" was "all about authenticity and reality."[733] Kyra Kyles of the *Chicago Tribune* perceptively commented:

Lay off, you plead. They're just dolls for 8-year-olds, you say. To you, I say: Have you seen Tre? Done up in a Kangol knockoff and shorts so baggy they practically hang outside the box, he looks more like a drug-dealing pimp. In fact, he looks like a drug-dealing pimp that is his own best customer. Is this the image of an African-American hip-hopper Mattel would like 8-year-old girls to embrace?[734]

Of the Flava character Kiyoni Brown, Kyles wrote, "Here's a girl who needs literal plastic surgery. The doll looks like Lil' Kim after a domestic dispute with Mike Tyson." Of the others, "These dolls pander to the most unimaginative stereotypes about hip-hop and our increasingly multicultural society.... By putting hip-hop in a graffiti-covered box, Mattel contradicts the very 'individualism' it claims to embrace..."[735]

Mattel's promotional statement had declared that "just like real teens, Flavas reflects true individuality," "reflecting how today's teens change their looks based on their personality and mood of the moment..." The "mood of the moment" would normally be regarded as some type of fractured mental disorder. However, since we now have a sliding scale of over one hundred genders to select from, depending on one's "mood of the moment," all is transient. With every facet of one's life in a state of constant change, commodity markets become matters of infinite variation. While the global corporations like to spin that they respond to "consumer demand," the demand is entirely manufactured by marketing and advertising agencies, just as Edward Bernays' created a market for cigarettes among women, in the name of "freedom." UNICEF is at least candid in stating that it is the global corporations that mold attitudes, referring to "the power to influence" that "advertising and marketing" have over "individual and community beliefs" in their "ways of thinking and

---

[732] Newsweek Staff, "Toys: Flavas of the Week."
[733] Howard, "Ads crank up the volume."
[734] Kyles, "Mattel's hip-hop Flava dolls flop."
[735] Ibid.

behaviours." It is good to know that children the world over have in UNICEF such a guardian against their exploitation.

At the time of Flavas' release the chairman and CEO of Mattel (2000–2011) was Robert Eckert, who had been with Kraft Foods and McDonalds. He was a member of the Trilateral Commission, one of the globalist think tanks established by David Rockefeller; the Asia Society, another Rockefeller initiative, Business Council; and on the board of the Los Angeles branch of the World Affairs Council,[736] another part of the globalist network. The present chairman of Mattel is Israeli businessman Ynon Kreiz.[737] The rivalry between MGA and Mattel has been a litigious bitch-fight.[738]

After a hiatus, "Bratz" was relaunched in 2018. MGA's PR blurb played the predictable tune: how "independent" a little girl can be if she just follows the Pied Piper of corporate sales gimmickry. Their "new mantra" (sic) was: "It's good to be yourself, it's good to be Bratz." Now girls could "discover and express their true selves"—which would also be a boon for the manufacturers of makeup and slutty fashion: a vast new class of consumers. "Bratz is back to arm girls with the confidence to know that it's good to be yourself, and it's good to be a Bratz."[739]

Around the same time as "Flavas" was launched (2002–2003), Mattel produced a doll of Shakira, the Latina MTV celebrity. MTV commented:

> *Leather-and-wrist-band look Shakira sported in her "Objection (Tango)" video sure excited many of her fans. It also thrilled the doll department of Mattel, which will immortalize the jalapeno-Latin performer with her doll in March.... The toy giant chose the singer because of her multicultural appeal and will market the doll internationally...*[740]

The relationship between Mattel and MTV is symbiotic. In 2018 Mattel produced a board game of MTV series, "Jersey Shore Family Vacation," in association with Viacom Nickelodeon Consumer Products (part of the MTV Entertainment Group), "the party game for meatballs, fist pumpers and prank war champions." Mattel stated it is "always looking for culturally relevant trends." [741] The themes of this "reality-show" seem to be multiracialism and retardation.

---

[736] IU News Room, "Mattel, Inc. chairman and CEO."
[737] Jewish Business News, "Mattel Appoints Israeli Ynon Kreiz as Chairman."
[738] MGA Entertainment, Inc. v. Mattel, Inc. (2019).
[739] License Global, "MGA Unveils New Bratz."
[740] Wiederhorn, Jon. "Make Shakira Dance for You."
[741] Mattel, "Mattel produces MTV's 'Jersey Shore Family Vacation' Board Game."

In 2021 Mattel and MTV "teamed up" to produce and assist in promoting respectively, "Music Producer Barbie," in an effort to encourage more females to enter music production.742 The doll is produced in several "race" types.

MTV is the primary promoter of Hip Hop and Rap. MTV sponsored the Hip Hop Open, an annual (2000 to 2015) event in Germany. "Yo MTV Raps" was a two-hour program that aired from 1987 to 1995, first in Europe and the following year in the USA. The show was crucial in the promotion of Hip Hop across the world.

Jeff Chang, editor of *Total Chaos*, wrote of the globalizing impact of Hip-Hop behind the familiar facade of "rebelling against authority," writing of Hip-Hop promoter Dana Burton's "Iron Mic" shows:

> *His artists performed a mini history of hip-hop, from its urban American beginnings to its Chinese apotheosis. It was the perfect brew—an African-American entrepreneur promoting a Polish vodka owned by a French corporation using Chinese performers practicing an Afro-Latin-influenced art form that originated in the inner cities of the United States. Welcome to hip-hop's new world.743*

Chang sees Hip Hop as part of a "progressive" movement, yet also states that it is both financially lucrative, and a form used by NGOs to promote their agendas:

> *But one thing about hip-hop has remained consistent across cultures: a vital progressive agenda that challenges the status quo. Thousands of organizers from Cape Town to Paris use hip-hop in their communities to address environmental justice, policing and prisons, media justice, and education. In Gothenburg, Sweden, nongovernmental organizations (NGOs) incorporate graffiti and dance to engage disaffected immigrant and working-class youths. And indigenous young people in places as disparate as Chile, Indonesia, New Zealand, and Norway use hip-hop to push their generation's views into the local conversation.744*

---

742 Mattel Newsroom, "Barbie Launches New Music."
743 Chang, "It's a Hip-Hop World."
744 Ibid.

Chang does not see the paradox, but in the next paragraph does state precisely what the purpose is in "engaging" these "disaffected youth":

> More than 59 million rap albums were sold in the United States alone last year. But that number represents only a small part of hip-hop's influence. It sells an estimated $10 billion worth of trend-setting luxury and consumer goods every year—not just in movies, shoes, and clothing but in everything from snack crackers and soda drinks to cars and computers. This "urban aspirational lifestyle" market is expected to continue to grow exponentially.[745]

From what Chang writes, it should be evident that Hip Hop as a form of genuine dissent, is as phony as the New Left revolt against the "Establishment." It is, like the Left, a *controlled opposition*, and a *channeled rebellion*.

The same year Chang wrote his article for *Foreign Policy*, the US State Department started using Hip-Hopper Toni Blackman as the "US's first official hip-hop ambassador, tasked with using her music to help spread American values around the world."[746] Jazz and Abstract Expressionism had the same function during the Cold War. Blackman's role is analogous to that of Louis Armstrong during the Cold War era.[747] Blackman received a fellowship from of George Soros's Open Society Institute. She is touted among Establishment institutions and academia for her "Hip hop social activism."

The Doll as Fetish Figure

The modern play-doll has been imbued with the characteristics of a fetish figure, possessing powers to reshape the child according to the will of the maker.

In describing a fetish figure from the Congo held by the Horniman Museum, ethnographer Victoria Hobbs wrote that "The priest would order a wooden figure from the carver and then endow it with its power during a ritual at which time medicines or magically-charged materials were attached."[748]

---

[745] Ibid.
[746] CBC Radio, "Why the US State Department."
[747] Vulliamy, Ed. "'Rockers and spies.'"
[748] Hobbs, "The Function of a 'Fetish' Figure."

The place of the "priest" in the Late West is taken by the corporation executive; "medicines" and "magically-charged materials" are the electronic media whose message through sound and imagery, subliminally invades the mind of the target.

With its attachments the figure is imbued with an empowering spirit also known as *nkisi*.

Accoutrements such as make-up and attire are charged with meaning, impelling the child to want the doll and perhaps even to become a reflection of the doll. Incantations take the form of advertising catchphrases such as "it's good to be like a Bratz," empowering the figure with an influence over its possessor with a desire that will probably not be quenched until satisfied. Money thereby accrues to the maker of the figure, and even more so, power over the mind of the child.

Nkisi is conceived as a power emanating from the unseen world of the dead, an omniscient force which is otherwise inaccessible to human perception.

Neither parents nor child are fully aware of the "power emanating from the unseen world" of manufacturing, marketing and advertising, "an omniscient force which is otherwise inaccessible to human perception." UNICEF has openly referred to this fetish power, stating that it has "the power to influence [the] ways of thinking and behaviours" of children.

An appropriately empowered figure was selected, and through chanting, singing and dancing, the *nkisi* spirit would be called upon to act.

A selected figure is empowered through the sounds and words of advertising and marketing, including singing and dancing, and the chanting of advertising jingles and slogans repetitively, until a desire is created from outside to within the child, whose "thinking and behavior" are changed according to the will of the "priests" of marketing and advertising. An induced feeling of *fetishism* overwhelms the child, which is like only to dissipate and leave with age, at which time another fetish figure is imposed by marketing wizardry to restart the process.

Global Exploitation

Globalization means the free flow of capital, resources and labor (in the name of "replacement migration") across the world. This is the "open society" of George Soros and other oligarchs. It is also the internationalism of the UN and its organs, and a vast network of interlocking NGOs, euphemistically called the "civil society," which act as a *de facto* world government.[749]

We have seen how UNICEF works for the globalization process in conjunction with the transnational corporations. "Diversity and inclusion" is the catchphrase, like "human rights." "The rights of the child" is a euphemism for the reconstruction of children as consumers and "world citizens." It is analogous to the "rights of women" which is a euphemism for the deconstruction of woman as mother and her reconstruction as factory fodder; likewise with the "rights of migrants," and the "rights of ethnic minorities" who become the "vast new consuming public" of Harry Oppenheimer's post-apartheid vision, in the name of "liberation."

As we have seen, all of these supposedly protected groups have a myriad of organs within the UN and "universal declarations" to redefine who they are in the name of their "rights." UNICEF has shown itself to be unequivocally committed to the redefinition of what it is even to be a "child," where even to "play" becomes a mechanism for indoctrination and reconstruction. UNICEF overtly states that global corporations are a primary driving force behind this process.

Among the companies cited for commendation for their "inclusion and diversity" policies by UNICEF are those that have long been accused of using cheap labour, including child labor. Globalization enables relocating manufacturing to low cost states where wages and labor practices are exploitive. While these companies posture with their good causes of "inclusion and diversity," or what they call "corporate responsibility," their products, for which they are commended by UNICEF, are manufactured in the low cost states.

A report on global corporations in low cost states summarized the situation with these toy companies as they pertain to conditions in China. Note that three of the companies referred to, Mattel, Disney, and Crayola, are praised for their promotion of "diversity and inclusion" in the UNICEF Playbook. The report states:

> *Hundreds of thousands of young Chinese migrant workers toil away in factories making toys for major international brands. A recent report by China Labor Watch (CLW) exposed dozens of violations in four factories that make toys for Mattel, Fischer-Price, Disney, Crayola, and others. Violations included unpaid wages, lack of safety training, excessive overtime, poor living conditions, environmental pollution, and lack of fire safety.*

---

[749] See: Howard, *The Open Society Playbook*.

> Like electronics, toy manufacturing can also be very chemically intensive, requiring various hazardous inks, solvents, paints and phthalates (used in plastics). While potentially dangerous for consumers, these chemicals are even more dangerous for workers who are exposed on a regular basis in higher concentrations, often without safety training or protective equipment, as found by CLW. Additionally, the management in these factories can be very abusive. A worker named Hu Nianzhen killed herself in November 2014 after working at a Mattel factory for two years because of the demanding conditions of her work and the verbal abuse and threats from her superiors.[750]

The comeback of such corporations is that their manufacturing is subcontracted to factories over which they have no oversight. The rationale for relocating their manufacturing from Western states to China and the Third World is precisely because of the sweatshop conditions that drive down costs and maximize profits. That is the character of globalization. What other reason do corporations have for relocating to low cost states for manufacturing if not to maximize their profits?

A recent article in the *New York Post* is particularly insightful in castigating Nike for its posturing on "social justice issues" while having a long record of being condemned for its use of sweatshop labor, including child labor, in China and the Third World. Steven Mosher wrote of Nike in 2020:

> *Woke companies are constantly hectoring America on its failings.*
>
> *The Social Justice Warriors who run Nike, for example, pompously inform us that they are fighting "against discrimination in communities worldwide." Not only that but they are "work[ing] every day to erase the stain of racism and the damage of injustice."*
>
> *Really, Nike? Then why do you have your shoes made by an oppressive, morally bankrupt regime? China is the ugly poster child, the living exemplar, for all of the evils that you are so quick to condemn America for.*

---

[750] O'Connell, "8 Things You Didn't Know."

> *Right now, at this very moment, the Chinese Communists are eliminating the Uyghurs, a Turkish-speaking people who live in China's Far West, from the face of the earth.*
> *…But it's even worse for Nike, the wokest of woke companies.*
> *It turns out that some of these Uyghurs have been slaving away making basketball shoes with the famous swoosh on them.*
> *An Australian Strategic Policy Institute report published this March, "Uyghurs for sale," found Uyghur slave labor working in factories supplying 83 well-known global brands in the technology, clothing, shoe and automotive sectors, including Apple, GM, Gap—and Nike.*
> *Nike contracts with a Qingdao company, for example, that as of January of this year had 600 Uyghurs cobbling together its shoes.*
> *Yes, the same company that funds organizations asking for reparations for a practice that ended in the US in 1865 has actually used slave labor in China to make its products—and its profits—for many years.*[751]

Mosher refers to Nike's sponsorship of Colin Kaepernick, lauded in the UNICEF Playbook as an example to the corporate world:

> *Like Nike, the pro-sports officials, owners and athletes of the NFL and the NBA who are making big money off the China market have also turned a blind eye to the brutal oppression of minorities there, all the while making woke noises about how racist America is.*
> *The poster child for all of this anti-American demagoguery is NFL quarterback Colin Kaepernick, who in 2018 signed a multi-million-dollar contract to become a megaphone for Nike products.*
> *I wonder if the same man who kneels to protest America's slave-owning past might one day stand for the freedom of slaves in China. It would only be fitting. It was Uyghur slaves, after all, who might have stitched his Kaepernick brand of Air Force 1 shoes together.*[752]

---

[751] Mosher, "Nike should quit lecturing."
[752] Ibid.

Mosher points to the wide divergence between Nike's corporate sponsorship in the USA in the name of "human rights" and its use of the sweatshops of Asia.

As for Nike, it has pledged to donate "$100 million over the next 10 years to organizations dedicated to ensuring racial equality, social justice and greater access to education."

But I have a better idea, Nike. Why don't you take the blood money you have earned from employing slave labor in China and open a factory in the US? Choose a site in the inner city, employ minorities, and provide jobs and a way out of poverty.

That would go a lot further toward ensuring racial equality and social justice, not to mention hope for the future of America, than anything else you could do.[753]

In 2006 it was reported that MGA's "Bratz" was "made in a sweatshop in China, where women are routinely forced to work seven days and 94 ½ hours a week, for wages of just 51 ½ cents an hour, $4.13 a day."

As bad as conditions are now, they are about to get worse. The factory wants to fire all the workers and then bring them back as temporary workers with contracts of just one to eight months, which would strip them of any legal rights they might have. As it is, the workers are denied sick days as well as work injury and health insurance.[754]

The toy manufacturing industry not only makes vast profits for the corporate elite, but more importantly, reconstructs children in the image of the "inclusive" "global citizen," from the youngest possible age. As we have seen, UNICEF is well aware of the influence that manufacturing, advertising and marketing have in reshaping children, and regard the opportunities as laudable rather than as exploitive or abusive. Here we have the means by which children can be reconstructed beyond the influence of parents, according to a global corporate culture that converges with than of UNICEF and vast globalist networks that we have been considering, whether as UN organs, NGOs, or corporate boardrooms. There is a convergence of aims and doctrines, and this is indicated by the UNICEF Playbook.

The lesson for the "children of the world" is that there is no sense of permanence and attachment to be had; that all is in a state of flux, or what might here be called "fashion" and "trend." This *global cultural nihilism* means that children can be treated as consumers, whose play, attire and diet become as transient as any other commodity, and hence in need of

---

[753] Ibid.
[754] China Labor Watch, "Made in China."

continuous renewal—of production and consumption. That is the reality behind the catchphrases of the "rights of the child," the child as an "individual" (while obsessing about the latest trends and fashions) with his or her own "personality or "attitude," all shaped by marketing and advertising, as UNICEF has stated.

Jeff Chang's description of the globalization process is particularly cogent: "the perfect brew...[of] an African-American entrepreneur promoting a Polish vodka owned by a French corporation using Chinese performers practicing an Afro-Latin-influenced art form that originated in the inner cities of the United States." Black, Polish, French, Chinese, Latino... all such identities cease to exist in this "perfect brew"—the melting-pot—the crucible of globalization. One is no longer Chinese, French, African, or Latino, but a part of the production and consumption process, behind the facade of a bogus "individuality."

Globalization of Labor: Origins and Aims of the United Nations Global Migration Compact

> "Each country has its own culture, language, way of life, and it is better for people to live in their own country."
>
> Dalai Lama (2018)

Behind humanitarian gestures such as "open borders" and the "rights of refugees" stands the need for a detached and uprooted mass of laborers and technocrats to keep the global economic treadmill operative. Decades of social breakdown, reinforced by liberal ideology, has helped to cause a demographic decline in the industrialized states that threatens the obsession with a perpetual growth economy. In its zeal to fully integrate women into the "inclusive economy" via "liberation" from family and home, with its backing of feminism and "reproductive rights," the oligarchy has created a demographic crisis now scrambles to replenish the workforce. The excess populations of the under-industrialized states is a means of doing so. The so-called "far right" has been vilified for referring to such Third World population shifts to the West as "The Great Replacement," yet the United Nations calls the same phenomenon by a similar term, "Replacement Migration." These population shifts are taking place while at the same time there are moves to strengthen "hate speech" laws to stifle dissent. The UN Global Compact for Migration, like "hate speech laws," is proceeding behind the facade of "human rights" but for the benefit of globalized capitalism.

The United Nations Global Compact for Safe, Orderly and Regular Migration was signed on December 19th, 2018 by 164 members of the UN General Assembly. Twenty-nine UN member states did not sign the compact, including the USA, Hungary, Austria, Italy, Poland, Slovakia, Chile, Israel and Australia. It is notable that the USA, where the Compact had its origins, was not a signatory nation in 2018, having been resisted by the Trump Administration, which was eschewing various globalist entanglements. The ironic scenario was reminiscent of the US Senate's rejection of membership in the League of Nations, one of the prime architects having been President Woodrow Wilson. At the time the Trump Administration issued a strong statement that eloquently exposed the globalist agenda:

> *The United States did not participate in the negotiation of the Global Compact for Safe, Orderly, and Regular Migration ("the Compact"), objects to its adoption, and is not bound by any of the commitments or outcomes stemming from the Compact process or contained in the Compact itself. The Compact and the New York Declaration for Refugees and Migrants, which called for the development of the Compact and commits to "strengthening global governance" for international migration, contain goals and objectives that are inconsistent and incompatible with US law, policy, and the interests of the American people.*
>
> *The United States proclaims and reaffirms its belief that decisions about how to secure its borders, and whom to admit for legal residency or to grant citizenship, are among the most important sovereign decisions a State can make, and are not subject to negotiation, or review, in international instruments, or fora. The United States maintains the sovereign right to facilitate or restrict access to our territory, in accordance with our national laws and policies, subject to our existing international obligations.*
>
> *We believe the Compact and the process that led to its adoption, including the New York Declaration, represent an effort by the United Nations to advance global governance at the expense of the sovereign right of States to manage their immigration systems in accordance with their national laws, policies, and interests.*[755]

Apologists for the agreement state that it does not undermine national sovereignty, that it will make migration a more ordered, humane process, and eliminate people smuggling. The legal advice to the New Zealand government was that the compact is "non-binding," and the apologists have used this to repudiate opposition.[756]

---

[755] "National Statement."
[756] Devlin, "New Zealand Votes."

Lord Bates, Britain's Minister of State at the Department for International Development, stated: "The compact 'protects every state's right to determine its own immigration policies, including in areas such as asylum, border controls and returns of illegal migrants.'"[757] At the time, New Zealand's foreign affairs minister and deputy prime minister, Winston Peters, head of the populist New Zealand First Party, and part of the Labour Government coalition, having based his political career largely around stricter migration control since the founding of NZ First, in his role as apologist for the Labour Government, and as the New Zealand representative who signed the Compact, adopted the line of Lord Bates, Angela Merkel, et al. Like Merkel and other European leaders who have blamed the "Right" for spreading false information, Peters claimed that the "Alt Right" in New Zealand has been responsible for spreading misinformation about the Compact, but what he thinks the alt right is in New Zealand is uncertain. What was real is the backlash from among his own party grassroots. If Peters had been in opposition he would surely have been the most vociferous opponent of the Compact. For his compromise he was out of Parliament the following general election.

The Nature of UN Declarations and Covenants

However, when viewed from the perspective of how the UN functions, and how its declarations and compacts are implemented, it is pure cant for politicians to claim that there is no justification for popular misgivings. While the declaration is called "non-binding" on signatory states, and it supposedly does not subvert national laws, myriad UN declarations have become "international law," and it is "international law" to which the Migration Compact appeals.

The Migration Compact is sold with Orwellian "double-speak." Human Rights and Race Relations Acts, implemented across the world, are examples of the types of "international law" to which the Migration Compact alludes, which were based on the 1948 UN Declaration on Human Rights. These acts are draconian and biased.

New Zealand, and of course the other UN members are signatories to many UN "covenants" and as such are "obligated" (sic) to report to the UN regularly in regard to how these "covenants" are being implemented. Under "universal periodic reviews" these include the International Covenant on Civil and Political Rights; International Convention on the

---

[757] Goodman, "What's the UN Global Compact."

Elimination of All Forms of Racial Discrimination; Convention Relating to the Status of Refugees; United Nations Declaration on the Rights of Indigenous Peoples, and others. What is a UN "universal periodic review"? In regard to UN conceptions on "human rights," for example, the New Zealand Government explains:

> *Under this mechanism, the human rights situation of all UN Member States is reviewed every 5 years. 42 UN Member States are reviewed each year in Geneva during three sessions dedicated to 14 States each. These three sessions are usually held in January/February, April/May and October/November.*[758]

The Ministry of Foreign Affairs and Trade also explains UN sanctions against states that do not abide by "international law."[759] When sanctions do not work, the bombing tends to start. Since the Migration Compact is a reflection and outcome of UN "international law," it is nonsense to claim that this does not impact on state sovereignty and the right of states to determine their own migration policies.

That the Migration Compact is based around other UN "covenants" that have become "international law," with UN sanctions against those states deemed offenders, is indicated by the Compact's "preamble."[760] As with other UN declarations and covenants, much of the Migration Compact outlines the monitoring of compliance by signatory states. Sections entitled "follow-up" and "implementation" are devoted to this. The International Organization for Migration is the UN policing agency that enforces it.

In arguing for an increase of draconian measures against states deemed to be in violation of "international law," particularly on how "human rights" is defined by the UN, Buhm Suk Baek of Cornell, points out that while the UN claims not to intervene in the internal affairs of members states:

> *Humanitarian intervention is based upon the doctrine that there are limits to the freedoms states have in dealing with their own nationals. It should be distinguished from actions to protect a state's own nationals abroad. When this doctrine was defined by Dutch international scholar Hugo Grotius and other 17th century legal scholars, it allowed one or more states to use force to*

---

[758] "Universal Periodic Review."
[759] "UN Sanctions," ibid.
[760] "Global Compact for Safe, Orderly and Regular Migration," Preamble (2).

prevent another state from mistreating its own nationals in circumstances so brutal and widespread that they shocked the conscience of the international community. Such interference in a state's domestic affairs is defended by the argument that if certain practices continue to take place in a state despite protest and objections by neighboring states, then humanitarian considerations outweigh the prohibition of intervention and justify a decision to interfere.[761]

It is double-speak when the UN states that it does not intervene in a state's internal affairs, whether by economic sanctions, or by armed force. As is often the case, "atrocity propaganda" is a prelude to the invasion of a targeted state that somehow offends the "international community." It was the liquidation of the supposed tyrant Qaddafi that created a refugee crisis from Africa into Europe, of which Qaddafi had warned:

Tomorrow Europe might no longer be European, and even black, as there are millions who want to come in. What will be the reaction of the white and Christian Europeans faced with this influx of starving and ignorant Africans.... we don't know if Europe will remain an advanced and united continent or if it will be destroyed, as happened with the barbarian invasions.[762]

The UN Global Compact for Migration is intended to bring order to the chaos that globalist intervention has wrought on Libya and Syria, and wherever else the nebulous "international community" meddles.

In calling for an increase in the powers of intervention by the UN Buhm Suk Baek concludes that, "Admittedly, humanitarian intervention had been abused in the past by strong states to pursue other political, economic or military objectives."[763] Baek approvingly cites the example of the way Yugoslavia was targeted and reduced to ruin in the name of "human rights":

Under Security Council Resolution 757, the Council imposed a wide range of economic sanctions on the Federal Republic of Yugoslavia (Serbia and Montenegro) on May, 1992. These sanctions are also related to the protection of human rights as the Council announced its concern for the continued expulsion of

---

[761] Baek, "Economic Sanctions."
[762] Murphy, "How the Fall of Qaddafi."
[763] Baek, "Economic Sanctions," 19 (2.3),

non-Serb civilians and noted the 'urgent need for humanitarian assistance and the various appeals made in this connection' under the former Resolution.[764]

Serbia is a particularly poignant example of how the "human rights" ploy was used to dismember a state for the purposes of privatizing and globalizing its economy, with particular reference to the mining region of Kosovo, where the privatization of the economy was made an official war aim. The Rambouillet Peace Agreement that paved the road to war, states: *"the economy of Kosovo shall function in accordance with free market principles."*[765] Prior to the decision to target Serbia for "regime change," for years the Kosovar Albanian separatists were known for their anti-Serbian and anti-Orthodox terrorism. It did not take long for "the international community" to change terrorists and narco-gangsters into "freedom fighters" defending the oppressed Kosovar Albanians.[766] In 2011 the Israeli newspaper *Haaretz* reported on how international capital, in conjunction with the UN in 2006, celebrated "the conclusion of the biggest privatization deal signed since the end of the war with Serbia, involving the Drenas mining complex, shut down by NATO bombs during the war."[767] That is the reality behind wars waged by the "international community" in the name of "human rights."

UN Global Migration Compact

So, what does the Migration Compact state? The fundamental premises are that (1) humans should have the right to move across the earth without regard to barriers, (2) this is a natural part of the economic globalization process, (3) international capital has a significant role to play in this, (4) the compact is part of "international law" and "global governance."

When the UN General Assembly adopted a resolution on global migration in 2017, affirming the New York Declaration on Refugees and Migrants in 2016, it did so with the explicit statement that this involves "global governance," refers to "actionable commitments," and formalizes

---

[764] Ibid., 31 (3.2.3), Sanctions against the Federal Republic of Yugoslavia.
[765] "Rambouillet Agreement," Article I (1), 1.
[766] Bolton, *Babel Inc.*, 161-173.
[767] Blau, "Israel Black Hole."

what appears to be a policing role for the UN International Organisation for Migration.[768]

Like UN declarations in general, the Migration Compact uses the language of Orwellian double-speak. Hence, while apologists allude to the compact being "non-legally binding," it states of this that the compact upholds "the sovereignty of States and their obligations under international law."[769] On "implementation," the Compact states that, "We reaffirm our commitment to international law and emphasize that the Global Compact is to be implemented in a manner that is consistent with our rights and obligations under international law."[770]

The "sovereignty of states" is meaningless when confronted by "international law." The UN has operated behind this duplicity since its founding.

The first "vision and guiding principle" of the Compact states:

This Global Compact expresses our collective commitment to improving cooperation on international migration. Migration has been part of the human experience throughout history, and we recognize that it is a source of prosperity, innovation and sustainable development in our globalized world, and that these positive impacts can be optimized by improving migration governance.[771]

...We learned that migration is a defining feature of our globalized world, connecting societies within and across all regions, making us all countries of origin, transit and destination....[772]

This is the crux of the issue: the real aim buried among the usual moralizing. Economic globalization necessitates open borders and is a primary means of destroying the barriers to international capital, not only economically, but socially, culturally, and ethnically. This explains why the international oligarchs hatched this Compact, for what is called "social investment." While the UN refers to the integrity of the states, this is more double-speak as it also refers to states being fluid and without fixity of heritage or destiny, "making us all countries of origin, transit and

---

[768] "Resolution by General Assembly."
[769] "Global Compact for Safe, Orderly and Regular Migration," (7).
[770] Ibid., (41), 32.
[771] Ibid., (8) Our Vision and Guiding Principles.
[772] Ibid., (10) Common Understanding.

destination." This means a globalized mass humanity without roots, able to be relocated across the world as marketing and labor needs require.

While "national sovereignty" is affirmed[773] in Orwellian manner, again the concept is negated with the next passage, "that the State, public and private institutions and entities, as well as persons themselves are accountable to laws that are publicly promulgated, equally enforced and independently adjudicated, and which are consistent with international law."[774] These are the repressive laws that have been enacted in many states, based on "legally non-binding" UN covenants, where criticism of immigration policies can result in the jailing of dissidents. It is why increasingly repressive "hate speech" laws are being enacted. This is affirmed where:

> *The Global Compact is based on international human rights law and upholds the principles of non-regression and non-discrimination. By implementing the Global Compact, we ensure effective respect, protection and fulfilment of the human rights of all migrants, regardless of their migration status, across all stages of the migration cycle. We also reaffirm the commitment to eliminate all forms of discrimination, including racism, xenophobia and intolerance against migrants and their families.*[775]

Any dissent is called "racism and xenophobia," and the legal prohibitions have long been enacted through race relations and human rights laws, while the news media in all Western states can be relied on to make pariahs out of those who object. A primary "objective" is the utilization of data to promote global migration agendas. The Compact also alludes to cooperation between a broad range of "stakeholders," including trades unions, media, academia, civil society, and business in what is called a "whole of society approach."[776] It seems evident that the purpose is a mobilization against the specter of "populism," which drove the oligarchy and its leftist fodder into fear and frenzy with the election of Donald Trump, and with the ever present Russian bugbear of Putin, and other "populists" such as Orbán in Hungary, who speak not only of preserving "Christian Europe," but of resisting globalist oligarchs such as George Soros.

---

[773] Ibid., (15) National Sovereignty.
[774] Ibid., Rule of law and due process.
[775] Ibid., Human Rights.
[776] Ibid., 4 (15).

Politicians are selling the Migration Compact with the idea that its aim is to reduce "refugees" by ensuring they are not compelled by their home states to seek refuge in other states. This is being used to implement another UN initiative, the 2030 Agenda for Sustainable Development. The whole of Objective 2, "Minimize the adverse drivers and structural factors that compel people to leave their country of origin," is designed to restructure states socially and economically. This means "private and foreign direct investment" (d), and there can be little doubt that the aim is to allow predatory capital to take over a state's resources and utilities under the guise of the UN definition of "human rights," "inclusive economy," "gender equity," etc. This is precisely what Serbia was subjected to and reduced to ruin by NATO bombs when it rejected the imposition of the Rambouillet Peace Agreement.

Labor Market Fodder

The Compact refers to using migration to facilitate "labour market needs," "labour mobility agreements," "free movement regimes," "visa liberalization," to speed up visa and permit processing, [777] and to address "demographic realities," meaning the demographic decline of the European states through migration, by "consultation with the private sector and other stakeholders," changing the character of states according to the requirements of global capital.

Objective 16 aims to integrate migrants into host communities, while ensuring their own identities are retained. Hence, there remains the quandary of whether a society is to be a melting pot or multicultural. The ultimate aim remains an "inclusive economy," as the oligarchic think tanks call it, where the laws of social production will level out any dissimilarities between hosts and migrants, especially after several generations, in the hope that a standardized population will have emerged based on production and consumption, where the population is a nebulous *Homo Economicus*. "Labour market integration"[778] is a key aim and ultimately the real aim.

---

[777] Ibid, Objective 5: Enhance availability and flexibility of pathways for regular migration, 11.
[778] Ibid., Objective 16: Empower migrants and societies to realize full inclusion and social cohesion, 23.

Indoctrination

Objective 17 aims at the remolding of the attitudes of the host peoples:

> *We commit to eliminate all forms of discrimination, condemn and counter expressions, acts and manifestations of racism, racial discrimination, violence, xenophobia and related intolerance against all migrants in conformity with international human rights law.... We also commit to protect freedom of expression in accordance with international law, recognizing that an open and free debate contributes to a comprehensive understanding of all aspects of migration.*[779]

This is unadulterated cant; again, Orwellian double-speak. It is precisely the terminology used by the New Zealand Ministry of Justice for the "hate speech proposals," while in the next breath saying that criticism of multiculturalism will be prohibited. Any criticism of open borders, and defense of the host people is called "racism and xenophobia" by UN "international human rights laws." Under the UN covenants there never has been "freedom of expression" for dissent. There have been jail sentences and crippling fines for speaking out.

Paragraph (c) of this section states that the news media should be used as an indoctrination utility to ensure that there is standardized reporting in support of migrant globalization:

> *Promote independent, objective and quality reporting of media outlets, including internet based information, including by sensitizing and educating media professionals on migration-related issues and terminology, investing in ethical reporting standards and advertising, and stopping allocation of public funding or material support to media outlets that systematically promote intolerance, xenophobia, racism and other forms of discrimination towards migrants, in full respect for the freedom of the media.*[780]

Again, this is precisely what the New Zealand Labour government has undertaken by subsidizing the news media for the purpose of what is

---

[779] Ibid., Objective 17 (33): Eliminate all forms of discrimination and promote evidence-based public discourse to shape perceptions of migration, 24.
[780] Ibid., 17. 33 (c), 24.

euphemistically called "democracy." The news media has been put on the government payroll to propagate the state's dogma.

How can there be "independent, objective and quality reporting of media outlets," and "full respect for the freedom of the media," when the aim is to impose a common standard of journalism and eliminate anything deemed "racist" or "xenophobic"; smear words applied to dissent? Again, it is pure cant. Although the news media in the Western world has long been compliant anyway, it is part of an indoctrination program, aimed at:

> ...awareness-raising campaigns targeted at communities of origin, transit and destination in order to inform public perceptions regarding the positive contributions of safe, orderly and regular migration, based on evidence and facts, and to end racism, xenophobia and stigmatization against all migrants.[781]

Interference in the internal political process is also urged, to suppress and smear any sign of political resistance:

> Engage migrants, political, religious and community leaders, as well as educators and service providers to detect and prevent incidences of intolerance, racism, xenophobia, and other forms of discrimination against migrants and diasporas and support activities in local communities to promote mutual respect, including in the context of electoral campaigns.[782]

Again, this appears to be an appeal to mobilization against political dissidence. The National Endowment for Democracy, Freedom House, the Soros network, and many others, have been adept at interfering in the internal politics of states, and it is notable that the UN Compact openly urges interference in "political campaigns." While governments are encouraged to inhibit political campaigning, at street level organizations such as Antifa and Black Lives Matter can be violently used to confront "populist" reaction. What happened at Charlottesville in 2017 when lawfully assembled citizens attempted to defend their heritage, and were confronted not only be street mobs, but opposed by police, courts, and media, is an example of the "engagement" recommended by the UN.

---

[781] Ibid., (f).
[782] Ibid., (g), 25.

What is Behind the UN Global Compact?

The UN Global Migration Compact is an initiative of global capital. The aim is the free flow of labor, in addition to the free flow of resources and capital to benefit an international oligarchy. The Migration Compact refers frequently to the role to be played by private business. In implementing the Compact, it is stated:

We decide to establish a capacity-building mechanism in the United Nations, building upon existing initiatives, that supports efforts of Member States to implement the Global Compact. It allows Member States, the United Nations and other relevant stakeholders, including the private sector and philanthropic foundations, to contribute technical, financial and human resources on a voluntary basis in order to strengthen capacities and foster multi-partner cooperation.[783]

The philanthropic foundations are the long established means by which globalist oligarchy pursues its agendas, now called "social investment" by creating and funding a vast international network of NGOs called "civil society."

The Migration Compact originates from the New York Declaration for Refugees and Migrants. The Compact states: "This Global Compact presents a non-legally binding, cooperative framework that builds on the commitments agreed upon by Member States in the New York Declaration for Refugees and Migrants." The International Organisation for Migration (IOM), the monitoring organization for the Compact, also states: "...Annex II of the New York Declaration set in motion a process of intergovernmental consultations and negotiations culminating in the planned adoption of the Global Compact for Migration at an intergovernmental conference on international migration in 2018."[784]

The seeding of the New York Declaration, and hence the UN Migration Compact, leads back to a Rockefeller Foundation's plan for city crisis management across the world. The plan originates with a concept called "100 Resilient Cities," established in 2013, funded by the Rockefeller Foundation, "and managed as a sponsored project by Rockefeller Philan-

---

[783] "Global Compact for Safe, Orderly and Regular Migration," Implementation, (43), 32.
[784] "Global Compact for Migration."

thropy Advisors with support from the Brookings Institution." Resilient Cities submitted to the UNHCR:

> Heads of state and government gathered at the UN General Assembly in New York last month against the backdrop of a burgeoning refugee crisis in South Asia and a lingering one across the Middle East and Europe. City leaders from across the globe also convened to discuss the role that cities play in providing assistance to refugees.
> These discussions were facilitated by two major events. The Brookings Institution—together with the International Rescue Committee and 100 Resilient Cities—Pioneered by The Rockefeller Foundation—convened a high-level working group to elicit best practice recommendations for local communities grappling with displacement-related challenges. At the same time, New York City convened a Global Mayors Summit on Migration and Refugee Policy and Practice designed to uncover how cities overcome obstacles to implementing policies that promote, among other things, refugee integration, rights protection, and empowerment.[785]

Among the "platform partners" of Resilient Cities is the Anti-Defamation League (ADL), the century-old Zionist smear-mongering and private investigation organization. Why does Resilient Cities need the partnership of the ADL? It is notable that while the ADL and other Zionist entities throughout the world are in the forefront of opposing immigration restrictions and advocating for "refugees," this does not apply to Israel, which has not signed the UN Migration Compact.[786]

Another Resilient Cities partner is the Asia Society, formed by the Rockefeller dynasty. Another partner is the World Bank. Most explicitly *Bloomberg* reports:

> The Global Compact for Safe, Orderly and Regular Migration gets backing from global business community.
> Numerous leaders of major multinational companies endorsed the Global Compact for Safe, Orderly and Regular Migration (Global Compact for Migration) today at the second annual Bloomberg Global Business Forum, a gathering of more

---
[785] Brookings Institution, "Engaging City Leaders."
[786] "Netanyahu: Israel Won't Sign."

than 70 heads of state and delegation, and 200 of the world's most prominent business leaders, to strengthen economic prosperity and collaborate on trade issues, globalization, innovation, and competition.

In a press conference with the Presidents of Switzerland and Mexico, Alain Berset and Enrique Peña Nieto, whose Permanent Representatives to the United Nations led the negotiations, Michael R. Bloomberg, the Founder of Bloomberg L.P. and Bloomberg Philanthropies, and Mayor of New York City (2002–2013), announced the first wave of support from global business leaders for the Global Compact for Migration. These founding signers include Jim Coulter and Jon Winkelried, Co-CEOs of TPG; Dawn Fitzpatrick, Chief Investment Officer of the Soros Fund Management; Joe Gebbia, Co-founder and Chief Product Officer of Airbnb; Dara Khosrowshahi, CEO of Uber; Rich Lesser, CEO of BCG; Hamdi Ulukaya, Founder, Chairman and CEO of Chobani; and John Zimmer, President and Co-Founder of Lyft.[787]

Bloomberg proceeds to unequivocally state the purpose behind the rhetoric, albeit still retaining some of that rhetoric in regard to "national sovereignty," and the "rule of law":

Every nation has a role to play in addressing this crisis, and this Compact is designed to help guide them. It provides a framework for how the international community can reap the economic benefits of immigration without sacrificing national sovereignty or rule of law—and I want to thank all of the government and business leaders who are supporting its implementation.[788]

President Berset of Switzerland, who has combined a career as a financial adviser with that of being a social democratic politician, in a nexus between capital and socialism that has been common, also stressed the economic motive for migration: "Without the foreign labor force, many of our industries would not function as they do now. Notwithstanding difficulties, migration must be seen as an enrichment—economically and culturally."[789]

---

[787] Bloomberg, "Renowned Business Leaders Welcome."
[788] Ibid.
[789] Ibid.

"Deterritorialization" and "Reterritorialization"

It is an "enrichment" of the international financial and economic system of predatory capital that aims at what sociologists have called "deterritorialization" and "reterritorialization" as part of the process of globalization. One might also say identities are deconstructed and reconstructed.

An identity is reterritorialized by the processes of social production, accelerated by the advent of cyber and other technology making the feeling of distance, place, and space seem of decreasing importance in terms of human relationships, which also happen to be paradoxically increasingly remote rather than personal. Identities, both individual and collective, are redefined according to the new realities imposed by technologies and economics, and hence are "reterritorialized." Dr. Zdravko Mlinar, a founder of "spatial sociology," whose career includes service with UN organs, states that while traditional identities are being made redundant by "progress," new identities ("reterritorialization") are formed. Mlinar concluded in an early paper on the subject:

> *The growing use of new information, communication and transportation technologies is radically altering the meaning of space and spatial distance. The decline of the role of space as a barrier to connectedness is the focus of attention. Less often it is observed that the protective function of space is also weakening and that this is mobilising people, goods and ideas and threatening the survival of sepociaic territorial (cultural) identities.* [790]

These "new identities" that arise in a "contradictory process" involving "internationalization and globalization," "strengthen small social groups and individuals," while "these undermine the particular territorial (cultural) identities we have known..." This is a process of both "homogenization and diversification."[791] Mlinar sees increased "diversification" among individuals, forming new communities and "subgroups" based around "goods and ideas."[792]

---

[790] Mlinar, "Deterritorialization.," 150.
[791] Ibid.
[792] Ibid., 151.

The traditional bonds of family, faith, homeland, and ethnos will be replaced by detaching and reattaching individuals to new identities formed around globalization; and it will be called "freedom."

Migrants Used to Break European Identities

Defining the forming of new communities according to the processes of production is a Marxist analysis in the service of global capitalism. Marx approvingly saw the internationalization of labor as proceeding from the internationalization of the means of production as part of the dialectics of history, "owing to the development of the freedom of commerce, to the world market, to uniformity in the mode of production, and to the conditions corresponding thereto."[793] What Marx wrote in 1848 on the "internationalization" of the production processes leading to socialism, seems similar to what is now stated on the inexorability of globalization under the aegis of capitalism. Both lead to global standardization in the interests of production and to the detriment of authentic identities.

Migrants have been used in this process in the interests of both US geopolitics and of international capital, often working in tandem. Traditional Islam (not the *Wahhabist* sect backed by the USA's Saudi allies), remains an obstacle to globalization. However, the USA aims to detach and secularize Muslim migrant youth so that they might become part of the amorphous mass of *Homo Economicus*.

In 2011, *The Globe and Mail* reported that "leadership programs" sponsored by the US Embassy in France focused on "potential leaders in Muslim groups and other minorities," via the International Visitor Leadership Program. A large proportion of the participants since 2010 have been Muslims.[794] Then Secretary of State Hilary Clinton commented that many of the Egyptians in the program had become active in the riots that overthrew the regime in Egypt as part of the well-orchestrated "Arab Spring."[795]

Garrett Martin stated that US Embassies across Europe are under instruction to "court second and third generation" Muslims,[796] that is to say, those who have been uprooted from their traditions. These de-Islamized youth are to be the fodder of globalism.

---

[793] Marx and Engels, *Communist Manifesto*, 71-72.
[794] Elash, "US accused." See Bolton, *Babel Inc.*, 192.
[795] Martin, "In Smart-Power Shift."
[796] Ibid.

The omnipresent globalist speculator George Soros has a migrant plan: "The Soros Plan." Soros has drafted a plan that includes the European Union taking a million migrants from Africa and the Levant annually, "for the foreseeable future," with each given a grant of 15,000 Euros. The costs involved could be met by EU borrowing due to its AAA credit rating.[797] Hence, international finance gains (1) a vast labor source, (2) a means of destabilizing nation-states, and (3) interest accrued through the funding of the program by the banks.

Another arch plutocrat, the late Peter Sutherland, was in the forefront of open border advocacy for Europe. Sutherland had been Attorney General of Eire, director general of GATT and the World Trade Organization, honorary European chairman of the Trilateral Commission, member of the Bilderberg Group steering committee, on the advisory board of the Council on Foreign Relations, and a chairman of Goldman Sachs, which is the primary corporate contributor in funding the Afro-Levantine demographic shift to Europe.[798] Sutherland was also United Nations Special Representative of the Secretary General for International Migration. Sutherland explained the agenda for the use of the Afro-Levantine migrants into Europe as being to break down the national-cultural consciousness of Europe such as it exists:

> *This will demand, first and foremost, that EU leaders overcome the forces that have so far impeded action. One obstacle is anti-migrant populism, which has intensified owing to the serious economic challenges that Europeans have faced. With far-right political parties nipping at their heels, most mainstream politicians avoid taking a stance on migration that might make them seem "soft."*[799]

Sutherland stated that the migrants provide labor and taxes.[800] Further:

> *The 21st century is built on mobility: capital, goods, and information circulate at low cost and lightning speed. Yet, paradoxically, international migration has become more perilous. It is governed by outmoded notions about human*

---

[797] Soros, "Rebuilding the Asylum."
[798] Kottasova, "Google, Goldman Sachs Donate."
[799] Sutherland, "Dying for Europe."
[800] Sutherland, "Lower the Costs."

mobility. It is hampered by inadequate policy and legal frameworks. And it is stifled by overriding security concerns.[801]

"Mobility of capital, goods, and information at low cost and lightning speed" is the aim of globalization.

Hungarian Prime Minister Viktor Orbán has accused Soros of being a "prominent member of a circle of 'activists' trying to undermine European nations by supporting refugees heading to the continent from the Middle East and beyond." In an interview on public radio "Kossuth" Orbán said of Soros:

> *His name is perhaps the strongest example of those who support anything that weakens nation states, they support everything that changes the traditional European lifestyle. These activists who support immigrants inadvertently become part of this international human-smuggling network.*[802]

Soros responded by stating that Orbán's "plan treats the protection of national borders as the objective and the refugees as an obstacle. Our plan treats the protection of refugees as the objective and national borders as the obstacle."[803]

---

[801] Ibid.
[802] Gergely, "Orban Accuses Soros."
[803] Ibid.

Kalergi's Plan?
Europe and Antieurope

"Our manners, our civilization, and all the good things which are connected with manners and with civilization, in this European world of ours, depended for ages on two principles, and were, the result of both combined: I mean the spirit of a gentleman and the spirit of religion."

Edmund Burke (1790)

Antieurope stands *vis-à-vis* to Europe as the Antichrist stands *vis-à-vis* to the Christ; a counterfeit and a deceit. Rootless cosmopolitans such as European Union bureaucrats, businessmen, and politicians can talk of "European values" because the EU was founded on the doctrines of European decay. Freemasonry played a significant role in crafting what became the European Union, not as a resurgence of Europe after the fratricidal two world wars, but in the image of the eighteenth and nineteenth century doctrines that we have considered.[804]

Of Europe's present "values" and purpose, these are celebrated in the person of Count Richard von Coudenhove-Kalergi, founder of the Pan-European Union. This became a Masonic focus. According to Dr. Marian Mihaila, Assistant Grand Master of the Romanian Grand Orient, Kalergi was a Mason, funded by US Masons who aimed to create "on the American model"—which he calls "the first Masonic state in history"—"the United States of Europe."[805] A current Austrian Masonic chronology states of this: "1922: Admittance of Richard Coudenhove-Kalergi to the Lodge

---

[804] For details on the Masonic role in the founding of the EU see: Bolton, *The Occult & Subversive Movements*, 227-247.
[805] Mihaila, "European Union and Freemasonry," *Masonic Forum*, I: 6. The link seems to have been made to disappear. Dr. Mihaila does not seem much in evidence either. The link is cited in Bolton, *The Occult & Subversive Movements*, 230-231.

'Humanitas.' His Pan-European ideas are considered the origin of the idea of a European Union and are supported by the Grand Lodge."[806]

Kalergi alluded to his funding:

> *Early in 1924 Baron Louis Rothschild*[807] *telephoned to say that a friend of his, Max Warburg, had read my book and wanted to meet me. To my great astonishment Warburg immediately offered a donation of 60,000 gold marks to see the movement through its first three years. Max Warburg was a staunch supporter of Pan-Europe all his life and we remained close friends until his death in 1946. His readiness to support it (the movement) at the outset contributed decisively to its subsequent success.*[808]

Thorpe in his thesis on Kalergi refers to this financial backing, stating that Kalergi was invited to tour the USA in 1925 and, *"while there formed an American Committee headed by the director of the 'Institute of International Education' with backers including Felix and Paul Warburg (brothers of Max)."*[809] We might here see the start of Europe's subordination to both the USA and international finance, using the facade of a counterfeit Europe to impose a regional domination within the context of a world order.

Kalergi's vision was of a Europe populated by "a "diversity of individuals" of *Eurasian-Negroid* descent, he being of European-Japanese parentage, and of cosmopolitan upbringing. He wrote of this:

> *The man of the future will be the cross-breed. The Pan-European will be of the Eur-Asian Negroid race, similar in appearance to the ancient Egyptians, and of these the Jews will form a new aristocracy of spiritual grace.*[810]

The novelist Thomas Mann, a member of the Pan-European Union, described Kalergi as "Half Japanese, half mixed from the breed of Europe's international nobility, he really represents, as one knows, a Eurasiatic type of noble cosmopolite."[811] According to Mann, the "average German" would feel provincial by comparison.

---

[806] "The Eventful History of Freemasons in Austria," Entry: 1922.
[807] Head of the Austrian branch of the dynasty.
[808] Coudenhove-Kalergi, *Pan Europe*.
[809] Thorpe, *The Time and Space*, 17.
[810] Coudenhove-Kalergi, *Praktischer Idealismus*, 20, 23, 50
[811] Mann, *Pariser Rechenschaft*, 46; quoted by Thorpe, op cit., 18.

Kalergi was an enthusiast for Woodrow Wilson's internationalism for the post-1918 world, and particularly the concept of the League of Nations, writing on the prospect of a world order:

> *On the ruins of this old world a new world seemed to rise: democratic, republican, socialist and pacifist.... [M]y thoughts were fixated on this new world, on the glorious vision of a League of Nations uniting all nations and continents of the world in peaceful collaboration. A League that would replace international anarchy by order, arms by arguments, aggression by justice, revenge by understanding. Could anything more beautiful be imagined?*[812]

On the character of this new world order, there is more of a neo-Jacobin influence, Kalergi referring to his doctrine as "international humanitarianism,"[813] than anything of European tradition, Kalergi zealously proclaiming this future:

> *The emblem under which the Pan-Europeans of all states will unite, is the Solar Cross [das Sonnenkreuz]: the red cross on a golden sun, the symbols of Humanity and of Reason. This banner of love and of the spirit will wave one day, from Poland to Portugal, above a united World Empire of Peace and Freedom!*[814]

This counterfeit "pan-Europe" was (and remains) intended as a part of a world state, no different in substance from that envisioned by the Bolshevik leader Leon Trotsky when he wrote of a "Republican United States of Europe, as the foundation of the United States of the World," as the development of a historical process begun by capitalism.[815] With the League of Nations proving abortive, Kalergi considered Pan-Europe as an alternative road for internationalism.[816] Nonetheless, there was a working relationship between the League of Nations Secretariat and the Pan-

---

[812] Coudenhove-Kalergi, *An Idea Conquers the World*, 67.
[813] Coudenhove-Kalergi, "Die Pan-Europäische Bewegung," *Paneuropa*, 20; quoted by Thorpe, op cit., 40.
[814] Coudenhove-Kalergi, *Pan-Europe*, 193.
[815] Trotsky, *The Bolsheviki and World Peace* (1918). Trotsky wrote of the capitalist powers having *"expanded beyond the limits of the national state [feeling] intolerably cramped within its boundaries. The national Great Power must go and in tis place must step the imperialistic World Power."* Trotsky's answer was not a repudiation of the process, but the development of it. (Preface).
[816] Thorpe, op cit., 14.

European movement,[817] indicating the importance of Kalergi to internationalism. In 1925 Kalergi had sent the League Secretariat a memorandum, *World Organisation and Pan-Europe*,[818] which had been well received.

Although Kalergi failed in his erstwhile efforts to isolate and stop Hitler,[819] and the Axis had thwarted the Pan-European project as a component of a world state, the defeat of the Axis provided the impetus for the creation of the United Nations Organization and much of what has followed. Thorpe stated of Kalergi during the war years:

> *The goal of Pan-Europe had drifted from the prevention of a European war to a means of ensuring that the coming war would be Europe's last. This engagement with the Anglophone world, solidified during a politically active wartime exile in New York from 1940 to 1946, was to profoundly influence post-war plans for European unity, but by then the Young Count had become a 'grand seigneur', and had sidelined the PEU in favour of a new venture: the European Parliamentary Union.*[820]

While efforts have been made by adherents of Kalergi to trace the origins of Europe over the centuries to great monarchs, warriors, and statesmen,[821] and to claim that Kalergi was one among these, he rejected such a foundation for the establishment of Pan-Europe, opening the liens of his seminal Pan-Europe with: *"The eyes of Europe are turned backwards instead of forwards,"*[822] while nonetheless also drawing on great Europeans of the past to give his version of European some historical legitimacy, subjected to what Thorpe has accurately discerned as Kalergi's "progressivism."[823] Thorpe aptly quotes Catholic English scholar Christopher Dawson, himself a proponent of authentic Europe, in complaining of such tactics by those who bogusly proclaim "Europe" for their cause that they:

> *...with few exceptions are as oblivious of the European tradition as their opponents [i.e. nationalists]. They put their faith in an abstract internationalism which has no historic foundation, and*

---

[817] Ibid., 24.
[818] Coudenhove-Kalergi, *World Organization and Pan-Europe*. Cited by Thorpe, op cit., 24.
[819] Thorpe, op cit., 34.
[820] Ibid., 35.
[821] Ibid., 76. Thorpe provides a list, from Charlemagne to Nietzsche.
[822] Coudenhove-Kalergi, op cit., xii.
[823] Thorpe, op cit., 73.

consequently they provoke a fresh outburst of nationalist sentiment which is in some respects more excessive than anything the nineteenth century experienced.[824]

Thorpe concludes his thesis by stating that Kalergi's ideas have been distorted and mistranslated into a conspiracy theory by those on the "extreme right," "neo-Nazis," and "holocaust deniers." He states that this misrepresentation of the so-called "Kalergi Plan" was started in 2005 with the publication of *Goodbye, Europe: The Kalergi Plan: A Legal Racism*, by Austrian "holocaust denier" Gerd Honsik "in which," writes Thorpe, Honsik "argued that the real goal of European union, masterminded by Coudenhove-Kalergi, was that 'through ethnic mixing, the White race must be replaced by an easily controllable mestizo race.'"

Thorpe next cites the *Identitarians* in giving this theory further traction, by relating it to the immigration policies of the European Union, "attacking the present-day European policies by which this Plan was supposedly being put into action: namely, EU policies for integration, the protection of minorities, and the alleged encouragement of mass nonwhite immigration." He states in a footnote that, "The first such example was an Italian blog post on 11 December 2012 by Riccardo Percivaldi on the website Identità.com."[825]

As for this writer, I do not know Messrs Honsik or Percivaldi. While the *Identitarians*, a right wing youth movement that has spread across Europe and beyond, and has been subjected to much state harassment, were quite recently accused of misrepresenting the UN Global Compact on Migration, I have attempted to detail and document the meaning and context of this. Certainly, it was the *Identitarians* who publicized this project, and for this they should be praised, not damned, yet the UN said strangely few words on it. Likewise, while the "Right" has been accused of inventing a bogus "Great Replacement" theory on the displacement of *Homo Europaeus* through immigration, the UN refers to the same process, even using a similar phrase: "Replacement Migration." We have considered these matters, citing the publications and statements of both the UN and the EU. In searching for the origins of the project one comes necessarily upon Coudenhove-Kalergi. Much of what Thorpe states in his thesis, confirms, rather than repudiates, what he finds abhorrent in the rightist commentary.

---

[824] Dawson, *The Making of Europe*, xxiv-xxv.
[825] Thorpe, op cit., 277. Referring to Percivaldi, "The Kalergi Plan."

However, Thorpe errs in tracing the expose of the "Kalergi Plan" to an "Austrian holocaust denier" in 2005. In 1955, Captain Arthur Rogers O.B.E. wrote an article, "Warburg and the Kalergi Plan," subheaded "Warburgs pushed for Kalergi Plan for World Government through European Union and racial mingling." Captain Rogers refers to Kalergi naming in his memoirs the Warburgs as his financial patrons. He cites Kalergi's *An Idea Conquers the World*, and his 1923 book *Pan Europe*, where Kalergi had referred to his associations with Louis Rothschild and the Warburgs. He cites Kalergi's pamphlet *Pacifism* on the future "Pan-European" being Eurasian-Negroid. Rogers explains the role of Paul Warburg in the establishment of the Federal Reserve Bank in the USA, and of Max Warburg's role as chief financial adviser to Kaiser Wilhelm, and his role in funding Lenin and helping to facilitate his return to Russia in 1917. Rogers then cites the role of Winston Churchill is supporting Kalergi and in being the first president of the United Europe Movement. [826]

One is surely justified in asking why Louis Rothschild and the Warburg banking dynasty, including its members in the USA, Felix and Paul, were such enthusiastic patrons of Kalergi? This is likely to be beyond the scope of Thorpe, but it provides an added context that is missing in his thesis. However, one interprets such matters whether as a process; as a "conspiracy;" by "connecting the dots," as American historian Richard B. Spence calls it;[827] or as "network theory," as British historian Niall Ferguson explains certain events;[828] a dismissive attitude, especially when much of it is confirmed by one's own research, is hardly conducive to scholarship. Spence mentions that "real history" is often a matter of discussing "possibilities," and that "speculation, as educated guesswork, is the driving force of investigation." [829] Presumably, among a certain type of academic (probably, that is, the majority) one cannot speculate into areas that are beyond the pale.

---

[826] Rogers, "Warburg and the Kalergi Plan." Capt. Rogers served on the Imperial General staff during World War I, and became one of Britain's top officers in Military Intelligence.
[827] Richard Spence, *Wall Street and the Russian Revolution 1905–1925*, 2. Spence, a historian of note, states that there is "conspiracy *theory*" and "conspiracy *fact*." "*Simply put, conspiracy is not the exception in human behaviour, it is the norm.*" (p. 3).
[828] Niall Ferguson, "The Square and the Tower." In ridiculing "conspiracy theorists" as "invariably" misunderstanding and misinterpreting events, Ferguson states that rather than "elite networks" controlling "formal power structures," they "*usually have a highly ambivalent relationship to established institutions, and sometimes even a hostile one.*" (xix). Yet this is precisely what "conspiracy theorists" contend; that there are "elite networks" that promote their own revolution against certain institutions. Ferguson gives the World Economic Forum as an example of an "informal network" and how at Davos Nelson Mandela was persuaded to repudiate nationalization in favor of the privatization of the South African economy. (Ferguson, 311-315). Whether one calls this part of a "conspiracy" or "informal networking," the result is the same and the players are the same.
[829] Ibid., 2.

One is surely justified also in seeking the meaning and origins of the "European values" of which EU bureaucrats speak in conjunction with EU policies on "replacement migration." As Thorpe himself shows, Coudenhove-Kalergi is lauded as the "father" of the EU and his doctrines are the basis of E.U.'s so-called "European values."

After Kalergi visited Turkey and had seen its Westernization under Ataturk, he saw this as "paving the way for a complete reconciliation between Europe and the Near East."[830] While Dr. Kadioglu condemns the backlash against non-European immigration and the repudiation of Turkey as a "European" nation even by mainstream politicians such as Sarkozy in France, Germany opened its borders to a million Levantine and African migrants. Chancellor Angela Merkel, recipient of the "prestigious" Kalergi Prize awarded by the European Society Coudenhove-Kalergi in 2010,[831] was praised by the mainstream media for having adopted a policy of assimilation of Levantine and African migrants that has successfully turned them into "Germans." The question, however, is: what is a *"German"*? (or any other nominally European nationality), according to the E.U.? The answer is provided by a report from the Center for Global Development: A *German* (or Frenchman, Swede, Italian, is someone who works and pays taxes and is fully integrated in the labor market:

> *In 2015, large numbers of refugees fleeing war and terrorism in Syria, Afghanistan, and Iraq arrived on Europe's shores. Fear and uncertainty reigned—who would give these people asylum and how would they integrate? The German Chancellor, Angela Merkel, remained undaunted. "We can do this!" she announced in August of that year. And do this, they did. In 2015 and 2016, Germany received over one million first-time asylum applications.*
>
> *Five years later, over half of these refugees have found a job, and public support for immigration remains high....*[832]

The report states that "Germany needs to institute policies that target specific barriers to full labor market integration, such as training and the certification of existing skills." Here is the bottom line: *replacement migration* and "full market integration." By 2018 there were 1.8 million with a "refugee background" in Germany, states the report. Further, these

---

[830] Coudenhove-Kalergi, *Europa Erwacht* (1934), cited by Ayse Kadioglu, "What Stories Does Europe Tell?", 14.
[831] "European Prize for the Chancellor."
[832] Keita and Dempster, "Five Years Later."

migrants are "badly needed within an aging German labor market, which is facing skill shortages and needs trained migrant labor."

This is the cosmopolitan "Europe" envisaged by Kalergi; a landmass populated by a new breed of Eurasian-Negroid mixture. Of note is the decline of the initial anti-immigration sentiment, and the high proportion of Germans who reportedly actively support the integration process of migrants:

> *A survey by the Allensbach Institute for Public Opinion Research suggests that 55 percent of Germans have contributed to the integration of refugees since 2015, either financially or through their own involvement in supportive actions.*[833]

Since no part of *Homo Europaeus* has been subjected to the worldwide process of self-loathing more than the Germans, the German will-to-death is not surprising. A report from a media source at the start of the "refugee crisis" commented:

> *Germany still harbours a remarkable sense of guilt about the country's WWII regime and the Holocaust, which itself caused enormous flows of refugees, and indirectly the founding of the state of Israel. The younger generation of German voters was born 50 years after the war, but the sense of collective responsibility remains with the older generation, which in other countries tends to be more anti-immigration.*[834]

E.U.'s Neo-Jacobin Charter

What, then, are the "values" of "Europe," as promulgated by the European Union?

The *Charter of the Fundamental Rights of the European Union* was adopted in December 2000. Even the title puts us on familiar ground, with the Declaration of the Rights of Man, and the *Universal Declaration on Human Rights*. The Preamble refers not to "European values" but to "universal values":

---

[833] Ibid.
[834] Bird, "Germany's History Explains."

> *The peoples of Europe, in creating an ever closer union among them, are resolved to share a peaceful future based on common values.*
>
> *Conscious of its spiritual and moral heritage, the Union is founded on the indivisible, universal values of human dignity, freedom, equality and solidarity; it is based on the principles of democracy and the rule of law. It places the individual at the heart of its activities, by establishing the citizenship of the Union and by creating an area of freedom, security and justice.*[835]

The Charter refers to Europe's "spiritual and moral heritage," and proceeds to place these within the context of "indivisible, universal values of human dignity." They are "Europe's values" only so far as they proceed from the epoch of "Enlightenment," of Locke, Rousseau, Voltaire, Diderot, et al., the purpose of which was to overthrow and destroy Europe's traditional heritage. Europe's "spiritual and moral heritage" is Catholicism, and the ideal of "Europe" as an organism emanates from Catholicism and the High Culture epoch of Europe.[836] For better or worse, depending on one's perspective, the church and crown were overthrown by the "Age of Reason."

The EU Charter even adapts the slogan of Jacobinism and the Grand Orient de France: "freedom, equality and solidarity." It is the cosmopolitan doctrine of Kalergi, et al.

Like the Jacobin Declaration, the UN Declaration on Human Rights, etc., the E. U. Charter is a social contract, not between the component peoples of Europe, but between individuals, entered into on their behalf by states, which are themselves necessarily regarded as "social contracts" among their "citizens" ("citizen" being the term used in the French Republic, deriving from the social contract theory of Rousseau et al) analogous to "comrade" among the left). It is then, imbued with liberalism, the E. U. Charter stating, "It places the individual at the heart of its activities, by establishing the citizenship of the Union."[837] In enshrining these "rights of the citizen"—based on individual rather than organic identities—advocacy of European ethnicities is going to be a breach of the "social contract," subjecting not only member states but individuals to "human rights" and "race relations" laws. Hence, the "right to asylum" is guaranteed:

---

[835] *Charter of the Fundamental Rights of the European Union*, Preamble.
[836] Belloc, *Europe and the Faith*.
[837] *Charter of the Fundamental Rights of the European Union*, Preamble.

The right to asylum shall be guaranteed with due respect for the rules of the Geneva Convention of 28 July 1951 and the Protocol of 31 January 1967 relating to the status of refugees and in accordance with the Treaty on European Union and the Treaty on the Functioning of the European Union (hereinafter referred to as "the Treaties").[838]

Further, any policy of repatriation by a member state is prohibited: *"Collective expulsions are prohibited."*[839] The Charter establishes the basis for national legislation prohibiting the self-defense of Europeans, reiterating, as in much else, U. N. charters, and enshrining by force of law multiculturalism on every state:

1. *Any discrimination based on any ground such as sex, race, colour, ethnic or social origin, genetic features, language, religion or belief, political or any other opinion, membership of a national minority, property, birth, disability, age or sexual orientation shall be prohibited.*
2. *Within the scope of application of the Treaties and without prejudice to any of their specific provisions, any discrimination on grounds of nationality shall be prohibited.*[840]

Hence "Europe" is obliged to become a multicultural entity, which is reiterated with the axiom: "The Union shall respect cultural, religious and linguistic diversity."[841] Those who object to this *Antieurope* are subjected to state laws "prohibiting" (sic) any such resistance.

With the typical *double-speak* the sundry "rights" enshrined in the charter can be withdrawn to prohibit dissent:

Any limitation on the exercise of the rights and freedoms recognised by this Charter must be provided for by law and respect the essence of those rights and freedoms. Subject to the principle of proportionality, limitations may be made only if they are necessary and genuinely meet objectives of general interest

---

[838] Ibid., Article 18.
[839] Ibid., Article 19 (1), Right to Asylum.
[840] Ibid., Article 21 (1) (2), Non-discrimination.
[841] Ibid., Article 22, Cultural, religious, and linguistic diversity.

recognised by the Union or the need to protect the rights and freedoms of others.[842]

---

[842] Ibid., Article 52 (1), Scope and Interpretation of Rights and Principles.

Antipodean Social Laboratory: A Case Study of Official Europhobia and Slow-Motion Anglocide

"Permit me then to continue our conversation, and to tell you what the freedom is that I love, and that to which I think all men entitled. This is the more necessary, because, of all the loose terms in the world, liberty is the most indefinite. It is not solitary, unconnected, individual, selfish liberty, as if every man was to regulate the whole of his conduct by his own will. The liberty I mean is social freedom. It is that state of things in which liberty is secured by the equality of restraint. A constitution of things in which the liberty of no one man, and no body of men, and no number of men, can find means to trespass on the liberty of any person, or any description of persons, in the society. This kind of liberty is, indeed, but another name for justice; ascertained by wise laws, and secured by well-constructed institutions."

Edmund Burke (1789)

New Zealand's official narrative lauds itself as one of the world's most successful multicultural societies, maintaining the facade with increasingly repressive laws, social engineering, and indoctrination. The following reflects aspects of the New Zealand situation which sees the state at war with the majority ethnicity: New Zealand Europeans, who are blacklisted to go the way of the Afrikaners. New Zealand has historically been regarded as a "social laboratory." What happens here is a signpost for what is intended further afield. The Tarrant Mosque shootings in 2019 provided the key to open the Pandora's box of state repression against the European remnant in the Antipodes. Events continue to unfold at an accelerated pace.

The *Encyclopaedia of New Zealand* alludes to how New Zealand was widely regarded during the social reform epoch of circa 1890 to 1920, referring to the observations of overseas visitors: "The impact of such visitors was to confirm in the minds of New Zealanders that their country was the 'social laboratory of the world.'"[843]

Of a Fabian-socialist opinion, it is stated:

Sidney and Beatrice Webb were Fabian socialists who visited New Zealand in 1898 and recorded their views in a diary. Like the other socialist visitors, the Webbs were impressed by the reforms and particularly praised the industrial arbitration system. They also approved of the "independent" manner of the working class and the fact that there were neither millionaires nor slums. They found New Zealand in general "delightfully British," but as well-educated people they thought the country lacked intellectual life. They bemoaned the absence of public libraries and thought that (despite his undoubted political achievements) Premier Richard Seddon was gross, uneducated and rough.[844]

The latter named Premier Richard Seddon had been a former gold digger. His Liberal Party, like the old-style Labour Party of New Zealand and other countries, was a far cry from what is today called "liberalism." Seddon was one of the most vociferous opponents of Chinese immigration, not only in New Zealand but throughout the British Empire.

The Labour Party, which continued the social reform epoch of liberal governments, was also, like its Australian counterpart, committed to the maintenance of New Zealand as a White outpost.

In particular, Labour's most iconic figure, Michael Joseph Savage, was a proponent for "White New Zealand." It is relatively well-known that the primary champions of the "White Australia Policy" until the mid-twentieth century were the Labour Party and the trades unions. W. G. Spence, labor leader and union organizer, stated the attitude of the time that "true patriotism should be racial." In South Africa the Labour Party and unions fought for the White workers against the mine owners that wanted to exploit Chinese and Bantu labor. The miners' revolt on the Rand in 1922, the slogan being "White workers of the world unite, for a White South Africa," saw the Smuts government put down the revolt militarily and hang the leaders. The brutality caused such a groundswell of opinion that it resulted in the election of the Nationalist Party in alliance with the Labour Party, and the implementation of laws designed to protect labor against

---

[843] "Social Laboratory of the World," 3.
[844] Ibid.

monopolists, which developed into the much maligned apartheid system.[845]

For Seddon and the labor movement, as in other states, the matter of immigration restriction was a conflict with capitalism and the interests of the British Foreign Office, which did not want to offend its non-White subjects and allies.

Savage Racism

In a somewhat odd situation, the matter of Mickey Savage's "racism" came to public attention by a letter from the Auckland Ratepayer's Alliance, seeking assurance from the Auckland City Council that a statue of Savage will *not* be removed without public consultation, given that the statue was funded by ratepayers. The association's letter states:

> *Savage was an appalling anti-Chinese racist—exhibiting the worst of the racist treatment by the trade union and labour movements against Asians after the end of the First World War. But like for colonial leaders it is difficult to judge historical figures by today's standards and we shouldn't rip down memorials that are a part of our city's fabric.*[846]

Although the press release by the association states the predictable banalities about "racism," the writer does have the intellectual acumen, lacking in most academics and journalists, to realize the absurdity of *presentism*: using the dominant moral outlook of the present to judge the actions of the past. *Presentism* is an affront to scholarship, and negates the responsibility of researchers to understand historical events in the *context of their times*. However, *presentism* justifies political agendas and ideological dogmas, and eliminates the need for critical thinking. It is an essential component of the modernist outlook.

In alluding to Savage as "an appalling anti-Chinese racist" the Alliance president cites her source as a Trotskyite website, *Redline*. Here the author writes that at the time (2015) the Labour government was "playing the anti-Chinese card" in reference to the "Chinese sounding names" of those taking over the housing market.

The *Redline* writer, Philip Ferguson, states that Labour's housing spokesman Phil Twyford's reference to Chinese-sounding names harkens

---

[845] Bolton, *Babel Inc.*, 85-87.
[846] "Auckland Council Must Not Destroy."

back to the racism within Old Labour, the worst of whom was Labour hero Michael Savage. In his bizarre twist of history, necessitated by being hidebound to Bolshevik dogma, Ferguson stated that the Labour movement sided against its own class interests and with the middle class in attacking Chinese immigration, because it was dominated by "bourgeois ideology":

> ...However, the domination of the labour movement by bourgeois ideology also ensured that a number of trade unions and the early Labour Party were enthusiastic advocates and campaigners for White New Zealand. A number of unions excluded the Chinese from membership and national gatherings of trade unionists demanded tighter restrictions. From the early 1900s they often explicitly adopted the middle and upper class language of race and these privileged elements' calls for a White New Zealand.[847]

To the contrary, these "privileged elements" were demanding Asian labor. It is perhaps because it is the Marxist left that is dominated by "bourgeois ideology" that Ferguson, et al. are unable to understand this. It was the merchant class who were pushing for Chinese immigrants, as they still do. Ferguson continues:

> Labour gatherings after World War I indicate that both industrial unions and the party were strong supporters of the White New Zealand policy, increasingly using racial rather than economic arguments as justification.
>
> For instance, the 1919 LP conference featured a remit from the Auckland Printers' Machinists Union, "that conference appoint a committee to approach the Government with a view to prohibiting members of any colored race from entering New Zealand; failing this a more severe test of education should be placed on Hindoos." Instead of opposing such blatant racism, Savage and Holland succeeded in getting a motion passed to establish a committee to examine the immigration question....
>
> At the start of June 1920, Auckland watersiders decided not to work ships carrying "Asiatic" migrants.... The Auckland watersiders also warned of the danger of a "pibald population" if "Asiatics" and whites merged.

---

[847] Ferguson, "Labour's Racist Roots."

In April 1920 Labour MPs Michael Joseph Savage, Bill Parry and Frederick Bartram telegrammed Reform Party prime minister Massey asking that "steps be immediately taken to deal with (the) menace" of an "alarming influx of Asiatics and other classes of cheap labour." The Labour figures argued that this influx inevitably involved "the lowering of the living standards of our people, as well as the probable deterioration in the physical standard of all races mixing indiscriminately..."[848]

White New Zealand Policy

When the committee on immigration reported back to the Labour conference in 1920 on the need to assure restrictions, Pat Hickey, "firebrand" of the Red Federation of Labour, and a leading Labour Party figure, called for the report to be adopted without further ado and accentuated the racial argument. The party's newspaper, *The Maoriland Worker*, summarized Hickey as arguing that "It was as far as possible their duty to keep New Zealand white. Internationalism did not mean a reckless intermingling of white and coloured races."[849]

During the parliamentary debates on the 1920 Immigration Restriction Act, Savage stated that the issue was not only one of economics, but the "very law of life itself," referring to the geopolitical factor that, "we are living practically within a stone's throw of teeming millions, who continue to increase by millions annually, and [in Australia and NZ] there are millions of acres of uninhabited territory." Labour criticized the bill for not being sufficiently restrictive. There was also forceful repudiation of any suggestion that the Labour Party was committed to internationalism before racial integrity.

As Dan Sullivan (Labour Member for Avon) put it: "What I want to say quite definitely to the House is this: the Labour Party is just as keen as any member of this House, or as any person or party in the country, to maintain racial purity here in New Zealand. There can be no question at all about that..."[850] James McCombs (Labour, Lyttelton) then read from the Labour conference report of July 1920:

---

[848] Ibid.
[849] Ibid.
[850] Ibid.

That for the proper development of the country it is essential that the white population of the country should be increased by immigration...that a more adequate check should be placed upon Asiatic immigration...[and] that the presence of Asiatics in this country in any number and as permanent residents would result in an intermingling of the races detrimental to all.[851]

Ferguson provides other examples of Labour Party "racism," including that of Labour Party leader, Harry Holland. The 1920 Immigration Restriction Act was passed.

Predictable Bedfellows

The Bolsheviks were joined in their anathema towards Labour's "racist past" by fellow "anti-racists," the "liberal conservatives" at *The BFD*, which states that it offers a "center-right" voice.[852]

Actually, for the most part those who are called "right-wing" in New Zealand (as well as other Anglophone states, where Thatcherism and Reaganism are called "right-wing") are usually Whig-liberals, whose nineteenth century notions of individualism and free market economics eschew racial kinship as "socialistic," in the spirit of Ayn Rand, who called "racism" "the lowest form of collectivism."[853] There stands only the individual, detached from ancestors, heritage, without a nation, and in the moment. This repudiation of kinship bonds parallels the extreme left position of the Frankfurt School in regard to "the primary ties" of family, homeland, and race as restrictions on individual self-actualization. The nihilism of "left and right" proceeds from the detachment of the individual from any organic bond. That is why, for example, the pseudo-right in promoting melting pot assimilation under the "one nation" slogan, now jumps on the leftist bandwagon of decades past in condemning state programs for Maoris as "apartheid" separatism; they are in accord with the left in vilifying the Afrikaners. Having examined these special Maori programs herein, my position is that of the traditional right which in decades past resolutely defended the Afrikaner and his method of apartheid as the best policy and doctrine for the South African situation, when there was no confusion as to where the lines were drawn between

---

[851] Ibid.
[852] Slater, "Why Does the Prime Minister."
[853] Rand, "Racism," in *The Virtue of Selfishness*, 126.

the left/plutocracy and the right.[854] *The problem is not that the Maoris are set on a course of "separatism" with government backing, as seen in the He Puapua proposals, but that New Zealand Europeans are not accorded the same rights in regard to their heritage and future.*

Seeing an opportunity to attack the Labour Party, National Party hitman Cam Slater pointed out that Prime Minister Jacinda Ardern has a portrait of Savage in her office, whom he describes as "an appalling anti-Chinese racist," providing a link to Fergusons's article in *Redline*. Outdoing their anti-racist communist allies in the vitriol against Savage, the *BFDers* call him "not just a racist, but a nasty little eugenics type racist," "advocating for South African style racism," by golly (or perhaps not "golly"). "Quite the nasty spiteful, little racist," if the reader has by now not quite understood that what calls itself "right-wing" in New Zealand can out-anti-racist the anti-racists of the left. But worse still, Savage "held despicable anti-Semitic views as well." Again Slater refers to the communist *Redline's* "About" page as his source, linking a 2016 article.

In the *Redline* article Phil Duncan states that the first Labour government under Savage was very restrictive in regard to accepting Jewish refugees from Europe at the time of the Nazi ascent. An internal document within the Labour government stated that the preferred refugees were "Dutch, Belgian, and French," "as the more suitable type of immigrant." Others were not likely to have their applications accepted, according to the document.[855]

Now, Ardern more than any other Labour Prime Minister, has set a fanatical course to make amends for Labour's past, and has fast-tracked New Zealand on a path of European dispossession.

---

[854] When the Afrikaner still held his own homeland the right in New Zealand as elsewhere, organized in their defence around groups such as the Friends of South Africa, and the Southern Africa Friendship Association. There was no apologia about being "White."
[855] Duncan, "First Labour Government wanted."

Humpty Dumpty Laws

"'When I use a word', Humpty Dumpty said in rather a scornful tone, 'it means just what I choose it to mean—neither more nor less.'
  The question is,' said Alice, 'whether you can make words mean so many different things.'
  'The question is,' said Humpty Dumpty, 'which is to be master—that's all.'"

Lewis Carroll (1871)

The Human Rights Commission oversees the Race Relations and Human Rights laws in New Zealand. A campaign has been inaugurated by the Commission to purvey the impression that there is widespread "racism," whether "conscious" or "unconscious." Hence, the need to introduce further repressive laws that will prohibit political dissent, especially in regard to other measures being introduced by the government such as *He Puapua*, the "new school histories curriculum," and compulsory critical race theory in schools and public service.

The Human Rights Commission's campaign "Give Nothing to Racism" shows that New Zealand justice minister Andrew Little's professed purpose for enacting a "hate speech" law is not to curb violence and abuse. The aim is to extinguish dissent.

The Human Rights Commission campaign features media advertisements touting the Commission's "Voice of Racism" audio documentary, with the speak-over by filmmaker/actor Taika Waititi. The expectation of something horrendous is built up by a warning that the contents are not suitable for younger listeners, and that those who find the experience too much to withstand can escape by clicking on a heart-shaped image. Here one is assured: "If this website experience has been distressing for you please ask for help." Several "help" links are provided. Headphones are recommended, presumably lest some unsuspecting snowflake overhear and evaporate in shame, remorse, and self-guilt for harboring "unconscious bias" and being the beneficiary of "White privilege." Hence proceed with caution, all who dare, for here be a toxic brew of race-hate.

Waititi intones phrases that we are assured are from real life experiences: "everyday racism felt by real people." The Human Rights Commission explains:

> To create the Voice of Racism, more than 200 people shared their experiences of racism in New Zealand. These were curated into a collection of everyday experiences, to represent the racism that exists in the lives of many. These experiences include things that were said to them verbally and through people's actions, and the internalised racism they live with. These moments became "the Voice of Racism," one collective voice that articulates the racism people exhibit both intentionally and unintentionally.

Proceeding intrepidly, we find, among others equally as banal:

> "I've tried to pronounce it right but I can't."
> "Are you sure? Can you check with the manager?"
> "Your daughter has a long name. Anything shorter?"
> "Sorry I didn't realise you were in a que."
> "I don't understand what you are saying."
> "I'm afraid we can't help you."
> "You don't look like a lawyer."

Souring Relations

There are various categories on the Human Rights Commission website, each containing examples of what are regarded as different types of "racism." Nothing is placed in context. What is consistent is that for New Zealand Europeans the position is "damned if you do; damned if you don't." Whatever you say is going to be "unconscious bias," condescending, or aggressive. The snowflake SJW might be just as reprehensible in her friendliness (unconscious bias, patronizing), as the most offensive skinhead; because both the bourgeoisie-hipster liberal schoolteacher and the booze-soaked, unemployed skinhead have profited from "White privilege." Atonement for all New Zealand Europeans is an ongoing process.

The examples are so broad as to make frank and open relationships between Whites and "others"—such as existed prior to liberal interference—difficult, if not impossible. How is one supposed to have an open exchange when perpetually self-conscious of "slipping up" and perhaps offending sensibilities in some "unconscious" manner, and wondering whether one might be "dobbed in" to the Human Rights Commissariat by the network of informers that the government aims to cultivate through the establishment of emergency call-in centers should a "racist" comment—whether conscious or unconscious—be heard at a workplace, shop, bar, or café? The outcome can only be retardation of communication; guarded comments which themselves could be construed as "unconscious bias," aloofness, or awkwardness towards the "other."

State Supported Hit-List

Among the "anti-racist" organizations that the Human Rights Commission recommends is *Paparoa*. This is a far left web portal that serves primarily as a hit-list to identify those considered "racists," to be sacked from jobs, harassed by police, smeared by the press, and made into pariahs. It publishes photos of individuals and seeks their identification. Is that the type of organization that should be recommended by a government agency? Apparently so.

Paparoa and its leftist ilk refer to the dissident right as "Nazi accelerationists," a euphemism for "terrorism"; hence the dissident right is criminalized. The far left prepares the way for the state's "hate speech" laws.

Dissident rightists, and really anyone who is vaguely "conservative," are condemned for hiding their identities, with the insistence by the left that this can only be for terroristic purposes. Yet *Paparoa* explains that its supporters are anonymous because of the supposed "psychosis" (sic) of the right. Here we see a clear example of psychological *projection*. There are no examples of the left being targeted by the right. Conversely, there is a witch-hunt mentality. This report is worth quoting in full, as it shows precisely what type of regime is being foisted in the name of "human rights":

> A man lost his job after making comments about Muslims following the Christchurch terror attack.

Thomas Knight-Wagener now says he regrets what he said and is gutted to have lost his job at Placemakers Albany after just four days in the role.

Knight-Wagener, who got the job through labour hire organisation Tradestaff, said he and some colleagues were chatting about the terror attack the day after it happened when he decided to put his two cents in.

"Having an intellectual conversation about the comprehensive state of the Islamic movement on a global scale; got me fired."

"I didn't talk much about the Christchurch shooting, but that's how the conversation started."

Knight-Wagener said while talking about the shooting he digressed to mention what he had seen in news reports about the behaviour of Muslims living in the United Kingdom that "had been shown to be violent and destructive."

"I elaborated on the current state of the UK in regards to the growing Islamic community and the crimes against the people in these communities," he said.

"I said no swear words and was not abusive or aggressive in my manner. I was simply stating facts, of which no one wanted to hear obviously."

He then shut the conversation down and carried on with his work.

Knight-Wagener, originally from Kaitaia, said he returned to work on the Tuesday but when he went in on the Wednesday, he was told by the manager he had been assigned a new job by Tradestaff.

When he questioned why he had been moved on, he claimed the manager replied "something was said on Saturday about the Christchurch shooting."

He claimed the manager said one of the team members were offended by his comments and that Knight-Wagener didn't fit in with the team.

"Loose lips sink ships. It is a fair reason for dismissing someone, in my opinion, but only if it is an ongoing issue," Knight-Wagener said.

He said he knew as soon as the words came out of his mouth that he'd said the wrong thing.

"I was just remarking on what I'd heard on the news ... and as I said it, I thought it's just appalling the way it sounds as it's *coming out of my mouth and I thought I'm gonna stop talking about it."*

When questioned whether he was a right-wing radical, Knight-Wagener said he wasn't sure what right or left wing was but he was a supporter of Milo Yiannopoulos—a far-right British speaker who was last week banned from Australia after he blamed the Christchurch terror attack on "extremist leftism and barbaric, alien religious cultures."

He said he liked Yiannopoulus due to his opinion which created debates. However, he said he had no problem with Muslims, didn't condone the attack and said people shouldn't be dying.

Losing his job meant he was now having to move down to Bay of Plenty and pick fruit, a situation he says was not ideal given he was a qualified engineer.

"It's a shambles, to say the least."

He admitted he was known to be "a bit outspoken" and had decided to speak out to warn others about keeping their opinions on the issue to themselves.

"I'm just wondering how many other people this has happened to? It was just gossiping about what happened...and I lose my job."

A PlaceMakers spokesperson said she couldn't comment on specific employment cases within the business.

"But we have clear company values which include being respectful of our fellow employees, customers and the community. Expressing or spreading prejudiced views against any religious or ethnic group does not fit with our culture."[856]

This is an example of the informer network that the government aims to formalize.

Paparoa links to *Fightback*, a web portal aligned to Trotskyist-communism. *Paparoa* also features a Trotskyite academic, Scott Hamilton, who comes from a fractious political milieu on the extreme left. However, while this "scholar" a few years ago seemed to be poised to replace sociologist Dr. Paul Spoonley as the media's chief go-to academic for anti-right hatchetry, Spoonley has maintained that position. In his retirement he threatens to write another book on the "extreme Right" as a sequel to *Politics of Nostalgia* (1987), the book that established his career

---

[856] "Tradie's Muslim Comments," Emphasis added.

as an anti-right crusader, while being a notable international expert on immigration and multiculturalism as fundamental to the globalized growth economy.

Portrait of an Anti-Racist Academic: Dr. Spoonley's Damascus Moment

In the aftermath of the Tarrant Mosque shootings in 2019 Spoonley came into his own, advocating for new "hate speech" laws, a Herald column stating:

> *Academic expert on ethnicity and extremist politics, Massey University's Paul Spoonley, is also very supportive of the introduction of specific laws to outlaw hate. Talking to Newstalk ZB, he said, "I don't think we can delay, because if you delay, then the changes of something else occurring like the events of last week might be a possibility."*
>
> *Spoonley has been very active in the debate on hate speech, and in another article is cited explaining that hate speech "provides an enabling environment which green lights racial and religious vilification." He says it's a problem because it "provides unfiltered ideas and arguments for those who are pliable and interested. And it tells others what you have done and got away with."*[857]

Spoonley's is a simplistic notion, and as much was said by another academic, Dr. Paul Moon, whose Maori descent has not prejudiced his ability for actual scholarship on New Zealand history that often does not accord with liberal notions:

> *...arguing that "while a desire for censorship was an instinctive response to hate-based events, it would not address the root cause of the problem." He [Moon] agrees that there is a need "to re-evaluate the limits of free speech in New Zealand," but believes that "stifling speech could often create a dangerous climate of isolation" which could make things worse. Moon says: "Censorship would be fruitless as a means of prevention because*

---

[857] Edwards, "Political Roundup."

it addresses only a small part of the symptom, rather than the underlying cause."[858]

Spoonley mispresented himself to conservatives and rightists during the 1980s as "an academic with no axe to grind," in researching *Politics of Nostalgia*. On his own account Spoonley's epiphany on the road to anti-racism came in Britain during the 1970s. He claims that he was shocked by a White racist attack at a time when Black violence was overwhelming, as it still is. However, the defining moment for his career was the National Front march in Lewisham, 1977. Recently Spoonley, in trying to relate this to the New Zealand situation, in his decades-long quest to find an elusive "far right threat" in New Zealand, wrote:

When I was a student at the University of Bristol, there was a violent incident just blocks from my home. A young Asian man was held down while a swastika was carved into his stomach with a razor blade. It was 1977, and I was looking for a topic for my dissertation. I had found it. The level of hate puzzled me. Why would anyone do something like that because someone else was different? I went on to do my research on the National Front and (British) National Party. I was there in Lewisham later that same year when about 4000 National Front supporters yelled abuse at the local non-white community—protected by 5000 police.[859]

Spoonley by the 1980s, back in NZ, was very definitely someone who had "an axe to grind." He sought out the right-wing menace on which to build his career, and found such wild-eyed fanatics as the "1000 member" League of Rights, (in reality the League was an incorporated society limited to a membership of twelve), a middle-aged, middle class group of mainly world war veterans, based on the social credit theory of Major C. H. Douglas, and a commitment to the Crown Commonwealth of Nations. The League's "Action Seminars" taught the terroristic methods of writing to newspapers. The tone of attacks on the right was established around 1970 when the newspaper of the New Zealand Communist Party, *People's Voice*, reported that a wheelchair bound paraplegic demonstrator was attacked by a member of the League of Rights wearing a swastika armband.[860] As readers might discern, the smears against the dissident

---

[858] Ibid.
[859] Spoonley, "I Thought There Had Been a Decline."
[860] As I clearly recall reading it, when a subscriber to *People's Voice* as a youngster.

right by academics, journalists, and their psycho-left allies have not changed.

Spoonley's Damascus moment seems to be contaminated by *False Memory Syndrome*. Where his nightmare vision is of "4000" racists attacking the hapless non-White community with the assistance of police, in the real world the "4000 NF supporters" amounted to 500.[861] The so-called "Battle of Lewisham," as it is called in leftist mythology, was a confrontation between thousands of anti-NF demonstrators, spearheaded by the Trotskyite Socialist Workers Party, and the police. The Antifa heroes continue to celebrate their cowardly attacks and allude with pride to the way they entrapped the "NF honour guard."[862] Here is how one NF member described the situation:

> *I was trapped against a brick wall as the mob burst through. My legs gave way and I ended up on the ground. After being picked up by two policemen I sat on a wall at the side of the road. A black rioter aimed a brick at me but missed.... A white protestor said that this is what happens to "Nazis."*[863]

That was the experience of Esther Sizer, seventy-two, apparently a "far right thug" who would today be called a "Nazi accelerationist."

The 1977 Lewisham march, a legally sanctioned event by Britain's fourth largest political party, had an anti-mugging theme. The primary NF banner declared "Stop the muggers! 80% of muggers are black. 85% of victims are White." Of the area today, still the most violent in Britain: "NHS staff are being targeted by muggers trying to steal their identity badges so they can use them to obtain the free food and drinks being offered to doctors and nurses tackling coronavirus."[864]

Is Spoonley's expertise as a scholar any more reliable than that of Scott Hamilton, or the administrators of the *Paparoa* hit-list that is sanctioned by the Human Rights Commission as a valuable resource?

---

[861] This is the usual figure. See for example: Rippingdale, "Lewisham, London 1977: Notes on Fighting Fascism."
[862] Ibid.
[863] Sizer, "Don't let them intimidate you."
[864] Campbell, "NHS Staff Warned to Hide ID."

Ideological Roots of HRC Comrades:

Applying the methodology used by the generic *antifa* and its academic, parliamentary, and journalistic friends when smearing the right, might we then say that *Paparoa*, because of its overt Troskyite links, is part of an ideological lineage that includes the "militarisation of labour," subjugation of trades unions, torture, and liquidation en masse, and the creation of concentration camps? That is to say, all the stuff the left claims defines *fascism*.

Trotskyism, named after Leon Trotsky, commissar for foreign affairs and chief of the Red Army during the first phase of Bolshevik Russia, is the dominant faction—albeit itself typically fractured—of the far left in New Zealand. Trotsky in replying to the socialist critic of Bolshevism, Karl Kautsky, insisted on the necessity of "state terror."[865] On press freedom and "truth": "...our problem is not to punish liars and to encourage just men amongst journalists of all shades of opinion, but to throttle the class lie of the bourgeoisie and to achieve the class truth of the proletariat, irrespective of the fact that in both camps there are fanatics and liars."[866] On the regimentation of labor: "The very principle of compulsory labour service is for the Communist quite unquestionable. 'He who works not, neither shall he eat.'"[867]

Islam a "Rotting Piece of Cloth"—Trotsky

The left shed tears for Muslims after the Christchurch shooting atrocity in 2019. Auckland Imams joined the platform with Trotskyite eminence Joe Carolan of Socialist Aotearoa; Organise Aotearoa; the LGBT-Marxist Love Aotearoa-Hate Racism, et al. It is touching to see how the Christchurch madness enabled the godless to embrace Allah.[868] How is it that atheists can stridently mince forth as the champions of religious minorities? Suddenly, the Muslim community had newfound friends among far left transvestites and atheists who clambered aboard the same bandwagon as Imams in proclaiming Prime Minister Ardern's slogan, "They are us."

---

[865] Trotsky,"Terrorism and Communism," Chapter 4.
[866] Ibid. Chapter 8.
[867] Ibid.
[868] Bolton, "NZ in Wake of Mosque Shootings."

The early Bolsheviks also feigned sympathy for Islam, insofar as an insurrection of Muslims and other colonial peoples could be used to extend the influence of Bolshevism. What the Bolsheviks actually thought of Islam however, can be seen from Trotsky's speech at the 1924 congress of the Communist University of the Toilers of the East, an institution established to manipulate colonial peoples:

> *Even today we can still observe in the East the rule of Islam, of the old prejudices, beliefs and customs but these will more and more turn to dust and ashes. Just as a rotting piece of cloth, when you look at it from a distance, it seems to be all of a piece, all the pattern is there and all the folds remain but a movement of the hand or a puff of wind is enough for the whole cloth to turn to dust. And so in the East the old beliefs which appear to be so deep are actually but a shadow of the past: in Turkey they abolished the caliphate and not a single hair fell out of the heads of those who violated the caliphate; this means that the old beliefs have rotted and that with the coming historical movement of the toiling masses the old beliefs will not present a serious obstacle.*[869]

Given that "hate speech" laws are intended to be extended to criticism of religion, will such opinions be prohibited should they come from the left? The answer can only be in the negative, since the actual reason for the laws is to "target" genuine dissent, of which the left is not. Historically, the right has been aligned with Islam. It is only in recent years that factions of the right have been beguiled by Islamophobic propaganda emanating from well-funded pro-Israeli think tanks. The likes of Geert Wilders, Pam Geller, Daniel Pipes, David Horowitz, Tommy Robinson, et al. do not emerge from a historical rightist milieu.[870] Prohibiting the dissident right, as Paul Moon indicated, will not solve any problem. Indeed, had Tarrant and Anders Breivik been properly informed, perhaps they would not have even seen Islam as a problem, and would have directed their attention to the causes of Western decline? On the other hand, converts to Islam such as René Guénon, and those who have considered Islam favorably such as Julius Evola, have remained influential among the dissident right. How could it be otherwise, when both Islam and the right share so much in

---

[869] Trotsky, "Perspectives and Tasks in the East."
[870] Bolton, *Zionism, Islam and the West.*

common in confronting the modern epoch of decay, atheism, and materialism?

While all this seems to have taken us a long way from the HR Commission, this is the ideological and historical lineage of organizations that are portrayed as civic-minded and well-meaning by the Commission.

Why does the Human Rights Commission, a state agency, endorse a far-left blacklist targeting individuals on political grounds? It is enough for David Seymour, leader of the libertarian Act Party, to disagree with Green Party Member of Parliament Golriz Ghahraman in parliamentary debate over "hate speech" laws, for Seymour to be accused of inciting "White supremacist violence."[871] If Seymour's remarks critiquing Ghahraman's support for the repression of political dissent are regarded as inciting violence then any criticism of the state's liberal agendas will be regarded as "hate speech" and liable to prosecution. Ghahraman's histrionic posturing indicates that Seymour was accurate in calling her a "menace to freedom," as are the others behind the facade of "human rights." It is just such exaggerations to the point of absurdity that are compiled by the likes of Paul Hunt and Paul Spoonley as "evidence" of a "far right threat." David Seymour has been consigned to the ranks of the "White supremacist menace," while Paul Hunt likens sporadic hooliganism to a Nazi invasion of Britain.

Despite the combined police-media dragnet following the mosque shootings, no sign of a "White supremacist" terrorist cell was discovered, and no connections to Tarrant were found. Those are the facts whatever smoke and mirrors Spoonley, et al. produce to evoke a "Nazi" specter. It is disgraceful scaremongering for a repressive political agenda. The only terrorist cell ever found operating in New Zealand was among Urewera Maori separatists in alliance with Anarcho-psychotics. So far from repudiating these lunatics, the left united in solidarity.[872]

HRC Report Shows Hate Speech Law *Not* Needed

In 2019 the HRC published a report signed off by HR Commissioner Dr. Paul Hunt, "It Happened Here: Hate Crimes 2004–2012." The title is plagiarized from a 1966 British alternative history movie on the Nazi invasion of Britain.[873] That the HRC likens sporadic acts of mostly petty hooliganism to a Nazi invasion indicates that the mentality at the

---

[871] Small and Bracewell-Worrall, "Women MPs Urge David Seymour to Apologise."
[872] "Revealed: What Cops Filmed in Ureweras."
[873] Hunt, "It Happened Here."

Commissariat is akin to the delusions of their psycho-left colleagues at *Paparoa*.

The approach is no better than Ghahraman's liking little David Seymour to a "White supremacist terrorist." It is such histrionic nonsense that is being used to build a supposed case for the extension of the "human rights" laws and being called an "academic" does nothing to mitigate the moronic character of the "research."

Among the sundry examples of genocidal hatred we find that of Nic Miller in 2004. Miller, a member of the National Front, was assaulted and robbed by Somali youths when walking through Newtown, Wellington; a particularly multicultural area, which includes Somali gangs that have been kept in check by Maori gangs. For such a provocative crime against the poor Somalis Miller was tried twice, unsuccessfully; a matter which is not mentioned in Hunt's report. That the Somalis themselves were later beaten by those other than Miller indicates more about the racial dynamics of Newtown than the specter of "White racism." In Auckland Tongan and Somali youth fight for street supremacy.[874]

The report continues with examples that seldom give background and context, and do not indicate any discernible organizational involvement by the "far Right."

Using the same methodology, might we compile a list of crimes by Maori, Somali, Chinese, Tongan, Samoan, and other "ethnic" gangs and identify them as "hate crimes"? Shall we place the thuggery in a political context and state that it is aligned with the left? The presence of Black Power and the Mongrel Mob at the foundation of the Maori Party in 2004, their frontline presence in rioting against police during the 1981 Springbok Tour, and their support for the cynically politicized state rallies after the Christchurch mosque shootings, provide a more convincing association than the *non-sequiturs* of Hunt, Spoonley, et al. in their desperate attempts to justify their existence.

For example: are the violent muggings of Asians by Maori in Auckland hate crimes? If White hooligans had been involved, they would surely have been listed as such by Paul Hunt.[875] Of this race conflict, "Whau Local Board deputy chairwoman Susan Zhu said the incidents have caused widespread fear among the Chinese community, who felt vulnerable and helpless in the wake of the attacks."[876] However, because the assailants were Maori, so far from there being condemnation for this racial abuse, Auckland Mayor Phil Goff reassuringly stated that "it was important that

---

[874] Collins, "Residents Share Tales of Terror."
[875] Tait, "More Teens Arrested."
[876] Tait, "Brutal Assaults Scaring Auckland's Asian Students."

the young people arrested were supported and given help to change their behaviors."[877] Further:

> *Auckland University Chinese Student Society (AUCSS) president Phillip Wang said Chinese international students might be targeted because criminals thought they came from rich families. "I think it's more like a stereotyping thing. I think people think international students, or Asians in general, are rich, or have rich families. I think the criminals, they want to target international students or Asians in general instead of other people." Other Chinese students at the university were scared to walk home at night, Wang said.*[878]

The other notable targets, for many years, have been Indian dairy owners. The perpetrators are usually Maori or "Pasifika." While commenting on the brutal killing of a dairy owner, an Indian report indicated the widespread character of the violence:

> *West Auckland dairy-owners are struggling to cop-up with the recent rise of aggravated armed assaults in their stores. Many shop owners and workers have started equipping them with arms and bats, a practise that Police would discourage. Kamaljit Singh who has run a dairy store for [the] last 30 years is upset to see all this happen. His store was recently invaded by young thugs armed with machetes.*[879]

What Hunt's report on "hate crimes" unwittingly shows is that laws already exist for prosecuting any violence and abuse based on racial antagonism. The examples he cites were for the most part convicted under existing laws. So, what is it that the government and its allies want in implementing a "hate speech" law? There only remains the criminalization of any manifestation of pro-European dissent and criticism of globalist agendas. If stated outside the House, would David Seymour's criticism of Ghahraman have been prosecuted as "hate speech," especially given that he was accused of inciting "White supremacist threats" against her?

---

[877] Tait, "International Students Seen."
[878] "Chinese Students to Meet."
[879] Grewal, "The Family of Slain Auckland Dairy Owner."

Lamingtons and Rugby

While the likes of *Paparoa* state that the dissident right's appeal to "identity, community and purpose" is a strong attraction, what is laudable for every other race becomes toxic when appealing to White youths. The HRC asks on the Voice of Racism project for "Western and Pakeha culture" to be "challenged" as the "norm." What is this Eurocentric "norm," this legacy of colonialism and buttress of "White privilege"? Ghahraman recalls when settling in New Zealand from Iran as a youngster:

> *Aotearoa New Zealand as I encountered it during the 1990s was a starkly monocultural society. Pakeha history and culture dominated the national identity and was presented to us newcomers as "Kiwi." Kiwi food was pies and lamingtons, the language was English, kiwis loved rugby in winter and cricket in summer, the books I read through my school years were by English or American authors with a bit of Katherine Mansfield or Janet Frame...*[880]

Ghahraman regards this as White cultural hegemony, where all other races were invisible. However, what is she describing other than the banalization of "Western and Pakeha culture," defined as pies, lamingtons, rugby, and cricket? In her own words, she has described the reduction of European culture in New Zealand to a level beyond the puerile.

---

[880] Becraft, *The Big Questions*, 167.

Behind the Global Witch-Hunt

"A witch-hunt is an attempt to find and punish a particular group of people who are being blamed for something, often simply because of their opinions and not because they have actually done anything wrong."

Collins English Dictionary

The Tarrant Mosque shootings were used as a pretext to smear and repress dissidents throughout the world, tighten social media censorship, ban books, prohibit organizations, confiscate guns, and enact laws in a witch-hunt that continues.

Since it was discovered that Christchurch mosque shooter Brenton Tarrant gave a small donation to Martin Sellner of Generation Identity in Austria over a year ago, and consequently a couple of e-mails were exchanged in acknowledgement, a witch-hunt was launched against the "Far Right" in a cynical use of the Muslim deaths. In particular Sellner was targeted because of his articulate and professional manner. It is claimed that Sellner was of such influence that Generation Identity's campaign against the United Nations Migration Compact was responsible for several states not signing as the result of what is called "fake news" and "lies" about the Compact being "binding." As we have examined in a previous chapter,[881] the *Identitarian* contention that the UN Compact is indeed binding and enforceable on signatory states under international law is correct. It is a lie—"false news"—to pretend otherwise.

In New Zealand a journalist, Patrick Gower, became fixated with Sellner. Gower, if remembered at all, will probably be so because of the irredeemable fool he made of himself in his "interview" with Lauren

---

[881] Globalization of Labor: Origins and Aims of the United Nations Global Migration Compact.

Southern and Stefan Molyneux,[882] when they arrived in New Zealand for a speaking engagement that was cancelled due to extreme left threats.

While the media remains mute on the long history of violence from the left against the right, Gower, et al with the assistance of the supposed "experts" such as Paul Spoonley, have sought to show that New Zealand has long been "terrorized" by the right which, despite the media's and police's endeavors, remains elusive. The only examples given during the course of a television series promising to expose a long running campaign of violence by the "Right" were the psychotic antics of a gang called the Fourth Reich, which supposedly "terrorized" Nelson and the West Coast of the South Island. According to an "expert," the Fourth Reich "were responsible for the murders of young Māori man Hemi Hutley, gay man James 'Janis' Bamborough, Korean tourist Jae Hyeon Kim, and Christchurch woman Vanessa Pickering."[883]

Gower's "experts" failed to explain that the Fourth Reich gang was comprised of those of Chinese, Maori, and "Pasifika" descent. Whether there was a token White in the membership is unknown. Nonetheless, with a name like Fourth Reich, that must have been motivated by rightist ideology, like the Maori street gangs that wear the swastika. According to Gower and his experts, there is some type of historical and ideological continuity between the Fourth Reich, Tarrant, local critics of the UN Compact on Migration, and Sellner. Gower and other journalists, and their experts, failed to come up with anything that justifies the hysteria that they and the government have tried to generate amidst gun confiscations, demands for "hate speech" laws, the sacking of a Dominion Movement organizer from his job, [884] and a police "black list" that was leaked to the media and then leaked to the psycho-left *Paparoa*, which has the endorsement of Gower, Human Rights Commissioner Paul Hunt, and even the police.

After Gower's fiasco in trying to take on Southern and Molyneux he tried to redeem himself. A *Newshub* television series called *Because It Matters* fronted by Gower, attempted to show that Sellner's influence is "pervasive" (sic) in New Zealand politics, and that it is "Identitarian" ideology largely emanating from Sellner that prompted the Tarrant

---

[882] Newshub, "Full Interview: Lauren Southern and Stefan Molyneux."
[883] Gower, "Revealed: How White Supremacists."
[884] Dominion Movement was an *Identitarian* youth movement that after the Tarrant shootings was pilloried by the media, *doxed* by the left, and sought by the police. The movement had no connection, directly, indirectly, or philosophically, with Tarrant, and was a completely legal organization. Because of their success in recruiting among the young however, their demise was sought and obtained. Remnants regrouped as Action Zealandia, which has surpassed its predecessor.

shootings. The only "dangerous" "White supremacist" that Gower and his crew were able to uncover was Phil Arps, jailed for having shared Trarrant's video footage of the shootings. Arps was shown to have been present at an anti-UN rally in Christchurch, where he called out that New Zealand First Party leader and deputy Prime Minister, Winston Peters, widely seen as having compromised himself for the sake of a coalition with Labour, should be executed for "treason."[885]

Other than this were typically childish internet threats against Green Member of Parliament Golriz Ghahraman. She drew some ire because of her advocating the introduction of "hate speech" laws. Her support for "identity politics" is based on uniting "persons of color" against "White privilege." The threats allowed Ghahraman to posture for a few days, and receive a police escort since her life was supposedly at stake.[886] Ghahraman was also conspicuous for her participation in a violent effort to stop the New Zealand National Front's annual (and only) activity in October 2017, at its "Flag Day" rally, which was blocked by an alliance of anarchists and communists with Ghahraman to the fore.[887] Violent confrontation against political opponents is apparently acceptable to her.

When Gower's attempt to redeem himself after the Southern/Molyneux fiasco with a television series on "White supremacist terrorism" in New Zealand also flopped, generating mostly mirth and derision from viewers, he tried with a third attempt, this time to show how European "Identitarianism," and particularly Sellner, became "pervasive" (sic). Sellner and the long arm of the Austro-Nazi international conspiracy reached the halls of power, the proof being the rejection by the National Party of the United Nations Migration Compact. Peters, who has made his political career out of demanding immigration restrictions and hyping a supposed "Muslim threat," since he and his colleagues partnered with the Labour government, called on national opposition leader Simon Bridges to resign because of his supposedly being influenced by the "Austrian neo-Nazis" (sic).[888]

---

[885] "Police Investigating Death Threats."
[886] Vance, "Security Escort for Green MP."
[887] Devlin, "National Front Members Chased Away." (They were not "chased away"; they were simply mobbed by numbers).
[888] "'Absolutely' Links Between European Far-Right and New Zealand Extremists."

Identitarianism and UN Global Compact

According to Peters and Gower, Sellner launched a worldwide campaign against the UN Migration Compact, which through "lies" about it being "binding" on signatory states succeeded in dissuading some states from signing. Notably absent in this scenario is any mention of Israel refusing to sign on the very basis that it would undermine their sovereignty.[889] Is it because it would be difficult to portray Israel as being influenced by "Austrian Neo-Nazis" rather than simply following its own historic path of Judeo-centricity, which might be construed as "Jewish Nazism"? Indeed, while the liberals, leftists, and their oligarchic stringpullers squawked about "Austrian Neo-Nazis," the actual source of Islamophobia—influential and well-funded pro-Israel *neocon* think tanks—remained unmentioned amidst the hysteria. The pro-Israel attitudes of certain of the supposed "Far Right" in New Zealand also went unmentioned.[890]

My own knowledge of the UN Migration Compact was prompted by frequent comments made by radio talkback host Bruce Russell, a news commentator altogether more thoughtful than Gower, et al. Even then, it took me some weeks to look at whether Russell's warnings about the Compact were accurate, and I had heard nothing of any resistance to it from any "Far Right" in New Zealand, was unaware of the details of Mr. Sellner's campaign against it, and was not able to find any extensive analysis on it from any supposedly right-wing organization in New Zealand. But Gower, Peters, et al. alleged that the Compact was derailed by a well-oiled scare-mongering campaign by Sellner and the Austrian "Nazis," whose "lies" even fooled governments. However, it should be enough to read the UN Compact to readily see that it is indeed binding on signatory states, despite whatever legal advice to the contrary that was supposedly given to the government.

The "Great Replacement" and "Replacement Migration"

There has been much histrionics on the rightist, *Identitarian* campaigns against the "Great Replacement." Again, because the phrase was used by Mosque shooter Brenton Tarrant, the term reached a

---

[889] "Netanyahu: Israel Won't Sign."
[890] Bolton, "Islamophobia: The Trojan Horse Amidst the Right."

notoriety implying genocide. The rightist claim that Europeans are being replaced in their own homelands by alien migrants and refugees is lambasted as a "lie," and in the words of the ever-dubious *Wikipedia* as a "nationalist right-wing conspiracy theory." Again, Sellner is blamed for spreading the theory across the world.[891]

Yet from at least 2001 the United Nations started referring to "Replacement Migration." The theory laid the foundation for the UN Migration Compact. The UN document "Replacement Migration, Is It a Solution to Declining and Ageing Populations?" statistically examines the demographic trends of "developed" states. The issue is that of aging populations due to low fertility and the increasing duration of life expectancy. Hence, a looming economic crisis with the demographic imbalance. The solution is to replenish the labor market with migrants, by population transfers from the developing to the developed states. The preamble to the document states:

> *United Nations projections indicate that over the next 50 years, the populations of virtually all countries of Europe as well as Japan will face population decline and population ageing. The new challenges of declining and ageing populations will require comprehensive reassessments of many established policies and programmes, including those relating to international migration.*
>
> *Focusing on these two striking and critical population trends, the report considers replacement migration for eight low-fertility countries (France, Germany, Italy, Japan, Republic of Korea, Russian Federation, United Kingdom and United States) and two regions (Europe and the European Union). Replacement migration refers to the international migration that a country would need to offset population decline and population ageing resulting from low fertility and mortality rates.*[892]

The right uses the term the "Great Replacement," the UN uses the term "Replacement Migration'; either way, the references are to the "replacement" mainly of European indigenes by drawing on the burgeoning "third world" population. Is that, or is it not, precisely the aim of the UN Migration Compact? If not; how is it not? If so, how has Sellner, et al. "lied" and "misrepresented" the issue? The UN document concludes:

---

[891] Rossi, "'Great Replacement' Ideology Is Spreading."
[892] "Replacement Migration."

328 | The Tyranny of Human Rights

> *Finally, the new challenges being brought about by declining and ageing populations will require objective, thorough and comprehensive reassessments of many established economic, social and political policies and programmes. Such reassessments will need to incorporate a long-term perspective. Critical issues to be addressed in those reassessments would include (a) appropriate ages for retirement; (b) levels, types and nature of retirement and health-care benefits for the elderly; (c) labour-force participation; (d) assessed amounts of contributions from workers and employers needed to support retirement and healthcare benefits for the increasing elderly population; and (e) policies and programmes relating to international migration, in particular replacement migration, and the integration of large numbers of recent migrants and their descendants. In this context, it should be noted that immigrants to one country are emigrants from another country. As such, international migration must be seen as part of the larger globalization process taking place throughout the world, influencing the economic, political and cultural character of both sending and receiving countries. While orderly international migration can provide countries of origin with remittances and facilitate the transfer of skills and technology, it also may entail the loss of needed human resources. Similarly, international migration can provide countries of destination with needed human resources and talent, but may also give rise to social tensions. Effective international migration policies must therefore take into account the impact on both the host society and countries of origin.*[893]

The concluding sentences refer to:

1. The integration of large numbers of recent migrants and their descendants.
2. International migration...as part of the larger globalization process taking place throughout the world, influencing the economic, political, and cultural character of both sending and receiving countries.
3. International migration [that] may give rise to social tensions.

These are all factors posed by the right, yet raised first in 2001 by the UN The problems of "orderly international migration" discussed in the 2001

---

[893] "Replacement Migration." Conclusions and Implications, op. cit.

document are all addressed in the UN Migration Compact. Where were Sellner, et al. "lying" in these matters?

The UN document refers to problems that have supposedly hitherto been unknown to history. Nonsense. It is more a matter that the UN "experts," NGOs, leftists, academics, journalists, and their oligarchic string-pullers do not know history. They do not have a sense of the historical. They see only "human progress," like a tapeworm creeping along towards some utopian "end of history." Rather, the demographic crisis in the West has been seen in prior civilizations, and the desperate answer was the same: to fill the population void with migrants. It is in this that we might discern the end of civilizations, not their embarking on a bright new future.

Polynius (born ca. 200BC) said of the Greeks:

In our time all Greece was visited by a dearth of children and generally a decay of population...and a failure of productiveness results. ...For this evil grew upon us rapidly, and without attracting attention, by our men becoming perverted to passion of show and money and the pleasures of an idle life, and accordingly, not marrying at all, or, if they did marry, refusing to rear the children that were born, or at most one or two of a great number, for the sake of leaving them all well off or bringing them up in extravagant luxury...

The Greek elite become effete, and indeed were regarded as being "feminized" by the influences of an already decadent Persian civilization. The answer of Alexander was to expand the empire and integrate Persian corruption—"cultural enrichment" and "diversity," as it is now called—with the aim of forming a new world order.[894] Of Rome, Augustus recognized the demographic catastrophe caused by the corruption of traditional Roman virtues, asking, "How can the commonwealth be preserved if we neither marry nor produce children?" He referred to the city being given up to foreigners, and to liberating slaves "chiefly for the purpose of making out of them as many citizens as possible..."[895] Tacitus remarked that despite state efforts, "childlessness prevailed."[896] At the beginning of the second century Pliny the Younger wrote that his was "an age when even one child is thought a burden preventing the rewards of childlessness." Hierocles remarked that most people seemed to regard

---

[894] Bolton, *The Decline and Fall of Civilisations*, 198-199.
[895] Dio, *Dio's Rome*, Book IV, 86. Cited in Bolton, op cit., 205.
[896] Tacitus, iii, 25. Cited in Bolton, op cit.

siring children as interfering with their lifestyles. Prostitution became so widespread it became a substitute for marriage. Homosexuality and bisexuality had become common,[897] as did abortion. Many women became infertile. Birth control methods were widely used.[898] The cities were "populated by strangers."[899] How modern all this sounds. Of Western civilization in its modern epoch of decay, philosopher-historian Oswald Spengler wrote that "the destiny of being the last of the line is no longer felt as doom."[900]

There are causes for this demographic crisis that are not in the interests of the globalists to raise. They include the social pathologies that they have spent decades promoting, such as feminism, abortion, birth control, hedonism, and now a mania for a "sliding scale of gender." This "progress" has been seen before in the decaying epochs of prior civilizations over the course of millennia. Much of this was supposed to create a global "inclusive economy," as the corporations and NGOs call it. For decades the globalists have sought to fully integrate women into the work force by "liberation" from the "burden" of motherhood. Now there is a demographic crisis, and the globalist answer is "replacement migration," as per Rome and Greece.

These are the problems that the international oligarchy and their leftist fellow-travelers do not want discussed.

Institute for Strategic Dialogue

A primary question to be asked is the whence of the media's information on the "Far Right"? It is the Institute for Strategic Dialogue (ISD). Here we reach that much-abused term, "conspiracy theory." Indeed, following the "Far Right" and "White supremacist" websites, according to the ISD, "conspiracy theory" websites were most responsible for spreading Sellner's so-called "lies" on the UN Migration Compact. However, the news media and their globalist think tanks had their own theory about an "international Austro-Nazi conspiracy," which is so pervasive, well-placed, and funded as to be determining the policies of major political parties and governments. Gower cited the ISD as his source on the "Far Right":

---

[897] Stark, *The Rise of Christianity*, 117.
[898] Ibid., 118-121. See Bolton, op. cit., 208-209.
[899] Ibid., 156.
[900] Spengler, *The Decline of the West*, Vol. II, 103-104.

> An investigation by the Institute for Strategic Dialogue, which monitors extremism online, found: "Far-right and right-wing populist influencers... began spreading large-scale distorted interpretations and misinformation about the UN migration pact."[901]

Who is going to investigate the character of the Institute for Strategic Dialogue? According to Gower it is some type of definitive authority "monitoring" "extremism online," and almost sounds official, like a branch of Interpol. The ISD had embarked on an international smear campaign against Generation Identity and Sellner. It is pertinent to ask whether this has been undertaken precisely because Sellner and GI upset the proverbial applecart in regard to the UN Migration Compact; a cause that happens to be a part of the ISD agenda?

Among the major smears against GI and Sellner, the Freidrich-Ebert-Stiftung features an interview with Jakob Guhl, "Project Associate at the Institute for Strategic Dialogue (ISD), where he mainly works with the Online Civil Courage Initiative, a project that aims to improve and promote civil society reactions to hate speech and extremism on the Internet."[902] Guhl claims in regard to the UN Migration Compact that:

> While the agreement was barely talked about on social media until mid-September, far-right and right-wing populist influencers "discovered" the issue in mid-September and began spreading large-scale distorted interpretations and disinformation about the UN migration pact...and far-right representatives such Martin Sellner played a big role in shaping the discussion about the migration pact online. His "Stop Migration Pact" petition was the most shared URL link in our dataset until the end of October.[903]

Guhl complained that there was insufficient information about the Compact, until the "far Right" discovered it. That the UN was negligent in providing information on the Compact is surely an indictment on that body, not on the "far Right," which sought to address the information void. Indeed, it was the "far Right" that seems to have helped publicize the very scant information that the UN did provide, which enabled one to make an informed judgment based on the presentation of both sides, which clearly

---

[901] Gower, "Exclusive: Police Investigating White Supremacist's Death."
[902] "Too Little, Too Late."
[903] Ibid.

the UN and its allies were unwilling to do. Of the Friedrich-Ebert-Stiftung (FES), on their "About us" page, it is:

> ...the oldest political foundation in Germany with a rich tradition in social democracy dating back to its foundation in 1925. The foundation owes its formation and its mission to the political legacy of its namesake Friedrich Ebert, the first democratically elected German President.

There is nothing new about a leftist outfit taking its party line from a plutocratic think tank such as the ISD. In good social democratic fashion, the Ebert Foundation promotes NATO, trans-Atlantic free trade, and generally how to keep Germany subservient to the USA.

A report at *Politico* covers similar ground.[904] A report in the *New Zealand Herald* states that:

> European investigators are digging deeper into possible links between far-right ideologues and the suspected Christchurch mosque gunman, who sent at least two donations to an anti-Muslim group with branches around Europe.... "One of the dangers of this ideology is that it creates an imminent threat from the outside: a coming war if we don't do anything about it," said Austrian right-wing extremism researcher Julia Ebner, with the London-based Institute for Strategic Dialogue. "A violent escalation is part of their ideology."[905]

What nonsensical scare-mongering, posing as "expertise." As GI showed in a detailed response to media smears and Establishment repression, there was no violent intent.[906]

A report in *The Washington Post* included the widespread theme that there were "extensive" links between Sellner and Tarrant, citing Jacob Davey, "the author of a forthcoming Institute for Strategic Dialogue paper on the subject";[907] meaning, there were three brief emails in regard to Trarrant's small donation. *Post* columnist Anne Applebaum, introducing a Judeo-centric dimension, added:

---

[904] Cerulus, "How the UN Migration Pact Got Trolled."
[905] "Probe Into Links Between Accused Christchurch Gunman."
[906] Generation Identity.
[907] Applebaum, "Opinion: How Europe's 'Identitarians.'"

The obsession with the Jewish financier George Soros, a feature of far-right propaganda everywhere from Hungary to Alabama, is linked to this set of ideas. And when President Trump or Italian Interior Minister Matteo Salvini talk about immigrant "invasions," they are nodding and winking to Identitarianism, too.[908]

An "anti-Semitic" conspiracy theory can never be too far away for such commentators: *reductio ad Judaeum*. But since Applebaum has mentioned Soros, let us take a look behind the ISD, and if we find Soros lurking there are we supposed to overlook the fact lest it indicates an "anti-Semitic obsession"?

The "partners and funders" of the ISD are high-powered globalist corporations. From their website, they include: Facebook, Google, Twitter, Jigsaw, M&C Saatchi, Microsoft, Love Frankie, Asia Foundation, Carnegie Corporation NY, Eranda Rothschild Foundation (part of the famous banking dynasty), Gen Next, Open Society Foundations (yes, Soros), Robert Bosch Foundation, Vodafone Foundation.

Love Frankie is a Saatchie-sponsored "social change" project in Asia. Among those who "Love Frankie" are the US State Department, USAID, World Bank Group, Facebook, Google, sundry UN agencies, et al.[909]

Other partners of the ISD include the US State Department, International Republican Institute, Brookings Institution, Chatham House, the London School of Economics "Arena" project that targets anti-globalists; Royal United Services Institute, etc.

The ISD is a globalist institution founded to agitate for the suppression of opposition to globalization. They exist to target anti-globalization as "fascistic." That is their terminology, as laid out on their "About" page:

> *We believe it is the task of every generation to challenge such divisive, fascistic movements and to invest in the ongoing edification of open, democratic, and free civic culture, without which there can be no lasting protection of the rights of others, no cohesion and no lasting peace.*

Of its programs ISD has "advised 40 governments," reached 120 "strong cities network members," indoctrinated eighty thousand youth in "education programs," presided over seventy-five reports and policy

---

[908] Ibid.
[909] "Love Frankie."

briefings, and "trained over 32,000 activists," according to their "programmes" page. "Activists" is usually a euphemism for psychotics of the *Antifa* variety. Is this what ISD is referring to? Via their "Far-Right Extremism" page:

> *Based on our far-right analysis and research we briefed and advised a range of national and regional policy makers, ministries and security and intelligence agencies on the latest trends in online and offline extremism. Our research and analysis featured across major international and national news outlets and informs our engagement with tech firms and civil society.*

This is where governments and media receive their smear briefings, and it should be noted, "security and intelligence agencies," which might explain the nonsensical character of the police witch-hunt for elusive "far Rightists" in New Zealand, and the half-witted questions police posed after intrusive invasions of households on the basis of nothing.[910]

Among ISD "partners" we find sundry organizations that have been involved in "regime change" and "color revolutions" on behalf of the US government and/or international plutocracy. The International Republican Institute was established to promote the USA's version of democracy and culture-pathology worldwide. Its aim is US global hegemony. IRI funders, via their website, include USAID, The Bush Institute, Freedom House, National Democratic Institute, Solidarity Center of the AFL-CIO, Australian, Canadian, and British governments, and many others. IRI overtly states that it influences the formation and policies of political parties around the world.[911] It encourages "civil society organizations";[912] that is, it establishes subversive organizations in states marked by the USA for "regime change" of the type that were expelled from Russia and Hungary. It uses "the digital revolution" that has been a major factor in facilitating "color revolutions" across the world. While IRI boasts of its global interference in the internal affairs of states, they have the audacity to moralize via their "Beacon Project" (founded to suppress

---

[910] This author was questioned by two armed police, as were many other New Zealanders, following the Tarrant shootings. The Arabic translation of my book *Zionism, Islam and the West* did not conform to their instructions on the "far right." Their primary interest was in tracing members of Dominion Movement, none of whose identities were known to me. The extensive police questioning of so many unconnected New Zealanders did not render any sign of a "far right" terror network, but facts have not impeded the continuing portrayal of a "far right threat"; the bogey-man necessary for justifying state repression.
[911] "Link Political Parties."
[912] "Bringing Citizens Together."

alternative views over the internet), that "IRI is launching a new program aimed at countering the increasing threat of Russian soft power and propaganda."[913] What is the IRI other than an agency to purvey the "soft power and propaganda" of the USA?

Other ISD sponsors, Gen Next, Facebook, and Google, were among the founders of Movements.org, a globalist project aiming to use digital technology to foment "regime change" in states targeted by globalists and/or the USA. Its original name was Alliance of Youth Movements. Corporate sponsors of Movements.org have included Howcast, Edelman, Music TV, Meetup, Pepsi, CBS News, Mobile Accord, You Tube, MSN/NBC, National Geographic, Omicom Group, Access 360 Media. Public partnerships are Columbia Law School and the US State Department. Representatives at the organization's summits have included those from the Rand Corporation, World Bank, National Democratic Institute, You Tube, Freedom House, et al. Movements.org was particularly active in the "Arab Spring," where a string of regimes were toppled in quick succession.[914]

ISD initiated its own youth focused digital project similar to Movements.org, YouthCAN (Youth Civil Activism Network).

Conclusion

The ISD is part of a large, worldwide network of NGOs, so-called "civil society" that promotes globalization. The part the ISD plays is to help suppress dissent in the name of combating "racism," "xenophobia," and "fascism." Open borders and so-called "inclusive economies" are primary aims. Those who dissent from this process must be eliminated by being demonized, delegitimized, and smeared as a prelude to the actual banning of dissidents with the use of terms such as "hate speech," and "counter-terrorism." This is the function of the ISD.

There are multitudes of useful idiots in politics, academia, and media who play their part whether through banal idealism or plain opportunism. While the globalists and their allies discount as "conspiracy theorists" those who object that globalism means plutocratic exploitation and the reducing of humanity to a nebulous globule of economic units, they proffer their own theory of an "international Austro-Nazi conspiracy." They have used the Tarrant atrocity to cynically justify a witch-hunt against

---

[913] "Beacon Project Shines."
[914] Bolton, *Revolution from Above*, 235-240.

dissidents. Is the term "witch-hunt" an exaggeration for what is taking place? Consider this from New Zealand:

> *Firearm licence applicants are being checked for shaven heads, Nazi symbolism and camouflage clothes after the March 15 terror attack. Stuff has learned police issued a new directive informing vetting staff to be wary of the "extreme right," which includes white supremacy and far right ideology. Signifiers of the extreme right include tattoos, Celtic or Norse symbolism, books on the Third Reich, confederate flags, and reference to Norway mass-shooter Anders Breivik.*[915]

A New Zealand branch of the Norse folk religion *Asatru* had been grossly vilified because Tarrant had painted a rune on his firearm. That was enough for the media. In a small victory, the *Asatru* group successfully filed a complaint with the Media Council.[916] *The Otago Daily Times* carried a feature portraying the South Island Independence Movement as part of this "Far Right" "racist extremism." Opposition to the government's fringe antics is enough to get one blacklisted.[917] Such was the widespread disdain for this trash journalism that the newspaper's online public feedback forum was quickly taken down.

Had such actions of police, state, and media towards the elusive New Zealand "Far Right," "White supremacists," critics of the UN, gun-owners, and admirers of Donald Trump, been taken against the "Far Left," there would have been a reaction of outrage with cries of "McCarthyism" and "witch-hunt." In the present situation, however, things are totally different. The twelve-year-old girl, surrounded by armed police on a farm while she was shoveling horse dung with a pitch-folk, did not receive an apology from police, or sympathy from the media.[918] Likewise with the family of the Russian army veteran with post-traumatic stress disorder, who killed himself thanks to police antics emanating from the mass hysteria.[919] The mass hysteria that the news media and state generated led to the suicide of a young father, Jesse Anderson, who had been smeared as a "White supremacist" by Marc Daalder, a journalist specializing in smear-mongering. In a hit-piece on opposition to the UN Migration Compact,

---

[915] Manch, "Police Check Firearm Licence."
[916] "Thor-Worshiping Article Unfair."
[917] Hudson, "Racist Concerns."
[918] Palmer, "David Seymour Calls Out Police."
[919] Sherwood, "Ex-Russian Soldier Dies."

Daalder had written of Anderson, associating him with "White supremacy" and "anti-Semitism" in the most tenuous of ways:

> *When I spoke with NZ Sovereignty's Jesse Anderson about the planned march and his broader movement, however, he insisted it was neither racist nor right-wing. "We have no tolerance for racism, for sexism, for any of that. If we see anyone who is expressing awful views, we will ask them to move along," he vowed. Anderson later added, in response to questions about NZ Sovereignty's political leanings, "I don't see patriotism as right-wing, I don't see nationalism as right-wing."*
>
> *But everything the movement stands for is straight out of the far-right playbook. The conspiratorial assertions that the UN pact will result in censorship of the press or an influx of migrants originated on alt-right forums and news sites. The naked Islamophobia, homophobia, anti-Semitism and other despicable views are characteristic of the modern far-right. Protestations to the contrary are worth little in the face of self-evident facts.*[920]

In the world of Daalder, et al. it is enough to oppose the UN to be labelled an "anti-Semite" and "White supremacist." The Daalder article was used to deny Jesse Anderson child access. The young father consequently killed himself. A political colleague wrote:

> *I've seen it said that he lost a custody battle for his son, but that wasn't the case. The custody battle was about to begin, and he had won the last one. This time things were a little different though, and the weaponisation of Oranga Tamariki against him by his political enemies visibly shook him. He always treated everyone with respect, including those with opposing views, but the fact there are such evil people out there who would target his family to get at him caught him by surprise.*[921]

---

[920] Daalder, "The Furious World."
[921] de Boer, "In Memory of Jesse Anderson."

Multiculturalism in Practice: First Annual Europhobic Hatefest Turns on Itself

"Isn't it rich?
Are we a pair?
Me here at last on the ground,
You in mid-air.
Send in the clowns."

Stephen Sondheim, "Send in the Clowns"

New Zealand ethnic communities joined together with academics and human rights advocates in what was supposed to be a show of solidarity against "White supremacist terrorism" and the formulation of "hate speech" laws to enforce multicultural harmony. The result was recriminations between representatives of Jewish and Islamic communities in a replay of overseas conflict, as "anti-Semitism" collided with "Islamophobia" and without a "White racist" in sight.

Over the course of June 15th and 16th, 2021, the first "hui"[922] on "Countering Terrorism and Violent Extremism" was supposed to bring together in single accord a gaggle of "experts" and ethnic representatives. The idea of an annual "hui" to discuss terrorism was mooted in recommendations to government by the commission of inquiry into the Tarrant shootings. The primary focus was intended to be on what "experts" are calling "White identity terrorism."

The actual danger is that by demonizing any and all White dissent and denigrating any and all traces of New Zealand's settler heritage, some individuals might be pushed into a position where violence is considered the only remaining option. If they act on their desperation that in turn will

---

[922] *Hui* = meeting (Maori)

feed further state repression. The consequences of a deliberate policy of *White youth alienation* are not discussed or studied. Any grassroots initiative to address this alienation is itself condemned as "White identity extremism." The Euro-New Zealander, and particularly White youth, have been pushed into a no-win situation. The state is aggravating the "Lone Wolf" scenario and deflecting from its own responsibility. The "White extremist" is actually a red herring.

No Far-Right Terrorist Network—Only Far Left

Regardless of the reams of banality produced by the Commission of Inquiry, the annoying fact for these parasitic milkers of the public purse is that the only terrorist network that has ever been found in recent decades is a bizarre assortment of Maoris and anarchists in the hills of the Ureweras in 2007. Some of these psychotics are still at the forefront of the far left, and advocate state repression against the dissident right—for terrorism. In fact, Val Morse, a longtime anarchist of a particularly histrionic character, who was implicated in the Urewera camps, was present at the "anti-terrorism hui" presumably as an "expert" on "the far right." Those tried became a *cause celebre* of the left; "The Urewera Four," while in contrast Tarrant was repudiated by all rightist groups. In 2014 police apologized for "unnecessarily frightening" people during the raids, the police conduct report commenting: "The road block at Ruatoki was intimidating to innocent members of that community, particularly in view of the use of armed Police officers in full operational uniform."[923]

No such enquiry was ever contemplated in regard to the dozens of individuals visited by armed police "in full operational uniform," asking half-witted questions in pursuit of the willow-the-wisp of "White terrorism." No seminars were inaugurated, media features produced, government enquiries established, to investigate the alliance between Maori separatists and leftist extremists; while the left and Maori still squawk about the "injustice" of police raids in regard to guerrilla warfare training. No apologies were ever received from the blundering plods who invaded the homes of many New Zealanders in the aftermath of Tarrant, not on the basis of any terrorist threat, but on the basis of their views that dissent from government policy. Expressing support on social media for the then American president, or criticizing some aspect of the New

---

[923] "Report Into Operation Eight."

Zealand government was enough to be put on the police blacklist which ended up in the hands of the far left.

However, the counter-terrorism hui was not intended as anything other than a facade to examine ways in which barely discernible expressions of dissent might be thwarted. Paul Hunt, chief Human Rights Commissioner, can be relied on to produce voluminous annual reports showing that "White supremacist hate speech" and *ipso facto* potential terrorism exist by the simple expedient of banal nonsense as indicated by his less than impressive little study called "It Happened Here" (dramatically named after a 1960s low budget movie in which Germany invades Britain with the help of a fifth column of indigenous fascists, Mosley-style).[924]

Moses off Script

The Europhobic hui started with utopian hopes that did not last the day. When one puts a cat among pigeons, what can be expected? However, it would not be possible to organize such an event without a Zionist presence. A lack thereof would be implicit anti-Semitism. Hence the presence of Juliet Moses, representing the New Zealand Jewish Council. Had Moses kept to the Europhobic script about "Nazis" and "White identity terrorism," everything would have proceeded swimmingly. Yet it seems that Moses could not resist referring to Muslim terrorism, which is not what the hui was about. Keep to the script: *White extremists, White terrorists*. It would have seemed to the delegates from the Islamic Federation that Moses was raising precisely those matters that we are told had radicalized Tarrant, and the Muslims walked out, claiming "racism." A media report stated:

> *The walkout happened today during a panel addressing the causes of terrorism after a comment from NZ Jewish Council spokesperson Juliet Moses about the Israel-Palestine conflict sparked a commotion. Moses had told the crowd that leaders should be consistent in condemning terrorism.*
>
> *"We need to hear leaders condemn all support for terrorism and all terrorism equally whatever the source, target, and circumstances, and even when it is not politically expedient to do so. Hezbollah and Hamas, their military wings are proscribed*

---

[924] Hunt, "It Happened Here."

terror organisations in New Zealand but we saw a rally in support of Hezbollah on Queen St in 2018."

Her remarks caused a strong response from members of the Muslim community including victims of the Christchurch mosque attacks, as people shouted: "Free Palestine." Federation of the Islamic Associations of New Zealand (FIANZ) chair Abdur Razzaq said the hui was about "discussing social cohesion ... we came here to discuss ways to peace"...

Moses said she was only "stating fact" and did not believe her comments were controversial and that she was referring to the 2018 march, not the one that happened in Auckland this year.[925]

The Islamic Federation had placed itself in such a predicament when it jumped aboard the "antiracist" bandwagon, participating in so-called *aroha* (Maori = "love") rallies organized in the aftermath of Tarrant by sundry *militant atheists*, Trotskyites, and other communists. The Islamic Federation, after Tarrant, started spouting the most arrant liberal nonsense. This does not do service to the Islamic tradition in trying to co-opt the most debased elements of the modern West and attempting to appear as liberals in Muslim garb. They seem to have departed far from the roots of the Albanian Muslim migrants, anti-communists as one should expect from such a traditionalist religion, who established the Islamic Federation under the patronage of Mazhar Shukri Krasniqi, of whom Abdullah Drury, former PR man for the Federation, writes: "He was opposed to communism and was arrested by either the Albanian and Yugoslav security agencies at one point or another between 1945 and 1950, especially when he tried to escape the socialist utopia."[926]

A further media report states:

Moses told RNZ she had been correct to use her speech on Tuesday to reference a "Hezbollah rally" in Auckland's Queen St in 2018, when she cautioned it had not been condemned and that leaders should be consistent when confronting terrorism. She said Jews in New Zealand faced a number of threats, including that from Lebanese group, Hezbollah ...[927]

One might ask, is Moses implying that the Lebanese community in New Zealand constitute a "threat" to Jews in New Zealand? She is placing the

---

[925] Foon, "Hui on Countering Terrorism."
[926] Drury, "Mazherberg: An Albanian Exile."
[927] "Jewish Council Spokeswoman."

"threat" in a specifically New Zealand context. The importation of foreign quarrels is a feature of multiculturalism.

White Identity Bad; Jewish Identity Good

Apparently, there are a "large number of threats" to New Zealand Jews. Such impending "threats" are the lifeblood and *raison d'etre* of Zionism.[928] Any less of an image means the loss of the Zionist grip over Jewish communities, and a threat to Jewish existence, not by way of pogroms but through *out-marriage*.

Of the latter, Jewish dating sites aim to match Jew-to-Jew. In New Zealand *JSingles*, listed as a resource on *One Community Chronicle*, online successor to the *NZ Jewish Chronicle*, states: "JSingles NZ has been set up as a service for the NZ Jewish community to allow Jewish singles to easily meet other like minded people who share the same faith, background and values."[929] Replace "Jewish" with "White" and imagine the reaction from Stuff media, Patrick Gower, Newshub, Paul Spoonley, Human Rights Commission... NZ Jewish Council...

Further, the by-line of the NZ Jewish Council is that of supporting "Jewish awareness and identity."[930] That is to say the NZJC is an "identitarian" movement, as is Zionism *per se*. *Identitarianism* is only a "problem" when it is European. Then it becomes "White identity terrorism." As for the roots of Jewish identitarianism in Palestine, Stern, Irgun, Palmach, the King David Hotel, Count Bernadotte, and Deir Yasin, become part of a "liberation struggle," rather than a process of "ethnic cleansing."

"Rise in Anti-Semitism" Preludes Hui

Moses just a week prior to the "human rights" hui laid the foundation for her comments by claiming that the month previously had seen a significant increase in "anti-Semitic incidents" in New Zealand, relating this to what she was going to say at the hui a week later:

> While we haven't experienced the violent Jew-hatred seen recently in the United States and Europe, New Zealand has also

---

[928] Bolton, *Zionism, Islam and the West*, 33-62.
[929] "JSingles NZ."
[930] "New Zealand Jewish Council."

had a significant rise in antisemitic incidents **relating to the war between Hamas and Israel**.

Last year, 2020, saw 33 antisemitic incidents recorded in New Zealand—the highest number since records began in 1990. Last month alone, we recorded 16 incidents. They ranged from targeted, private antisemitic abuse of Jewish students online to a man giving the Nazi salute outside a synagogue.

Moses said those 16 incidents don't include public antisemitic social media posts from New Zealanders or on Kiwi forums, and the NZJC also noticed an increase of those.[931]

Moses quotes Green Party Member of Parliament Ricardo Menéndez tweeting in March "from the river to the sea, Palestine will be free." She states that this intrinsically means the destruction of Israel. But surely it could mean no more than that Menéndez supports the premise of the Balfour Declaration: a Jewish homeland in Palestine, to the extent that it does not encroach on the Arab indigenes? However, Zionist apologia, including that of Moses in her "glossary" for "leftie" critics of Israel, claims that Jews are the indigenes, "returning home" after centuries of exile, writing in the right-wing (?) *Australian Spectator*: "Colonisation: ...In relation to Israel, it means indigenous people regaining sovereignty over part of their ancestral homeland..."[932]

Hence Zionists can claim "solidarity" with indigenes in other states where it suits them, but obviously not extending to indigenous Europeans; that's "White identity extremism."

The extent to which the alleged upsurge in "antisemitism" in New Zealand is attributed to the "far right" is obscure. Much seems to emanate from the anti-Zionist left. Moses, on behalf of the NZJC, chastised Irish Bolshevik import Joe Carolan for chanting: "'Intifada, Intifada, globalise the Intifada' through a megaphone, [with] the crowd repeating the chant," at an anti-Israel rally in Auckland in May 2021. Moses continued: "It is even more alarming that Carolan, the co-founder of 'Love Aotearoa Hate Racism,' should be the person inciting such violence."[933] "Love Aotearoa Hate Racism" is one of the far-left fronts formed after the Tarrant shootings, Imam jumping aboard the bandwagons set up by those with a hatred towards Islam and all other religions. Carolan is an organizer of the *Unite* union, which has always been full of Trotskyites. Moses called on *Unite* to repudiate Carolan. He is also head of Socialist Aotearoa, a

---

[931] "New Zealand Not Immune."
[932] Moses, "The A-Z of Palestinian Oppression."
[933] "NZ Jewish Council Condemns."

Trotskyite faction. The Carolan antics helped set the stage for Moses at the Europhobe hui a week later, about which she commented:

> *It is worth noting that it is less than two days before this country's inaugural hui on Countering Terrorism and Violent Extremism. The Jewish Council calls on all leaders who are committed to ensuring that Aotearoa New Zealand never again falls prey to terrorism or violent extremism to condemn this brazen incitement to violence, which particularly threatens the Jewish community.*[934]

Could it be that the Zionists did not wish to be upstaged in the persecution stakes by Muslims even at an event that was supposed to be focused on the Tarrant mosque shootings?

It appeared to some that Zionists seemed to be placing Muslims in the same category as dissident Whites as a common "threat" to New Zealand Jews. The *Herald* quoted the Islamic Federation spokesman:

> *Razzaq said the remarks and the politicisation of the hui by Moses had been inappropriate, divisive and hurtful. He said Moses had used the Hezbollah "bogie" to promote fear and the "securitisation of Islam." Razzaq had told Radio NZ he felt sad for people who brought baggage from overseas and dumped it in New Zealand. He said Moses' comments had been a calculated attempt to denigrate Muslims present, including Palestinians, and "wipe out the memory" of those killed in the Christchurch mosque massacres.*
>
> *Moses rejected the claims and said she was there to raise concerns of her community...*[935]

So here we have Moses stating that she was there representing "her community," New Zealand Jews who, it would seem, at least according to the position of the NZ Jewish Council, consider certain Muslims a potential danger to their "community," as Tarrant considered Muslims a danger to European communities. Is the comparison unfair or exaggerated? Might one perceive a commonality of outlook between Tarrant and Zionists? Razzaq seems to have thought so when he said of Moses' comments, that they "had been a calculated attempt to denigrate

---

[934] Ibid.
[935] "Jewish Council Spokeswoman."

Muslims present, including Palestinians, and 'wipe out the memory' of those killed in the Christchurch mosque massacres."[936] It is also of interest that while Razzaq was outraged by Moses' implicit Islamophobia, which he called the "securitisation of Islam," this is precisely the tactic of the Islamic Federation, when it made the dissident right synonymous with "terrorism" in its submission to the government inquiry on counter-terrorism. The Federation's submission to the Royal Commission on Counter Terrorism, states:

> *There is not one universal—trans-historical, cross-cultural—political spectrum on which all ideologies can be graded. Ideologies are spectral. There are extremes on the spectra of liberalism, socialism, conservatism, Islamism, nationalism, and other political ideologies. Some political ideologies are inherently extreme, insofar as they are, often self-consciously, so far beyond the norms of the social contexts which they aim to change, that they have no popular or legitimate paths to power. They champion their cause through violence, or exit away from mainstream society. RWE ranges over forms of extremism on the spectra of ideologies on the political right, and rightist political ideologies that are inherently extreme—particularly white supremacy.*[937]

The Federation states that there can be extremes even in Islam, but it is only "rightist political ideologies that are inherently extreme."[938] Hence the Federation seeks to delegitimize rightist dissent. The submission in hyping up "resurgent Right-wing extremism in the global threatscape,"[939] deflects attention away from the widely perceived belief that it is Islam that is "inherently extreme," hence the dissident right serves Muslims as a red herring.

Yet, the stoush between Moses and Razzaq, chairman of the Federation's submission committee, ruined the moment when Moses put the "terrorism" issue back onto the Muslims. And that after the Federation's submission had tried ingratiate Jews by disparaging notions of a "Jewish conspiracy" as being peculiar to "right wing extremists,"[940] rather than being a significant preoccupation among Muslims. Moreover,

---

[936] "FIANZ Submission," 19.
[937] Ibid.
[938] Ibid.
[939] Ibid., 25.
[940] Ibid., 20 (4).

the Muslim submission goes so far as to cite the Anti-Defamation League of B'nai B'rith as a credible source for information on the "extreme right." Ironically, it was at the first annual "hui" on counter-terrorism that any show of Jewish-Muslim solidarity quickly fell apart.

Among the recommendations of the Islamic Federation is "to create a register for all these organisations and deem them as terror organisations. If it is identified officially, then we can get easy surveillance."[941] Perhaps the Islamic Federation hopes that if the state's surveillance is focused on an elusive "extreme right-wing threat," there will be no surveillance of Muslims?

The Federation has projected the accusations that have been made about "Muslim terrorism," by helping the state to manufacture an "extreme right-wing threat," on the *non-sequitur* basis that "rightist political ideologies are inherently extreme." This is a variation on what pro-Israeli organizations and individuals have been saying: that "Islam is inherently extreme." Ironically, Islamophobia is not a view that is intrinsic to the "extreme right." The historical relationship between the British people and Muslims (i.e. Arabs) is exemplified by the legendary Lawrence of Arabia,[942] not Tommy Robinson. If that relationship has now soured then perhaps the Muslim communities should undergo some self-assessment and stop projecting, scapegoating, and deflecting with the red herring of "right wing extremism."

"Baggage From Overseas Dumped in New Zealand"

Razzaq is quoted as stating that he "felt sad for people who brought baggage from overseas and dumped it in New Zealand."[943] While he was referring to Moses, she had been prompted to make her statements regarding perceived support for Hezbollah among New Zealand Muslims. From an outsider's viewpoint, both had "brought baggage from overseas and dumped it in New Zealand"; this is precisely the character of multiculturalism, and a premise as to why it is rejected by the dissident right. Each unassimilable group that constitutes its own "community," also constitutes a micro-nation. Migrants from the Middle East and Asia, and even the Pacific Island states, can be expected to bring their own "baggage from overseas and dump it in New Zealand." Yet is the melting-pot, "one nation" doctrine of the *pseudo-right* a better option than

---

[941] Ibid., 208.
[942] Lawrence, *Seven Pillars of Wisdom*. Introduction by K. R. Bolton.
[943] "Jewish Council Spokeswoman."

multiculturalism? Both involve ethnocide, ultimately at the behest of globalization.

Moses attended the Europhobic hui to represent *her* community, New Zealand Jews. She seems to have felt obliged to make a criticism of New Zealand Muslims a theme of her talk on a panel discussion about "terrorism," whereas the state apparatus that sponsored the hui did so for the purposes of establishing premises for the criminalization and suppression of *White dissent* against government policies. Yet because the hui was supposed to represent multicultural Aotearoa (as New Zealand is increasingly called) and that this could not be undertaken without including both Muslims and Jews, the actual character of multiculturalism was going to be inexorably outed. Europhobia was not sufficient to unite such disparate interests. The first lesson of the first annual Europhobic hatefest: "unity in diversity" is a fallacy.

Hate Speech and Human Rights: Imposing the Europhobic State

"Liberating tolerance, then, would mean intolerance against movements from the Right and toleration of movements from the Left. As to the scope of this tolerance and intolerance: ... it would extend to the stage of action as well as of discussion and propaganda, of deed as well as of word.

Withdrawal of tolerance from regressive movements before they can become active; intolerance even toward thought, opinion, and word, and finally, intolerance in the opposite direction, that is, toward the self-styled conservatives, to the political Right--these anti-democratic notions respond to the actual development of the democratic society which has destroyed the basis for universal tolerance."

Herbert Marcuse, New Left guru (1965)[944]

Professor Herbert Marcuse dedicated his essay "Repressive Tolerance" to his students at Brandeis University. It was published three years before the epochal New Left revolt that defined a generation. In the name of "freedom" at its most destructive, following the doctrine of the critical theorists, who included Marcuse, that the "primary ties" of family, religion, race, home, and homeland must be destroyed before one can self-actualize nirvana, the impact of the "68 Generation," and specifically those who created and manipulated it, have not only remained but intensified. Their doctrines have been mainstreamed.[945]

Marcuse's essay is an elaboration of the "social contract" theories that were enshrined, as we have seen, in Jacobin, communist, UN and EU statements and their localized variants, that ensure "freedom" within the bounds of what is being imposed as the "general will." Once the "general

---

[944] Marcuse, "Repressive Tolerance," 95-137.
[945] Bolton, *Perversion of Normality*.

will" is established, whether it is called "the dictatorship of the proletariat," or "human rights," anything outside its bounds is regarded as a breach of the "social contract," and punishments are enforced. The ultimate sanction in such a "democracy" is, as Rousseau advocated, death.

The left, such as today's Antifa, seek to repress any sign of dissent in the name of "freedom" and the "defense of democracy," according to the dialectics by Marcuse. Hence, the histrionic screams from the Antifa of "no platform for racists/Nazis, fascists," which Marcuse explains includes any dissent whatever, including that of scholarly research or conservative opinion ("Withdrawal of tolerance from...the self-styled conservatives"). Eventually, the process turns on itself, and self-destructs in the pursuit of an elusive human "perfectibility" within an egalitarian utopia. A dramatic example was the guillotining of Maximilien Robespierre, the architect of the French Revolution's Reign of Terror, and the new round of executions that followed.[946]

The repression of dissent is enacted internationally and nationally, in the name of "human rights"; a process that we have seen developing since the eighteenth century. New Zealand is an example of how this process unfolds, with repressive legislation justified by scare-mongering and the de-legitimization of dissidents.

Since at least 2017 the human rights bureaucrats, according to the Race Relations Commissioner of the time, Susan Devoy, have sought the extension of the human rights commissariat and the enactment of laws on "hate speech"; to the extent that this prohibits criticism of multiculturalism, "replacement migration," and the imposition of a Maori overclass, while enshrining the denigration, dispossession, and displacement of the New Zealand European. The following is this author's submission to the government inquiry on "hate speech" legislation, intended to outline the flaws in the doctrinal premises of the proposals, but without any naive belief that the submission will be taken into consideration. We are, after all, dealing with the same sacrosanct dogma that has been maintained for 240 years by the guillotine, the bullet to the back of the head, and US-NATO bombs, in the name of "liberty, equality, fraternity"; "the dictatorship of the proletariat," and "making the world safe for democracy."

---

[946] Maximilien Robespierre, the architect of the French Revolution's Reign of Terror, which guillotined over 17,000 "enemies of the revolution," was arrested on July 27th, 1794. The following day he was guillotined, with twenty-one of his adherents, before a cheering mob in the Place de la Revolution in Paris. Under the regime of the Directory, anarchy prevailed, until Napoleon's coup restored order in 1799.

Submission by Kerry R. Bolton

Ministry of Justice
humanrights@justice.govt.nz
16 July 2021

I am a "New Zealand European," according to the Government ethnic classification, aged 64. My maternal great-great-great-grandparents, a wheelwright and a laundress, arrived in Petone in 1840. My maternal great-grandfather arrived here in 1873. My paternal grandfather was a seaman from Leith, Scotland, my paternal grandmother, a match-girl from Bethnal Green.

I have authored seventeen books, and hundreds of papers on a variety of subjects that have been published in scholarly journals such as *The Journal of Social, Political & Economic Studies*; *World Affairs*; *India Quarterly*; *Journal of Russian Studies*; *Journal of Social Economics*, etc., and I have served as a peer reviewer for scholarly journals. My papers have been translated into Farsi, Arabic, Vietnamese, Tibetan, among others. I am not a member of any party or group.

I wish to address concerns regarding the proposals to extend the Human Rights and Race Relations laws.

Introduction

The premises are flawed. It is assumed that social cohesion can be legislated into existence for the purpose of sustaining a multicultural society. Social networks are formed around "nodes" through *assortativity*, or "like attracts like," which can have many variations, including race and ethnicity.

When a regime seeks to impose a dogma and requires laws in order to try and make this dogma work, the result is increasingly draconian and divisive.

It is ironic that the nebulous term "far right" is being used to support the extension of "hate speech" laws, and that this ill-defined "far right" is equated with "White supremacy." Yet the legal, moral and political concepts that are the basis of "human rights" laws are of Western liberal invention. They are imposed on the assumption that they are universal, but they have no counterparts in non-European custom. Sometimes these supposedly "universal human rights laws" are imposed with US, NATO, or

UN bombs. This is a form of cultural hegemony. It is part of the globalization process.

Example of New Zealand Chinese

It is an odd situation when the Islamic Federation jumps aboard the Western liberal bandwagon to ask for laws that could theoretically stifle their own views on gender or on Israel, for example.

Ian Bing, the first Chinese hotelier in New Zealand, who was honored with the unveiling of a bust in Picton in 2019,[947] whose grandfather came here as a gold fossicker, spent many years trying to warn of the direction in which New Zealand was heading. In 1989 he filed a submission to the Royal Commission on Social Policy, stating that the success of the Chinese in overcoming discrimination and animosity in the early days of their settlement was based on "minding their own business":

> *Theirs was to dedicate themselves to bringing up their children in the better-known Chinese customs and traditions and to be constantly reminded of their cultural heritage, disciple in the home – but away from home and when mixing with European company, conduct was always to be exemplary and nothing would be done that would bring shame or discredit to our ethnic group.... The emphasis being that any wrongdoing, reported or otherwise, group-shouldering of guilt and shame were to be carried by all...*[948]

The success of Chinese settlement into New Zealand did not include a grievance culture, but what amounts to *de facto* communal and cultural autonomy without imposition on others, based on what Mr. Bing called "home guidance and discipline."[949]

It is now expedient to blame "colonialization" and "White privilege" on the lack of such "home guidance and discipline" within New Zealand's many ethnic communities. Yet the New Zealand European is probably the only ethnicity that lacks a communal and cultural support network. When one looks at the social, political, economic, and cultural network of the Maori for example, it exists from hapu to Maori Council, with many intermediaries, in a parallel autonomy. If that is not working, and sixty-

---

[947] Trigger, "Fire Crackers, Chickens and the Chinese Publican."
[948] Bing, "Submission made to the Royal Commission," 4.
[949] Ibid.

nine billions of Maori assets[950] are not being wisely managed, then that requires *self-appraisal* rather than looking for scapegoats. Such networks provide the basis for each ethnic community to have a large measure of self-determination without imposition upon others, starting from what Mr. Bing called "self-assessment."[951]

Mr. Bing cautioned against the types of imposition that are now proceeding apace, and of scapegoating for one's own failings, writing:

> *I have yet to come across a single case where our folk either in organisation or combined effort made any call or demand for the abolishing of discriminatory practices and/or demands for racial equality. Yet again, I have yet to hear of any of our kin blaming the "white man" for our own shortcomings or failings.*[952]
>
> *Although New Zealand society is undergoing change, in many respects regrettable, I feel by and large, most of us will not forget the wisdom of our elders who have constantly reminded us of the need to be proud of our cultural heritage—but at the same time to accept the best of both worlds and to recognise qualities in ruling patterns and of other ethnic groups.*[953]

He stated that "we have not in any way sought or demanded changes in legislation and/or of education to make our lot easier."[954]

The New Zealand European serves as a scapegoat and a red herring to deflect from the causes of problems. In that respect, Mr. Bing commented on the early discriminatory measures towards Chinese, "certain writers would have their readers develop guilty consciences. I stress very strongly that I do not share those narrower views, less still yearn for sympathy." That "combined resolve" made the Chinese community stronger.[955] He rejected the now predominate view that "only the Caucasoid may not have pride in race," and alluded to the Race Relations acts in this regard, adding: "In labouring the point, compassionate racism is acceptable—if not even admirable—bigoted racism regrettable."[956] By "compassionate racism" Mr. Bing was referring to the "pride in race" that is, for example, a stated aim of the NZ Maori Council. ("Maori Community Development Act 1962" 18: 1: b (ii)). Mr. Bing rejected the allegations of "discrimination"

---

[950] Pullar-Strecker, "Reserve Bank Report."
[951] Bing, "Submission Made to the Royal Commission," 4-5.
[952] Ibid., 6.
[953] Ibid., 7.
[954] Ibid., 4.
[955] Ibid., 5.
[956] Ibid., 5.

directed at the "Caucasian," and the assumption that "the Caucasian is not discriminated against."[957]

Mr. Bing in making his submission in 1989 concluded with the belief that "the Chinese minority may well hold the key and serve as an example for the means towards a more tolerant society." That key, he stated, was "self-assessment," without imposing demands on others.[958]

Perhaps if Ian Bing were alive today, he would be facing the prospect of a fifty thousand dollars fine or three years jail for expressing such views.

Reality Behind the Facade

I knew Ian Bing during the 1980s, and he significantly influenced my outlook. He was keenly aware of the economic factors that are involved in what is now called globalization. One would assume that Muslims would also be aware of these factors, but they have been stampeded by the Tarrant atrocity, to jump aboard bandwagons that they would normally reject.

The traditional social structure of cultures breaks down under the impact of an economic system that is based on an "inclusive economy," behind the facade of "human rights." So far from seeking alternatives to the economic treadmill that sacrifices all cultures, "human rights" is the method which enforces social control.

Professor Noam Chomsky, who presumably will not be described as a "far right terrorist," explained the process:

Capitalism basically wants people to be interchangeable cogs, and differences among them, such as on the basis of race, usually are not functional. On the long term you can expect capitalism to be anti-racist—but because it is anti-human. And race is in fact a human characteristic—there's no reason why is should be a negative characteristic. So therefore identifications based on race interfere with the basic ideal that people should be available just as consumers and producers, interchangeable cogs who will purchase all the junk that's produced – that's their ultimate function, and any other properties they might have are kind of irrelevant, and usually a nuisance.[959]

---

[957] Ibid., 7.
[958] Ibid., 8.
[959] Chomsky, *Understanding Power*, 88-89.

Would this affirmation of race and description of the anti-human nature of capitalism be outlawed as "hate speech," because it questions the premises on which multiculturalism are based? It exposes the contradiction inherent in multiculturalism: the aim of (a) "inclusiveness" in an economy that, as Chomsky describes it, refashions individuals as "interchangeable cogs," detached from "identifications of race," while (b) demanding that "identifications of race" be maintained as a "human right."

Thought Crime

That multiculturalism is intended as a sacrosanct dogma is implicit in the summary of the discussion document, where it is stated that the incitement provisions of the Human Rights legislation "target speech that would have others believe that a society made up of different ethnic groups cannot function effectively."[960] However the primary discussion document, as distinct from the summary document, neglects to mention this. Why the obfuscation?[961]

What the summary document is stating is that *it is the intent to outlaw any critique of multiculturalism as a viable concept.* To "target," as it is said, anyone who questions the viability of a multicultural society is to criminalize that person. It is to make criticism of multiculturalism a thought-crime. Hence, we see academic apologists for the system becoming today's *Lysenkos* in propounding state-enforced dogmas that do not work, and it is called "science," while all other research is suppressed.

The rationalization for this is that "this type of speech seeks to turn people against each other and create separation between communities."[962] The premise is that any questioning of multiculturalism is "hate speech," and should be prohibited because it is likely to incite violence. The assumption is that critiquing multiculturalism means that, "some groups of people have less value than others. There could be a belief that these groups should not have the same rights and be treated differently and excluded from wider society."[963] It is then stated that "it is important to note that these proposals don't lower the threshold for criminalizing speech or prevent public debate on important issues."[964]

---

[960] "Proposals Against Incitement," summary statement, 6.
[961] "Proposals Against Incitement," 10.
[962] Ibid.
[963] Ibid.
[964] Ibid.

To make criticism of multiculturalism synonymous with incitement to hatred and even terrorism, has no logical basis. Anything can be taken to extremes. Should we judge Judaism on the actions of Baruch Goldstein, of Islam on Osama bin Laden, of Christianity on Jim Jones, of Hinduism on the Thuggee, or Buddhism on the kamikaze? In that case, the Labour Party shares a common ideology with Pol Pot.

Was the Dalai Lama inciting "hate" when he stated in 2018 (and other times) of refugees in Europe: "Each country has its own culture, language, way of life, and it is better for people to live in their own country."[965]

How do the proposals *not* lower the threshold of public debate, when it is explicitly stated that those who question multiculturalism are going to be *"targeted"* (sic)?

Stifles Scholarly Research

Will the new laws prohibit criticism of immigration? Will it be prohibited to critique the United Nations Compact on Global Migration and what the UN calls "replacement migration," because this questions the viability of multiculturalism? While the so-called "far right" has been condemned and even outlawed for critiquing what it calls "the great replacement," the UN's own term of "replacement migration" is not only similar but refers to the same demographic problems that the "far right" sought to discuss. How can any issue be a "debate" when only one side is enabled by law, and the other is prohibited on threat of three years jail or a fifty thousand dollars fine?

Such issues are implicit to wider questions such as whether the present treadmill growth economy is preferable to a sustainable economy, with immigration intended to feed the growth economy.

Shall referencing scientific papers be outlawed when these question some aspect of multiculturalism? I refer as one significant example to a recent meta-analysis of all the major studies on ethnic diversity and social trust, the abstract stating:

> *Does ethnic diversity erode social trust? Continued immigration and corresponding growing ethnic diversity have prompted this essential question for modern societies, but few clear answers have been reached in the sprawling literature. Taking this as point of departure, this article reviews the existing literature on the relationship between ethnic diversity and social trust through*

---

[965] "His Holiness the Dalai Lama."

a narrative review and a meta-analysis of 1,001 estimates from 87 studies. The review clarifies the core concepts, highlights pertinent debates, and tests core claims from the literature on the relationship between ethnic diversity and social trust. Several results stand out from the meta-analysis. We find a statistically significant negative relationship between ethnic diversity and social trust across all studies...[966]

Wouldn't the paper by Dinesen, et al. be classifiable as "speech that would have others believe that a society made up of different ethnic groups cannot function effectively"?

We have already seen how scientific papers that do not seem to accord with some aspect of the dogma result in suppression. For example, in 2008 Dr. Greg Clydesdale, Faculty of Management and Business, Massey University, wrote a paper for presentation at an overseas scholarly conference, on the question of the place of Pasifika migrants in New Zealand's de-industrialized economy. One would think that a scholarly consideration of the problems emerging for the Pasifika communities would be welcomed. Far from it. Clydesdale was lambasted by the news media, academia, and politicians, and was investigated by Race Relations Commissioner Joris de Bres.[967]

It is not only what is stated in the proposals, but what is inferred; the toxic atmosphere that hangs over discussion on such issues. Augment this with a fifty thousand dollars fine or three years jail, and the atmosphere becomes stifling beyond endurance.

In regard to the proposed changes on transgenderism, this also proceeds from the premise that to question its normalization is a heresy that must be outlawed. The amendments to the Human Rights laws are presumably intended to work in conjunction with the *Prohibition for Conversion Therapy Bill.* This Bill *dishonestly* equates all forms of counselling that do not encourage gender transformation as akin to exorcism. However, despite the impression given by that bill, the scholarly research on the subject is far from concluded.

Given that the aforesaid bill criminalizes professional counselling, without making a differentiation between professional medical consultation and faith-based interventions, the Human Rights amendments will augment this by outlawing, or at least discouraging, scholarly discussion.

---

[966] Dinesen, Schaeffer and Sonderskov, "Ethnic Diversity and Social Trust."
[967] "Economists stands by underclass comments."

Already we can see how the state has attempted to shut down Family First, whose submissions and papers are based on scholarly citations, by trying to have its charitable status withdrawn.[968]

Internal Contradictions

How are the Human Rights laws going to be applied to ethnic and religious customs that are not compatible with modern Western liberal society?

We have already seen an example of the contradictions that arise when the Prime Minister adorned herself with a *hijab*. She was criticized by Muslim feminists who stated that they consider the *hijab* a symbol of "oppression." One New Zealand Muslim stated:

> *Unfortunately, it was uncool for the non-hijab-wearing women in my circle of friends, and I'm talking about consistent and practising Muslims who had cried their eyes out over the mosque attacks. For the zillionth time, they were made to witness their faith being politicised and reduced to a piece of cloth.*[969]

This is an example of the muddle that is intrinsic to a multiplicity of values inherent in multiculturalism, which are all supposed to become part of a harmonious mosaic, while also somehow according with modern Western liberal concepts of civic virtue.

Are Muslims who object to the normalization of transgenderism in schools going to be subjected to the Human Rights laws? In such circumstances, whose "human rights" predominate, those of the transgendered or of religious communities? For example, in Birmingham in 2019 Muslims demonstrated against transgender education in schools.[970] What if the situation arose here, since transgenderism is also part of the New Histories curriculum?

Shall we see the jailing of Imam for condemning homosexuality, or for criticizing Israel and Zionism? Or will that be ignored in the wider interests of community relations, and the law applied only to New Zealand Europeans and Christian conservatives?

The inherent contradictions of multiculturalism arose at the first annual hui on hate speech and terrorism on June 15th and 16th, which was

---

[968] For example: Whitehall, "Children transitioning."
[969] Shakir, "Don't let Jacinda Ardern's."
[970] Parveen, "Birmingham School Stops LGBT Lessons."

supposed to focus on the nebulously defined "far right." The Muslim delegates walked out due to a speech by Juliet Moses of the Jewish Council, in which she alluded to New Zealand Muslim support for terrorism in the Middle East. She was condemned for being "racist." A spokesman for the Islamic Federation said that "Moses' comments had been a calculated attempt to denigrate Muslims present, including Palestinians, and 'wipe out the memory' of those killed in the Christchurch mosque massacres."[971]

It was the view of the Muslims present that Moses' comments had been "a *calculated attempt* to denigrate Muslims." Had the proposed Human Rights amendments been operative, shouldn't Ms. Moses be prosecuted? One can imagine the international outcry if she was jailed for Islamophobia. Alternatively, were the Muslim delegates being anti-Semitic? Will Muslims be subjected to prosecution for criticizing Israel, since Zionists consider any criticism to be anti-Semitic?

Among feminists there is debate over the nature of transgenderism, with a faction objecting to males assuming female gender identity. In New Zealand we see this with the organization *Speak Up for Women*, a left-wing organization—far removed from the "far right" or Christian conservatives—which was recently denied council facilities to hold meetings. Will this faction of feminism be subjected to prosecution because of its criticism of transgenderism, or is it only conservative lobbies that are intended for "targeting" (sic)?[972]

Europhobia

Could it be that the difficulties among various communities will be side stepped by the "hate speech" laws through the expedient of enforcing the laws only against New Zealand Europeans and certain Christians? The Race Relations and Human Rights laws have never been applied equitably.

Human Rights Commissioner Dr. Paul Hunt's sensationally entitled report on "hate crimes" "It Happened Here" (named after a low budget 1960s movie on the German invasion of Britain with the assistance of Fascist fifth columnists) strains to compile a list of supposed "hate crimes" based mostly on media reports, and without any context. For example, he states several times that "skinheads" (plural) attacked Somali youths in Wellington. The actual case was that of a lone White youth who was mugged by two Somali youths in Newtown. The victim is turned into the

---

[971] "Jewish Council Spokeswoman."
[972] McNeilly, "Controversial Women's Group."

villain on the basis that he is a New Zealand European, and guilt is assumed.[973] Dr. Hunt in referring to the incident on page 3, alludes to a hung jury and a retrial scheduled for 2006. Yet he fails to mention that this retrial returned a not guilty verdict.

There has never been a time when the Human Rights and Race Relations laws were *not* biased against New Zealand Europeans (that was the intention) as admitted by then Race Relations Conciliator Walter Hirsh in his 1988 interview.[974] The following year (April 1989) Alister Grant resigned from the Equal Opportunities Tribunal, stating that the Race Relations Office and the Human Rights Commission practiced "reverse racism." Mr. Grant had observed that "people of color," to use a present social construct, were considered by those Offices as always right regardless of the facts.

"Hate Speech" Review Considered Two Years Before Tarrant

In 2017 Race Relations Commissioner Susan Devoy condemned an attempt to establish the Auckland University European Students Association. At around the same time she also condemned a small group called Western Guard that had posted a few stickers. It seems likely that each group would not have had more than a half dozen members. Ms. Devoy stated that the groups were "full of hate and vile." She stated that laws about "hate speech" were being reviewed; that, "We are looking at the statutory limitations, we are reviewing the legislation."[975]

Given Ms. Devoy's comments about the review of laws on "hate speech" being under consideration in 2017, it seems that Tarrant serves as a cynically manipulated justification for draconian legislation that was planned long before the Mosque shootings.

When the Auckland University European Students Association had obtained permission to establish a stall during Orientation week, its declared aims included medieval reenactments, feasts, and hiking. The harassment of the embryonic group quickly drove it to oblivion. Yet on campus there is the Australasian Union of Jewish Students, which described itself as "a cultural, political and religious club, advocating for Israel and Judaism on campus."[976]

---

[973] Hunt, "It Happened Here."
[974] Quoted on page 112.
[975] "University Group Rejects 'White Pride.'"
[976] "Australasian Union of Jewish Students."

Why is it acceptable for an association to call itself "Jewish," and indeed Zionist, but unacceptable for one to be called "European," even though "New Zealand European" is an officially designated ethnic group? The New Zealand Maori Council has as its aim for Maori "to assume and maintain self-reliance, thrift, pride of race, and such conduct as will be conducive to their general health and economic well-being."[977]

There are dozens of organizations advocating for ethnic communities, yet vitriolic objections by the Human Rights Commission arise when there is any positive mention of the "New Zealand European."

"Not Okay to Be White"

We see the implicit Europhobia in the reactions from the news media when anyone so much as chalks up "it's okay to be White," the implication being that *it is not okay to be White*. Even stating "White lives matter" is objectionable; hence clearly for those who object, *"White lives do not matter."*

Double think must be employed to describe such slogans as "it's okay to be White" and "all lives matter" as "hate speech." For example, the Human Rights Commission opined in 2019 in regard to items adorned with "it's okay to be White" being sold on Trade Me that, "it seems likely that the stickers and T-shirts are intended to convey a message of intolerance, racism and division. There is no place for that in New Zealand." The same article refers to outrage in 2017 from the Napier mayor when "it's okay to be White posters" appeared in the city.[978]

It is only the New Zealand European whose heritage is denigrated and who is denied the same rights to identity that are encouraged for all others. The New Zealand European is, to the contrary, imbued with xenophilia and self-loathing. For example, Chester Borrows, former government minister and chairman of a review of the judicial system, stated on June 21st, 2021 on the Facebook page of Maori Party MP Ngarewa-Packer:

> *More pakeha accept that Maori make pakeha unique in the world and are proud of that aspect of coming from this country… otherwise we might as well be the progeny of any bland Anglo-Saxon nation around the world.*[979]

---

[977] "Maori Community Development Act 1962," 18: 1: b (ii).
[978] NZ Herald, "Trade Me defends selling."
[979] Given that these are the type of "public servant" who chair reviews into health, education, justice, etc., it is no wonder that the conclusions invariably blame "colonialism."

Apply that xenophilic attitude onto at least 90 percent of parliamentarians, teachers, academics, journalists, church ministers, bureaucrats, and an attitude of indifference and cultural disconnect onto the rest, and one might begin to understand that *the New Zealand European is certainly unique: it is the only designated ethnicity that does not have any identity other than a meaningless name for the purpose of census counting.* The New Zealand European is unique in not being represented as an ethnicity in parliament, on local bodies, nor having a voice in the media. Those who are "White" complexioned who attain such positions in no way represent the New Zealand European: they are *Pakeha-Maori*. Like Chester Borrows, they are disconnected from their heritage, know nothing of their culture, and couldn't care less. Like Chester Borrows, they can only see the New Zealand European existing relative to the Maori. While it could be said that Mr. Borrows is a deeply stupid, uneducated, uncultured little man, he and his type are products of a system that has indeed made the Anglo-Saxon heritage seem bland by disconnecting it from the spirit and soul that is encouraged for all other ethnicities.

It seems that the intention is to categorize the New Zealand European as "the other," as a means of unifying disparate and even traditionally antagonistic ethnic communities around a common contempt for the European. There is nothing more effective than to have a common enemy around which to unite. The New Zealand European also serves as a scapegoat for perceived injustices, diverting attentions away from causes. With the *chester borrows* and *paul spoonleys* dominating enquiries into social problems the conclusions are based on Europhobic or xenophilic reductionism that requires little or no more than referring to key words such a "colonialism" and "neocolonialism." The concept of "White privilege" serves as a red herring to distract from flaws in the economic system. An "inclusive multicultural society" is a synonym for an "inclusive growth economy," that requires feeding by what the United Nations calls "replacement migration."

The Six Proposals

1. Add more protected groups to the hate speech laws. This extends the range of suppression for debate, including scholarly research. Reject.
2. Add "hate speech" to the Crimes Act. This extends police powers for the purposes of suppression. Reject.

3. Increase punishments up to $50,000 fines and three years jail. This equates with criminalizing debate and opinion when contrary to state dogma. Reject.
4. Add "incitement" and "normalizing hatred" to the civil provision. This extends a draconian system, without precision of definitions. Reject.
5. Add "incitement to discriminate," which would extend the authority of the Human Rights Commission. The Commission is demonstrably biased, and intrinsically so. Reject.
6. Add "gender identity" to the Human Rights Act. As with ethnicity, this would impose repression, prohibiting or at least discouraging, debate on questions that are far from resolved by science. Reject.

Conclusion

In conclusion, all six proposals should be rejected as repressive, totalitarian, imposing a party line, and a sacrosanct dogma. Any ideology that requires increasingly repressive laws to be upheld is intrinsically flawed. When people are imposed on each other by threat of law the result is resentment, not goodwill.

Heresy

"It took them only an instant to cut off that head, but France may not produce another like it in a century."

Joseph Louis LaGrange (1794)

So said the mathematician LaGrange on the guillotining of Antoine-Laurent de Lavoisier immediately following a brief hearing. Lavoisier had intervened for LaGrange to save him from arrest and confiscation of property that was being undertaken by the revolution against those born in enemy states. However, Lavoisier, the "father of modern chemistry," had drawn the ire of Marat for opposing the revolutionary icon's membership to the French Academy on the basis that Marat had no merit as a scientist. Lavoisier thereby fell afoul of the "general will," he had breached the "social contract," and one of history's greatest scientists was doomed by the people's judgment—the Revolutionary Tribunal.

On the passing of his death sentence, Lavoisier stoically asked the Revolutionary Tribunal one favor; to be permitted to live long enough to complete an experiment that he had begun. The judge of the Tribunal interrupted Lavoisier's appeal with a quip: "The Republic needs neither scientists nor chemists; the trial cannot be restrained."[980]

The judge's quip could be adapted as a universal axiom for Western academia. Certainly, it expresses the sentiment of the iconic leftist "philosopher," Professor Herbert Marcuse, who justified intellectual repression in his 1965 essay "Repressive Tolerance." This "repressive tolerance" has also been enshrined in the "human rights" statements and laws, as shown herein, of the UN, EU and member states. What Marcuse advocated has become mainstream, where:

---

[980] For a cogent biography see: "Antoine Lavoisier."

> ...intolerance even toward thought, opinion, and word, and finally, intolerance in the opposite direction, that is, toward the self-styled conservatives, to the political Right ... This means that previously neutral, value-free, formal aspects of learning and teaching now become, on their own grounds and in their own right, political: learning to know the facts, the whole truth, and to comprehend it is radical criticism throughout, intellectual subversion. [981]

"The facts" and the "whole truth" are then defined by Marcuse to be in the service of "radical criticism" and "intellectual subversion." This dialectical double think is how the "heckler's veto" is rationalized by those who stifle freedom of expression and enquiry in the name of "liberty," whether in town halls or lecture rooms and academic journals.

While the world continues to stand aghast at Hitler's expulsion of a remnant of Germany's "intelligentsia," the exodus of that part of the intelligentsia included the likes of Marcuse, Adorno, Fromm, and the whole coterie of the Frankfurt School, sponsored by the Rockefeller Foundation and Columbia University, who have dominated the social sciences of the West ever since.[982] This "university in exile" has been about as positive for Western culture and learning as those who were released by Castro from Cuba's jails and mental asylums to enter the USA as "refugees."[983]

Essentially the same position was insisted upon in the USSR, to the extent that geneticists were regarded as heretical and replaced by Trofim Lysenko, an obscure plant breeder from Odessa, who almost brought Soviet agriculture to collapse by his insistence that new strains of crops could be created by environmental conditioning. Lysenko claimed that one species of wheat could be converted to another by subjecting it to external influences, a process he called "vernalization." Thereby, winter wheat could be transformed into spring wheat by subjecting it to cold, which would shock it into germinating another variety. Those Soviet scientists who rejected Lysenko's ideas were removed from their positions. In 1940 N.I. Vavilov, first president of the Academy of Agricultural Sciences, whose team proved that Lysenko's notions on wheat breeding were fallacious, was arrested. He died of a heart attack in solitary confinement in 1943. Mendelian genetics was smeared as "Nazi," and the Seventh International

---

[981] Marcuse, "Repressive Tolerance."
[982] See: Bolton, *The Perversion of Normality*.
[983] Cockburn, "Criminals 'In Exodus From Cuba.'"

Congress of Genetics, which was to be held in Moscow in 1937, was cancelled.[984]

Liberal Repression

While the USSR freed itself from the Lysenko dogma, its Western equivalents in the social sciences of Franz Boas, et al.,[985] have remained dominant in Western academia, and implicitly in Western policy making. Those who challenge these dogmas are smeared and purged.

Repression of heretical scientists in the West might be more subtle (but not invariably so), such as the denial of funds if research does not accord with orthodoxy. It was the imposition of such biases in funding that prompted the formation of the Pioneer Fund in New York in 1937, "to advance the scientific study of heredity and human differences," by providing grants to institutions for specific studies that are unable to obtain money from "government sources or from larger foundations." Recipients have included H. J. Eysenck, Arthur Jensen, William Shockley, Ernest van der Haag, and J. Philippe Rushton, according to their website. Most or all of these scientists have been subjected to verbal and physical assaults for their research in a situation that shows that the bounds of scholarly inquiry in the West are very limited. The Pioneer Fund comments on this situation on their website:

> *Some of those who strongly oppose behavior genetic and psychometric research have sometimes made bizarre and false charges against scientists who conduct these studies, subjecting them to harassment, including dismissal and threats of dismissal, stalled promotions, mob demonstrations, and threats of physical violence, even death. Some physical attacks have actually occurred. These politically motivated attacks on the Pioneer Fund and its grantees are documented in* The New Know-Nothings *by Morton Hunt; and* Race, Intelligence and Bias in Academe *by Roger Pearson.*

The following are some examples of scientists who have endured the stigma of heresy.

---

[984] Medvedev, *The Rise and Fall of T.D. Lysenko*.
[985] Bullert, "Franz Boaz as Citizen-Scientist."

William Shockley

Shockley, a Nobel Prize-winning physicist, applied science to the question of Negro and Caucasian IQ discrepancies, and supported eugenics. Hence, he suddenly became a "broken genius."[986] Dr. Shockley was reduced to appearing at lectures holding a placard upon which he wrote a couple of basic points about race and IQ, or writing a few points on a blackboard, as frenzied leftists, analogous to today's Antifa, shouted him down.[987] Ed Brayton, a liberal commentator who agreed that Shockley should have been opposed, yet was troubled by some of the methods, wrote:

> *After he won the Nobel Prize he became interested in eugenics and became one of the leading voices of racism in the US. Wherever he went, he was the object of fierce protests—as well he should have been.*
>
> *But in many places those protests did not merely register their disagreement and disgust with Shockley's views, they also tried—and often succeeded—in preventing him from speaking. They did this in a variety of ways, from drowning him out with bullhorns to storming the stage to intimidating the groups that invited him to withdraw their invitation. This was especially true on college campuses.*
>
> *...In 1973, Shockley was invited to speak at Staten Island Community College but was unable to do so because a group of students, predominately white, made it impossible for him to be heard.*
>
> *...The following year, Shockley was scheduled to debate Roy Innis of the Congress on Racial Equality at Yale. Once again, protesters managed to prevent the event from being held. The head of the Progressive Labor Party at Yale declared freedom of speech to be a "nice abstract idea used to enable people like Shockley to spread racism." A local minister in New Haven called for a demonstration to take place that would be "as peaceful as possible and as violent as necessary" to prevent Shockley from speaking.*

---

[986] Shurkin, *Broken Genius*.
[987] "Students Protest Shockley's Racist Theory."

> *With such threats of violence and disruption, the Yale Political Union decided to withdraw the invitation to take part in the debate. A second campus group stepped in to extend an invitation, but they too ended up withdrawing under the intimidation of threats of violence from those on campus. A third potential sponsor likewise withdrew under pressure, and the debate never took place.*[988]

Frank Ellis

A lecturer in Russian and Slavic studies at Leeds University, Ellis was pushed into early retirement in 2006 after being suspended earlier that year, pending disciplinary proceedings. He had opined that Black IQ scores are lower. Ellis's heresy is that he had stated in a BBC 5 Live interview[989] that he supported the views in the book *The Bell Curve*,[990] by eminent American psychologists Richard Herrnstein and Charles Murray.[991] Ellis had expressed private views that had not been associated with Leeds University, stating that he had become interested in the way issues are suppressed after studying Soviet and post-Soviet regimes.

Leeds University Secretary Roger Gair said that Ellis had the right to express his opinions but not the right to discriminate against students and colleagues, an odd comment since this was not in question.

James Watson

The co-discoverer of the molecular structure of DNA, for which he jointly won a Nobel Prize in 1962, Watson was, at the age of 79, harassed into a publicly humiliating retraction after stating that Black Africans lack creative intelligence. In an apology reminiscent of Galileo's apology to the Inquisition for his comments about heliocentricity, Watson stated:

> *I am mortified about what has happened. More importantly, I cannot understand how I could have said what I am quoted as having said. I can certainly understand why people, reading those words, have reacted in the ways they have. To all those who*

---

[988] Brayton, "William Shockley and Free Speech."
[989] "Tutor Defends 'Racist' Stance."
[990] Herrnstein and Murray, *The Bell Curve*.
[991] "Racism Row Lecturer Retires Early."

have drawn the inference from my words that Africa, as a continent, is somehow genetically inferior, I can only apologize unreservedly. That is not what I meant. More importantly from my point of view, there is no scientific basis for such a belief.[992]

The Federation of American Scientists said it was outraged that Watson "chose to use his unique stature to promote personal prejudices that are racist, vicious, and unsupported by science." Cold Spring Harbor Laboratory, Long Island, New York, removed Watson as Chancellor.

Yet while Watson took fright and claimed he could not understand how he made such a statement he had not long previously written in his autobiography:

There is no firm reason to anticipate that the intellectual capacities of peoples geographically separated in their evolution should prove to have evolved identically. Our wanting to reserve equal powers of reason as some universal heritage of humanity will not be enough to make it so.[993]

Watson's latter views are consistent with his political evolution. Starting as a leftist professor at Harvard, where he was among the faculty who declared themselves for America's withdrawal from Vietnam,[994] Watson rejected the left because of its fundamental opposition to the genetic foundations of human behavior. He stated in 2007: "I turned against the left wing because they don't like genetics, because genetics implies that sometimes in life we fail because we have bad genes. They want all failure in life to be due to the evil system." [995]

Francis Crick, another of the three Nobel Laureates who discovered the DNA double-helix, had expressed views similar to those of Watson. Crick was combative, and during the controversy of American psychologist Arthur Jensen's paper in the *Harvard Educational Review* on IQ differences among races, Crick threatened to resign as a Foreign Associate of the American National Academy of Sciences if steps were taken to "suppress reputable scientific research for political reasons." He supported the research of both Shockley and Jensen.[996] Crick's correspondence shows he had a significant interest in eugenics and the

---

[992] "DNA Discoverer Apologizes for Racist Remarks."
[993] Watson, *Avoid Boring People*.
[994] Jacobs, "Faculty Support Grows For Anti-War Proposal."
[995] Richardson, "James Watson, What I've Learned."
[996] Crick, "Letter to William Shockley."

question of IQ hereditability. For example, he wrote to Dr. John T. Edsall of the Fogarty International Center, National Institutes of Health, in discussing Shockley and Jensen, that:

> *As to your point about the I.Q. results on American Indians being mainly due to their cultural tradition, this may be so, but personally I doubt it. How do you explain the relatively poor I.Q. performance of the children of middle-class American Negroes?*[997]

In particular, in 1969, in a talk on the "Social Impact of Biology," Crick stated, as he described it to Lord Snow:

> *As far as I remember I said that the biological evidence was that all men were not created equal, and it would not only be difficult to try to do this, but biologically undesirable. As an aide I said that the evidence for the equality of different races did not really exist. In fact, what little evidence there was suggested racial differences.*[998]

Probably feeling that he had nothing left to lose, Watson repudiated his *galileo-apology* in 2019, the media reporting:

> *Nobel Prize-winning American scientist James Watson has been stripped of his honorary titles after repeating comments about race and intelligence.*
> *In a TV programme, the pioneer in DNA studies made a reference to a view that genes cause a difference on average between blacks and whites on IQ tests.*
> *Cold Spring Harbor Laboratory said the 90-year-old scientist's remarks were "unsubstantiated and reckless."*
> *Dr Watson had made similar claims in 2007 and subsequently apologised....*
> *Dr Watson sold his gold medal in 2014, saying he had been ostracised by the scientific community after his remarks about race.*
> *In 2007, the scientist, who once worked at the University of Cambridge's Cavendish Laboratory, told the Times newspaper*

---
[997] Crick, "Letter to John T. Edsall."
[998] Crick, "Letter to Lord Charles Percy Snow."

that he was "inherently gloomy about the prospect of Africa" because "all our social policies are based on the fact that their intelligence is the same as ours—whereas all the testing says not really."

While his hope was that everybody was equal, he added, "people who have to deal with black employees find this is not true."

After those remarks, Dr Watson lost his job as chancellor at the laboratory and was removed from all his administrative duties. He wrote an apology and **retained his honorary titles of chancellor emeritus, Oliver R Grace professor emeritus and honorary trustee.**

But Cold Spring Harbor said it was now stripping him of those titles after he said his views had not changed in the documentary American Masters: Decoding Watson, aired on US public broadcaster PBS earlier this month.

"Dr Watson's statements are reprehensible, unsupported by science," the laboratory said in a statement, adding that they effectively reverse his apology....[999]

Chris Brand

Brand lectured in psychology at Edinburgh University for nearly thirty years (1970–1997). During the 1980's, he served on the UK's Council for National Academic Awards. His book *The g Factor* was published in 1996, where he stated that there are inherited differences in IQ between races. As a result of his views in *The g Factor*, Brand's lectures were disrupted by the Trotskyite-run Anti-Nazi League, and his book was withdrawn by John Wiley & Sons. Hence the merits of scholarship were determined by yobbery.

After a complaint from the Chaplain of Edinburgh University, who was a supporter of the riotous Anti-Nazi League, Brand was suspended, then dismissed for bringing the university into "disrepute," that is, discussing issues that fall outside the *de facto* limitations of inquiry imposed on academia by intellectually questionable, politically motivated, self-serving coteries.

After his removal from Edinburgh University, Brand ended up working as a waiter during 1998–1999 (while he was also Director of the

---

[999] BBC News, "James Watson: Scientist loses titles."

California-based Institute for the Study of Educational Differences), reminiscent of the way Germany's intelligentsia became menial laborers under the post-1945 process of "de-Nazification." Brand writes in summation:

> The case was to go before a Scottish Employment Tribunal in 1999; but Edinburgh University offered a settlement of the maximum that any UK court could have offered for "unfair dismissal," saying it was paying out "to prevent the airing of Brand's opinions and views at public expense"– a surprising attitude for a university. I accepted this settlement since to have proceeded to a trial would probably have been deemed "frivolous" by the Tribunal and put me at risk of paying what would have been the University's enormous costs.[1000]

The real reason for Brand's removal from Edinburgh was his book *The g Factor*. The circumstances include the following:

> Despite very favourable reviews (e.g. in Nature), The 'g' Factor fell foul of "political correctness" about race and IQ. In press interviews, Brand freely agreed there was a Black-White IQ difference, that the difference was substantially genetic.... On April 17, 1996, The 'g' Factor was withdrawn as "repellent" by Wiley & Sons (New York and Chichester). Wiley followed up their modern version of censorship by refusing to publish a new book on 'g' by Berkeley's Emeritus Professor Arthur Jensen—a proposal which Wiley had had under consideration for nine months.[1001]

So much for the credibility of Wiley as a scholarly publisher. As for Edinburgh University, Principal Sir Stewart Sutherland felt obliged to emphasize to the media that he regarded Brand's research as "false and personally obnoxious."[1002]

Andrew Fraser

A lecturer in law at Macquarie University, Sydney, Australia, Fraser was prevented from teaching after having written a letter to the local press

---

[1000] Brand, "Brief Curriculum Vitae."
[1001] "Christopher Brand: Race, Sex, Psychology and Censorship."
[1002] Ibid.

criticizing immigration from Black Africa.[1003] For this crime against humanity, "University vice-chancellor Professor Di Yerbury responded with a three-page memo to staff announcing that Professor Fraser would not teach until further notice."[1004] A report in *The Weekend Australian* stated:

> *Professor Fraser yesterday rejected an offer by the university to buy out his contract and launched a bitter attack on Vice-Chancellor Di Yerbury, describing her as an "intellectual coward." Professor Yerbury responded by suspending Professor Fraser from teaching, citing a report in The Australian yesterday in which he claimed a group called Smash Racism was planning to disrupt his classes.... "We have a duty to act decisively to protect his safety and that of others on campus," she said. Professor Yerbury told The Weekend Australian late yesterday that she would seek legal advice if he made further unauthorized public statements.... Yerbury said she was not bothered by Professor Fraser's personal attack on her. "I will wear that as a badge of honour," she said. "I made the apology because I was distressed and ashamed he had associated the university with views which so fundamentally contravened its position."*[1005]

(1) Apparently writing the letter to a suburban newspaper should have first been approved by the university; (2) the inquisitors in academia work in tandem with histrionic Marxist rioters to repress freedom of expression and inquiry.

In September 2005, the law journal of Deakin University was directed not to publish Professor Fraser's peer-reviewed paper "Rethinking the White Australia Policy."[1006]

Nicholas Kollerstrom

A physicist and historian of science specializing in astronomy, Kollerstrom was an honorary research fellow in Science and Technology Studies at University College London (UCL). In 2008, his fellowship was

---

[1003] Fraser, "The Path to National Suicide."
[1004] Mclean, "Outspoken academic banned from teaching."
[1005] Roberts, "Lecture ban for 'racist' professor."
[1006] "Professor Andrew Fraser: A Short Biography."

terminated after he had written articles for the Committee for Open Debate on the Holocaust (CODOH) critiquing aspects of the Auschwitz narrative the previous year. Kollerstrom appears to have been a leftist who belonged to the Green and Respect parties and the Campaign for Nuclear Disarmament. A press release from UCL curtly stated:

> *UCL has been made aware of views expressed by Dr. Nicholas Kollerstrom, an Honorary Research Fellow in UCL Science & Technology Studies.*
>
> *The position of Honorary Research Fellow is a privilege bestowed by departments within UCL on researchers with whom it wishes to have an association. It is not an employed position.*
>
> *The views expressed by Dr. Kollerstrom are diametrically opposed to the aims, objectives and ethos of UCL, such that we wish to have absolutely no association with them or with their originator.*
>
> *We therefore have no choice but to terminate Dr. Kollerstrom's Honorary Research Fellowship with immediate effect.*[1007][30]

According to *The London Jewish Chronicle*, there had also been disquiet at UCL regarding Kollerstrom's "conspiracy theories" involving the 9/11 attacks, and other issues.[1008]

Greg Clydesdale

Greg Clydesdale of Massey University,[1009] New Zealand, was declared heretical in 2008 by Members of Parliament, the news media, the Race Relations Conciliator, and academia for having written a paper that documented the obvious: Polynesians are an economic underclass in an economy whose manufacturing base has long since been wrecked by government policies. This was hardly a matter of blaming or disparaging Polynesians, but that of analyzing the economic factors, and the way the process had impacted on them.

Pointing out with statistical data the continuing underachievement of Polynesians educationally and professionally is analogous to the boy who

---

[1007] "Dr. Nicholas Kollerstrom."
[1008] Peled, "College Rejects Shoah Denier."
[1009] Clydesdale was at that time with the faculty of Management and Business at Massey University, Palmerston North, New Zealand.

cried out "the emperor has no clothes." Yet, the head of the "Pasifika" department at Massey, Sione Tu'itahi, castigated his colleague. The banal reaction was featured on Massey's website lest the university be mistaken as having endorsed empirical evidence rather than dogma. Massey demonstrated its malice against Clydesdale, commenting:

> *Massey University has welcomed the announcement by Race Relations Conciliator Joris de Bres that he will investigate Dr. Clydesdale's report. It is expected that several Massey academics and other staff will be pleased to participate in any review.*[1010]

Clydesdale was obliged to forego the presentation of his paper to an academic conference on economic development in Brazil: New Zealand's false image as a multicultural utopia could not be exposed to the outside world.

Richard Lynn

In 2018 the University of Ulster withdrew the title of emeritus professor from Richard Lynn who had taught psychology at the university. A news source stated:

> *The university said it had made its decision "following due process and considering all relevant information."*
>
> *"Ulster University has withdrawn the emeritus title from Professor Richard Lynn and notified the individual accordingly," it said.*
>
> *"Professor Richard Lynn does not work for Ulster University nor does he contribute to our research and teaching."*
>
> *The title of emeritus professor is often bestowed on retired academics who have been eminent at a particular university.*
>
> *In February, the university's students' union called on UU to end its association with the psychology professor.*
>
> *The union passed a motion alleging that Prof Lynn advocates views that are "racist and sexist in nature."*
>
> *Speaking on Saturday, the union's president Kevin McStravock said: "We'd welcome the fact they've considered the*

[1010] "Massey's Pasifika Director says." What became of the Race Relations Conciliator's enquiry is not known.

case and they've taken this action and I think it's clear they've made the right decision with that."[1011]

J. Philippe Rushton

J. Philippe Rushton died in 2012. In 2020, the Department of Psychology at the University of Western Ontario issued a shameful declaration against their late colleague, notable for its histrionic manner, biased conclusions, and questionable sources. The statement begins:

John Philippe ("Phil") Rushton was a faculty member in the Department of Psychology from 1977 until his death in 2012.

Although Rushton published on a variety of topics in the field of personality and individual differences, much of his research was racist, and attempted to find differences in intelligence between racialized groups and to explain them as caused by genetic differences between races.

Although Rushton ceased teaching for the Department of Psychology in the early 1990s, he continued to conduct racist and flawed studies, sometimes without appropriate ethics approval, for two more decades. There are other ethical concerns surrounding Rushton's research. In particular, much of this research was supported by the Pioneer Fund, a foundation formed in 1937 to promote eugenicist and racist goals. The fund was headed by Rushton himself for many years (2002–2012). Indeed, Rushton was the largest recipient of Pioneer Fund grants at the time of his death. Further, he directed funding from this foundation to editors of some of the journals in which he published. Rushton also created an offshore private promotional organization called the Charles Darwin Institute to promote his writings.[1012]

The statement itself is "deeply flawed," and in particular premised on dogmatism, rejecting out-of-hand genetic approaches to sociological and psychological research, as if the science has been proven and closed on the subject. This is far from the case. The Psychology Department at Western Ontario misrepresents the issues; particularly Rushton's application of *r/K selection theory* to human evolution. According to the declaration,

---

[1011] "Ulster University Withdraws Status From Prof Richard Lynn."
[1012] "Dr. Philippe Rushton."

this is reprehensible and absurd. However, Harvard biologist E. O. Wilson (co-discoverer of the *r/K selection theory*, and considered the father of the modern scientific synthesis of *sociobiology*), stated of Rushton:

> *I think Phil is an honest and capable researcher. The basic reasoning by Rushton is solid evolutionary reasoning; that is, it is logically sound. If he had seen some apparent geographic variation for a non-human species—a species of sparrow or sparrow hawk, for example—no one would have batted an eye.... [W]hen it comes to racial differences, especially in the inflamed situation in this country, special safeguards and conventions need to be developed.*[1013]

A scholarly outlook does not attempt to repudiate scientific enquiry with a mixture of ideological dogma and the smearing of those who dissent. However, when "human rights" becomes the premise of all science, the "scientific frontier" contracts rather than expands.

The declaration concludes with a familiar premise: Herbert Marcuse's double-think doctrine of "repressive tolerance," which has become the basis of liberal-dominated academia:

> *Academic freedom and freedom of expression are critical to free scientific inquiry. However, the notion of academic freedom is disrespected and abused when it is used to promote the dissemination of racist and discriminatory concepts. Scientists have an obligation to society to speak loudly and actively in opposition of such abuse.*[1014]

The declaration sources include the Southern Poverty Law Center, indicating the careless attitude these "scholars" maintain in regard to their own research, while having the audacity to disparage The Pioneer Fund as a disreputable source. The year prior to the declaration, the SPLC, long lauded as the paragon of liberal virtue, had been widely exposed by the mainstream news media as a lavish scam, an ex-employee agonizing: "Were we complicit, by taking our paychecks and staying silent, in ripping off donors on behalf of an organization that never lived up to the values it espoused?"[1015]

The cited SPLC reference for The Pioneer Fund is filled with rhetoric about "Nazi science," while Rushton, and indeed all scientists who

---

[1013] Cited in Knudson, *A Mirror to Nature*, "Rushton on Race," 190
[1014] Statement on Rushton.
[1015] Moser, "The Reconing of Morris Dees."

research race and genetics, is classified as a "White Nationalist." While the SPLC might be a convenient reference for some Antifa street thug wanting to rationalize his/her psychopathy, its citation as a credible reference by the Psychology Department at Western Ontario says something about the mental outlook of those who dominant academia.

Ricardo Duchesne

In 2019, ex-leftist Riccardo Duchesne, Professor of Sociology at the University of New Brunswick, was targeted by *Huffpost* as a "White supremacist." The article is illustrated with KKK imagery. He had previously been damned by "colleagues" at the University, pressuring for his dismissal for his criticism of multiculturalism. *Huffpost*, in a malicious hit-piece, stated that:

> Kerry Jang, a psychiatry professor at the University of British Columbia and former Vancouver city councilor...issued a formal complaint to UNB in 2015 calling into question Duchesne's academic credentials and his fitness to teach after reading his racist blog posts attacking Vancouver's Asian community over a plan to study the city's history of discrimination. Other professors followed suit, including 10 members of the university's own sociology department who months later issued an open letter rejecting Duchesne's views and calling them "devoid of academic merit."[1016]

Any non-conformist academic who questions multiculturalism and concomitant globalization is automatically going to be blacklisted. According to Jang, et al., "academic credentials" are to be judged on conformity to the dominant paradigms, regardless of scholarly merit. Following the article, 113 faculty members of the University sent a letter to *Huffpost* repudiating Duchesne's views. In May 2019, Duchesne submitted his early retirement to the University. A statement published by *Huffpost* reads:

> The University of New Brunswick has announced Ricardo Duchesne's early retirement from the university. The statement

---

[1016] Robins-Early, "The White Supremacist Professor Teaching at a Public University."

issued by Dr. Petra Hauf, the Vice President of Saint-John's campus, said:

> I write to advise members of the University community that Dr. Ricardo Duchesne, professor in the department of social science, has provided his notice of early retirement to focus on his own pursuits as an independent scholar. We respectfully accept his decision and thank him for his 24 years of service.
>
> Dr. Petra Hauf, UNB's Saint John's campus vice-president, said in a public statement, "I want to assure the community that we unequivocally condemn racism and misogyny, and do not support the dissemination of any kind of hate speech, or ideas that promote or inspire hatred." She went on to note that the university has a zero-tolerance policy for racism and discrimination.[1017]

Dr. Hauf and her *type* can get away with academic hooliganism by uttering Pavlovian-response buzzwords such as "hate speech," and the academic career of a serious scholar can be ended. Sensationalism from an online journal is sufficient to press the collective saliva button for academia to drool venom.

The Canadian Historical Association issued a statement in solidarity with the New Brunswick lynch mob: *"We share the signatories' concerns about Duchene's [sic] views and like them, distinguish between the important principle of academic freedom and indefensible and potentially dangerous arguments."*[1018] Again, we see the hovering spectre of Marcuse: the double-think of tyrants—"repressive tolerance."

Professor Kenneth Westhues[1019] made some very pertinent observations on the Duchesne case:

> Against the background of other mobbing cases I have studied, I would hypothesize two additional explanatory factors. First is the envy of excellence. First on my checklist of mobbing indicators is: "By standard criteria of job performance, the target is at least average, probably above average." A quick search for Ricardo Duchesne on Google Scholar shows a degree of scholarly productivity that I would guess excels that of at least three-quarters of UNB faculty in the social sciences. To judge

---

[1017] Martens, "Over 100 University of New Brunswick Faculty 'Condemn.'"
[1018] Cited by Westhues, "Making Fast Work of Ricardo Duchesnes."
[1019] Kenneth Westhues is Professor Emeritus, Sociology and Legal Studies University of Waterloo, Canada.

by ratemyprofessors, Duchesne excels in the classroom. It would be interesting to compare Duchesne, in scholarly stature and appreciation by students, to the 100 colleagues who signed the statement against him. My guess is that he would fare very well.

Having looked up Duchesne on Google Scholar, I spent a few hours perusing his work, studying in particular articles from 15 to 25 years ago, in order to grasp the transition he reports having made in his own career, from the standard leftist critique of European civilization to defense of it. I found it reassuring to follow the intellectual development of this independent-minded sociologist, charting his own path in what appears to be an honest search for truth—the value on which every university rests.[1020]

Several decades ago, Wilmot Robertson, author of *The Dispossessed Majority*, had a regular feature in his magazine, *Instauration*, entitled "Cultural Catacombs." In the dark age of this civilization the catacombs seem to be where real scholars will be increasingly driven.

[1020] Westhues, "Making Fast Work of Ricardo Duchesne," op. cit.

Denigration of Western Science

"For the historical outlook itself the data are always symbols. Scientific research, on the contrary, is science and only science. In virtue of its technical origin and purpose it sets out to find data and laws of the causal sort and nothing else, and from the moment that it turns its glance upon something else it becomes Metaphysics, something trans-scientific. And just because this is so, historical and natural science data are different."

Oswald Spengler (1918)[1021]

In 2021 the Ministry of Education released a Working Paper[1022] designed to give "parity" of "Maori knowledge" to Western science, which is derided as "Eurocentric." The introduction explains:

> Mana ōrite mō te mātauranga Māori means equal status for mātauranga Māori in NCEA[1023] and is particularly important when deciding what TMoA subjects to support at NCEA Levels 1-3. Our goal is to ensure parity for mātauranga Māori with the other bodies of knowledge credentialed by NCEA (particularly Western/Pākehā epistemologies). This parity needs to span English-and Māori-medium settings. The Ministry is committed to ensuring mātauranga Māori is explicitly and equitably valued in NCEA and that mātauranga Māori pathways are acknowledged and supported equally in NCEA.[1024]

[1021] Spengler, *The Decline of the West, Vol. 1*, 154.
[1022] Nippert. *Determining the NCEA Level.*
[1023] NCEA = National Certificate in Educational Achievement, a high school assessment administered by the New Zealand Qualifications Authority.
[1024] Ibid., Part I Policy objectives, Mana ōrite mō te mātauranga Māori, 3.

From a traditionalist viewpoint, this is laudable in theory: providing Maori an option within the context of their own heritage. However, as in all such measures, in practice it becomes something quite different:

1. The predicate is the denigration of the European.
2. Western science will be placed on parity with ju-ju, voodoo, and priestcraft.
3. No such options are available for New Zealand European students to learn their heritage, other than in derogatory terms.
4. The outcome will be to reinforce and extend Maori agitation and demands against the New Zealand European.

Across the education spectrum Maori learning whether in mathematics, physics, astronomy, or biology are "grounded in te ao Māori and mātauranga Māori," with "equal mana [for] subjects which reflect non-indigenous paradigms or knowledge bases."[1025]

A new subject, Te Reo Pākehā, that is, learning the English language for the purpose of serving Maori interests, is introduced: "In this new subject, ākonga[1026] study English through a distinctly te ao Māori perspective, gaining the skills required to navigate confidently and competently in te ao Pākehā."[1027] Of course, it is not that learning the English language is a new subject, but that it will be taught from a "Māori perspective," which will mean that students will be taught that they are learning the language of the "colonizers" so that they can attain the necessary skills for entering commerce and academia. "In contrast" to the present teaching of English to those whose first language is something other than English:

> ...Te Reo Pākehā presents the English language, through an ao Māori lens, as a communication tool that underpins social interaction, the expression of thoughts, and further academic learning. As a subject, it has the objective of empowering ākonga to navigate more successfully between te ao Māori and te ao Pākehā. It is grounded in the unique pedagogy of TMoA and is crucial to pathways for ākonga whose primary language of instruction is te reo Māori, as many tertiary and career options,

---

[1025] Ibid., Keep NCEA Level 1 as an optional level (12), 4.
[1026] Ākonga = students.
[1027] Ibid., Te Reo Pākehā, 2.8 (27), 35.

locally and abroad, demand fluency in and knowledge of academic and professional English.[1028]

However, with the introduction of the "Philosophy and History of Science" as a new "strand" in the teaching of Maori, we come to the Europhobic predicate:

> *Philosophy and History of Science is a unique strand in Pūtaiao, with no equivalent in NZC. It promotes discussion and analysis of the ways in which science has been used to support the dominance of Eurocentric views (among which, its use as a rationale for colonisation of Māori and the suppression of Māori knowledge); and the notion that science is a Western European invention and itself evidence of European dominance over Māori and other indigenous peoples. Pūtaiao allows opportunities to incorporate Māori perspectives and knowledge about the natural world into the classroom. In this regard, it decentres Western epistemologies and methodologies.*[1029]

This premises the other subjects insofar as it reduces all Western knowledge to that of rationalizing colonization. It broadens the attack—and an attack is what this is—behind the facade, again, of "human rights," to Europeans as the oppressors of not only Maori but "other indigenous peoples." It also "allows opportunities" to relegate Western empirical methodology to a subordinated and denigrated position.

This offensive against Western empirical methodology prompted concern from a small group of academics, whose objections have marked them as "heretics" within academia,[1030] and especially by the Royal Society of Aotearoa.

The scientists[1031] had written to *The New Zealand Listener* in response to the Ministry of Education proposals, and specifically the aim of "parity" for "mātauranga Māori" vis-à-vis "other bodies of knowledge credentialed by NCEA (particularly Western/Pākehā epistemologies)"; and of "discussion and analysis of the ways in which science has been used to

---

[1028] Ibid.
[1029] Ibid., 2.3 Pūtaiao (24), 21.
[1030] See the chapter "Heresy," for examples of how scientists are purged from academia for affronting some aspect of liberalism.
[1031] Kendall Clements, School of Biological Sciences; Garth Cooper, School of Biological Sciences; Michael Corballis, School of Psychology; Douglas Elliffe, School of Psychology; Elizabeth Rata, Professor of Critical Studies in Education; Emeritus Professor Robert Nola, Department of Philosophy; and Emeritus Professor John Werry, Department of Psychological Medicine, Auckland University.

support the dominance of Eurocentric views (among which, its use as a rationale for colonisation of Māori and the suppression of Māori knowledge); and the notion that science is a Western European invention and itself evidence of European dominance over Māori and other indigenous peoples," as quoted above.

Professor Clements, et al., responded that "this perpetuates disturbing misunderstandings of science emerging at all levels of education and in science funding. These encourage mistrust of science..."[1032]

To the denigration of Western science as a means of maintaining European hegemony and Eurocentrism, Clements, et al. replied:

> *Science itself does not colonise. It has been used to aid colonisation, as have literature and art. However, science also provides immense good, as well as greatly enhanced understanding of the world.... The future of our world, and our species, cannot afford mistrust of science.*

Likely the most heretical of the comments, and the one sin that cannot be forgiven, was that:

> *Indigenous knowledge is critical for the preservation and perpetuation of culture and local practices, and plays key roles in management and practices. However, in the discovery of empirical, universal truths, it falls far short in what we can define as science itself.*
>
> *To accept it as the equivalent of science is to patronise and fail indigenous populations; better to ensure that everyone participates in the world's scientific enterprises. Indigenous knowledge may indeed help advance scientific knowledge in some ways, but it is not science.*[1033]

The news media dutifully reported the Europhobic reactions, including those of academics whose method of response is the use of *ad hominem*. Hence, the scientists who questioned the Ministry of Education intent were themselves attacked as "neo-colonialists," including presumably Professor Rata, one of the signatories of the *Listener* letter:

[1032] Clements, "In Defence of Science."
[1033] Ibid.

Associate professor Ocean Mercier[1034] focuses on how mātauranga and science connect and relate, particularly in educational and environmental contexts. Mercier said what the professors outlined in the letter was not new and came up from time to time. "This is a very old argument, actually, that is coming from scientists who are very deeply steeped in a particular set of scientific norms that go back a long way, and they have their roots in colonialism," she said.[1035]

Further, "Many Māori are also outlining that non-Māori academics should not determine how or what mātauranga Māori is and that positionality is crucial when it comes to discussions about the Māori school curriculum."[1036] Any right-traditionalist should consistently support such an outlook. However, as usual, the contention only goes one way—against the European. One might conversely state that non-European academics should not determine how or what European knowledge is (whether in the hard sciences or metaphysics and spirituality) and *that* positionality is crucial when it comes to discussions about school curriculum. But to do so—need we state (?)—would be to bring opprobrium upon one as a "racist," "neo-colonialist," and "White supremacist." The only consistency in such matters is a duplicitous Europhobia. The aim, Mercier states, is to "decolonise" science:

> *I think if there is one thing this particular incident reminds us off is that there is need to decolonise first, to decolonise the science systems before we can create a safe space for mātauranga and indigenous knowledge. This is a reminder that this space is not completely safe.[1037]*

This is a euphemism for the politicization of science and of education, which becomes indoctrination and the maintenance of a party-line.

The Vice Chancellor of the University of Auckland, Dawn Freshwater, issued a statement that the letter from the seven scientists, "has caused considerable hurt and dismay among our staff, students and alumni. While the academics are free to express their views, I want to make it clear that they do not represent the views of the University of Auckland."[1038]

[1034] Mercier is a signatory of the letter condemning the seven scientists.
[1035] Dunlop, "University academics' claim that mātauranga Māori."
[1036] Ibid.
[1037] Ibid.
[1038] Ibid.

Dr. Freshwater's statement is itself an affront to the spirit of Western science, where she places boundaries within enquiry and opinion, on the basis of "hurt and dismay."[1039] Rather, she sees Auckland University, "this country's largest research institution," as being "at the forefront of this exciting exploration."[1040]

The *Stuff* article by Māni Dunlop cites Dr. Freshwater as stating that Auckland University "had respect for mātauranga Māori as a valuable knowledge system, and that it was not at odds with Western empirical science and did not need to compete."[1041] In which case, if mātauranga Māori "was not at odds with Western empirical science and did not need to compete," why is there a proposal by the Ministry of Education working paper that the teaching of a "new strand," "the philosophy and history of science," be based on:

1. "Discussion and analysis of the ways in which science has been used to support the dominance of Eurocentric views."
2. Depiction of Western science as "itself evidence of European dominance over Māori and other indigenous peoples."
3. "Opportunities to incorporate Māori perspectives and knowledge about the natural world into the classroom."

If, according to Dr. Freshwater, mātauranga Māori "was not at odds with Western empirical science and did not need to compete," why does the working paper from the Ministry of Education refer to the decentering of "Western epistemologies and methodologies"? Dr. Freshwater, like so many in academia, as indicated by the hundreds who signed the statement against the seven heretical scientists, does not herself seem to think in terms of Western empiricism, but rather in banalities, clichés, and slogans; and they congratulate themselves on being the "intelligentsia" who smirk, ridicule and smear at those who dissent. But the "democratic majority" is dogmatically held to be implicitly right, including in matters of science. That is the basis of democracy: consensus opinion, "the general will," although decision by majority vote is not yet permitted to chart the course of an ocean-liner, airplane, or space-craft.

[1039] Ibid.
[1040] Ibid.
[1041] Ibid.

Sloganeering

Hundreds of academics closed ranks to condemn the seven heretics, signing a statement in condemnation, which reads like a proclamation from the Committee of Public Safety, or the Supreme Presidium of a "democratic republic," an exercise in conformist sloganeering:

A letter signed by seven University of Auckland Professors/ Professors Emeritus, published in the New Zealand Listener (July 23) claims to be 'in defence of science' against what is described as an effort to "encourage mistrust of science."

We, the signatories to this response, categorically disagree with their views. Indigenous knowledges—this case, Mātauranga—are not lesser to other knowledge systems. Indeed, indigenous ways of knowing, including Mātauranga, have always included methodologies that overlap with 'Western' understandings of the scientific method.

However, Mātauranga is far more than just equivalent to or equal to 'Western' science. It offers ways of viewing the world that are unique and complementary to other knowledge systems.

The seven Professors describe efforts to reevaluate and revise the significance of Mātauranga in NCEA, including the acknowledgement of the role 'western' science has played in rationalising colonisation as contributing to "disturbing misunderstandings of science emerging at all levels of education and in science funding."

The Professors claim that "science itself does not colonise", ignoring the fact that colonisation, racism, misogyny, and eugenics have each been championed by scientists wielding a self-declared monopoly on universal knowledge.

And while the Professors describe science as 'universal', they fail to acknowledge that science has long excluded indigenous peoples from participation, preferring them as subjects for study and exploitation. Diminishing the role of indigenous knowledge systems is simply another tool for exclusion and exploitation.

The Professors present a series of global crises that we must "battle" with science, again failing to acknowledge the ways in which science has contributed to the creation of these challenges. Putting science on a pedestal gets us no further in the solution of these crises.

> Finally, they believe that "mistrust of science" is increased by this kind of critique. In contrast, we believe that mistrust in science stems from science's ongoing role in perpetuating 'scientific' racism, justifying colonisation, and continuing support of systems that create injustice. There can be no trust in science without robust self-reflection by the science community and an active commitment to change.[1042]

The dissident letter was a rare example of "robust self-reflection by the science community," yet the condemnatory statement implicitly condemns with *ad hominem* and *non-sequitur*, what was intended as a small gesture in questioning the motives of (1) placing Maori myth and legend on par with Western scientific methodology, (2) subjecting Western science to ideological, agenda-driven criticism, with doctrinal buzz-words such as "racism," "colonisation," "misogyny," and "eugenics." Indeed, "science" can be utilized in the pursuit of any number of ideologies, including those of liberalism and the left.

The Enlightenment *philospophes* of the seventeenth and eighteenth century literary salons claimed to be speaking in the name of "science" on the basis of speculative assumptions that transpired to be at odds with empirical observations. The myth of the noble savage, that emerged in the collective imagination of Enlightenment "scientists" and "philosophers," continues to be the basis of those academics who place ideology before the Western scientific methodology that they decry as "racist," "misogynist," and "colonialist." Marx, Engels, and Lenin were held to be the final arbiters of science in the communist states, and in the USSR a barely educated agronomist, T. D. Lysenko, held sway not only over Soviet agriculture, but the biological sciences, because his crackpot theories were deemed to accord more closely with Marxism than those of Mendelian genetics. Similar ideas continue to hold sway over Western social sciences, since Franz Boas was ensconced in Columbia University, and his teachings on what is analogous to the noble savage are maintained with the same fanaticism as those of Lysenko in the USSR.[1043] One might ask: what is the academic work of Paul Spoonley, one of the signatories of the Hendy statement, other than often a justification for the exploitation of migrants in the service of a globalized growth economy, behind the mantle of

---

[1042] Hendy, "An open response to 'In defence of science.'"
[1043] For example the esteem that was accorded to Boas' student Professor Margaret Mead, for her book *Coming of Age in Samoa*, and the vilification of Professor Derek Freeman, an honorary Samoan chief, whose book *Margaret Mead and Samoa: the Making & Unmaking of an Anthropological Myth* debunked Mead's research methodology and conclusions.

"human rights"? How many of those hundreds of academies who signed the Hendly statement were motivated primarily by political ideologies rather than primarily by science? Tze Ming Mok, for example, served as a spokesperson for an "antifa" anarchist front in 2004.

Royal Society

That an ostensibly scholarly society devoted to the pursuit of knowledge can succumb to the dominant "human rights" doctrine itself presents a challenge as to the influence of such ideologies, epically when they subvert what should be objectivity a detachment in the pursuit of knowledge, premises which are maligned as "Eurocentric," "racist," "colonialist." The Royal Society has ensured that it is thoroughly imbued with *taha Maori*.

A campaign was initiated urging the Royal Society to investigate and censure the seven dissident scientists in inquisitional manner. According to a news report:

> *Māori academics online have been encouraging people who do not agree with the letter to lodge a complaint to the Royal Society.*
>
> *The scientific academy said it had received numerous emails about the letter.*
>
> *In a joint statement, president Brent Clothier and academy executive committee chairwoman Charlotte MacDonald said they deeply regret the harm such a "misguided view" could cause.*
>
> *"The recent suggestion by a group of University of Auckland academics that mātauranga Māori is not a valid form of knowledge is utterly rejected by Royal Society – Te Apārangi.*
>
> *"The society strongly upholds the value of mātauranga Māori and rejects the narrow and outmoded definition of science outlined in* The Listener *letter to the editor."*[1044]

Garth Cooper, Michael Corballis, and Robert Nola, were notified on October 6th, 2021 that they would be investigated, however Dr. Michael Corballis, died shortly afterwards. Of five original complaints, three withdrew November 10th.

[1044] Dunlop, "University academics' claim that mātauranga Māori."

It seems that the decision of the Royal Society is pre-determined, again based on entrenched suppositions, or *dogma*, given the public statement that has been made. It is shameful that Dr. Corballis should end his career on such a note for speaking up on the integrity of the scientific method, in the face of what amounts to nothing other than the recurrence of the noble savage doctrine that was regarded as "science" during the seventeenth and eighteenth centuries. Here the "intelligentsia" and other denizens of literary salons of the era pronounced on the *assumed* virtues of the dusky races of mythic lands. Polynesians were among the first so honored.

While there is talk of "outmoded" ideas, what is one to make of the same doctrines now being imposed by the Ministry of Education, Royal Society, TEU, state-funded news media, and every educational institution in New Zealand from kindergarten to university, and enforced by commissariats for "human rights" and "race relations"? Is the liberal ideology any less pervasive than those of Jacobin France, the People's Republic of China, or the Democratic People's Republic of Korea? Yes, all such states are called "democratic."

Is the role assumed by the Royal Society any different from that of the Jacobin's Committee of Public Safety? The guillotine is missing, but is the intent any different? If so, how?

Is the intent, and even the process, far removed from those brought against N.L. Vavilov and other biologists because Mendelian genetics was regarded as contrary to Marxian "science," because genetics was labeled as being "connected with brutal fascism," and "bourgeois pseudoscience"?[1045] An unnamed member of the LAAAS Presidium told Vavilov in no uncertain terms that:

> *Marxism is the only science. Darwinism is only a part; the real theory of knowledge of the world was given by Marx, Engels, and Lenin. And when I hear discussion about Darwinism without mention of Marxism, it may seem on the one side, that all is right, but on the other, it's a horse of a different colour.*[1046]

In 1941 a military collegium of the Supreme Court rendered sentence on Vavilov as "belonging to a rightist conspiracy," spying for England, sabotaging agriculture, etc.[1047] He died of malnutrition several years later

---

[1045] Prezent, I.I, "On Pseudoscientific Theories in Genetics," *Yarovizatsiya*, January 1939, cited in Medvedev, *The Rise and Fall*, 53-54.
[1046] Medvedev, *The Rise and Fall*, 64.
[1047] Ibid., 71.

in a prison camp. Medical genetics came under scrutiny, and the eminent biologist N.V. Kol'tsov and other geneticists were condemned by Prezent for a "pseudoscientific and deeply reactionary concept which carried them into the arms of fascist ideology," and "bourgeois genetics."[1048] The Medico-Genetical Institute was shut down, the "foremost medical geneticist," S.S. Levit, and his co-workers were arrested and condemned in 1937 by Marxist "philosopher of science" Arnost Kolman[1049] in an article entitled the "Black Hundred delirium of fascism and medico-biological sciences."[1050] Members of the Fertilizer Institute became "enemies of the peoples," and "anti-grasslanders," because their views on the use of fertilizers did not accord with current doctrines.[1051]

From the USSR came references to "brutal fascism," "bourgeois pseudoscience," "rightist conspiracy," "deeply reactionary," "enemies of the people." Accused scientists were brought before tribunals and condemned *a priori*, on the basis of maintaining party-line. Democratic New Zealand eight decades later, pervaded with eighteenth and nineteenth century doctrines masquerading as "science," and seven scientists who dissent from the party-line are condemned with terms such as "Eurocentric," "colonialist," "racism," "misogyny," "eugenics," "exploitation," "mistrust," "scientific racism," "narrow and outmoded." The Royal Society assumes the role of an inquisitorial tribunal, and hundreds of academics eagerly show themselves to be loyal to party-line dogma.

Return of the Noble Savage

Associate Professor Ocean Mercier evokes a familiar allegation against the dissidents, that their thinking is, as quoted previously, "very deeply steeped in a particular set of scientific norms that go back a long way, and they have their roots in colonialism." One hears the same theme repeated until it becomes a cliché: "outmoded," "extinct," "regressive," an affront to "modern science." The variations of Marxism, post-Marxism, and liberalism that remain dominant in academia and much of the rest of Western society, trace their origins back centuries. Since they are dogmas, while they are subject to revision, the premises are impervious to challenge. Criticism is met with denunciation, whether from academia, press, pulpit, or parliament.

[1048] Ibid., 80.
[1049] Kolman recanted and sought asylum in Sweden in 1976.
[1050] Ibid., 82.
[1051] Ibid., 92.

While John Dryden poetically referred to the noble savage running free, "as nature first made man," in *The Conquest of Granada* (1672) it was the first professional female novelist, Aphra Behn, who wrote the novel *Oroonoko* lauding the virtues of the noble savage in 1688, which was made into a tragedy of the same name by the English dramatist Thomas Southerne in 1695. While Jean-Jacques Rousseau is often mistakenly regarded as the father of this fanciful notion, his *Discourse on the Origin of Inequality Among Men* (1755) did philosophize on the same theme, the state of "natural man." Speculating that "compassion" is a universal trait of nature, he speculated on ideas that have again become mainstream within academia and politics. Hence crime results from laws, rather than laws originating to restrain innate criminal tendencies, and we might discern the familiar insistence of the "progressive" (whose doctrinal origins trace back to eighteenth century theorizing) that the reform of society is the panacea for all ills. Rousseau, the father of much of what is today called "progressive," and "modern," opined:

> *It must, in the first place, be allowed that, the more violent the passions are, the more are laws necessary to keep them under restraint. But, setting aside the inadequacy of laws to effect this purpose, which is evident from the crimes and disorders to which these passions daily give rise among us, we should do well to inquire if these evils did not spring up with the laws themselves...*[1052]

From here is but little distance to the charge against Western civilization that its laws and ethos are intrinsically flawed. Of slavery, Rousseau concludes that such a state does not exist in "nature," but that servitude commences with the social polity, before which there is only the free individual:

> *...it is impossible to make any man a slave, unless he be first reduced to a situation in which he cannot do without the help of others: and, since such a situation does not exist in a state of nature, every one is there his own master, and the law of the strongest is of no effect.*[1053]

[1052] Rousseau, *Discourse on Inequality*, 21
[1053] Ibid., 23.

Already in his dissertation Rousseau had "proved that the inequality of mankind is hardly felt, and that its influence is next to nothing in a state of nature," yet he states soon after that in proving his hypothesis he has "nothing to determine my choice but conjectures..."[1054] This state of natural innocence was destroyed, according to Rousseau, preceding Marx and Engels by close to a century, with the first notion of private property:

> *The first man who, having enclosed a piece of ground, bethought himself of saying This is mine, and found people simple enough to believe him, was the real founder of civil society. From how many crimes, wars and murders, from how many horrors and misfortunes might not any one have saved mankind...*[1055]

Yet, "nothing is more gentle than man in his primitive state, as he is placed by nature at an equal distance from the stupidity of brutes, and the fatal ingenuity of civilised man."[1056]

While such naiveté from the imaginings of an eighteenth century philosopher might now seem quaint, the ideological impetus they gave to Jacobinism, Marxism, and liberalism has caused the misery for which he indicted "civilization." What he did not see in his drawing room speculations was "nature red in tooth and claw" and rejected out of hand contrary opinions of philosophers such as Hobbes. As Lothrop Stoddard showed in his aptly titled *Revolt Against Civilization*, such a doctrine had provided the rationalization for mass sociopathy behind the facade of "human rights," "social justice," "democracy," "liberty, equality, fraternity."

It is the ideological spectre that pervades academia. This doctrine became fashionable among the literati and their aristocratic patrons, who were titillated by the prospect of a society without the constraints of civilization, or what one might say by that time over-civilization. In particular New Zealand's own neck of the ocean became a focus with the exploration of James Cook and others. It is reflected in a poem, waxing lyrical:

> *When Cook-lamented, and with tears as just*
> *As ever mingled with heroic dust,*
> *Steer'd Britain's oak into a world unknown,*
> *And in his country's glory sought his own,*

[1054] Ibid.
[1055] Ibid.
[1056] Ibid., 26.

Wherever he found man, to nature true,
The rights of man were sacred in his view[1057]

Tertiary Education Union: Activism Before Scholarship

The Tertiary Education Union has pronounced against the dissidents, writing to them that:

> ...*their letter to the editor was damaging and ill-advised. TEU said to some members it seemed designed to attack and offend, rather than present a reasoned academic argument. It said members found the letter offensive, racist, reflective of a patronising, and neo-colonial mindset.*
>
> *"Your letter neglected to engage with or mention the many highly accomplished scholars and scientists in Aotearoa who have sought to reconcile notions of science, mātauranga Māori, and Māori in science," the TEU letter stated.*
>
> *"Our members worry that you have undermined the mana of many indigenous scientists and scholars who are working to understand the ways in which knowledge accumulates. Your letter will do little to encourage (and much to discourage) Māori to engage with science."*[1058]

Again we see the time-honoured use of *ad hominem* and slander by the TEU. The dissidents are condemned as "racist," "offensive," "neo-colonialist." Claiming that the dissidents' letter "seemed designed to attack and offend, rather than present a reasoned academic argument," is pure projection. Where did the TEU, Royal Society, or any other critic present a reasoned argument against the dissidents? The response from the academic Establishment seems to have been nothing other than to slander, with buzz-words such as "racist," and "neo-colonialist."

My experience with the TEU involves a complaint I made to Waikato University (Hamilton) regarding a master's thesis that was replete with falsely cited references. The thesis had garnered first class honors, and was supervised and graded by supposedly "eminent scholars," the former including Israel's primary apologist in New Zealand, Professor Dov Bing, who publically termed the farcical thesis, "sound scholarship." A tribunal

---

[1057] Cowper, "Charity."
[1058] Dunlop, "University academics' claim that mātauranga Māori."

was set up to investigate the complaint. The role of the TEU was to threaten that if my complaint was upheld a strike would be called. Hence, although the tribunal recommended that the thesis grade be downgraded, the Vice Chancellor of the time, Dr. Crawford, lied by claiming that the tribunal had upheld the thesis as "sound," and refused to make the tribunal's report public. That is the character of "scholarship" in New Zealand: its efficacy can be determined by the threat of a union strike.

Where is the "science"; where is the reasoned argument, the dialectical critique? What should we make of this "scholarly" response, for example, from Professor Joanna Kidman on her Twitter account, July 24th, 2021?

Oh settlers! Opened the Letters page of the Listener to find a bunch of University of Auckland professors, incl Liz Rata, denying that Mātauranga Māori is science. Where do these shuffling zombies come from? Is there something in the water?

Kidman describes herself on her Twitter bio as, "Professor. Indigenous sociology. Māori education. Settler-colonial racism researcher."

"In response to the accusations of racism, signatory Elizabeth Rata said it was not worthy of a response," continued the *Stuff* article. "'I actually don't have a response. My response is what that deserves.'"[1059]

However, signatory Douglas Elliffe stepped down as acting dean of the psychology faculty at Auckland University,[1060] a familiar scenario within academia throughout the West.

Sovietization

At other times and places the present histrionics against scholarly dissent manifested in Red Guards dragging teachers from their classrooms, subjecting them to verbal abuse, beatings, torture, and at times death, as "class enemies."

[1059] Dunlop, "University academics' claim that mātauranga Māori."
[1060] Kerr-Lazenby, "University of Auckland professor relinquishes role."

Erasure of Memory: Delenda est Europaeus

"Who controls the past controls the future."

George Orwell (1949)

Such is the total war against European humanity that ethnic erasure is desired, and self-loathing Whites are among the vanguard of those who would erase the memory that *Homo Europaeus* ever walked the earth. The aim is that Europeans forget who they are, and without roots and identity, continue on the path to oblivion, rejoicing in their own demise.

One of the most conspicuous manifestations of the erasure of *Homo Europaeus* is the destruction of historic monuments reflecting the heritage of Europe and its far-flung outposts.

When the Jacobins overthrew the French church and crown, they sought the destruction of the art, monuments, architecture, and churches that recalled the old regime. When Mao assumed control of China, he sought to destroy all monuments and books of Confucianism. The destruction of monuments reflecting European heritage has proceeded over several decades, but in the last few years has accelerated. Where once there was criminal vandalism by individuals or groups there is now a program of official vandalism. An American commentator writes of this:

> *Throughout history and across cultures, regime change always begins and ends with the destruction and removal of symbols. Iconoclasm is one of the most powerful strategies for Cultural Revolution. From the French Revolution to the Bolshevik Revolution to the Islamic State, regime change has been accompanied by the destruction of statues, paintings, monuments,*

sacred objects and other symbols identified with the previous government.[1061]

Dawn Perlmutter relates the acceleration of the process to the election of Trump:

> For several years there have been numerous incidents of vandalism of Confederate statues, fallen officer memorials, and veterans' monuments. The widespread desecration of statues and memorials throughout the country directly corresponds to the increase in anarchist, socialist, communist, anti-police, anti-government and anti-Trump movements.
>
> The iconoclasm campaign had its first big success in July 2015 when the Confederate flag on South Carolina's statehouse grounds came down after 54 years at the Capitol. During the debates over its proposed removal dozens of confederate statues were vandalized. Walmart, Sears, Amazon and other companies removed Confederate merchandise from thousands of stores across the US Organizers discovered the power of iconoclasm and began targeting statues, names and memorials…[1062]

A further impetus for vandalism and erasure, both unofficial and official, was the aftermath of the Charlottesville "Unite the Right" rally, in which a legally permitted and peaceful demonstration in support of preserving the Southern heritage was attacked by both police and leftist mobs. The actions of mob vandalism against monuments have often indicated mass psychosis:

> Immediately after the Charlottesville rally, Confederate statues and plaques were removed from public parks, cemeteries, plazas and government buildings in cities across the country. Politicians are calling for the removal of all Confederate monuments from public spaces and legislation is being introduced to remove Confederate statues from the US Capitol building. Other statues were vandalized and destroyed. In Durham, NC protesters toppled a bronze statue of a Confederate soldier outside the Old Durham County Courthouse. They did not just remove the statue. They lynched it. Video of the incident shows a woman climbing a

---

[1061] Perlmutter, "American Iconoclasm."
[1062] Ibid.

ladder to the top of the statue and tying a rope around the soldier's neck. Dozens of other activists participated in the lynching, pulling the statue to the ground, cheering and taking turns kicking, spitting and standing on the fallen soldier. This went beyond vandalism. It was a collective ritual execution.[1063]

Hundreds of Confederate monuments were not the only targets. Christopher Columbus is undoubtedly the most despised of any European for having put the America within the purview of Europe. In June 2020 statues of Columbus were vandalized in Minnesota, Boston, Miami, and Virginia.[1064] The same month statues of the Pioneer Mother and the Pioneer Man at the University of Oregon were toppled and put into storage.[1065] A commentator on the New Zealand situation writes:

Statues of "dead colonial white guys" have been compared to the much maligned Confederate War Memorials in the Southern United States and the wholesale removal of "controversial historical landmarks" has been mooted in the media.

These "Anti-Colonialist" activists have in the last twenty years or so been successful in destroying, vandalising or banishing a number of monuments. The Chinese mayor of Gisborne, Meng Foon announced late last year that a statue of Captain James Cook would be removed into museum storage, saying that it was "about time we're celebrating the local history as well."[1066]

Gisborne Mayor Meng Foon shortly after became the Race Relations Commissioner.

The explorer Captain James Cook, an English working class lad who made good by his own efforts, is a subject of particular hatred by those who would erase the European heritage from "Aotearoa." His monuments are subjected to frequent defacement. In July 2019 his statue in Gisborne was desecrated with painted slogans: "this is our land" and "thief pakeha."

Statues of Queen Victoria, in whose reign our colony was founded, have also been targeted. Dunedin's statue has had to have its nose and crown replaced after Anglophobic mongrels

---

[1063] Ibid.
[1064] "Confederate and Columbus Statues Toppled."
[1065] "University Statement on Pioneer Statues."
[1066] Spoonlet, "Anti-White Iconoclasts."

attacked it, leaving behind anti-colonial messages. Wellington's has been graffitied and vandalised too, and so have Auckland's and Christchurch's.

Zealandia, the personification of our country, has not been spared from this anti-white action either.

A memorial in Auckland to the fallen of the New Zealand Wars, hundreds of soldiers and civilians that we are supposed to forget, has been the target of vandalism from radical leftists several times.

There is, in the city bearing his name, a statue dedicated to Captain John Fane Hamilton, killed leading his men during the Battle of Gate Pah. In 2018, a Maori activist named Taitimu Maipi, inspired by anti-white columns on Stuff, attacked the statue with a hammer and then covered it in paint. Maipi was not charged with vandalism, or any other crime. It's apparently completely legal to openly attack monuments to white history. The ethnomasochist mayor of Hamilton Andrew King said that "we do have to sit back and listen very carefully to the message that's behind this." The message, Andrew, is that white people are bad. King then went a step further and started a campaign to change the name of the city, because obviously Hamilton is problematic now that a single Maori is upset about it. He also initiated a review of all the street names in the city, reviewing them for "cultural appropriateness." Which culture do you think they have to be appropriate for? Names that were brought up included Bryce,[1067] Grey[1068] and von Tempsky[1069].

Physical reminders of this country's white history and culture are not the only things that need to be changed. Auckland University lecturer Hirini Kaa is more concerned about how "place names are used to honour and memorialise historic misdeed and their doers," saying that European-derived place names are a "potent form of colonization."[1070]

The writer cites many other examples of vandalism of memorials to those killed in the New Zealand Wars.

[1067] Minister of Native Affairs (1879–1884).
[1068] New Zealand governor.
[1069] Heroic military commander during the New Zealand Wars.
[1070] Spoonlet, op. cit.

While Human Rights Commissioner Paul Hunt strains to compile a list of so-called "hate crimes" and "hate speech," none of these expressions of Europhobia are mentioned, and never will be.

Other than our monuments, there is our literature and theatre, until nothing remains as a sanctuary for European culture. Will it be driven to the catacombs? Doctor Watson in modernist renditions of Arthur Conan Doyle's *Sherlock Holmes* becomes Black or even a Chinese woman. Television series set in the medieval epoch usually have Africans mingling about the streets, if not featuring as main characters.

> The co-creator of Midsomer Murders, Brian True-May, is to step down from his role at the end of the current series after he sparked a race row by suggesting there was no place in the programme for ethnic minorities.
>
> True-May, the co-creator and producer of Midsomer Murders which began on ITV in 1997, described the show as the "last bastion of Englishness" and said it "wouldn't work" if ethnic minorities appeared on screen.
>
> The programme's production company All3Media, which launched an investigation into his comments in an interview with the Radio Times earlier this month, said True-May had been "reinstated" as producer of the show.
>
> But ITV said it understood True-May would step down from his role at the end of the current production run.
>
> An ITV spokesman said: "We welcome the apology from Brian True-May and understand that he will step down from his role on Midsomer Murders at the end of the current production run."
>
> True-May told last week's edition of Radio Times: "We just don't have ethnic minorities involved. Because it wouldn't be the English village with them. It just wouldn't work."
>
> "Suddenly we might be in Slough. Ironically, Causton (one of the main centers of population in the show) is supposed to be Slough. And if you went into Slough you wouldn't see a white face there.
>
> 'We're the last bastion of Englishness and I want to keep it that way."

> ITV said at the time that it was "shocked and appalled" at the sentiments which were "absolutely not shared by anyone at ITV."[1071]

Like a "class enemy" in Mao's China, Brian True-May had to confess guilt and express contrition but was nonetheless purged.

Of course, Doctor Seuss is a "racist" whose books are purged:

> *Six Dr. Seuss books—including* And to Think That I Saw It on Mulberry Street *and* If I Ran the Zoo—*will stop being published because of racist and insensitive imagery, the business that preserves and protects the author's legacy said Tuesday.*
>
> *"These books portray people in ways that are hurtful and wrong," Dr. Seuss Enterprises told* The Associated Press *in a statement that coincided with the late author and illustrator's birthday.*
>
> *"Ceasing sales of these books is only part of our commitment and our broader plan to ensure Dr. Seuss Enterprises' catalogue represents and supports all communities and families," it said.*
>
> *The other books affected are* McElligot's Pool, On Beyond Zebra!, Scrambled Eggs Super!, *and* The Cat's Quizzer.[1072]

Moreover, Shakespeare is a "racist" and a misogynist—a fascist all-rounder—who should not be taught in schools:

> *William Shakespeare, thou hast been getting canceled.*
>
> *An increasing number of woke teachers are refusing to study the Bard—accusing his classic works of promoting "misogyny, racism, homophobia, classism, anti-Semitism, and misogynoir."*
>
> *A slew of English literature teachers told the School Library Journal (SLJ) how they were ditching the likes of "Hamlet," "Macbeth," and "Romeo and Juliet" to instead "make room for modern, diverse, and inclusive voices."*
>
> *"Shakespeare was a tool used to 'civilize' Black and brown people in England's empire," insisted Shakespeare scholar Ayanna Thompson, a professor of English at Arizona State University.*

[1071] Plunkett, "Midsomer Murders Creator To Step Down."
[1072] Pratt, "Six Dr Seuss Books Won't Be Published."

> Teachers also need to "challenge the whiteness" of the assumption that Shakespeare's works are "universal," insisted Jeffrey Austin, who is head of a Michigan high school's English literature department.
>
> Former Washington state public school teacher Claire Bruncke told SLJ she banished the Bard from her classroom to "stray from centering the narrative of white, cisgender, heterosexual men."[1073]

Is there anyone or anything other than Europhobic street mobs and compliant local politicians behind the erasure of the historic monuments? One finds the putrescent hand of oligarchy funding and pushing the crusade. Rajiv J. Shah, director of the Rockefeller Foundation, boasted of the role of the Foundation in *starting the process* in 2017 for the erasure of monuments to heroic Americans:

> *A few months after I started at the Rockefeller Foundation in March 2017, I was in New Orleans where I met Mayor Mitch Landrieu. We talked about how New Orleans, like many cities around the country, was not only plagued by systemic racism and violence but also stained by monuments to the Confederacy. Mayor Landrieu asked that The Rockefeller Foundation provide a grant to help take down four Confederate monuments, including a towering statue of Robert E Lee.*
>
> *…So, when I woke up in New Orleans the next morning, I went for a short jog to see the statue of Lee, which had stood cross-armed and defiant since 1884.*
>
> *As I stood there in the shadows of both the Confederacy and my own experience, I decided that I wanted to do what I could to ensure children in New Orleans no longer had to walk to school under the watchful eye of a Confederate general. I wanted to use the newfound authority in my role to make a statement. So, Rockefeller made the grant—and one month later to the day the statues came down.*
>
> *From that day forward, our country engaged in a debate about monuments and statues—and other communities followed New Orleans' lead.*[1074]

[1073] Brown, "William Shakespeare Ditched."
[1074] "Remarks by Rajiv J. Shah."

Other statues that were eliminated were those of Confederate President Jefferson Davis, General P.G.T. Beauregard, and a monument to the Crescent City White League—several thousand Confederate army veterans, who for three days in 1874 overthrew the Reconstruction era Louisiana government, then based in New Orleans, and its integrated police force. Thus, a monument honoring the veterans of a heroic fight against a corrupt and tyrannical government was obliterated.[1075]

In 2020 the Andrew W. Mellon Foundation pledged $250,000,000 over five years to "help *reimagine* the country's approach to monuments and memorials, in an effort to better reflect the nation's diversity and highlight buried or marginalized stories."

> *The Monuments Project, the largest initiative in the foundation's 50-year history, will support the creation of new monuments, as well as the relocation or rethinking of existing ones.*
>
> *And it defines "monument" broadly to include not just memorials, statues and markers but also "storytelling spaces," as the foundation puts it, like museums and art installations.*[1076]

Among the eleven trustees of the Mellon Foundation at least four are drawn from the oligarchy: Kathryn A. Hall, Chair, Founder and Co-Chair, Hall Capital Partners LLC; Katherine G. Farley, Former Senior Managing Director, Tishman Speyer; Joshua S. Friedman, Co-Founder, Co-Chairman and Co-Chief Executive Officer, Canyon Partners, LLC; Kelly Granat, Managing Director and Portfolio Manager, Lone Pine Capital.[1077]

Across Britain monuments reflecting anything of Britain's imperial heritage are being removed.

Statues, busts and the name of Sir John Cass, a primary figure in the Royal African Company, have been removed from various institutions. He had been prominent in establishing schools and his legacy continues, but the Cass Foundation changed its name to the Portal Trust to purge itself of the memory of its founder.

The Imperial College London has stopped using its Latin motto, which can be translated as "scientific knowledge, the crowning glory and the safeguard of the empire," because of the imperial reference.

University of Liverpool renamed Gladstone Hall.

[1075] Hedin, "Fiscal Sponsor's Bold Role."
[1076] Schuessler, "Mellon Foundation to Spend."
[1077] "Trustees," Andrew W. Mellon Foundation.

Four streets—John Hawkins Square in Plymouth, and in London, Havelock Road, Black Boy Lane and Cassland Road Gardens—are being renamed. Councils across Scotland, England, and Wales are actively consulting on a further 21 streets.

Statues have been removed from two schools in England, six have changed their names because of links to slavery and colonialism, while seven others have removed "inappropriate" house names within schools.

There are also audits and reviews under way into monuments and landmarks across the country.

In November, the Welsh government identified 209 monuments, buildings or street names linked with slavery. The first minister, Mark Drakeford, said the audit was part of "a much bigger piece of work" that would consider how the nation moves forward.[1078]

Boy Scout founder Baden Powell's statue has been "boarded up," after threats of vandalism.[1079] Campaigns are afoot to erase the memory of other British heroes, such as Cecil Rhodes, Sir Francis Drake, Robert Clive, Robert Peel... Hamlet has been given a black face and lives in West Africa,[1080] God is a Black man.[1081] Cinderella has become Black, the Prince is a Filipino, the Queen is Black, and the King European.[1082]

Anne Boleyn is portrayed by "a woman of color," and it could only be a Black woman who could object to this *cultural appropriation* in the public arena.

Last fall, UK broadcaster Channel 5 announced that Jodie Turner Smith, a Black woman and star in comedy-thriller "Queen & Slim," would play Anne Boleyn, the second, doomed wife of Henry VIII, in an upcoming historical drama series called "Anne Boleyn." Smith's casting and her acting have been widely praised, but of course, that hasn't stopped an onslaught of racist backlash in response to her playing a white, English queen from the 16th century.

This week, a new voice entered the chat on Smith's casting, as conservative firebrand Candace Owens weighed in via tweet.

[1078] Mohdin and Storer, "Tributes to Slave Traders."
[1079] "Poole's Baden-Powell Statue."
[1080] Papaa Esideu, see "The First Black Actor to Play Hamlet."
[1081] Morgan Freeman.
[1082] *Cinderella*, Disney, 1997.

"I'm actually totally fine with Jodie Turner playing the role of Anne Boleyn so long as the radical left promises to keep their mouth shut if in the future Henry Caville [sic] is selected to play Barack Obama and Rachel McAdams can play Michelle," Owens wrote. "Not double standards- K?"[1083]

But to the *avant garde* culture-critics a Black playing a famous White character is not the same as a White playing a Black figure. Not at all, because Whites will forever have to atone for millennia of "racism." "People of color" thereby have *carte blanch* to denigrate, dispossess, and culturally appropriate a "Whiteness" that we are assured is nothing but a *social construct* quite recently invented by a ruling class to enslave that very tangible race called "people of color." Writes an Asian feminist "with a passion for movement journalism," scapegoating the mass of Whites who have never had a part of any "White supremacist power structures," much less the entertainment industry whose dominant ethnicity seldom identifies as "White"[1084]:

> *Owens, as usual, has remarkably missed the point, here, which is that people of color playing white historical figures or famous people isn't the same thing as white people playing people of color. The former poses a meaningful challenge to white supremacist power structures, and helps begin to make up for years of entertainment industry whitewashing—the latter simply builds upon said entertainment industry whitewashing. Very different things.*[1085]

Returning to New Zealand, indicative of the fanaticism and the extent to which Europhobia aims to expunge every vestige, every memory of *Homo Europaeus*, being largely enacted by *oikophobes* in influence, there is an intent to change the name of New Zealand's nation football team, the All Whites. A news report provides the background:

> *The All Whites could be no more.*
> *New Zealand Football (NZF) are contemplating dropping the All Whites moniker for the men's national team.*

[1083] Cheung, "Candace Owens: If a Black Woman."
[1084] Gabler, *An Empire of Their Own.*
[1085] Cheung, "Candace Owens: If a Black Woman."

> *The potential change is part of a wider process NZF is going through to ensure they are up to the mark when it comes to cultural inclusivity.*
>
> *It comes on the back of the heightened worldwide awareness around racism and racial inequality, and the name's potentially racist connotations, and RNZ [Radio New Zealand] understands the national body began gauging feedback on the potential change more than six months ago.*
>
> *NZF chief executive Andrew Pragnell declined an interview, with the organisation instead issuing a short statement.*
>
> *"As with many other national bodies, New Zealand Football is on a journey around cultural inclusivity and respecting the principles of Te Tiriti o Waitangi."*
>
> *"As part of our Delivery and Sustainability Project announced last year, we are in the process of working with stakeholders across the game, as well as people from outside football, looking at all areas of the organisation to make sure they are fit for purpose in 2021 and beyond."*
>
> *"It is too early in the process to speak about any outcomes but this is an important piece of work as we strive to be the most inclusive sport in Aotearoa."*
>
> *The All Whites name came about during the team's qualifying run ahead of the 1982 World Cup in Spain.*[1086]

Notice that the name "New Zealand" is not even used. This is increasingly common especially from the news media and government departments. The name is being gradually changed to Aotearoa—now often provisionally called Aotearoa-New Zealand—without any referendum or formal declaration, just as Rhodesia became Zimbabwe-Rhodesia in transition, and finally Zimbabwe. Note how the push for a name change is being undertaken as part of world-wide "inclusivity," which is a euphemism for the expurgation of any and all things European. The very color *white* is offensive because it might suggest a certain "race." As in many issues in New Zealand the name change will be looked at as a double standard, since not only is the national rugby team named the All Blacks, but that in addition there is the race-selected "Maori All Blacks."

The offensiveness of the color "white" was mooted in 2015 by an "activist and writer" ("activist" generally being a euphemism for an adherent of the psycho-left) Mara Weiss, an American import, writing:

[1086] "Football: No More All Whites?"

> *New Zealand does not consider itself to be racist. But what we don't seem to understand is that the act of choosing that name was an act of **passive racism**. "Whites" is a term that has always been used to mean "white people," especially in the context of segregated societies like apartheid South Africa and the southern United States. "All-Whites" sounds uncomfortably like a sign over a door inscribed "Whites Only." As an American living in New Zealand it is hard for me to understand why the colour of the uniform was so important and how the name ever got approved in the first place.*[1087]

The name is an example of "passive racism." If something that even vaguely suggests by way of word association the *European* is not flagrant "racism," then it is "passive racism," "implicit racism," "unconscious bias." With the name Mara Weiss (Mara: Hebrew = "bitter") could it be that she is expressing another form of "passive racism"?

The obliteration of all things "White," all things European, suggests a fanaticism no less implicit in character than that of *jihadists* who tear down the monuments of the ancient past in Egypt, Iraq, and Afghanistan; of Mao's Cultural Revolution that sought out for destruction all things Confucian, of the Bolsheviks who exploded the Orthodox Cathedrals, and the Jacobins who expunged Catholicism from France.

[1087] "Guest Blog: Mara Weiss." Emphasis added.

"Taking the Knee": Reintegrative Shaming

"The white race is the cancer of human history; it is the white race and it alone."

Martin Duberman (1967)[1088]

What more dramatic representation of European self-degradation do we need than the recent manifestation of "taking the knee"? The action is one of subservience, denigration, enslavement, shame, humiliation, of *wakiinama*, of *kau tau*, of *sajdah*, of *ukukhothamela*... What more do we need to show in this epoch of putrescent decay that *Homo Europaeus* is anything other than humiliated and defeated? It is the perfect gesture of the PTBO "snowflake," of the *oikophobe* and *xenophile*. It is the fantasy of the sick who thrill at the prospect of European extinction; of their own humiliation and extinction. Bow before the colored world, White man, bend your knee, and then bend your head for the final death blow. Exalt in the blood of Natasha Glenny, while wailing over the death of George Floyd.

On the origins of "taking the knee," the scribbling class explains with the enthusiasm of a titillated masochist that has become the new "normal":

> *Taking the knee originates from the US. The anti-racism protest was first performed by American footballer Colin Kaepernick, who took the knee during the national anthem before a match in 2016. He said he could not stand to show pride in the flag of a country that oppressed black people.*
>
> *"After hours of careful consideration, and even a visit from Nate Boyer, a retired Green Beret and former NFL player, we came to the conclusion that we should kneel, rather than sit...during the anthem, as a peaceful protest," said Eric Reid, a*

[1088] Duberman, "What's Happening to America?" 57-58.

US football player who adopted the protest. "We chose to kneel because it's a respectful gesture. I remember thinking our posture was like a flag flown at half-mast to mark a tragedy."

The statement has become a prominent symbol in sport and during anti-racism protests in the UK and abroad. It came to wider prominence during the Black Lives Matter demonstrations of 2020 following the murder of George Floyd.[1089]

George Floyd has become a new saint for Europhobia, the martyr crucified by "White racism" and "White supremacy." He joins Martin King and Nelson Mandela, and one day might be part of a pantheon for a new world religion. Given that Mandela was deified in honor of his role in planning the death of White South Africans, it is consistent that George Floyd would be sanctified, as it is criminals from the category of "persons of color" who are the heroes of this epoch, where once there were those of the *Iliad* and the *Sagas*; of Rorke's Drift, Roland, The Alamo, Thermopylae, and Stamford Bridge. Instead we are told of the Song of Floyd, the Saga of Mandela, and the Odyssey of King. That the sanctification of petty thug George Floyd and terrorist organizer Mandela become important to the present "world historical narrative" and a new and enforced code of morality means that *Homo Europaeus* is fit only for enslavement and ultimate extinction, and the deaths of Europeans by black and brown criminals do not matter. They are of no account. The genocide of the Afrikaner is a "far right conspiracy theory."

White individuals might aspire to joining the sanctified if they are killed while in the process of trying to assault other Whites: hence the sanctification of Heather Heyer at Charlottesville in 2017,[1090] and Blair Peach at Southall, London in 1979, both praised eternally, with memorials erected for their roles in far-left violent confrontations against legal political events by pro-White groups.

Taking the knee is an assertion that one accepts the shame and humiliation of "being White," and is trying to make amends for it. "Shaming" is an important method of social control. In a normal society a

---

[1089] Butterworth, "What Is the History of Taking the Knee?"

[1090] A cogent comment on this, states: "Now comes the trial of James Alex Fields, who came under attack by Antifa as he was trying to find his way out of Charlottesville, which was a city unfamiliar to him. A leader in a Marxist group that likes to portray themselves as "good ol' boys" or Southern rednecks, pointed a rifle at Fields. Fields turned away from this hick Marxist leader on to a one-way road. On that road, his car was attacked by bat-swinging Antifa members. The crash happened because Fields didn't see the stopped cars ahead of him because his view of them were blocked by massed Antifa, who were still illegally gathered in the city. (It is also possible that for a moment Fields wasn't looking where he was going.)" Jenab6, "The James Alex Fields Chapter."

feeling of shame prevents the individual from assuming actions beyond the norms long established to maintain a healthy social organism. There are taboos, customs and derivative laws. In the modern dysfunctional society, shame is used to impose conformity in the pursuit of the destruction of *Homo Europaeus* and the creation of a "new world order" that is not encumbered by traditional cultures. From a sociological and anthological perspective:

> ...*shame focuses on collective guilt as a consequence of some group act or historical event. It is the shared outcome or identity of such actions, which has both personal and group consequences, that create collective guilt. This condition influences both a personal and group identity and shapes how others identify and act with and around them. At times, collective shame may be self-generated. Acting in some form of collective misconduct may result in one's understanding of the extreme inappropriateness of their actions, recognition of which is most often based upon their own moral standards. However, in most instances of collective shame, it is not self-actualization that labels a group's action as shameful, it is the evaluation of others that produces that label.*[1091]

The "collective guilt" of *Homo Europeaeus*, symbolized by "taking the knee" is a ritual of self-humiliation, when the European sees himself and is seen by others as humiliated in defeat. He is told that he is the "cancer of the world" and must atone. He performs an act of submission. Sociologists Bates and LaBrecque, in a paper on the sociology of shaming, cite the example of "Southern Shame" that is particularly apt for our subject:

> ...*Many southerners have had to deal with the stigma associated with slavery and racial discrimination in the South. Though bigotry and racial hatred knew no geographic boundaries in America, as exemplified by race riots, anti-busing actions and open discrimination in numerous non-south communities, the former Confederate states have born the collective stigma of racial injustice. For example, the actions of the head of the Alabama Department of Public Safety, Bull Connor in unleashing police dogs on Catholic nuns, African American veterans and*

[1091] Bates and LaBrecque,"The Sociology of Shaming," 5.

> others in the Selma to Birmingham civil rights march in 1968 helped to transform a protest into a symbolic moral crusade which labeled southerners as collectively shame-worthy. Thus, a shared sense of shame is an on-going stigma that most southerners have to address as part of their regional identity.[1092]

"Shame" for slavery, segregation, and "White supremacy" have been instilled into generations of Southerners by the manipulation of history. Shame premises the Southerners "collective regional identity." The pulling down of Southern monuments and the elimination of the Southern flag become further acts of ritual atonement.

Bates and LaBrecque consider that methods by which social agendas become the new normal by challenging tradition as a source of "shame." As we have seen the efficacy of this challenge is enabled by such social agendas being sponsored by interests that are at least as powerful, and one might argue more so, than the state. The authors unwittingly describe the methods by which the New Left and civil rights movements of prior generations, and today's BLM, Antifa, et al., are utilized by interests above the state who aim to redirect society. Shaming is used not to maintain traditional values, but to destroy them.

> Whereas traditional shaming was designed to reinforce existing social norms and values, modern shaming has emerged as a tool for political and social change. In social movements such as the civil rights, women's and gender acceptance movements, astute students of attitude and social change initially challenged the traditional positions as antiquated and immoral. A constant barrage of information and examples of how the majority position violates higher standards of morality and social justice contributes to a less clearly defined and supported public standard. The tactic of nonviolent protest served both Ghandi and Martin Luther King Jr. well by positioning their causes as the higher moral ground (Miller, 1985). The protests and the harsh reactions by agents of the status-quo further contributed to the delegitimizing of the moral standards of the dominant society.[1093]

[1092] Ibid., 5.
[1093] Ibid., 7.

The authors refer to *"A constant barrage of information and examples of how the majority position violates higher standards of morality and social justice."* Such a "constant barrage" does not emanate from street level "activists," but from what is often part of the so-called "Establishment" that such "activists" imagine they are resisting: globalist news and digital media, CBS, NBC, *Washington Post*, *New York Times*, Facebook, Rockefeller Foundation, Ford Foundation, Open Society, Hollywood, MTV, Twitter, Amazon.com, Google, and others around the world, that no longer even act subtlety in suppressing views that are oppositional.

> *Similar actions by the Women's and Gay Rights Movements created environments conducive of social change. Encouraging unreasonable responses by agents of social control was a vital component of shaming a control group and questioning their legitimacy in the eyes of the larger society. Selma, the Chicago Democratic Convention and the Stone Wall Bar became symbols of society's intolerance and a source of shame for the status-quo which were effectively transformed into effective means for social change.*[1094]

"The Women's and Gay Rights Movements" and the Black civil rights operations mentioned by the authors, could not have achieved anything without the sponsorship of Rockefeller, et al.[1095]

> *In the case of these successful social movements, reintegrative shaming was employed as an effective mechanism of encouraging the society to largely accept new definitions morality or correctness. In these instances, the movement's actions created environments conducive to reintegrative shaming. That is, the movements sought change, but they wanted their opposition to accept the change and establish a new moral order that would shape future interactions.*[1096]

The moral landscape is captured by slogans emanating from the central theme of "human rights," and what was in former generations regarded as

---

[1094] Ibid., 7.
[1095] For detailed documentation on how the oligarchs have backed left movements, see: Bolton, *Revolution from Above*; and *The Perversion of Normality*.
[1096] Bates and LaBrecque, "The Sociology of Shaming," 7.

deviant or absurd has become the new normality through the use of "reintegrative shaming."

The bottom line is that the mere existence of *Homo Europaeus* is a "crime against humanity," "humanity" being defined solely in terms of "persons of color." *Homo Europaeus* is guilty by mere existence. Hence, White deaths are of no consequence, while the death of a single Black criminal is a thing of eternal lamentation. *Homo Europaeus* bends his knee in an induced humiliation and guilt, a "collective shaming," while his symbols and monuments are toppled, his kin assaulted and killed, as he sings in praise of his own obliteration.

Conclusion

"By destroying traditional social habits of the people, by dissolving their natural collective consciousness into individual constituents, by licensing the opinions of the most foolish, by substituting instruction for education, by encouraging cleverness rather than wisdom, the upstart rather than the qualified, by fostering the notion of getting on to which the alternative is a hopeless apathy, liberalism can prepare the way for that which is its own negation: the artificial, mechanized or brutalized control, which is a desperate remedy for its chaos."

T. S. Eliot (1939)[1097]

E pluribus unum
Novus ordo seclorum

These are the dictums that have appeared on the Great Seal of the USA since the eighteenth century revolutionary epoch. Ever since Thomas Jefferson and his party of Republican-Democrats enthused over France's Jacobins and wished to emulate their revolution with a second of their own, there has been a struggle for the control of the USA between those holding to the legacy of George Washington and Alexander Hamilton, and those who remain zealots for the world revolutionary mission enunciated by Jefferson's party.[1098] The dominant party is, apart from occasional *interregna* such as that of Trump (who failed to effect a national populist revolution), that of Jefferson's American Jacobins, the so-called *Liberal Establishment*, which includes most of the USA's oligarchy.

While *E puribus unum* is indeed a laudable aim for what was to be forged into a nation from a multiplicity of often contending states, reflecting the tradition of the American nationalism of Washington and

---

[1097] Eliot, *The Idea of a Christian Society*, 16-17.
[1098] For the struggle between the Washington/Hamilton Federalist Party and Jefferson's Jacobin Republican-Democrats see: Ron Chernow.

Hamilton, when combined with the globalizing slogan, *Novus ordo seclorum*, what confronts the world is precisely what Washington and Hamilton rejected: the USA as the citadel of world revolution which, like Jacobin France and Bolshevik Russia, attempts to remake the world in its own image: *Novus ordo seclorum* in the name of democracy and of *la droit humain*.

E pluribus unum—"Out of Many, One"—behind the banner of equality, democracy, and human rights for all races and nations, as Woodrow Wilson enunciated in his *Fourteen Points*,[1099] and Franklin Roosevelt in the *Atlantic Charter*,[1100] and thereafter the *UN Charter*[1101] and a thousand and one declarations and treaties stemming therefrom, liberalism steamrolls over all, and by this leveling process, what emerges from "many" is "one" universal mono-world—cynically undertaken in the name of "diversity."

Homo Europaeus is regarded as *passé* in this globalization process working towards *Homo Economicus*.[1102] What is not yet realized is that this process is no respecter of any race. The "people of color" who form a broad coalition based on a recent social construct to serve as a battering ram against the European, are being used as a dissolving agent to obliterate all races and reformulate a transhuman, amorphous mass whose identity will be as fluid as the 120-plus gender variations that are now said to exist: *from many, one*. In the quest for a multiplicity of identities, what will emerge from the chaos is a rootless new life form that can be molded as the requirements of global business require, on the assumption that the human mind is *tabula rasa*. A multiplicity of identities will render meaningless any depth of authentic identity, and from out of this dissolutive process humanity will be remolded into a nebulous automaton.

Since the doctrine of globalists—whether of the oligarchic or Marxist varieties—is based on the assumption that humans can be shaped by the forces of production, those who seek this Brave New World are confident that new managerial, technocratic, and menial classes can be formed into what has been called *the global me*, detached from race, gender, ethnicity, faith, culture, family, and homeland.

Typical of Machiavellian plans, such aims require a facade to conceal the real purposes. The doctrine of human rights, under various slogans over the course of several centuries, provides that facade. As Alexander

---

[1099] Wilson, *Fourteen Points*.
[1100] Roosevelt and Churchill, *Atlantic Charter*.
[1101] *United Nations Charter*.
[1102] It is notable that primary to both Wilson's Fourteen Points and Roosevelt's Atlantic Charter is that free trade must be the dominant form of economics over the world.

Hamilton, confronted by these forces of dissolution, warned in the first of *The Federalist Papers*:

> *A dangerous ambition more often lurks behind the spacious mask of zeal for the rights of the people than under the forbidding appearance of zeal for firmness and efficiency of government. History will teach us that the former has been found a much more certain road to the introduction of despotism than the latter, and that of those men who have overturned the liberties of republics, the greatest number have begun their career by paying an obsequious court to the people; commencing demagogues, and ending tyrants.*[1103]

Not since Jacobinism and Bolshevism has the world marched towards such tyranny in the name of equality and human rights, this time not so much reliant—other than as a final recourse—on the guillotine, the bomb, and the gun, but with smiling platitudes buttressed with increasingly draconian laws, in the name of "kindness," "inclusiveness," and "tolerance."

[1103] Hamilton, *The Federalist Papers*, No. 1, (fifth paragraph).

Bibliography

Foreword by Dr. Edward Dutton

Adams, James Eli. *Dandies and Desert Saints: Styles of Victorian Masculinity.* Princeton, NJ: Princeton University Press, 2018.
AntroBlogi. "Pseudotieteellisiä kuvitelmia kansanluonteesta." September 24, 2019. https://antroblogi.fi/2019/09/edward-dutton-ja-pseudotiede/
Benenson, Joyce F. "The development of human female competition: allies and adversaries." *Philosophical Transactions of the Royal Society* B, 368: 2013007920130079, 2013.
Dutton, Edward. *Making Sense of Race.* Whitefish, MT: Washington Summit Publishing, 2020.
Dutton, Edward. *Suomen vaiennettu raiskausepidemia: Miten suomalaiset valjastettiin rakastamaan hyväksikäyttäjiään (The Silent Rape Epidemic: How the Finns Were Groomed to Love Their Abusers).* Translated by Saara Sarvivuori. Oulu: Thomas Edward Press, 2020.
Dutton, Edward. *The Silent Rape Epidemic: How the Finns Were Groomed to Love Their Abusers.* Oulu: Thomas Edward Press, 2019.
Dutton, Edward. *Religion and Intelligence: An Evolutionary Analysis.* London: Ulster Institute for Social Research, 2014.
Dutton, Edward and Rayner-Hilles, J.O.A. *The Past is a Future Country: The Coming Conservative Demographic Revolution.* Exeter: Imprint Academic, 2022.
Dutton, Edward and Lynn, R. "A Negative Flynn Effect in Finland, 1997–2009." *Intelligence,* 41 (2013): 5.
Graham, J., Haidt, J. and Nosek, B. "Liberals and Conservatives Rely on Different Sets of Moral Foundations." *Personality Processes and Individual Differences,* 96 (2009): 1029-1046.
Hammond, R. and Axelrod, R. "The evolution of ethnocentric behaviour." *Journal of Conflict Resolution,* 50 (2006): 1-11.
Kanazawa, Satoshi. *The Intelligence Paradox: Why the Intelligent Choice Isn't Always the Smart One.* Hoboken, NJ: John Wiley and Sons, 2012.
Kirkegaard, Emil. "Mental Illness and the Left." *Mankind Quarterly,* 60 (2020): 487-510.
Lin, C. and Bates, T.C. "Each is to count for one and none for more than one: Predictors of support for economic redistribution." *PsyArXiv.* June 20, 2021. https://doi.org/10.31234/osf.io/3jq4c
Moss, J. and O'Connor, P. "The Dark Triad traits predict authoritarian political correctness and alt-right attitudes0." *Heliyon,* 6(7): e04453. 2020.
Ok, E., Qian, Y, Strejcek, B. and Aquino, K. "Signaling Virtuous Victimhood as Indicators of Dark Triad Personalities." *Journal of Personality and Social Psychology.* 2020. https://doi.org/10.1037/pspp0000329

Rushton, J. Philippe. *Race, Evolution, and Behavior: A Life History Perspective*. New Brunswick, NJ: Transaction Publishing, 1995.
Saini, Angela. *Superior: The Return of Race Science*. London: 4th Estate. 2019.
Suomen Uutiset. "Brittiantropologi Oulun raiskausepidemiasta: Suomalaisia on 'groomattu' rakastamaan hyväksikäyttäjiään." *Suomen Uutiset*, September 16, 2019. https://www.suomenuutiset.fi/brittiantropologi-oulun-raiskausepidemiasta-suomalaisia-groomattu-rakastamaan-hyvaksikayttajiaan/
Verhulst, B., Hatemi, P. and Martin, N. "Corrigendum to 'The nature of the relationship between personality traits and political attitudes.'" *Personality and Individual Differences*, 99 (2016): 378-379.
Waytz, A., Iyer, R., Young, L., Haidt, J. and Graham, J. "Ideological differences in the expanse of the moral circle." *Nature Communications*, 10 (2019): 1-12.

The Tyranny of Human Rights

"2020 Country Reports on Human Rights Practices: Russia." US Department of State. https://www.state.gov/reports/2020-country-reports-on-human-rights-practices/russia/.
Abbott, Catherine. "Communism, Marxism, and Socialism: Radical Politics and Jim Jones." https://jonestown.sdsu.edu/?page_id=64856.
"About the DA." Democracy Alliance. http://democracyalliance.org/about/.
"'Absolutely' Links between European Far-Right and New Zealand Extremists - Patrick Gower." *Newshub*, July 2, 2019.
Adorno, Theodore W., et al. *The Authoritarian Personality*. New York: Harper, 1950.
Aesop. "Washing the Ethiopian White." 600BC.
Alpaugh, Micah. "The Friends of Freedom and Atlantic Democratization." Age of Revolutions, August 6, 2018. https://ageofrevolutions.com/2018/08/06/the-friends-of-freedom-and-atlantic-democratization/.
"American Jewish Congress (AJC)." Stanford University. https://kinginstitute.stanford.edu/encyclopedia/american-jewish-congress-ajc.
ANC Daily News Briefing, June 27, 2001.
"Annual Reports & Finances." The Sentencing Project. https://www.sentencingproject.org/annual-reports-finances/.
"Antoine Lavoisier." Chemeurope.com. https://www.chemeurope.com/en/encyclopedia/Antoine_Lavoisier.html#_note-6/.
"Aotearoa New Zealand's Histories in the New Zealand Curriculum." Ministry of Education, 2021. file:///C:/Users/New%20User/Downloads/CO2716_MOE_Aotearoa_NZ_Histories_A3_FINAL-020%20(1).pdf.
"Aotearoa New Zealand's Histories in Schools and Kura." Ministry of Education, March 6, 2020. https://www.education.govt.nz/our-work/information-releases/issue-specific-releases/nzhistories/.
App, Austin J. *History's Most Terrifying Peace*. Takoma Park, Md.: Boniface Press, 1947.
Applebaum, Anne. "Opinion: How Europe's 'Identitarians' Are Mainstreaming Racism." *The Washington Post*, May 17, 2019. https://www.washingtonpost.com/opinions/global-opinions/how-europes-identitarians-are-mainstreaming-racism/2019/05/17/3c7c9a6e-78da-11e9-b3f5-5673edf2d127_story.html?noredirect=on&utm_term=.2641dfd32252.
Associated Press. "Mortars kill Serb 2 teens in US sector." *Deseret News*, August 17, 1999.

"Auckland Council Must Not Destroy Michael Joseph Savage Memorial." *Scoop Independent News*, June 12, 2020. https://www.scoop.co.nz/stories/AK2006/S00324/auckland-council-must-not-destroy-michael-joseph-savage-memorial.html.

"Australasian Union of Jewish Students." The University of Auckland New Zealand.. https://auckland.campuslabs.com/engage/organization/australasian-union-of-jewish-students.

Bacque, James. *Crimes and Mercies: The Fate of German Civilians Under Allied Occupation 1944–1950.* London: Little, Brown, 1997.

Bacque, James. *Other Losses: An Investigation into the Mass Deaths of German Prisoners at the Hands of French and Americans After World War II.* Toronto: Stoddard Publishing, 1989.

Baek, Buhm S. "Economic Sanctions Against Human Rights Violations." Cornell Law School Inter-University Graduate Student Conference Papers, April 14, 2008. https://scholarship.law.cornell.edu/cgi/viewcontent.cgi?article=1039&context=lps_cl acp.jkkukjnv.

"Baker, Ella Josephine." Stanford University. https://kinginstitute.stanford.edu/encyclopedia/baker-ella-josephine.

Bandele, Asha. "A Message From Our Partners at the Drug Policy Alliance." Center for Law and Justice, July 7, 2016. http://www.cflj.org/6182-2/.

Barnett, Clive. "The limits of media democratization in South Africa: politics, privatization and regulation." *Media, Culture & Society* 21, 5 (September 1999): 649-671. https://journals.sagepub.com/doi/10.1177/016344399021005004.

Barruel, Abbé A. *Memoirs Illustrating the History of Jacobinism.* London, 1798.

Bates, Rodger A. and Bryan LaBrecque, "The Sociology of Shaming." *The Journal of Public and Professional Sociology*, Vol. 12, No. 1, July 2020. https://digitalcommons.kennesaw.edu/jpps/vol12/iss1/3/.

BBC News. "James Watson: Scientist loses titles after claims over race." *BBC News*, January 13, 2019. https://www.bbc.com/news/world-us-canada-46856779.

BBC News. "Rule, Britannia! will be sung on Last Night of the Proms after BBC U-Turn." *BBC News*, September 2, 2020. https://www.bbc.com/news/entertainment-arts-53998584.

"Beacon Project Shines Light on Moscow's Meddling." IRI International Republican Institute, April 6, 2016. https://www.iri.org/web-story/beacon-project-shines-light-moscows-meddling.

Becraft, Andrew, David Brougham, Leoni Freeman, Theresa Gattung. *The Big Questions What is New Zealand's Future?* Penguin Books, 2018.

Belloc, Hilaire. *Europe and the Faith.* London: Black House Publishing, 2012 [1920].

Benner, Chris and Manuel Pastor. "Inclusive Economy Indicators. Framework and Indicator Recommendations." The Rockefeller Foundation, December 2016. https://www.rockefellerfoundation.org/wp-content/uploads/Inclusive-Economies-Indicators-Full-Report-DEC6.pdf.

Benson, Ivor. *This Worldwide Conspiracy.* Melbourne: New Times Ltd., 1972.

Benson, Ivor. *The Struggle for Africa: Undeclared War.* Perth: Australian League of Rights, 1978.

Bernerth, Jeremy. B. "You're Offended, I'm Offended! An Empirical Study of the Proclivity to Be Offended and What It Says About Employees' Attitudes and Behaviours." *Journal of Business Research*, No. 116, August 2020. https://www.sciencedirect.com/science/article/pii/S0148296320303416.

Binder, David. "In Yugoslavia, rising ethnic strife brings fears of worse civil conflict." *The New York Times,* November 1, 1987.

Bing, Ian. "Submission Made to the Royal Commission on Social Policy re Chinese in New Zealand." MS-Papers 10367. National Library of New Zealand. March 1989. https://tiaki.natlib.govt.nz/#details=ecatalogue.17316.

Bird, Mike. "Germany's History Explains Why It's So Accepting of Refugees – and Why It Wants Austerity for Greece." Business Insider Australia, September 10, 2015. https://www.businessinsider.com.au/germanys-history-explains-why-its-so-accepting-of-refugees-and-why-it-wants-austerity-for-greece-2015-9.

Bizot, Francois. *The Gate*. Vintage, 2004.

Blau, Uri. "Israel Black Hole in Kosovo." Haaretz, August 12, 2011. https://www.haaretz.com/1.5045281.

Block, Donna. "An Aristocrat of Africa." *Mail & Guardian*, November 26, 1999. https://allafrica.com/stories/199911260104.html

Bloomberg. "Renowned Business Leaders Welcome Landmark Agreement on International Migration." *Bloomberg*, September 26, 2018. https://gbf.bloomberg.org/news/renowned-business-leaders-welcome-landmark-agreement-international-migration/.

Boast, Hannah. "Briefing Note: Update on Aotearoa New Zealand's Histories Curriculum Changes." Ministry of Education, August 23, 2019. https://assets.education.govt.nz/public/Uploads/R-51-1226694-BN-Hipkins-Redacted.pdf.

de Boer, Dieuwe. "In Memory of Jesse Anderson 1994–2019." Right Minds NZ, March 9, 2019. https://www.rightminds.nz/articles/memory-jesse-anderson-1994-2019.

Bolton, Kerry R. "Aotearoa New Zealand Histories." *The Euroepan New Zealander*, January 3, 2021. https://theeuropeannewzealander.net/2021/01/03/aotearoa-new-zealand-histories/.

Bolton, Kerry R. *Babel Inc: Multiculturalism, Globalisation and the New World Order*. London: Black House Publishing, 2013.

Bolton, Kerry R. *The Banking Swindle: Money Creation and the State*. Black House Publishing Ltd, 2017.

Bolton, Kerry R. *The Decline and Fall of Civilisations*. London: Black House Publishing, 2017.

Bolton, Kerry R. "Islamophobia: Trojan Horse Amidst the Right." Arktos. https://arktos.com/2019/04/26/islamophobia-trojan-horse-amidst-the-right/

Bolton, Kerry R. "Karl Marx: Profile and Assessment in Troy Southgate (ed.)" *The Dialectics of Dictatorship*. London: Black Front Press, 2020.

Bolton, Kerry R. "NZ in Wake of Mosque Shootings." https://www.kerrybolton.com/new-zealand-in-wake-of-mosque-shootings/.

Bolton, Kerry R. *The Occult and Subversive Movements: Tradition and Counter-Tradition in the Struggle for World Power*. London: Black House Publishing, 2017.

Bolton, Kerry R. *The Parihaka Cult*. London: Black House Publishing, 2012.

Bolton, Kerry R. *The Perversion of Normality: From the Marquis de Sade to Cyborgs*. London: Arktos Media Ltd., 2021.

Bolton, Kerry R. *The Psychotic Left: From Jacobin France to the Occupy Movement*. London: Black House Publishing, 2013.

Bolton, Kerry R. *Revolution from Above*. London: Arktos Media Ltd., 2011.

Bolton, Kerry R. *Stalin: The Enduring Legacy*. London: Black House Publishing, 2012.

Bolton, Kerry R. *Zionism, Islam and the West*. London: Black House Publishing, 2014.

Boyd, E.B. and Rachel Z. Arndt. "Jason Liebman on Creating Space for Digital Activists." Fast Company, April 20, 2011. http://www.fastcompany.com/1747612/jason-liebman-creating-space-digital-activists.

Boyd, Julian P., ed. *The Papers of Thomas Jefferson*. Volume 14. *Thomas Jefferson to John Trumbull*, 14:561. New Jersey: Princeton University Press, 1958.

Brand, Christopher R. "Brief Curriculum Vitae." November 13, 2004. http://bussorah.tripod.com/brandbio.html.

Brayton, Ed. "William Shockley and Free Speech." February 5, 2008. https://www.patheos.com/blogs/dispatches/2008/02/05/william-shockley-and-free-spee/.

Breitbart Tech. "Jack Dorsey, BLM's DeRay Mckesson Claim They Want Twitter To Represent 'Every Voice.'" *Breitbart*, June 2, 2016. http://www.breitbart.com/tech/2016/06/02/jack-dorsey-blms-deray-mckesson-claim-they-want-twitter-to-represent-every-voice/.

"Bringing Citizens Together." IRI International Republican Institute. https://www.iri.org/program/bring-citizens-together.

Brinkley, Douglas. "The Man Who Kept King's Secrets." *Vanity Fair,* January 19, 2014. https://www.vanityfair.com/news/politics/2014/01/clarence-jones-martin-luther-king-jr-secrets.

Broden, Stephen E. "Warning: The Real Power and Purpose Behind the 'Black Lives Matter' Movement." Black Community News, March 4, 201. http://blackcommunitynews.com/the-real-power-and-purpose-behind-black-lives-matter-movement/.

Brookings Institution, International Rescue Committee, and 100 Resilient Cities. "Engaging City Leaders in the Global Compact Process: Recommendations for Action." UNHCR, October 19, 2017. https://www.unhcr.org/events/conferences/5a05aa787/engaging-city-leaders-global-compact-process-recommendations-action.html.

Brown, Lee. "William Shakespeare Ditched by Woke Teachers Over 'Misogyny, Racism'." New York Post, February 16, 2021. https://nypost.com/2021/02/16/shakespeare-ditched-by-woke-teachers-over-misogyny-racism/.

Brown, Steven. "What Can We Do To Prevent the Next Killing?" July 7, 2016. http://www.urban.org/urban-wire/what-can-we-do-prevent-next-killing.

Browning, Robert. "The Pied Piper of Hamelin."1842.

Bullert, Gary. "Franz Boas as Citizen-Scientist: Gramscian-Marxist Influence on American Anthropology." *Journal of Social, Political and Economic Studies*, July 1, 2009. https://www.semanticscholar.org/paper/Franz-Boas-as-Citizen-Scientist%3A-Gramscian-Marxist-Bullert/0bb5480f5643925eff373bef85fc2a1a4eb1c1fa.

Burke, Edmund. *Reflections on the Revolution in France*. 1790. https://socialsciences.mcmaster.ca/econ/ugcm/3ll3/burke/revfrance.pdf.

Burnett, Thom and Alex Games. *Who Really Runs the World? The War Between Globalization and Democracy*. London: Collins and Brown, 2005.

Bush, George H. W. *Address Before a Joint Session of the Congress on the State of the Union*. January 29, 1991. https://www.govinfo.gov/content/pkg/PPP-1991-book1/pdf/PPP-1991-book1-doc-pg74.pdf.

Bush, George H. W. *Address Before a Joint Session of the Congress on the Cessation of the Persian Gulf Conflict*. March 6, 1991. https://www.govinfo.gov/content/pkg/PPP-1991-book1/pdf/PPP-1991-book1-doc-pg218-3.pdf.

Butterworth, Benjamin. "What Is the History of Taking the Knee? Origins of the Aanti-Racism Gesture – and Why England Players Do It." July 14, 202. https://inews.co.uk/news/uk/taking-the-knee-what-history-orgin-meaning-why-england-players-explained-1103131.

"Cabinet Paper Material Proactive Release." Ministry of Education, September 9, 2019. https://www.education.govt.nz/assets/Documents/Ministry/Information-releases/2019-releases/NZ-Histories/R2-1-124-125-Redacted.pdf.

Campbell, Denis. "NHS Staff Warned to Hide ID After Spate of Targeted Muggings." *The Guardian*, March 25, 2020. https://www.theguardian.com/world/2020/mar/25/nhs-staff-warned-to-hide-id-after-spate-of-targeted-muggings.
Carlyle, Thomas. *The French Revolution: A History*. 1837.
Carlyle, Thomas. *Past and Present*. 1843.
Carnegie, Andrew. "The Gospel of Wealth." 1889.
Carol, Steven. *From Jerusalem to the Lion of Judah & Beyond: Israel's Foreign Policy in East Africa*. Bloomington, iUniverse Inc., 2012.
Carroll, Lewis. *Through the Looking Glass*. 1871.
CBC Radio, "Why the US State Department is backing hip hop diplomacy." *CBC Radio*, January 24, 2020; https://www.cbc.ca/radio/thecurrent/the-current-for-jan-24-2020-1.5438975/why-the-u-s-state-department-is-backing-hip-hop-diplomacy-1.5439554.
Cerulus, Laurens and Eline Schaart. "How the UN Migration Pact Got Trolled." *Politico*, March 3, 2019. https://www.politico.eu/article/united-nations-migration-pact-how-got-trolled/.
Chang, Jeff. "It's a Hip-Hop World." *Foreign Policy*, October 12, 2009. https://foreignpolicy.com/2009/10/12/its-a-hip-hop-world.
Chang, Jeff. *Total Chaos: The Art and Aesthetics of Hip-Hop*. New York: Basic Civitas Books, 2007.
Chang, Jung and Jon Halliday. *Mao: The Unknown Story*. Jonathan Cape, 2005.
Charter of Fundamental Rights of the European Union. Official Journal of the European Union, December 7, 2000. https://eur-lex.europa.eu/legal-content/EN/TXT/?uri=CELEX:12012P/TXT.
Chernow, Ron. *Alexander Hamilton*. Penguin, 2004.
Chesterton, A. K. *Candour* (Liss, England) July 22, 1960.
Cheung, Kylie. "Candace Owens: If a Black Woman Can Play Anne Boleyn Then a White Man Should Play Obama." Salon, June 4, 2021 https://www.salon.com/2021/06/04/candace-owens-anne-boleyn-black-obama-white/.
China Labor Watch. "Made in China: The Sweatshop Behind the Bratz." *China Labor Watch*, December 21, 2006. https://chinalaborwatch.org/made-in-china-the-sweatshop-behind-the-bratz/.
"Chinese Students To Meet With Police After Rush of 'Predatory Gang' Attacks." *Stuff*, March 30, 2016. https://www.stuff.co.nz/national/crime/78356002/four-attacks-in-a-week-but-international-students-not-being-targeted–police?rm=m.
Chomsky, Noam. *Understanding Power*. New York: The New Press, 2002.
"Christopher Brand: Race, Sex, Psychology and Censorship." http://www.cycad.com/site/Brand/index.html.
Cicero, Marcus T. *De Divinatione*. Loeb Classical Library, 1923.
Cleaver, Pauline. "Aide Memoire New Zealand's Histories in Schools and Kura." Ministry of Education, September 6, 2019. https://www.education.govt.nz/assets/Documents/Ministry/Information-releases/2019-releases/NZ-Histories/R2-2-1204767-AM-Hipkins-Redacted.pdf.
Cleaver, Pauline and Kiritina Johnstone. "Aide Memoire New Zealand's Histories in Schools and Kura." Ministry of Education, September 6, 2019. https://www.education.govt.nz/assets/Uploads/SIGNED-REDACTED-1204768-AM-signed.pdf.
Clements, Kendell, et al. "In Defence of Science." *New Zealand Listener*, July 24, 2021. https://www.fsu.nz/in_defence_of_science_article.

Coates, Ta-Nehisi. "What We Mean When We Say 'Race is a Social Construct.'" *The Atlantic*, May 15, 2013. https://www.theatlantic.com/national/archive/2013/05/what-we-mean-when-we-say-race-is-a-social-construct/275872/.

Cockburn, Patrick. "Criminals 'In Exodus From Cuba': US Fears Castro emptying His Jails—Into Florida." *Independent*, August 28, 1994. https://www.independent.co.uk/news/criminals-exodus-cuba-us-fears-castro-emptying-his-jails-florida-1386288.html.

Collins, Simon. "Residents Share Tales of Terror From Youth Gangs in 'Dead End' Street." NZ Herald, January 31, 2007. https://www.nzherald.co.nz/nz/news/article.cfm?c_id=1&objectid=10421675.

"Confederate and Columbus Statues Toppled by US Protesters BBC News, June 11, 2020. https://www.bbc.com/news/world-us-canada-53005243.

"Constitutional Issues and Human Rights. International Human Rights." Justice.govt.nz. https://www.justice.govt.nz/justice-sector-policy/constitutional-issues-and-human-rights/human-rights/international-human-rights/.

Conway-Smith, Erin. "South African Framers Fearing for Their Lives." The Telegraph, December 1, 2012. http://www.telegraph.co.uk/news/worldnews/africaandindianocean/southafrica/9716539/South-African-farmers-fearing-for-their-lives.html.

"Convention on the Rights of the Child." United Nations Human Rights, September 2, 1990. https://www.ohchr.org/en/professionalinterest/pages/crc.aspx.

Cortwright, David. "Black GI Resistance During the Vietnam War." Vietnam Generation, vol.2, no. 1, GI Resistance: Soldiers and Veterans Against the War. https://digitalcommons.lasalle.edu/cgi/viewcontent.cgi?article=1052&context=vietnamgeneration.

Coudenhove-Kalergi, Richard N. *Pan-Europe*. Vienna: Pan-Europa Verlage, 1923.

Coudenhove-Kalergi, Richard N. "Die Pan-Europäische Bewegung." *Paneuropa* 1, No. 2 (1924).

Coudenhove-Kalergi, Richard N. "Praktischer Idealismus." Wien and Leipzig: Pan Europa Verlag 1925.

Coudenhove-Kalergi, Richard N. "World Organization and Pan-Europe: A Memorial to the League of Nations." LoN, 39/45485/45485. 1925.

Coudenhove-Kalergi, Richard N. *Europa Erwacht!* Zurich/Vienna/Leipzig: Paneuropa Verlag, 1934.

Coudenhove-Kalergi, Richard N. *An Idea Conquers the World*. London: Hutchinson, 1953.

Courtier-Forster, R. "Bolshevism, Reign of Terror at Odessa," *London Times*, December 3, 1919.

Cowper, William. "Charity." 1781.

Crick, Francis. "Letter to John T. Edsall, Fogarty International Center." US National Library of Medicine, Februaty 22, 1971. http://resource.nlm.nih.gov/101584582X196.

Crick, Francis. "Letter to Lord Charles Percy Snow." US National Library of Medicine, April 17, 1969. http://resource.nlm.nih.gov/101584582X19.

Crick, Francis. "Letter to William Shockley." US National Library of Medicine, April 18, 1969. https://collections.nlm.nih.gov/catalog/nlm:nlmuid-101584582X363-doc.

Cropley, Ed. "Winnie Mandela, tarnished 'Mother' of post-apartheid South Africa." *Reuters*, April 3, 2018. https://www.reuters.com/article/us-safrica-winniemandela-idUSKCN1H91A6.

Daalder, Marc. "The Furious World of New Zealand's Far Right Nationalists." The Spinoff, February 2, 2019. https://thespinoff.co.nz/politics/02-02-2019/will-the-far-right-movement-rise-in-new-zealand/.

Dalton, Deron. "The Three Women Behind the Black Lives Matter Movement." Madame Noire, May 4, 2015. http://madamenoire.com/528287/the-three-women-behind-the-black-lives-matter-movement/.

Davies, C. "Downfall of the Devil's Dandy Landlord." *Camden New Journal*, February 20, 2003.

Dawson, Christopher. *The Making of Europe: An Introduction to the History of European Unity*. London: Sheed & Ward, 1946 [1932].

Declaration of the Rights of Man and the Citizen. National Assembly of France, August 26,1789. https://www1.curriculum.edu.au/ddunits/downloads/pdf/dec_of_rights.pdf.

Dell, N. "Can the Army Afford to go Woke, Benign Social Progress or National Security Threat." Knowledge Enabled Army. https://web.archive.org/web/20210702035433/https:/kea-learning.nz/editors-pick/new-zealand-chief-of-army-writing-competition-winner-of-the-new-zealand-defence-force-private-writing-category-can-the-army-afford-to-go-woke-benign-social-progress-or-national-security-threat/.

Devlin, Collette. "National Front Members Chased Away From Parliament." Stuff, October 28, 2017. https://www.stuff.co.nz/national/98328741/national-front-members-chased-away-from-parliament.

Devlin, Collette. "New Zealand Votes for UN Migration Compact after Legal Advice." Stuff, December 19, 2018. https://www.stuff.co.nz/national/politics/109486713/new-zealand-votes-for-un-migration-compact-after-legal-advice.

Díaz del Castillo, Bernal. *The True History of the Conquest of New Spain*. London: Hakluyt Society 1908 [1568].

Dinesen, Peter T., Merlin Schaeffer, and Kim M. Sønderskov. "Ethnic Diversity and Social Trust: A Narrative and Meta-Analytical Review." Research Gate, September 2019. DOI:10.13140/RG.2.2.20314.70081. https://www.researchgate.net/publication/335924797_Ethnic_Diversity_and_Social_Trust_A_Narrative_and_Meta-Analytical_Review.

Dio, Cassius. *Dio's Rome*. Kessinger, 2004.

"DNA Discoverer Apologizes for Racist Remarks." *Fox News*, October 19, 2007. https://www.foxnews.com/story/dna-discoverer-apologizes-for-racist-remarks.

"Dr. Nicholas Kollerstrom." UCL News, April 22, 2008. http://www.ucl.ac.uk/news/news-articles/0804/08042202.

"Dr. Philippe Rushton." Western Social Science Department of Psychology. https://psychology.uwo.ca/people/faculty/remembrance/rushton.html.

"Drug 'Reduces Implicit Racial Bias,' Study Suggests." University of Oxford, March 8, 2012. http://www.ox.ac.uk/news/2012-03-08-drug-reduces-implicit-racial-bias-study-suggests.

Drury, Abdullah. "Mazharbeg: An Albanian Exile." Waikato Islamic Studies Review, June 2020, vol. 6, no. 1. https://www.waikato.ac.nz/fass/UWISG/review/Waikato-Islamic-Studies-Review-Vol-6-No-1.pdf.

Dryden, John. *The Conquest of Granada of the Spaniards in two parts: acted at the Theatre Royall.* 1672. http://name.umdl.umich.edu/a36610.0001.001.

Duberman, Martin, et al. "What's Happening to America?" A Symposium. *Partisan Review* 34, no. 1, 1967. http://archives.bu.edu/collections/partisan-review/search/detail?id=326075.

Duncan, Phil. "First Labour Government Wanted 'Aryan' Immigrants not Jewish Refugees From the Nazis." Redline Contemporary Marxist Analysis, January 26, 2016. https://rdln.wordpress.com/2016/01/26/first-labour-government-wanted-aryan-immigrants-not-jewish-refugees-from-the-nazis/.

Dunlop, Māni. "University academics' claim that mātauranga Māori is 'not science' sparks controversy." *Stuff*, July 28, 2021. https://www.stuff.co.nz/pou-tiaki/300368356/university-academics-claim-that-mtauranga-mori-is-not-science-sparks-controversy.

"Economist Stands by Underclass Comments." Stuff, January 31, 2009. http://www.stuff.co.nz/national/463023/Economist-stands-by-underclass-comments.

Edwards, Bryce. "Political Roudoup: Outlawing Hate Speech and Hate Crimes." NZ Herald, April 1, 2019. https://www.nzherald.co.nz/nz/political-roundup-outlawing-hate-speech-and-hate-crimes/LF6PHAS2JK3JN3KB3XDJKFE36M/.

Eliot, T. S. *The Idea of a Christian Society*. London: Faber & Faber, 1939.

Elash, Anita. "US Accused of Meddling in France’s Immigrant Policies." The Globe and Mail, 17 February 16, 2011. https://www.theglobeandmail.com/news/world/us-accused-of-meddling-in-frances-immigrant-policies/article566737/.

Engels, Friedrich. *The Condition of the Working Class in England*. 1844.

Engels, Friedrich. "Democratic Pan-Slavism." Neue Rheinische Zeitung, No. 222, February 1849. https://marxists.architexturez.net/archive/marx/works/1849/02/15.htm.

Ernie Lazar FOIA Collection. https://archive.org/details/ernie1241_general.

"European Prize for the Chancellor." The Federal Government, January 13, 2011. https://archiv.bundesregierung.de/archiv-en/hidden-hier-nur-knoten-verlinken-die-auch-publiziert-sind-fuer-preview-elemente-test-etc-nur-preview-hidden-node-verwenden/homepage/european-prize-for-the-chancellor-477196.

Evola, Julius. *Revolt Against the Modern World*. Rochester: Inner Traditions, 1995.

Evola, Julius. *Men Among the Ruins: Post-War Reflections of a Radical Traditionalist*. Rochester: Inner Traditions, 2002.

Ferguson, Karen. *Top Down: The Ford Foundation, Black Power, and the Reinvention of Racial Liberalism*. University of Pennsylvania Press, 2013.

Ferguson, Niall. *The Square and the Tower: Networks, Hierarchies and the Struggle for Global Power*. Penguin, 2017.

Ferguson, Philip. "Labour's Racist Roots." Redline Contemporary Marxist Analysis, August 24, 2015. https://rdln.wordpress.com/2015/08/24/labours-racist-roots-2/.

"FIANZ Submission to the Royal Commission of Inquiry Into the Attack on Christchurch Mosques." The Federation of Islamic Associations of New Zealand (Inc). https://fianz.com/wp-content/uploads/2020/12/FIANZ-RC-FORMAL-SUBMISSION-24-February-2020-FINAL-VERSION-Autosaved.pdf.

Finkelstein, Norman G. *The Holocaust Industry: Reflections on the Exploitation of Jewish Suffering*. New York: Verso, 2001.

Finn, Peter. "Serbs Killed Within Earshot of NATO Troops." *Washington Post*, July 25, 1999. https://www.washingtonpost.com/wp-srv/inatl/longterm/balkans/stories/balkans072599.htm.

Fitzsimmons, Michael P. "The Debate of Guilds Under Napoleon." *Journal of the Western Society for French History*, Vol. 36 (2008). http://hdl.handle.net/2027/spo.0642292.0036.010.

Fogel Robert. W. and Stanley L. Engerman. *Time on the Cross: The Economics of American Negro Slavery*. New York: W.W. Norton & Co., 1974.

Foon, Eleisha. "Hui on Countering Terrorism Sees Mass Walkout Over Hezbollah Comment." June 15, 2021. https://www.rnz.co.nz/news/national/444796/hui-on-countering-terrorism-sees-mass-walkout-over-hezbollah-comment.

"Football: No More All Whites? NZ Football Eye Change To Name." *New Zealand Herald*, August 23, 2021. https://www.nzherald.co.nz/sport/football-no-more-all-whites-nz-football-eye-change-to-name/EBPZDBJ2EDMESO7LZ2LKOT676Y/.

Fraser, Andrew. "The Path to National Suicide." Ironbark Resources, July 2005. http://www.ironbarkresources.com/articles/fraser2005pathtonationalsuicide.htm.
Freeman, Colin. "Nelson Mandela 'Proven' To Be a Member of the Communist Party After Decades of Denial." *The Telegraph*, December 8, 2012. http://www.telegraph.co.uk/news/worldnews/nelson-mandela/9731522/Nelson-Mandela-proven-to-be-a-member-of-the-Communist-Party-after-decades-of-denial.html.
Freeman, Derek. *Margaret Mead and Samoa: The Making and Unmaking of an Anthropological Myth*. Harvard University Press, 1983.
Fromm, Erich. *Escape from Freedom*. Farrar & Rinehart, 1941.
Gabler, Neal. *An Empire of Their Own: How the Jews Invented Hollywood*. Anchor, 1989.
Gaer, Felice. "Making a Difference: AJC's Advocacy for Human Rights in the United Nations Charter." *AJC The Jacob Blaustein Institute for the Advancement of Human Rights*. June 26, 2020. https://www.ajc.org/sites/default/files/pdf/2020-07/JBI%20REPORT%20ON%20AJC%20UN%20CHARTER.pdf.
Gandhi, Mahatma. *The Collected Works of Mahatma Gandhi, Vol. 3*. New Delhi: Publications Division Government of India, 1999.
Gelb, Leslie H. "US, Soviet, China Reported Aiding Portugal, Angola." *The New York Times*, September 25, 1975. https://www.nytimes.com/1975/09/25/archives/us-soviet-china-reported-aiding-portugal-angola-secret-funneling-of.html.
Generation Identity. https://www.identitaere-bewegung.at/unwahrheiten/
Gergely, Andras. "Orban Accuses Soros of Stoking Refugee Wave to Weaken Europe." *Bloomberg*. October 30, 2015. http://www.bloomberg.com/news/articles/2015-10-30/orban-accuses-soros-of-stoking-refugee-wave-to-weaken-europe.
Gerhart, Gail. M. and Clive L. Glaser. *From Protest to Challenge. A Documentary History of African Politics in South Africa 1882-1990*. Vol. 6: Challenge and Victory 1980–1990. Bloomington: Indiana University Press, 2010.
Germani, Clara. "Moscow's Academic Nightmare University in Decline: Patrice Lumumba University Once Was One of the Jewels of Moscow. Today, Like the Rest of Russia, the School—Now Renamed—Struggles Amidst Reform and Is a Shadow of Its Former Self." *The Baltimore Sun*, November 5, 1995. http://articles.baltimoresun.com/1995-11-05/news/1995309007_1_patrice-lumumba-dream-school-moscow.
Ghandnoosh, Nazgol. "Black Lives Matter: Eliminating Inequity in the Criminal Justice System." The Sentencing Project, 2015. https://www.sentencingproject.org/publications/black-lives-matter-eliminating-racial-inequity-in-the-criminal-justice-system/.
"Global Compact for Migration." International Organization for Migration UN Migration. September 16, 2016. https://www.iom.int/global-compact-migration.
"Global Compact for Safe, Orderly and Regular Migration." July 11, 2018. https://refugeesmigrants.un.org/sites/default/files/180711_final_draft_0.pdf.
Goff, Phillip Atiba. "Documenting Racial Disparities in the Police Use of Force." Open Society Foundations, July 12, 2016. https://www.opensocietyfoundations.org/voices/documenting-racial-disparities-police-use-force.
Gold, Matea. "Wealthy Donors on Left Launch New Plan to Wrest Back Control in the States." *Washington Post*, April 12, 2015. https://www.washingtonpost.com/politics/wealthy-donors-on-left-launch-new-plan-to-wrest-back-control-in-the-states/2015/04/12/ccd2f5ee-dfd3-11e4-a1b8-2ed88bc190d2_story.html.

Goldberg, Barry and Barbara Shubinki. "Black Education and Rockefeller Philanthropy from the Jim Crow South to the Civil Rights Era." Rockefeller Archive Center, September 11, 2020. https://resource.rockarch.org/story/black-education-and-rockefeller-philanthropy-from-the-jim-crow-south-to-the-civil-rights-era/.

Goodson, Stephen M. *Hendrik Frensch Verwoerd South Africa's Greatest Prime Minister*. CreateSpace Independent Publishing Platform, 2018.

Goodman, Jack. "What's the UN Global Compact on Migration"? BBC News, December 20, 2018. https://www.bbc.com/news/world-46607015.

"Govt Departments Teaching 'White Privilege.'" Scoop Independent News, May 26, 2021. https://www.scoop.co.nz/stories/PA2105/S00229/govt-departments-teaching-white-privilege.html.

"Govt's Denials About 'White Privilege' Don't Stack Up." Scoop Independent News, June 2, 2021. https://www.scoop.co.nz/stories/PA2106/S00022/govts-denials-about-white-privilege-dont-stack-up.html.

Gower, Patrick. "Revealed: How White Supremacists Terrorised New Zealand for Decade." Newshub, May 19, 2019. https://www.newshub.co.nz/home/new-zealand/2019/05/revealed-how-white-supremacists-terrorised-new-zealand-for-decades.html.

Gower, Patrick. "Exclusive: Police Investigating White Supremacists' Death Threats Against Winston Peters." Newshub, June 30, 2019 https://www.newshub.co.nz/home/new-zealand/2019/06/exclusive-police-investigating-white-supremacists-death-threats-against-winston-peters.html.

"Grand Orient de France: An Initiatory Approach and a Republican Commitment." https://www.godf.org/js/tinymce/source/avril-2021/GODF-7-points-en.pdf.

"Greens Draw up Their Own Anti-Smacking Bill." Scoop Independent News, October 6, 2003. https://www.scoop.co.nz/stories/PA0310/S00087/greens-draw-up-their-own-anti-smacking-bill.htm?from-mobile=bottom-link-01.

Grewal, Preetinder S. "The Family of Slain Auckland Dairy Owner Break Their Silence." SBS Punjabi, May 29, 2017. https://www.sbs.com.au/language/english/the-family-of-slain-auckland-dairy-owner-break-their-silence.

Griffin, G. E. *The Fearful Master: A Second Look at the United Nations*. Boston: Western Island, 1964.

Gromyko, Andrei. *Memories*. London: Hutchinson, 1989.

Grose, Peter. *Continuing the Inquiry: The Council on Foreign Relations from 1921 to 1996*. New York: Council on Foreign Relations, 2006. https://cdn.cfr.org/sites/default/files/book_pdf/Continuing_The_Inquiry.pdf.

"Guest Blog: Mara Weiss—Time to Change All Whites Name." The Daily Blog, August 1, 2015. https://thedailyblog.co.nz/2015/08/01/guest-blog-mara-weiss-time-to-change-all-whites-name/.

Guimarães, Andresen Fernando. "The United States and the Decolonization of Angola: the origins of a failed policy." UN Department for Peacekeeeping Operations. October 2003.

"Gunnar Myrdal, Analyst of Race Crisis, Dies." *The New York Times*, May 18, 1987. https://www.nytimes.com/1987/05/18/obituaries/gunnar-myrdal-analyst-of-race-crisis-dies.html.

Haines, Herbert H. *Black Radicals and the Civil Rights Mainstream, 1954–1970*. University of Tennessee Press, 1995.

Hamilton, Alexander. *The Federalist Papers.*"No. 1. https://guides.loc.gov/federalist-papers/text-1-10#s-lg-box-wrapper-25493264.

Hawkes, Marielle. "Briefing Note: Teaching of Te Tiriti o Waitangi Follow-up." Ministry of Education, June 14, 2019.

https://www.education.govt.nz/assets/Documents/Ministry/Information-releases/2019-releases/NZ-Histories/R-6-1194902-BN-Davis-Redacted.pdf.

Hawkes, Marielle. "Kai & Korero Chats About the Future of New Zealand." Beyond the Ballot, August 14, 2017. https://medium.com/beyond-the-ballot/kai-k%C5%8Drero-d6ca078b2be6.

Hayden, Tom. *Reunion: A Memoir*. London: Hamish Hamilton, 1989.

Hayden, Tom. "The CIA's Student Activism Phase." *The Nation*, November 26, 2014. https://www.thenation.com/article/archive/cias-student-activism-phase/.

He Puapua: Report of the Working Group on a Plan to Realise the UN Declaration on the Rights of Indigenous Peoples in Aotearoa/New Zealand. 2019. https://www.tpk.govt.nz/docs/undrip/tpk-undrip-he-puapua.pdf.

Hedges, Chris. "Kosovo's Next Masters? Inside the Kosovo Liberation Army." *Foreign Affairs*, May/June 1999. https://www.foreignaffairs.com/articles/europe/1999-05-01/kosovos-next-masters

Hedin, Mark. "Fiscal Sponsor's Bold Role in Removing Confederate Statues From New Orleans." Fiscal Sponsor Directory, November 17, 2017. https://fiscalsponsordirectory.org/?p=3852.

Helper, Hinton. R. *The Impending Crisis of the South: How to Meet It*. 1857.

Herrnstein Richard J. and Charles Murray. *The Bell Curve Intelligence and Class Structure in American Life*. New York: The Free Press, 1994.

Hendy, Shaun, et al. "An open response to 'In defence of science' New Zealand Listener (July 23)." https://docs.google.com/forms/d/e/1FAIpQLSdRwHTSKURHaalXZSNo2oluN9OjuDxK6UDG4gb6t7NhAPO3Zg/viewform.

"His Holiness the Dalai Lama's Response to a Question About the Refugees." Rotterdam, September 17, 2018. https://www.dalailama.com/news/2018/his-holiness-the-dalai-lamas-response-to-a-question-about-refugees.

Hobbs, Victoria. "The Function of a 'Fetish' Figure." *Conservation Journal*, 31, April 1999. http://www.vam.ac.uk/content/journals/conservation-journal/issue-31/the-function-of-a-fetish-figure/.

"Hobson's Pledge. Moving Forward as One." https://www.hobsonspledge.nz/.

"Holden Roberto Dies at 84, Fought to Free Angola From Portuguese Rule." *New York Times*, August 4, 2007. https://www.nytimes.com/2007/08/04/world/africa/04roberto.html.

Howard, Scott. *The Open Society Playbook*. Antelope Hill Publishing, 2021.

Howard, Theresa. "Ads crank up the volume with tunes." *USA Today*, August 10, 2003. https://usatoday30.usatoday.com/money/advertising/adtrack/2003-08-10-track_x.htm.

Hudson, Daisy. "Racist Concerns Over SI Independence Site." Otago Daily Times, July 6, 2019. https://www.odt.co.nz/regions/racist-concerns-over-si-independence-site.

Humphrey, John. "Human Rights, the United Nations, and 1968." *Journal of the International Commission of Jurists*, Vol. IX, no. 1, June 1968, 1-13. https://www.icj.org/wp-content/uploads/1968/06/ICJ-Journal-IX-1-1968-eng.pdf.

Humphris, Rachel. "The Relevance of Jean-Jacques Rousseau 300 Years After his Birth." *UNHCR*, June 28, 2012; https://www.unhcr.org/news/latest/2012/6/4fec23bc6/relevance-jean-jacques-rousseau-300-years-birth.html.

Hunt, Paul. "It Happened Here: Reports of Race and Religious Hate Crimes in New Zealand 2004–2012." Human Rights Commission Te Kahui Tika Kangata, June 2019. https://www.hrc.co.nz/files/1515/6047/9685/It_Happened_Here_Reports_of_race_and_religious_hate_crime_in_New_Zealand_2004-2012.pdf.

"Interim Agreement for Peace and Self-Government in Kosovo (Rambouillet Accords)." United Nations Peacemaker, February 23, 1999. https://peacemaker.un.org/kosovo-rambouilletagreement99.

Irving, David. *The Destruction of Dresden*. London: Future Publications, 1980.

IU News Room. "Mattel, Inc. chairman and CEO to speak in Indianapolis at Kelley School lunch series." Indiana University News Room, February 11, 2008. https://newsinfo.iu.edu/news/page/normal/7456.html.

Jacobs, Scott W. "Faculty Support Grows For Anti-War Proposal." The Harvard Crimson, October 3, 1969. https://www.thecrimson.com/article/1969/10/3/faculty-support-grows-for-anti-war-proposal/.

Jefferson, Thomas. *Declaration of Independence of the Thirteen Colonies*. US Congress, July 4, 1776. https://uscode.house.gov/download/annualhistoricalarchives/pdf/OrganicLaws2006/decind.pdf.

Jenab6. "The James Alex Fields Chapter of 'The Innocent Get Convicted While the Guilty Go Free." Live Journal, December 4, 2018. https://jenab6.livejournal.com/81862.html.

Jewish Business News. "Mattel Appoints Israeli Ynon Kreiz as Chairman." *Jewish Business News*, February 11, 2018; https://jewishbusinessnews.com/2018/02/11/mattel-appoints-israeli-ynon-kreiz-chairman/

"Jewish Council Spokeswoman Stands by Comments After Christchurch Hui Marred by Walkout." NZ Herald, June 17, 2021. https://www.nzherald.co.nz/nz/jewish-council-spokeswoman-stands-by-comments-after-christchurch-hui-marred-by-walkout/VZKDLGGVJEJA7JH4ZQSERJN2FM/.

"John Minto to Visit Abahlali baseMjondolo on Saturday, 17 April 2009." Abahlali baseMjondolo. http://antieviction.org.za/2009/04/18/.

Jones, Winfield. *The South Occupied*. New York: Tocsin Publishers, 1941.

"JSingles NZ." https://jsingles.co.nz/

Kadioglu, Ayse. "What Stories Does Europe Tell? A View from Turkey." CES Open Forum Series 2019–2020. Center for European Studies Harvard. https://ces.fas.harvard.edu/uploads/art/Ayse-K.-Final-Version-10-17-2019.pdf.

Keita Sekou and Helen Dempster. "Five Years Later, One Million Refugees Are Thriving in Germany." Center for Global Development, December 4, 2020. https://www.cgdev.org/blog/five-years-later-one-million-refugees-are-thriving-germany.

Kelley, Francis Clement. *Blood-Drenched Altars: A Catholic Commentary on the History of Mexico*. Rockford, Ill.: Tan Books, 1987 [1935].

Kennedy, Emmet A. *Cultural History of the French Revolution*. New Haven: Yale University Press, 1989.

Kerr-Lazenby, Mina. "University of Auckland professor relinquishes role after claiming mātauranga Māori is 'not science.'" *Stuff*, July 29, 2021. https://www.stuff.co.nz/national/300368560/university-of-auckland-professor-relinquishes-role-after-claiming-mtauranga-mori-is-not-science.

"Kimihia Te Mea Ngaro - Maori Access to Capital." Reserve Bank of New Zealand Te Putea Matua. https://www.rbnz.govt.nz/financial-stability/financial-stability-report/fsr-may-2021/kimihia-te-mea-ngaro-maori-access-to-capital.

King, Martin L. Jr. "Letter From Birmingham Jail." April 16, 1963. https://www.csuchico.edu/iege/_assets/documents/susi-letter-from-birmingham-jail.pdf.

Kipling, Rudyard. "The Stranger." 1908. https://www.poetry.com/poem/33582/the-stranger.

Knudtson, Peter. *A Mirror to Nature: Reflections on Science, Scientists, and Society*; "Rushton on Race." Stoddart Publishing, 1991.

Korey, William. *NGOs and the Universal Declaration of Human Rights: A Curious Grapevine*. New York: St Martin's Press, 1998.

Kottasova, Ivana. "Google, Goldman Sachs Donate Millions To Help Refugees." CNN, September 11, 2015. http://money.cnn.com/2015/09/11/news/refugee-crisis-corporate-donations/.

Kyles, Kyra. "Mattel's hip-hop Flava dolls flop." *Chicago Tribune*, August 14, 2003. https://www.chicagotribune.com/news/ct-xpm-2003-08-14-0308140373-story.html.

Lasch, "What's Wrong with the Right?" *Tikkun*, no. 1, 1987.

Lau, Peter F. *Democracy Rising: South Carolina and the Fight for Black Equality Since 1865*. Lexington: University Press of Kentucky, 2006.

Lawrence, T. E. *Seven Pillars of Wisdom*. London: Black House Publishing, 2013.

"Le Chapelier Law." Liberty, Equality, Fraternity: Exploring the French Revolution, accessed October 24, 2021. https://revolution.chnm.org/items/show/480.

Leo XIII. *Rerum Novarum. Encyclical of Pope Leo XIII on Capital and Labor*. May 15, 1891. https://www.vatican.va/content/leo-xiii/en/encyclicals/documents/hf_l-xiii_enc_15051891_rerum-novarum.html.

Lemkin, Raphael. *Axis Rule in Occupied Europe*. Washington: Carnegie Council, 1944.

Lenin, Vladimir I. *The State and the Revolution*. New York, 1935.

Lévi-Strauss, Claude. "Rousseau: The Father of Anthropology." *The UNESCO Courier*, March 1963, 10-15.

Lewis, Arthur R. *Christian Terror in Southern Africa*. Salisbury: Rhodesian Christian Group, 1978.

Lewis, C. S. *God in the Dock: Essays on Theology and Ethics*. 1970.

License Global. "MGA Unveils New Bratz." *License Global*, April 6, 2018; https://www.licenseglobal.com/toys-games/mga-unveils-new-bratz

Linder, Douglas O. "The Nelson Mandela (Rivonia) Trial An Account." 2010. https://www.famous-trials.com/nelsonmandela.

"Link Political Parties and People." IRI International Republican Institute. https://www.iri.org/program/link-political-parties-and-people.

Lipstadt, Deborah E. *Denying the Holocaust: The Growing Assault on Truth and Memory*. London: Penguin Books, 1994.

Loeffler, James. "Becoming Cleopatra: The Forgotten Zionism of Raphael Lemkin." *Journal of Genocide Research* 19, no. 3 (July 2017): 340-360. https://doi.org/10.1080/14623528.2017.1349645

Loeffler, James. "The Zionist Founders of the Human Rights Movement." *The New York Times*, May 14, 2018. https://www.nytimes.com/2018/05/14/opinion/zionism-israel-human-rights.html.

Locke, John. *An Essay Concerning Human Understating*. London: Printed by Eliz. Holt for Thomas Basset, at the George in Fleet Street, near St. Dunstan's Church, 1689. https://www.gutenberg.org/files/10615/10615-h/10615-h.htm

Locke, John. *Second Treatise on Government*. https://www.gutenberg.org/files/7370/7370-h/7370-h.htm

"Love Frankie." https://lovefrankie.co/.

Ludovici, Anthony M. *A Defence of Conservatism: A Further Textbook for Tories*. Sacred Truth Publishing, [1927] 2015. http://anthonymludovici.com/dc_01.htm.

de Maistre, Joseph. *Considerations on France*. 1797.

Malone, Andrew. "Mugabe's British Henchman: One of Our Worst Slum Landlords, He Built a Monstrous Mansion in Sussex and Had a Rival Murdered. Now the Mail Can Reveal Nicholas Van Hoogstraten's Astonishing New Life." Daily Mail, July 26, 2013.

Updated September 6, 2013. https://www.dailymail.co.uk/news/article-2379698/Mugabes-British-henchman-One-worst-slum-landlords--built-monstrous-mansion-Sussex-rival-murdered-Now-Mail-reveal-Nicholas-Van-Hoogstratens-astonishing-new-life.html.

Manch, Thomas and Sam Sherwood. "Police Check Firearm Licence Applicants for Signs of 'Extreme Right' After March 15 Terror Attack." Stuff, June 29, 2019. https://www.stuff.co.nz/national/christchurch-shooting/113666061/police-check-firearm-licence-applicants-for-signs-of-extreme-right-after-march-15-terror-attack.

Mandela, Nelson. R. "The Shifting Sands of Illusion." *Liberation*, June 1953. http://www.speechwall.com/mandela-writings-1.html.

Mandela, Nelson. R. "Eulogy: Harry Oppenheimer." *Time*, September 4, 2000. http://content.time.com/time/subscriber/article/0,33009,997869,00.html.

Mann, Thomas. *Pariser Rechenschaft*. S. Fischer Verlag, 1974 [1926].

"Maori Community Development Act 1962." Parliamentaty Counsel Office, December 14, 1962. https://www.legislation.govt.nz/act/public/1962/0133/latest/DLM341045.html.

Markay, Lachlan. "Read the Confidential Document Left Behind the Democracy Alliance Meeting." *The Washington Free Beacon*, May 5, 2014. http://freebeacon.com/politics/jonathan-soros-left-a-confidential-document-at-his-donor-conference/.

Martens, Bailey. "Over 100 University of New Brunswick Faculty 'Condemn' Ricardo Duchesne's Extremist Views." Huffpost, May 29, 2019. https://www.huffpost.com/archive/ca/entry/ricardo-duchesne-unb-faculty-condemn_ca_5ceda269e4b0793c2346ca52.

Martin, James J. "Raphael Lemkin and the Invention of 'Genocide.'" *The Journal of Historical Review* 2, No. 1, Spring 1981. https://www.historiography-project.com/jhrchives/v02/v02p-19_Martin.php

Martin, Garret. "In Smart-Power Shift, US Now Actively Cultivating Muslim Minorities in the EU." The European Institute at the University of Maryland, December 31, 2018. https://www.europeaninstitute.org/index.php/123-european-affairs/ea-april-2011/1282-in-smart-power-shift-us-now-actively-cultivating-muslim-minorities-in-the-eu.

"Martin Luther King, Jr. A Current Analysis." Federal Bureau of Investigation, March 12, 1968. (FBI 104-10125-10133). https://www.archives.gov/files/research/jfk/releases/104-10125-10133.pdf.

Marx, Karl, and Friedrich Engels. *The Communist Manifesto*. Moscow: Progress Publishers, 1975 [1848].

Marx, Karl. "The Future Results of British Rule in India." *New-York Daily Tribune*, August 8, 1853. http://www.historyisaweapon.com/defcon6/works/1853/07/22.html.

"Marx To Engels In Manchester." Marx-Engels Correspondence 1862. [London], July 30, 1862. http://hiaw.org/defcon6/works/1862/letters/62_07_30a.html.

Mattel. "Mattel Introduces MTV's 'Jersey Shore Family Vacation' Board Game," *PR Newswire*, December 17, 2018. https://www.prnewswire.com/news-releases/mattel-introduces-jersey-shore-family-vacation-board-game-300767261.html

Mattel Newsroom, "Barbie Launches New Music Producer Doll to Highlight the Gender Gap in The Industry," Mattel, September 13, 2021. https://corporate.mattel.com/news/barbie-launches-new-music-producer-doll-to-highlight-the-gender-gap-in-the-industry.

McDonnell, Michael A. and A. Dirk Moses. "Raphael Lemkin as historian of genocide in the Americas." *Journal of Genocide Research* 7, no. 4, (December 2005): 501-529.

https://www.dirkmoses.com/uploads/7/3/8/2/7382125/moses__mcdonnell_lemkin_americas.pdf.

McDougall, Dan. "White Farmers 'Being Wiped Out.'" *The Times*, March 28, 2010. Reproduced at AmericanRenaissance.com, http://www.amren.com/mtnews/archives/2010/03/white_farmers_b.php.

McFadden, Charles. J. *The Philosophy of Communism*. New York: Benziger Bros., 1939.

McHardie, Stephanie. "Education Report: Including New Zealand's History Within the National Curriculum. Ministry of Education, August 30, 2018. https://www.education.govt.nz/assets/Documents/Ministry/Information-releases/2019-releases/NZ-Histories/R-4-1204074-ER-Hipkins-Davis-Redacted.pdf.

McLean, John. *Voyages of the Pioneers to New Zealand 1839–85*. Wellington: Winter Productions, 2015.

Mclean, Tamara. "Outspoken academic banned from teaching." *News.com.au*, July 29, 2005.

McNeilly, Hamish. "Controversial Women's Group Offered New Venue in Dunedin." Stuff, July 5, 2021. https://www.stuff.co.nz/national/politics/local-government/300350002/controversial-womens-group-offered-new-council-venue-in-dunedin.

Mead, Margaret. *The Coming of Age in Samoa: A Psychological Study of Primitive Youth for Western Civilization*. William Morrow and Company, 1928.

Medvedev, Zhores A. *The Rise and Fall of T. D. Lysenko*. New York: Anchor Books, 1971.

Meldrum, Andrew. "Tycoon Flees Zimbabwe After Falling Foul of Mugabe." *The Guardian*, June 9, 2006. http://www.guardian.co.uk/world/2006/jun/09/zimbabwe.topstories3.

Melgunov, Sergei. *The Red Terror in Russia*. Hyperion, 1975 [1927].

Mercury News. "Facebook hangs Black Lives Matter sign at its headquarters, plus other tech reaction to violent week." *Mercury News*, July 9, 2016. https://www.mercurynews.com/2016/07/09/facebook-hangs-black-lives-matter-sign-at-its-headquarters-plus-other-tech-reaction-to-violent-week/.

Mihaila, Marian. "European Union and Freemasonry." Masonic Forum, I: 6. (masonicforum.ro/en/nr27/european.html#b_22).

Ministry of Education. *Ministry Bulletin for Scool Leaders*, 89 (May 7, 2018): 15-16. https://www.education.govt.nz/assets/Documents/School/SchoolsBulletin/2018-Bulletins/Issue89Bulletin.pdf.

Mlinar, Zdravko. "Deterritorialization and Reterritorialization of Cultural Identifies." *Druzboslovne Razprave*, no. 15-16 (1994): 140-152. http://dk.fdv.uni-lj.si/dr/dr15-16Mlinar.PDF.

Mohdin Aamna and Rhi Storer. "Tributes to Slave Traders and Colonialists Removed Across UK." *The Guardian*, January 29, 2021. https://www.theguardian.com/world/2021/jan/29/tributes-to-slave-traders-and-colonialists-removed-across-uk.

"Montreal Statement of the Assembly for Human Rights March 22-27, 1968." *Journal of the International Commission of Jurists* IX, no. 1 (June 1968): 94-112. https://www.icj.org/wp-content/uploads/1968/06/ICJ-Journal-IX-1-1968-eng.pdf.

Moon, Paul. *Fatal Frontiers: A New History of New Zealand in the Decade Before the Treaty*. Penguin Books, 2006.

Morris, David Z. "Netflix and Twitter Execs Donate to Black Lives Matter Leader's Mayoral Campaign." *Fortune*, March 26, 2016. http://fortune.com/2016/03/26/netflix-twitter-black-lives-matter/.

Moser, Bob. "The Reckoning of Morris Dees and the Southern Poverty Law Center." *The New Yorker*, March 21, 2019. https:// www.newyorker.com/news/news-desk/the-reckoning-of-morris-dees-and-the-southern-poverty-law-center.
Moses, Juliet. "The A-Z of Palestinian Oppression: A Glossary To Help Lefties Launch Their Verbal Attacks on Israel." Spectator, June 5, 2021. https://www.spectator.com.au/2021/06/the-a-z-of-palestinian-oppression/.
Mosher, Steven W. "Nike should quit lecturing on social justice—and atone for using slave labor in China." *New York Post*, July 25, 2020. https://nypost.com/2020/07/25/nike-should-quit-lecturing-on-social-justice-and-atone-for-using-slave-labor-in-china/
Mostert, Cheslyn. "Reflections on South Africa's Restructuring of State-Owned Enterprises." Occasional Paper No. 5, March 2002. http://library.fes.de/pdf-files/bueros/suedafrika/07164.pdf.
Muggeridge, Malcolm. "The Great Liberal Death Wish." [Presentation at Hillsdale College]. Imprimis, Vol. 8, No. 5, May 1979. https://imprimis.hillsdale.edu/the-great-liberal-death-wish/.
Marcuse, Herbert. "Repressive Tolerance." From Wolff, Robert. P., Barrington Moore, and Herbert Marcuse. *A Critique of Pure Tolerance*. Boston: Beacon Press, 1969, https://www.marcuse.org/herbert/publications/1960s/1965-repressive-tolerance-fulltext.html.
"Massey's Pasifika Director says report fails to recognise wider contribution of Pacific people." Massey University, December 8, 2008. https://www.massey.ac.nz/massey/about-massey/news/article.cfm?mnarticle_uuid=27DC5253-96BF-57FE-AA70-353740D50ADE.
Murphy, Dan. "How the Fall of Qaddafi Gave Rise to Europe's Migrant Crisis." Christian Science Monitor, April 21, 2015. https://www.csmonitor.com/World/Security-Watch/Backchannels/2015/0421/How-the-fall-of-Qaddafi-gave-rise-to-Europe-s-migrant-crisis.
Myrdahl, Gunnar. *An American Dilemma: The Negro Problem and Modern Democracy*. Vol. 1. New York: Harper Bros., 1944.
"National Statement of the United States of America on the Adoption of the Global Compact for Safe, Orderly, and Regular Migration." United States Mission to the United Nations. December 7, 2018. https://usun.usmission.gov/national-statement-of-the-united-states-of-america-on-the-adoption-of-the-global-compact-for-safe-orderly-and-regular-migration/.
Ndlela, Dumisani. "Zimbabwe: Hwange Crisis – Gratifying Van Hoogstraten's Rancour." *Financial Gazette*, August 17, 2011. http://allafrica.com/stories/201108191237.html.
"Netanyahu: Israel Won't Sign Global Migration Pact, Must Protect Its Borders." The Times of Israel, November 20, 2018. https://www.timesofisrael.com/israel-wont-sign-global-migration-pact-netanyahu-announces/.
"New Zealand Chief of Army Writing Competition Winner of the New Zealand Defence Force Private Writing Category May 2021: Can the Army Afford To Go Woke, Benign Social Progress or National Security Threat [Mr. N. Dell]." Knowledge Enabled Army. https://kea-learning.nz/people-leadership/new-zealand-chief-of-army-writing-competition-winner-of-the-new-zealand-defence-force-private-writing-category-can-the-army-afford-to-go-woke-benign-social-progress-or-national-security-threat-2/.
"New Zealand Not Immune From Rise in Antisemitism." Scoop, June 10, 2021. https://www.scoop.co.nz/stories/PO2106/S00091/new-zealand-not-immune-from-rise-in-antisemitism.htm [Emphasis added].
Newshub. "Full interview: Lauren Southern and Stefan Molyneux." YouTube Video, 13:46. August 3, 2018. https://www.youtube.com/watch?v=mUR9U6Srj7g.

Newsweek Staff. "Toys: Flavas Of The Week." *Newsweek*, August 3, 2003. https://www.newsweek.com/toys-flavas-week-135565.

Ngo, Andy. *Unmasked: Inside Antifa's Radical Plan to Destroy Democracy*. New York: Center Street, 2021.

Nietzsche, Friedrich. *Beyond Good and Evil*. Penguin Books, 1984.

Nietzsche, Friedrich. *Thus Spoke Zarathustra*. Middlesex: Penguin Books, 1969.

Nippert, Hukarere, et al. *Determining the NCEA Level 1, 2, and 3 Subject Lists for Te Marautanga o Aotearoa*. Wellington: Ministry of Education, 2021. https://ncea-live-3-storagestack-53q-assetstorages3bucket-2021xte0r81u.s3.amazonaws.com/s3fs-public/2021-06/Technical%20Report%20TMoA.pdf?VersionId=DV_LCpfodqR2BeROrkVHghISsckS_Nuo.

NZ Herald. "Trade Me defends selling 'It's okay to be white' items." *Otago Daily Times*, May 22, 2019. https://www.odt.co.nz/news/national/trade-me-defends-selling-its-okay-be-white-items.

"NZ Jewish Council Condemns 'Unite' Union Leader's Incitement to Violence." New Zealand Jewish Council, June 12, 2021. https://www.nzjc.org/12-june-21-unit-union.

O'Connell, Elizabeth. "8 Things You Didn't Know Were Made with Sweatshop Labor." Green America, Accessed January 17, 2022. https://www.greenamerica.org/world-hurt/8-things-you-didnt-know-were-made-sweatshop-labor

"Operation Mayibuye." http://law2.umkc.edu/faculty/projects/ftrials/mandela/mandelaoperationm.html.

Oppenheimer, Harry. "Portrait of a Millionaire: 'I, Harry Oppenheimer.'" *Africa South* 4, no. 3 (April–June 1960): 7-16. https://www.sahistory.org.za/sites/default/files/archive-files2/asapr60.3.pdf

Orwell, George. *1984*. 1949.

Paget, Karen M. *Patriotic Betrayal: The Inside Story of the CIA's Secret Campaign to Enrol American Students in the Crusade Against Communism*. New Haven: Yale University Press, 2015.

Pallister, David, Sarah Stewart, and Ian Lepper. *South Africa Inc. The Oppenheimer Empire*. London: Corgi Books, 1988.

Palmer, Scott. "David Seymour Calls Out Police for 'Disturbing' Gun Raids." *Newshub*, May 11, 2019. https://www.newshub.co.nz/home/new-zealand/2019/05/david-seymour-calls-out-police-for-disturbing-gun-raids.html.

Parveen, Nazia. "Birmingham School Stops LGBT Lessons After Parents Protest." *The Guardian*, March 4, 2019. https://www.theguardian.com/education/2019/mar/04/birmingham-school-stops-lgbt-lessons-after-parent-protests.

"Past Programs." The Africa-America Institute. http://www.aaionline.org/programs/past-programs/southern-african-student-program-sasp-1961-%E2%80%93-1983/.

"Peabody Fund." *The Encyclopedia Britannica*, 1996.

Pedler, Frederick. *Main Currents of West African History, 1940–1978*. New York: Barnes & Noble, 1979.

Peled, Daniella. "College Rejects Shoah Denier." *The Jewish Chronicle*, April 24 2008.

Percivaldi, Riccardo. "The Kalergi Plan: The Genocide of the European Peoples." *Identità*, December 11, 2012. https://xn--identit-fwa.com/blog/2012/12/11/il-piano-kalergi-il-genocidio-dei-popoli-europei/.

Perlmutter, Dawn. "American Iconoclasm: the Destruction of Sacred Images." American Renaissance, August 21, 2017. https://www.amren.com/news/2017/08/american-iconoclasm-destruction-sacred-images/.

Peta, Basildon. "Van Hoogstraten to take over top bank and colliery in Zimbabwe." *Independent,* July 14, 2005. https://www.independent.co.uk/news/world/africa/van-hoogstraten-to-take-over-top-bank-and-colliery-in-zimbabwe-299066.html.

Peters, Ralph. "Constant Conflict." *Parameters* 40, no. 4 (2010): 126-134. http://press.armywarcollege.edu/parameters/vol40/iss4/16.

Phillips, Wendel. "Wendel Phillips on Reconstruction." *The New York Times,* December 29, 1864. https://www.nytimes.com/1864/12/29/archives/wendell-phillips-on-reconstruction.html.

Plessy v. Ferguson. Oyez. Accessed December 26, 2021. https://www.oyez.org/cases/1850-1900/163us537.

Plunkett, John. "Midsomer Murders Creator To Step Down at End of Current Series." *The Guardian*, March 23, 2011. https://www.theguardian.com/media/2011/mar/23/midsomer-murders-brian-true-may-english.

"Police Investigating Death Threats Made Against Deputy Prime Minister Winston Peters." NZ Herald, June 30, 2019. https://www.nzherald.co.nz/nz/news/article.cfm?c_id=1&objectid=12245284.

"Policy Immoral." *Evening Post,* Wellington, November 25, 1986.

"Poole's Baden-Powell's Statue Boarded up Instead of Removed." BBC News, June 12, 2020. https://www.bbc.com/news/uk-england-dorset-53020114.

Porter, Lindsay. *Who are the Illuminati*? London: Collins & Brown, 2005.

Pratt, Mark. "Six Dr. Seuss Books Won't Be Published for Racist Images." Stuff, March 3, 2021. https://www.stuff.co.nz/entertainment/books/300243163/six-dr-seuss-books-wont-be-published-for-racist-images.

"President's Five-Year Review & Annual Report 1968." The Rockefeller Foundation, January 26, 2001. https://www.rockefellerfoundation.org/wp-content/uploads/Annual-Report-1968-1.pdf.

Preston, Nikki. "World Record New Zealand Overtakes the UK's Title for the Most Rainbow Parliament." NZ Herald, October 17, 2020. https://www.nzherald.co.nz/nz/world-record-new-zealand-overtakes-the-uks-title-for-the-most-rainbow-parliament/CLEAKIDVKRIOQDF5ZO67EGIDCY/.

"Probe Into Links Between Accused Christchurch Gunman and European Far-Right Groups." NZ Herald, April 6, 2019. https://www.nzherald.co.nz/nz/news/article.cfm?c_id=1&objectid=12220026.

"Proceedings of the Kohimarama Conference, Comprising Nos 13 to 18 of the 'Maori Messenger.'" Victoria University of Wellington, 2009. http://nzetc.victoria.ac.nz/tm/scholarly/tei-BIM504Kohi.html.

"Professor Andrew Fraser A Short Biography." Ironbark Resources. http://www.ironbarkresources.com/articles/fraserbio.htm.

"Prohibition of Conversion Therapy Bill." Member's Bill. https://familyfirst.org.nz/wp-content/uploads/2020/10/PMB-Prohibition-of-Conversion-Therapy-Bill.pdf.

"Promote Digital Democracy." IRI International Republican Institute. https://www.iri.org/program/promote-digital-democracy.

"Pro-Palestine Group Slates New Conciliator." *Evening Post*, December 24, 1985.

"Proposals Against Incitement of Hatred and Discrimination." Ministry of Justice (New Zealand). https://apo.org.au/sites/default/files/resource-files/2021-06/apo-nid312994.pdf.

Proposals Against Incitement, Summary Document: Freedom of Expression is Protected but it is Subject to Reasonable Limits.

"Public Interest Journalism Fund: General Guidelines." April 30, 2021. https://d3r9t6niqlb7tz.cloudfront.net/media/documents/210429_PIJF_General_Guidelines_f4RtoKG_cRdUBNy_cLXUAKM.pdf.

Pullar-Strecker Tom. "Reserve Bank Report Tots up $69b of Assets in Maori Economy." Stuff, January 28, 2021. https://www.stuff.co.nz/business/124067350/reserve-bank-report-tots-up-69b-of-assets-in-maori-economy.

Putnam, Robert. D. "E Pluribus Unum: Diversity and Community in the Twenty-first Century The 2006 Johan Skytte Prize Lecture."
Journal of Scandinavian Political Studies, Volume30, Issue 2, June 2007, Pages 137-174. https://doi.org/10.1111/j.1467-9477.2007.00176.x.

Quigley, Carroll. *Tragedy & Hope: A History of the World in Our Time*. New York: Macmillan Co., 1966.

"Racism Row Lecturer Retires Early." BBC News, July 12, 2006. http://news.bbc.co.uk/2/hi/uk_news/england/west_yorkshire/5174010.stm.

"Rambouillet Agreement Interim Agreement for Peace and Self-Governance in Kosovo." Article I (1), 1. US Department of State, January 20, 2001. https://1997-2001.state.gov/regions/eur/ksvo_rambouillet_text.html.

Rand, Ayn. "Racism." In *The Virtue of Selfishness*. New American Library, 1964.

"Remarks by Rajiv J. Shah at the University of Pennsylvania Perelman School of Medicine Commencement." Rockefeller Foundation, 16 May 16, 2021. https://www.rockefellerfoundation.org/news/remarks-by-dr-rajiv-j-shah-at-the-university-of-pennsylvania-perelman-school-of-medicine-commencement/.

"Replacement Migration, Is It a Solution to Declining and Ageing Populations?" United Nations, 2001. https://www.un.org/en/development/desa/population/publications/ageing/replacement-migration.asp.

"Report Into Operation Eight (Urewera Raids) Finds Police Acted Unlawfully." IPCA Independent Police Conduct Authority, May 22, 2013. https://www.ipca.govt.nz/Site/publications-and-media/2013-Media-Releases/2013-May-22-Operation-Eight.aspx.

"Resolution Adopted by the General Assembly on 6 April 2017." United Nations General Assembly, April 17, 2017. https://www.iom.int/sites/default/files/our_work/ODG/GCM/A-71_280-E.pdf.

"Revealed: What Cops Filmed in the Ureweras." NZ Herald, September 28, 2011. https://www.nzherald.co.nz/nz/news/article.cfm?c_id=1&objectid=10754889.

RFE/RL. "Wesley Clark: We did the right thing in 1999." *Radio Free Europe/Radio Liberty*, April 11, 2010. https://www.rferl.org/a/Wesley_Clark_We_Did_The_Right_Thing_In_1999/2009039.html

Richardson, John H. "James Watson: What I've Learned." Esquire, October 19, 2007. http://www.esquire.com/features/what-ive-learned/ESQ0107jameswatson.

Richardson, Valerie. "No Racial Bias in Police Shootings, Study by Harvard Professor Shows." *The Washington Times*, July 11, 2016. http://www.washingtontimes.com/news/2016/jul/11/no-racial-bias-police-shootings-study-harvard-prof/.

Riddell, Kelly. "George Soros Funds Ferguson Protests, Hopes to Spur Civil Action." *The Washington Times*, January 14, 2015. http://www.washingtontimes.com/news/2015/jan/14/george-soros-funds-ferguson-protests-hopes-to-spur/.

Rilley, Katie. "Read Hilary Clinton's 'Basket of Deplorables' Remarks About Donald Trump Supporters." *Time*, September 10, 2016. https://time.com/4486502/hillary-clinton-basket-of-deplorables-transcript/.

Rippingale, James. "Lewisham, London 1977: Notes on Fighting Fascism." Al Jazeera, November 24, 2018. https://www.aljazeera.com/indepth/features/lewisham-london-1977-notes-fighting-fascism-181118080513964.html.

Roberts, Greg. "Lecture ban for 'racist' professor," *The Weekend Australian*, July 30 2005.

Roberts, Sam. "Rockefeller on the Attica Raid, From Boastful to Subdued." *The New York Times*, September 12, 2011. https://www.nytimes.com/2011/09/13/nyregion/rockefeller-initially-boasted-to-nixon-about-attica-raid.html.

Robins-Early, Nick. "The White Supremacist Professor Teaching At a Public University." Huffpost, May 18, 2019. https://www.huffpost.com/entry/ricardo-duchesne-white-nationalist-unb_n_5cdec3c8e4b09e057802c216.

Robinson, John. *He Puapua: Blueprint for Breaking Up New Zealand*. Wellington: Tross Publishing, 2021.

Robinson, John. *Unrestrained Slaughter: The Maori Musket Wars 1800-1840*. Wellington: Tross Publishing, 2020.

Rogers, Arthur. "Warburg and the Kalergi Plan: Warburgs pushed Kalergi Plan for world government through European Union and racial mingling." Originally published as "Power-Crazy One-Worlders & the Negro Invasion." *Free Britain*, no. 158, July 1955.

Roosevelt, Elliot. *As He Saw It*. New York: Duell, Sloan and Pearce, 1946.

Roosevelt, Franklin D. and Winston S. Churchill. *Atlantic Charter*. August 14, 1941. Yale Law School. https://avalon.law.yale.edu/wwii/atlantic.asp.

Roose, Holly. "Rosenwald Fund Schools (1912-10320." Black Past, June 7, 2011. https://www.blackpast.org/african-american-history/rosenwald-fund-schools-1912-1932/.

Rossi, Melissa. "'Great Replacement' Ideology is Spreading Hate in US and Across the Globe." Yahoo News, June 30, 2019. https://news.yahoo.com/great-replacement-ideology-is-spreading-hate-in-us-and-across-the-globe-140000230.html.

de Rougemont, Denis. *The Idea of Europe*. New York: Macmillan 1966.

Round, David K. *Truth or Treaty: Commonsense Questions About the Treaty of Waitangi*. Canterbury University Press, 1998.

Rousseau, Jean Jacques. *Discourse on Inequality*. 1755. https://aub.edu.lb/fas/cvsp/Documents/DiscourseonInequality.pdf879500092.pdf

Rousseau, Jean Jacques. *The Social Contract or Principles of Political Right*. 1762. https://socialpolicy.ucc.ie/Rousseau_contrat-social.pdf.

Rutgers, Catherine (ed.) *Promoting diversity and inclusion in advertising: A UNICEF Playbook*. UNICEF: United Nations Children's Fund, July 2021. https://www.unicef.org/media/108811/file/UNICEF-PLAYBOOK-Promoting-diversity-and-inclusion-in-advertising.pdf.

Sack, John. *An Eye for an Eye: The Untold Story of Jewish Revenge against Germans in 1945*. Arizona: Basic Books, 1993.

de Sade, Donatien A. F. *Philosophy in the Bedroom*. 1795.

Salinas, Rodrigo. "Human Rights and Freemasonry: Brief Reflections on the 60th Anniversary of the Universal Declaration on Human Rights." Huelen Lodge, Santiago, December 2008. https://www.geocities.ws/huelenlodge/200812HumanRightsandFM.pdf.

Sebak, Nened. "The KLA—terrorists or freedom fighters?" *BBC News*, June 28, 1998. http://news.bbc.co.uk/2/hi/europe/121818.stm

Schmitt, Carl. *The Concept of the Political*. University of Chicago Press, 1995 [1932].

Schuessler, Jennifer. "Mellon Foundation to Spend $250,000,000 to Reimagine Monuments." *The New York Times*, October 5, 2020. https://www.nytimes.com/2020/10/05/arts/mellon-foundation-monuments.html.

Shurkin, Joel N. *Broken Genius: The Rise and Fall of William Shockley, Creator of the Electronic Age.* Macsci, 2006.

Searle, G. R. *Morality and the Market in Victorian Britain.* Oxford: Clarendon Press, 1998.

Shahak, Israel and Norton Mezvinsky. *Jewish Fundamentalism in Israel.* London: Pluto Press, 1999.

Shah, Rajiv. J. "Reflecting on Violence Against Black Americans." The Rockefeller Foundation, June 6, 2020. https://www.rockefellerfoundation.org/blog/reflecting-on-violence-against-african-americans/.

Shakir, Ali. "Don't Let Jacinda Ardern's headscarf Send the Wrong Message." Stuff, October 2, 2019. https://www.stuff.co.nz/national/christchurch-shooting/116195738/dont-let-jacinda-arderns-headscarf-send-the-wrong-message.

Sheldrake, Rupert. "An Experimental Test of the Hypothesis of Formative Causation." *Rivista di Biologia – Biology Forum* 86 (3/4) (1992): 431-44. https://www.sheldrake.org/research/morphic-resonance/an-experimental-test-of-the-hypothesis-of-formative-causation.

Sherwood, Sam. "Ex-Russian Soldier Dies of Suspected Suicide After Police Standoff in Christchurch." Stuff, March 27, 2019. https://www.stuff.co.nz/national/crime/111596809/exrussian-soldier-dies-of-suspected-suicide-after-police-standoff-in-christchurch.

Shotwell, James T. "A Tribute." A World Charter for Human Rights. The American Jewish Committee. New York. http://www.ajcarchives.org/AJC_DATA/Files/HR5.PDF.

"Singapore's Approach to Diversity Has Created a Distinctive Identity Across Ethnic Groups: PM Lee Hsien Loong." The Straights Times, May 19, 2017. https://www.straitstimes.com/politics/singapolitics/pm-whether-chinese-malay-or-indian-a-singaporean-can-spot-a-fellow-citizen.

Sizer, Esther, "Don't let them intimidate you." *Spearhead*, no. 109 (September 1977).

Skousen, W. C. *The Naked Capitalist.* Salt Lake City, 1971.

Slater, Cam. "Why Does the Prime Minister Have the Portrait of a Racist and Anti-Semite Behind her Desk?" The BFD, June 17, 2020. https://thebfd.co.nz/2020/06/17/why-does-the-prime-minister-have-the-portrait-of-a-racist-and-anti-semite-behind-her-desk/.

Small, Zane and Anna Bracewell-Worrall. "Women MPs Urge David Seymour to Apologise for Golriz Ghahraman Remarks." Newshub, May 22, 2019. https://www.newshub.co.nz/home/politics/2019/05/women-mps-urge-david-seymour-to-apologise-for-golriz-ghahraman-remarks.html.

Smith, Margaret (ed.). *Relationships and Sexuality Education: A Guide for Teachers, Leaders and Boards of Trustees, Years 1-8.* Ministry of Education, 2020.

Socarides, Charles W. "Sexual Politics and Scientific Logic: The Issue of Homosexuality." *The Journal of Psychohistory*, Vol. 19, No. 3, Winter 1992. http://www.geocities.ws/kidhistory/homopolo.htm.

"Social Laboratory of the World 1890–1920" in *Story: Visitors' opinions of New Zealand.* Teara The Encyclopaedia of New Zealand, page 3. teara.govt.nz/en/visitors-opinions-about-new-zealand/page-3.

Solzhenitsyn, Alexander. "News of Christendom." No. 141. Lucs-sur-Boulogne, September 25, 1993. http://la.revue.item.free.fr/nouvelles_de_chretiente141_090808.htm.

Soros, George. "Rebuilding the Asylum System." Project Syndicate, September 26, 2015. http://www.georgesoros.com/essays/rebuilding-the-asylum-system/.

Spence, Richard. B. *Wall Street and the Russian Revolution 1905–1925*. Oregon: Trine Day, 2017.
Spengler, Oswald. *The Hour of Decision*. New York: Alfred A Knopf, 1934.
Spengler, Oswald. *The Decline of The West*. [1918, 1926] London: Allen & Unwin, 1971.
Spoonlet, Paul. "Anti-White Iconoclasts." Action Zealandia, July 29, 2019. https://action-zealandia.com/articles/anti-white-iconoclasts.
Spoonley, Paul. "I Thought There Had Been a Decline in Far Right Politics, I Was Wrong." Stuff, March 15, 2020. https://www.stuff.co.nz/opinion/120179211/i-thought-there-had-been-a-decline-in-far-right-politics-i-was-wrong.
Staff and agencies. "Winnie Mandela found guilty of fraud," *The Guardian*, April 24, 2003. https://www.theguardian.com/world/2003/apr/24/southafrica.
Stalin, Vladimir J. *Constitution (Fundamental law) of the Union of the Social Socialist Republics*. Moscow, December 5, 1936.
https://www.marxists.org/reference/archive/stalin/works/1936/12/05.htm.
Stark, Rodney. *The Rise of Christianity: A Sociologist Reconsiders History*. Princeton University Press, 1996.
Stern, Sol. "A Short Account of International Student Politics & the Cold War with Particular Reference to the NSA, CIA, etc." Ramparts Magazine, March 1967, 29-39. https://www.unz.com/print/Ramparts-1967mar-00029/.
Stoddard, Lothrop T. *The French Revolution in San Domingo*. 1914.
Stoddard, Lothrop T. *The Revolt Against Civilization: The Menace of the Under-Man*. London: Chapman & Hall, 1922.
"Students Protest Shockley's Racist Theory." *NBC News*, November 20, 1973.
Sunday Times, July 10, 1988.
"Supurb Excellence." Superb Enterprises. Accessed January 23, 2022.
http://www.supurbenterprises.com/supurb-excellence/.
Sutherland, Peter. "Dying for Europe." July 14,
2015. http://petersutherland.co.uk/article/european-union-articles/dying-for-europe/.
Sutherland, Peter. "Lowering the Costs & Amplifying the Benefits of Migration." July 4, 2014. http://petersutherland.co.uk/article/world-trade-articles/lowering-the-costs-amplifying-the-benefits-of-migration/.
Syberberg, Hans-Jürgen. *On the Fortunes and Misfortunes of Art in Post-War Germany*. Translated by Alexander Jacob. London: Arktos Media, 2017 [1990].
Szasz, Thomas. "The Shame of Medicine: The Case of General Edwin Walker." The Szasz Column # 17. https://www.iaapa.de/szasz_archive.htm#17.
Tacitus, Cornelius. *The Annals of Imperial Rome*.
Tackett, Timothy. *The Coming of the Terror in the French Revolution*. Cambridge: Harvard University Press, 2015.
Tait, Morgan. "Brutal Assaults Scaring Auckland's Asian Students." NZ Herald, March 30, 2016. https://www.nzherald.co.nz/nz/news/article.cfm?c_id=1&objectid=11613419.
Tait, Morgan. "International Students Seen as Easy Targets, Crime Expert Says." NZ Herald, March 30,
2016. https://www.nzherald.co.nz/nz/news/article.cfm?c_id=1&objectid=11614190.
Tait, Morgan. "More Teens Arrested in Relation to Attacks on Asians." NZ Herald, April 1, 2016. https://www.nzherald.co.nz/nz/news/article.cfm?c_id=1&objectid=11615300.
Taylor, Geoff. "Feeling the strain of the front line." *Dominion Post*, Wellington, April 7, 2007.
Tennyson, Alfred. "Locksley Hall." [1835] Poems, 1842.
Tennyson, Alfred. "Locksley Hall After Sixty Years." London: MacMillan, 1886.

"The Eventful History of Freemasons in Austria." Osterreichisches Freimaurer Museum Schloss Rossenau Austrian Masonic Museum. Entry: 1922. https://www.freimaurermuseum.at/en/history-of-freemasons-in-austria.html.

"The First Black Actor to Play Hamlet on the RCS On Why the Arts Needs More Than Tokenism." Yorkshire Post, January 15, 2018. https://www.yorkshirepost.co.uk/news/first-black-actor-play-hamlet-rsc-why-arts-needs-more-tokensim-1764824.

UNESCO. *The Race Concept: Results of an Inquiry*. Paris: UNESCO, 1952. https://unesdoc.unesco.org/ark:/48223/pf0000073351/PDF/073351engo.pdf.multi.

"The Road to Sharpeville; and the ANC's Orwellian Memoryhole." Why We Are White Refugees, March 21, 2010. http://why-we-are-white-refugees.blogspot.com/2010/03/road-to-sharpeville-and-ancs-orwellian.html.

The United Nations Declaration on the Rights of Indigenous Peoples: A Manual for National Human Rights Institutions. United Nations. https://www.justice.govt.nz/assets/Documents/Publications/UN-Declaration-on-the-Rights-of-Indigenous-Peoples.pdf.

"The United Nations in South Africa.The UN: Partner in the Struggle Against Apartheid." United Nations South Africa. https://southafrica.un.org/en/about/about-the-un.

Thomas, Melody. "Early Maori View on Sexual Fluidity Far More Liberal Than Previously Believed." Stuff, July 6, 2018. https://www.stuff.co.nz/life-style/love-sex/105284489/early-mori-view-on-sexual-fluidity-far-more-liberal-than-previously-believed.

Thompson, H. Keith. and Henry Strutz (eds.), *Doenitz at Nuremberg: A Re-Appraisal*. New York: Amber Publishing, 1976.

"Thor-Worshiping Article Unfair – Media Council." *Stuff*, July 6, 2019. https://www.stuff.co.nz/national/113961735/thorworshipping-article-unfair--media-council.

Thorpe, Benjamin James. *The Time and Space of Richard Coudenhove-Kalergi's Pan Europe, 1923–1939*. University of Nottingham, July 2018. http://eprints.nottingham.ac.uk/51778/1/Thesis%20%5B10.05.18%5D.pdf.

"Too Little, Too Late." Friedrich Ebert Stiftung, February 7, 2019. https://www.fes.de/en/displacement-migration-integration/article-page-flight-migration-integration/too-little-too-late/.

Towe, Thomas. E. "Fundamental Rights in the Soviet Union: A Comparative Approach." *University of Pennsylvania Law Review* 115: 1251-1274. https://scholarship.law.upenn.edu/cgi/viewcontent.cgi?referer=&httpsredir=1&article=6224&context=penn_law_review.

Tönnies, Ferdinand. *Gemeinschaft und Gesellschaft,* 2nd ed. Leipzig: Fues's Verlag, 1887.

Trachtenberg, Leo. "Philanthropy That Worked." City Journal, Winter 1998. https://www.city-journal.org/html/philanthropy-worked-12156.html.

"Tradie's Muslim Comments Get Him Axed From New Job." NZ Herald, March 15, 2019. https://www.nzherald.co.nz/business/tradies-muslim-comments-get-him-axed-from-new-job/BAE5K4DTJASJFDSW4VW5UEQXLY/.

Trigger, Sophie. "Fire Crackers, Chickens and the Chinese Publican Who Saved Picton's Crow." Stuff, June 25, 2019. https://www.stuff.co.nz/national/113466108/fire-crackers-chickens-and-the-chinese-publican-who-saved-pictons-crow.

Trotsky, Leon. *The Bolsheviki and World Peace*. New York: Boni & Liverigth, 1918.

Trotsky, Leon. "Perspectives and Tasks in the East." April 21, 1924. https://www.marxists.org/archive/trotsky/1924/04/perspectives.html

Trotsky, Leon. "Terrorism and Communism [Dictatorship versus Democracy]: A Reply to Karl Kautsky." 1920. https://www.marxists.org/archive/trotsky/1920/terrcomm/.

Trotsky, Leon. *The Revolution Betrayed.* Pathfinder Press, 1973 [1936].
"Trustees." The Andrew W. Mellon Foundation. https://mellon.org/about/trustees/.
"Tutor Defends 'Racist' Stance." BBC News, March 8, 2006.
  http://news.bbc.co.uk/2/hi/uk_news/education/4785574.stm.
"Ulster University Withdraws Status From Prof Richard Lynn." BBC News April 14, 2018.
"U. N. General Assembly, Resolution A/RES/31/6 A." 42nd plenary meeting, October 26, 1976, 10-11. https://undocs.org/en/A/RES/31/6.
UN General Assembly Resolution A/RES/96-I, 95 (I), Fifth Plenary Session, December 11, 1946. https://undocs.org/en/A/RES/96(I)
UN Security Council. "Report of the Secretary General Pursuant to Paragraph 2 of the Security Council Resolution 808 (1993)."
  https://www.icty.org/x/file/Legal%20Library/Statute/statute_re808_1993_en.pdf
United Nations. *Convention on the Prevention and Punishment of the Crime of Genocide.* General Assembly resolution 260 A (III). December 9, 1948.
  https://www.un.org/en/genocideprevention/documents/atrocity-crimes/Doc.1_Convention%20on%20the%20Prevention%20and%20Punishment%20of%20the%20Crime%20of%20Genocide.pdf
United Nations. "International Convention on the Suppression and Punishment of the Crime of Apartheid." General Assembly resolution 3068 (XXVIII)), 28 UN GAOR Supp. (No. 30) at 75, UN Doc. A/9030 (1974), 1015 UNT.S. 243. July 18, 1976.
  https://www.un.org/en/genocideprevention/documents/atrocity-crimes/Doc.10_International%20Convention%20on%20the%20Suppression%20and%20Punishment%20of%20the%20Crime%20of%20Apartheid.pdf.
Universal Declaration of Human Rights. United Nations. 1948.
  https://www.ohchr.org/EN/UDHR/Documents/UDHR_Translations/eng.pdf.
Universal Declaration on Human Rights at 70. United Nations Human Rights Office of the High Commissioner.
  https://www.ohchr.org/EN/NewsEvents/Pages/DisplayNews.aspx?NewsID=23997&LangID=E.
US Information Agency. "TRANSCRIPT: Jamie Shea Talks To The West Pacific." *Scoop.* July 16, 1999. https://www.scoop.co.nz/stories/GE9907/S00067/transcript-jamie-shea-talks-to-the-west-pacific.htm.
Utley, Robert M. *The Last Days of the Sioux Nation.* New Haven: Yale University Press, 1963.
"UNICEF Aotearoa." Unicef mo nga tagariki katoa.
  https://www.unicef.org.nz/feature/our-new-name.
United Nations Charter. United Nations. https://www.un.org/en/about-us/un-charter.
"Universal Periodic Review 2019." New Zealand Foreign Affairs and Trade.
  https://www.mfat.govt.nz/en/peace-rights-and-security/human-rights/universal-periodic-review-2019/.
"University Group Rejects 'White Pride' Accusations." RNZ Radio New Zealand, March 2, 2017. https://www.rnz.co.nz/news/national/325728/university-group-rejects-%27white-pride%27-accusations.
"University Statement on Pioneer Statues." University of Oregon, June 13, 2020.
  https://around.uoregon.edu/content/university-statement-pioneer-statues.
US Dept. of State, "Congo Crisis," Foreign Relations, 1961-63, Vol. XX, 13 January 1995.
  https://history.state.gov/historicaldocuments/frus1961-63v20.
Vance, Andrea. "Security Escort for Green MP Golriz Ghahraman After Death Threats." Stuff, May 21, 2019. https://www.stuff.co.nz/national/politics/112882626/security-escort-for-green-mp-golrizghahraman-after-acts-david-seymour-called-her-a-menace.

Verwoerd, H. F. Verwoerd Speaks: Speeches 1948-1966. Johannesburg: APB Publishers, 1966.

de Villiers, Dawid. *The Case for South Africa*. London: Tom Stacey Ltd., 1970.

"Voice of Racism the Everyday Racism Felt by Real People in Aotearoa New Zealand." NZ Human Rights. https://voiceofracism.co.nz/?gclid=EAIaIQobChMIjcD86cH06gIVlAsrCh15sAAHEAA YASAAEgIsDfD_BwE.

Vulliamy, Ed. "'Rockers and spies'—how the CIA used culture to shred the iron curtain." *The Guardian*, May 3, 2020. https://www.theguardian.com/us-news/2020/may/03/rockers-and-spies-how-the-cia-used-culture-to-shred-the-iron-curtain

Warriner, Virginia C.A. "Internationalisation of Maori Businesses in the Creative Industry Sector: Ko Te Rerenga o Te Koki a Tu, He Whare Oranga." Doctoral thesis. Massey University, 2009. https://mro.massey.ac.nz/bitstream/handle/10179/1244/02whole.pdf

Washington, G. Farewell Address (1796), https://avalon.law.yale.edu/18th_century/washing.asp.

Watson, James D. *Avoid Boring People: Lessons From a Life In Science*. Oxford University Press, 2007.

Westhues, Kenneth. "Making Fast Work of Ricardo Duchesne." https://www.kwesthues.com/Duchesne1906.html.

Whitaker, Ben. *The Foundations: An Anatomy of Philanthropy and Society*. London: Eyre Methuen, 1974.

Whitehall, John. "Children Transitioning: Childhood Gender Dysphoria A Paediatrician's Warning to New Zealand." Family First New Zealand, October 201. https://familyfirst.org.nz/wp-content/uploads/2018/10/REPORT-Children-Transitioning-Childhood-Gender-Dysphoria-Dr-John-Whitehall.pdf.

Wiederhorn, Jon. "Make Shakira Dance for You Whenever, Wherever." *MTV News*, November 5, 2002. https://www.mtv.com/news/1458520/make-shakira-dance-for-you-whenever-wherever/

Wiker, Benjamin. *10 Books that Screwed Up the World: And 5 Others that Didn't Help*. Simon & Schuster, 2008.

Wilson, Jason. "White farmers: How a far-right idea was planted in Donald Trump's mind." *The Guardian*, August 24, 2018. https://www.theguardian.com/world/2018/aug/23/white-farmers-trump-south-africa-tucker-carlson-far-right-influence.

Wilson, Woodrow. *Fourteen Points*. January 8, 1918. https://avalon.law.yale.edu/20th_century/wilson14.asp

Wilson, Woodrow. *War Message to US Congress*. April 2, 1917. https://www.khanacademy.org/humanities/world-history/euro-hist/american-entry-world-war-i/a/wilsons-war-message-to-congress-april-2-1917.

Wimpee, Rachel. "Funding a Social Movement: The Ford Foundation and Civil Rights 1965-1970." Rockefeller Archive Center, November 4, 2020. https://resource.rockarch.org/story/philanthropy-social-movements-ford-foundation-civil-rights-1965-1970/.

Windshuttle, Keith. *The Fabrication of Australian History*. Sydney: Macleay Press, 2002.

Witkowski, Jan. "Stalin's War on Genetic Science." *Nature* 454, July 2008, 577-579. https://doi.org/10.1038/454577a.

"Women and Children in White Concertation Camps During the Anglo-Boer War 1899–1902." South African History Online, https://www.sahistory.org.za/article/women-and-children-white-concentration-camps-during-anglo-boer-war-1900-1902.

Yockey, Francis P. *Imperium: The Philosophy of History and Politics.* [1948] Abergele: Wermod & Wermod, 2013.
Zachary, G. P. *The Global Me: New Cosmopolitans and the Competitive Edge: Picking Globalism's Winners and Losers.* New South Wales: Allen & Unwin, 2000.
Zelevansky, Nora. "The Big Business of Unconscious Bias." *The New York Times*, November 20, 2019. https://www.nytimes.com/2019/11/20/style/diversity-consultants.html.

About the Author

Kerry R. Bolton has certifications in historical theology, ethnography, and psychology. He is widely published in scholarly journals on a variety of subjects, including *India Quarterly, Geopolitika, Journal of Gothic & Horror Studies, Journal of Social, Political & Economic Studies, Journal of Social Economics, International Journal of Russian Studies, Occidental Quarterly*, etc. His books include *Revolution from Above, Russia & the Fight Against Globalization, Artists of the Right* (two volumes), *The Parihaka Cult, The Banking Swindle, Stalin: The Enduring Legacy, Peron & Peronism, The Occult & Subversive Movements, Opposing the Money Lenders, Geopolitics of the Indo-Pacific, The Psychotic Left, Zionism, Islam and the West, The Decline & Fall of Civilisations, Yockey: A Fascist Odyssey*, and *The Perversion of Normality*. He has translated, annotated, and edited an edition of Spengler's essays: *Oswald Spengler: Prussian Socialism & Other Essays*; and with John Morgan a collection of *Yockey MSS, The World in Flames*.

ENJOYED THIS BOOK?

TO READ MORE, VISIT US AT

ANTELOPEHILLPUBLISHING.COM

www.ingramcontent.com/pod-product-compliance
Lightning Source LLC
Chambersburg PA
CBHW021422070526
44577CB00001B/10